ISBN 978-1-330-64411-9
PIBN 10086648

English
Français
Deutsche
Italiano
Español
Português

www.forgottenbooks.com

Mythology Photography **Fiction**
Fishing Christianity **Art** Cooking
Essays Buddhism Freemasonry
Medicine **Biology** Music **Ancient
Egypt** Evolution Carpentry Physics
Dance Geology **Mathematics** Fitness
Shakespeare **Folklore** Yoga Marketing
Confidence Immortality Biographies
Poetry **Psychology** Witchcraft
Electronics Chemistry History **Law**
Accounting **Philosophy** Anthropology
Alchemy Drama Quantum Mechanics
Atheism Sexual Health **Ancient History**
Entrepreneurship Languages Sport
Paleontology Needlework Islam
Metaphysics Investment Archaeology
Parenting Statistics Criminology
Motivational

LENTEN SERMONS,

PREACHED CHIEFLY TO YOUNG MEN AT THE UNIVERSITIES,

BETWEEN

A. D. 1858—1874.

BY THE

REV. E. B. PUSEY, D.D.,

REGIUS PROFESSOR OF HEBREW, AND CANON OF CHRIST CHURCH.

LONDON:

A. D. INNES & CO.,

31 AND 32, BEDFORD STREET, STRAND.

1893

𝔒𝔵𝔣𝔬𝔯𝔡

HORACE HART, PRINTER TO THE UNIVERSITY

ADVERTISEMENT.

THERE is little to be noticed about the following Sermons, except that perhaps it may be said, that, being addressed to young men of intellect and education, allusions were made to intellectual temptations with which they were encompassed, and that the Sermons preached at S. Mary's, Oxford, being part of courses, selected by the late lamented Bishop of Winchester for the benefit of the young men, in whose well-being he took so deep an interest, they are not, all, on subjects, which, had they been single Sermons, the writer would have chosen for Lent.

CONTENTS.

b

SERMON XXIV.

ISAIAH; HIS HEAVINESS AND HIS CONSOLATION.

PREACHED AT S. MARY'S, OXFORD. LENT, 1869.

Isa. vi. 8, 10.

SERMON I^a.

LIFE, THE PREPARATION FOR DEATH.

HEB. ix. 27.

"It is appointed unto all men once to die, but after this the judgement."

WHY is there such awe in that brief word, "death?" Why, if we could see along this Church a long so-lemn funeral procession, in which one by one, those narrow dwelling-places, wherein our bodies shall one day resolve into their dust, should pass before us; each, as they shall one day be, as in God's sight they are, inscribed with our several names, the num-ber of our fleeting years, the year, month, day, which closed them; why should we look each with an awed gaze upon our own? Whence is that cold pang which brave men have felt on the battle eve? Or why do crowds fly, like scared sheep, before a pestilence? Is it only the heathen thought, that " linquenda tellus et domus et placens uxor?" Or is it a shrinking from the bodily circumstances of death, that " this sensible warm motion shall become a kneaded clod?" Or is it that life and its pros-pects are so bright, the thought of self-development

^a Preached at Great S. Mary's, Cambridge.

B

so grand, the pleasures of this life so dazzling, the joy of working among our fellow-men so satisfying, life itself so buoyant, that we should long to have our allotted threescore years and ten measured out to us, or the ten years of toil and sorrow which fill out the fourscore years? Life is joyous, because it flows from God, the source of life: duty, well-ful-filled, sheds peace on the soul, for it places us so far in harmony with God: pure love engoldens life, because love is the created image of the Being of God, Who is love, a ray from the essential bliss of God. But if we knew that we were to pass from joy to joy; that life was only to flow over the barrier which bounds our vision, then to glide on more brilliant and heaven-lit than before, who would not exchange this dying life for the land of the living? It is not the mere loss of this life or its joys, which gives that start of fear. Loss we may grieve over! It may make our "sun go down at noonday." It does not give that piercing shock of personal fear. The poet truly said, "Conscience does make cow-ards of us all." For the Apostle said, "The sting of death is sin."

Hence was it, that a brave man, sent on a forlorn hope, turned back to meet a disgraced death. Death confronted him; one deadly unrepented sin flashed on his mind; he dared meet death; he dared not meet an unreconciled God. Why did the sight of the decayed remains of his pious and beautiful queen so affect the young Duke of Gandia [b], that, for his thirty-three remaining years, he never forgot that sight, and at once died to the world, that at his

b S. Francis Borgia.

death he might live to God? Why did that haircloth
beneath the dress of the just-departed wife of Italy's
dearest hymn-writer[c], so move his soul, that he
thenceforth renounced the world whose pomps he
loved, and loved to be counted a fool for the love of
Christ? Why, in our own days, did that chance
glance at the morning dress laid aside for dinner,
awakening the thought of our laying aside this our
mortal frame, change in an instant the whole current of the life of a noble convert, while yet young,
and make him give his life, his all to God[d]?

What gives to death this solemn aspect?

The answer is simple. We can but die once.
Every error, negligence, ignorance, sin, can be, in
some sort, undone. Our dear Lord prayed for His
executioners; the guilt then of the Crucifixion of
the Son of God, the Redeemer, could be undone;
His Blood was shed for those who shed it; nay, it
overflowed to be the source not of cleansing only or
of healing, but of living union with Himself. "The
Blood which in their phrenzy they shed, believing
they drank," says St. Augustine so often. But if
we fail in death, it cannot be repaired. All of life is
summed up there. Men fall, rise, relapse, recover,
relapse again, and are again restored by the grace
of God in life. But what in death? "As the tree
falleth, so it shall be." It may have inclined this
way or that; the breath of God's good Spirit, the
impulse of His inspirations, the soft violence of His
grace, the strong blows of His merciful visitations
seemed to impel it one way. Inured habit bowed
it the other; it fell; it cannot rise. "Where it

[c] Jacopono da Todi.   [d] This history is printed, not published.

falleth, there it shall be[e]." "It is appointed unto all men once to die, and after that "—what, a second trial? a second plank after shipwreck? a fresh use of all the experience gained in life? However any may act, you too know that God saith none of these things, but, "It is appointed unto all men once to die, but after that, the judgement."

But, because death is an act so alone, so single, so distinct and separate in its nature and its issue from all besides in life, does it therefore stand insulated? If one were to judge from the ways and words of mankind, it must surely be so. It is the one thing in this life, which is absolutely certain! How long we shall abide here, what shall befall us to-morrow, in what way we shall pass out of this life; early, late, sudden, slow; with ease or pain; we can form no guess. The green leaf is rent off, while the sere yellow leaf, ready to drop of itself, remains. "With forethought," said the Heathen poet, "does God whelm with a murky night the issue of the future." Every other trial we may escape. This, this alone is certain. All depends on it. Eternity hangs upon the moment of death; eternal bliss, eternal woe. And yet who prepares for it? Were it any trial in this life, on which the provision for our future depended, what care would men take! Were it an examination in this place, which should give you good credentials in this life, every right means is used, every nerve is strained. And yet the judgement of after-life often reverses this judgement as to its outset. The loss may be repaired. But where the judgement is final, irreversible, irreparable, where

[e] Eccl. xi. 3.

the stake is infinite, endless, the bliss known to God Alone Who is the Bliss and Joy of His own, the loss unendurable; who well-nigh prepares, who thinks of it? The thought is an unwelcome guest, to whom men refuse entrance, if they can; if they cannot, they are fertile in excuses for dismissing him. One thing alone they never say, "Come again to-morrow." They would fain never think of him, till he comes to carry them to judgement. We know that we must die. Why embitter life with the thought of it?

"Præsentem rape lætus horam, et linque futura."

And yet how should it be, that every thing of moment in this life, which has to be done well, is to be studied, and that the weightiest act of all should need no study, no preparation? Is there no science of dying well? no "disce mori?" Has our merciful Father destined all our whole race to pass through this aweful irreparable ordeal, and shod our feet with no preparation, whereby we may tread unharmed on its bars of fiery iron? Does He guide us step by step through this life's wilderness, when our bodies are unworn, our minds in their full vigour, and does He leave that last act severed from all before, when the body is enfeebled by age, disease, approaching dissolution, and the soul distracted by pain, worn by sleeplessness, wearied by the weariness of its poor brother, the body, with which it is so mysteriously united, from which it is now about to be rent away,—does He leave us to enter upon that last decisive act with no preparation, no fore-arming, to seek for His grace, pardon, assisting strength, in what way we best can, aided by such prayers of the priest or of our sorrowing friends as we can get, and fortified by His sacrament?

To judge from men's ways, one should think that such was their belief. What else means this picture of death-bed repentance, which so many have in their minds, as though a man might live through this life without God, and then, by one act at its close, sever himself from all his past, and live with God for all eternity? How comes the name "death-bed repentance" to be so familiar to us, as to have become a sort of proverb? How is it, that we clergy so often content ourselves with the true warning, that no one knows that he shall have any death-bed, upon which to enact this his ideal of the close of life, this phantasm of repentance, as though, if death-bed there would surely be, men were not so mistaken in calculating upon it? True, that the very possibility that there should be no death-bed is aweful enough. What of those hundreds whom one explosion in a mine sent into eternity with just that moment's notice of the coming sound; what if, when the men of a whole village were last year so cut off at once, one man in that whole village had continued in sin, calculating on a death-bed repentance? Souls pass into eternity every day; "cut off even in the blossom of their sin," without one moment seemingly, to say one "Lord, have mercy." But to dwell on this alone would be almost to grant that if they had a death-bed, on which to repent, they would repent. I do not mean that there are *not* death-bed repentances. God has placed no limit to the wonderfulness, the unaccountableness of His mercies. His mercy outruns, overpowers, over-masters His justice; and I heartily believe, that He would not part, if He could, with one soul which He has made. Doubtless, the hour of death is an hour when God is very busy with the soul, because it is its last. When the tongue can give no utterance of its hope in Jesus; when friends have ceased to pray with it, as thinking it insensible; when human means are passed; when, perhaps, even friends have ceased to pray *for* it, as believing it to be gone; still often, while it yet lingers, God is pleading with it, and works in it what the Judgement Day alone will reveal. But taking into account more than all which experience tells us of the uncovenanted mercies of God; counting up all we know of those, whom devout fervent prayer has rescued out of the very jaws of the dragon, so that, at God's bidding, he departed from them[f], when already half-devoured, and thankfully adoring the incredible, fathomless depths of the Divine mercy and compassion; yet who has told us that these *were* mere death-bed repentances; that they stood in no connexion with any thing in the past life; that they were mere displays of the absolute sovereignty of Divine mercy; manifestations only of the unrestrained omnipotence of the Blood of Jesus, incompressible by any laws save of His Omniscient Wisdom? We see the fact, the marvellous, miraculous interposition of Divine

[f] See a history of the "July lately past," in S. Gregory's monastery. S. Greg. in Evang. Hom. i. 19. 7. Opp. i. 1514, 1515. He gives Hom. in Evang. i. 12. 7. the opposite history of a bad nobleman, Chrysaorius, who saw evil spirits ready to take him to hell; "he cried 'a truce but till to-morrow; a truce but till to-morrow' but while he was thus crying, he was torn from the habitation of his flesh."

love; the secret springs are hid in the depths of the
Divine knowledge.

It is almost a sacred proverb: "He cannot die
ill, who has lived well; and hardly does he die well,
who has lived ill." What then are we to think of
those aweful cases, where a man, who *seems* to have
lived well, dies ill? There was so much seeming
good, and yet the man died an apostate! The tortures were severe. But for God's grace, perhaps,
we too might all have failed under them. Yet he
died, denying Jesus, his only hope. Pelagius had
even a name of sanctity; he commenced his heresy in
his conception of man's perfectibility; we part with
him out of sight, anathematizing himself in hypocrisy[g]. Eutyches was all-but closing a venerated
life, chosen for seeming graces to be the head of
those who had forsaken all for Christ. He died,
the parent of a soul-destroying heresy, denying his
Lord Who bought him. Judas had faith to cast out
devils; he gave up all for Christ; we cannot even
imagine that he entered the Apostolate, already a
thief and a hypocrite, or with the matured will to
give the reins to that covetousness which destroyed
him. His guilt was unknown to all, except our Lord.
Graces he must have had, to justify our Lord's selec-
tion of him to that closest nearness to Himself, who
was among those of whom He said, "[h]Behold My
mother and My brethren." In these horrible cases,
we take refuge in the thought, that these were not
sudden unprepared apostasies. In Judas, the lurk-
ing evil has been revealed to us, lest the unexplained
terrific close should paralyse us. "Who then can

[g] At the Synod of Diospolis.   [h] S. Matt. xii. 49.

be saved," since one in such nearness to our Lord
perished? We cannot endure the thought that
"the grey-haired saint should fail at last." We
feel sure that, if he perished, we must have been
deceived about him. A life-long real service drop
blighted to the ground, when it seemed to be opening to flower in the Paradise of God, unless there
had been a cankerworm, buried deep at the heart,
which ate out its life, while all without was blossom-
ing with such hopeful show? It is too horrible!
The ground seems to be giving way under one's
feet; they seem well-nigh to have slipped from the
Rock of ages; one would seem to be walking amid
the slime-pits of the accursed cities, where to fall is
to sink into the abyss of Hell. But no; God has
shown us in Judas the preparations for that horrible
fall. He has told us, that, even amid that seeming
service, his was faith divorced from love; that he
was, at once (O, horrible mixture), an Apostle and
(so Jesus warned him) "[i] a devil."

But if then we may hope that in Judas we see the
secret of those horrible deaths, which close a life of
outward show; if in him we see the secret threads,
which, running through his life, twined themselves
continually closer and thicker and more consolidated,
until they bound him fast, and dragged him to his
eternal ruin; if we see in him the forerunners of
that seemingly sudden, hopeless fall; if we seem to
see, why, after the disappointment about the oint-
ment and our Lord's mild rebuke, he yielded himself to Satan, replaced the lost gain at the price of
his Master's life, and so already committed, was

[i] S. John vi. 70.

not melted by his Lord's humility in washing his feet, and received to his own damnation the Sacrament of his Lord's Body ; why, then, dare we think, that, in those opposite miracles of mercy, there were no forerunners of a partially accepted grace, even amidst a life of sin ?   If an impenitent death, after seeming good in life, is, probably, amid whatever green and gay freshness of the leaves, the end of an unfruitful life, barren of real good, why should we think that those stupendous miracles of mercy in death-bed conversions were not God's crowning gifts of mercy to souls, whom He had in lifetime secretly prepared to accept that mercy ?   Of course, there can be no question of merit, nor of grace of congruity, where the fitting sequel of a God-forgetting life were that dreadful place, into which the Psalmist says, " [k] the forgetters of God shall be cast."   Man cannot merit either God's justifying grace (since when unjustified, or forfeiting God's free gift of justification, he has " [l] great deserts, but evil ;"   he merits, not heaven but hell), or God's last crowning gift of final perseverance.   But merit is one thing, God's preparation of the heart is quite another. And we, who see not as God seeth, who discern not the secret springs which God alone moveth, how should we know that God had not all along, by secret inspirations of His grace, which were obeyed for the time, prepared the heart for that seemingly sudden change of a death-bed repentance ?   Sudden, at last, is ofttimes that last act of conversion, whereby

[k] Ps. ix. 17.   [l] " His [the Apostle Paul's] before his conversion were great, but evil." S. Aug. de grat. et lib. arb. n. 12. Opp. x. 724.

the fallen Christian is anew translated from the power of Satan into God. But God surrounds all with His exciting forecoming grace; and that last wave of grace, which bears the sinner back to God, has probably been preceded by many an eddy, in which the soul, now as it seems advancing, now falling back, has come within the sphere of that last mightiest grace, whereby God, in His mercy, " binds him fast To the bright shore of love."

But if any be (as we dare not say they are not) very hopelessly unlikely to be the objects of those rare manifestations of God's Almighy mercy, it would be, one should think, those, who should live an evil life, encouraging themselves by the hope of a death-bed repentance. For what is this but to sin in full light and with full choice, turning the grace of God into an encouragement to sin, choosing deliberately what would offend God, with the hope of bribing His aweful justice at the end by the mockery of an unfelt repentance?

Life, then, whether we will it or will it not, is a preparation for our death. Ceaselessly, noiselessly, swiftly, smoothly flows on and on and on the stream of time; it gathers strength with our weakness; slow perhaps in our early wondering years, rapid beyond all measure, as less and less of it remains to us; yet charged with every sin and folly, which stained its earlier course, and " darker as it downward bears, " unless its foulness have been cleansed by penitence and the Blood of Jesus. Of itself every day is the parent of the morrow. As day to day carries on the wondrous tale of the loving-kindness of God, so day transmits to day the gathering deepening sum of human sin. God gives grace on grace. The grace of God well-used is the pledge of enlarged grace. Man adds sin to sin. The sin of to-day is the preparation and earnest of to-morrow's sin, and that of to-morrow's and to-morrow's and to-morrow's, till that last day, which knows no morrow save eternity. To-day's evil-speaking of another, ensures to-morrow's; to-day's oath, or bad conversation, or freedom with Holy Scripture, or irreverent jest, or negligence in prayer, or forgetfulness of self-examination, or sloth, which leaves no time for the morning's prayer; or engrossment in the evening's occupation, which leaves the soul too dead-tired for the evening's; or slovenly preparation for Holy Communion, or still more slovenly thanksgiving after it, are so many moral earnests that the same will be on the morrow or on the next occasion. Much more will this week's deadly sin, but for some mighty interposition of God's grace, be the forerunner and forthbringer of the next week's or next month's deadly sin. And if so, when should it cease, if not now? Look back to past years. Did you think as to any negligence of any religious habit which you were taught in childhood, or as to any thing half-known to be wrong, that it would have lasted until now? The act of the child became the habit of the man. Why should not the habit of youth be that of middle age, and the wont of middle age be the inured custom of advanced age, and the inured custom of advanced age be the necessity of old age (if you ever see it), and wherever death should find you, the habit of that age be the ruling thought in death?

Life, will we, nill we, is the preparation for death. We live, but to die. Our death is not the end only, it is the object of our life. Our journey's end, not the journey itself, is that journey's object. It is this we have in view; this relieves its weariness, its monotony, its irksomeness. It was for this, that God sent us into the world; it is to this end, that He has been guiding us by all the varieties of His Providence; for this it is, that He has provided us with all the richness and prodigality of His grace; it is for this, that He has invented all the fertility of His resources to save us. For death knits in one our time and our eternity. Time and eternity meet in that one point. As we are in that last moment of time, such are we throughout eternity.

How then can we prepare for that moment, upon which our all hangs, and in which we can do so little, nay, in which almost all must be done for us? What can men do then mostly, but repeat what they have done before? What do we find, even in death-beds, where we hope that all is well? If they have confessed before in life, they make what confession they can, and hear once more the earnest of our Lord's absolving voice, "Thy sins be forgiven thee;" if they have communicated before, they fortify themselves once more for that last conflict, with their Redeemer's Body and Blood; they attend, as well as they can, to prayers said for them; they say, as they can, some words of old-remembered hymns, some fragments of prayers, some condensed words for mercy, "Jesus, Saviour, save me;" at last, they can say the one word, Jesu, or form it in their hearts, or look at some representation of Him, or gaze up to heaven where He is interceding for them, and long that He should have pity on them. All, good things in themselves. For He has said, "whoso cometh unto Me, I will in no wise cast out." Good, if by God's grace they are done sincerely; comforts to survivors. But are such few acts, even if God continue the grace to do them, are such few acts the turning-points of life and death? Would they replace a wasted life? Would they efface whole multitudes of life-long sins? Is a common-place end (such as experience shows that most ends are) a happy good-foreboding close of a common-place life, in which the sins of youth (diverted from their course by marriage) have issued in a respectable, meaningless, objectless life?

It has been said by some, with a holy boldness, that if one had the sins of the whole world upon him, and could by one mighty act, ensouled by the grace of God, will, for the love of God and in faith in Jesus, that they were all undone, and if he yielded up his soul in that act, they would be all forgiven. No one, who has known aught of God's mercy, could limit the possibilities of God's mercies; for he himself would be to himself the greatest marvel of God's forbearing mercy. I speak not of God's Omnipotence of mercy, but of the narrowness of man's reception of that mercy. And what do we see? What do we hear of? I speak not, I deny not, I believe a vast manifold work of God in that all-but-sacrament of death; that last moment, which God hath reserved to Himself, wherein to speak to the soul yet unwon by His grace, and say to it, "Wilt thou still reject Me? Why wilt thou die?" I believe that God will not part with any soul, which *will* be saved, seeing He has given His Son to die for it. But whatever mercies of this sort God has in store for the ignorant, for those who knew not what they did, for whom especially Jesus prayed, beholding them afar through all those centuries on His Cross— what have we to do therewith, who live in His Gospel's full light, on whom no blindness falls, unless self-created, whom He has fenced round from so many temptations, of whom so many, through their imaginations, become their own tempters?

But, apart from these, what do so many of those tranquil deaths look like? Is it the supernatural peace of God shed into the soul; the Presence of the Divine Comforter; the love which taketh away fear; the voice of Jesus bidding the soul to "Come?" Blessed souls, to which such deaths come in God's mercy, because they have ever had a reverent fear of death; because they have ever dwelt near the Cross of Jesus, and looked up to His Divine Eye of love, and the Precious Blood has bedewed, cleansed, healed, sanctified them. Then, it is the holy close of a life near to God. Death, meditated on, has done its work before its time. Jesus is with the soul in the valley of death, which has sought to live by His side in the world's varied pilgrimage.

But is death the only spot in this world, in which there is no room for self-deceit? Will those who, by saying, "[k] Lord, Lord," have, through life, compounded with themselves for not doing the things which Jesus said, awake of themselves to see, that they have made a life-long mistake? Will those—in

[k] S. Matt. vii. 21.

whom worldliness has stifled the life of God in the soul for years, and who have been on easy terms with God, owning Him respectfully, yet letting Him interfere very little with their outward lives, and not at all with their inward, open their eyes and see through the thick mist which they have gathered round them? Plainly they do not. For what more terrific than to find, at life's close, that life, amid imagined services, or, at least, not disservice of God, had been one real rebellion of self-will? And these are at peace.

Such easy deaths look like the unspiritual ends of unspiritual lives. A hopeful easy death is rather the sequel of a life passed in awe and fear. Fear of death in life is commonly taken away in death; but, short of absolute despair of God's mercy, I would rather witness any agony than see a spiritually un-fearing death as the sequel of a spiritually unfear-ing life. I would not dare to ask for an end, even spiritually painless; I would only ask for a sinless death, and leave the rest with God.

Death has a great work for grace to do, in itself, without weighting it with a work not its own. It is a startling prayer which the Church puts into our mouths by the graves of those we love, winding up its appeal for God's mercy in the solemn cadence, "O holy and merciful Saviour, Thou most worthy Judge eternal, suffer us not, at our last hour, for any pains of death, to fall from Thee." We should not have framed this prayer ourselves. Yet those who framed it, had had before their eyes death and the trials incidental to death.

Every sort of death has its own trials. Death

with sharp pain, lest it break endurance; death with lingering pains, lest it wear out patience. Then the Evil one has studied our characters all our life long, and applies the knowledge, with all his accumulated experience of ourselves, our weak points, whereby we most easily fall, and of others' death-beds, and his supernatural skill against us. It has become a sort of proverb, "The ruling passion strong in death." This too must come from large experience. What, if that ruling passion have been something antagonistic to simplicity of character, to the tranquil workings of grace? What, if it have been vain-glory, or love of praise, or vanity, or impatience, or love of ease, or again disputing, or censoriousness, what pitfalls there yawn on all sides for us, what opening in our armour (if spiritual armour we have) for Satan's deadly thrusts, what occasions for unreality, in the face of the Truth Itself, for loss of faith when faith is our all; for murmuring against Divine justice when about to appear at its bar! Probably those evil deaths after specious lives, have had this in common, that it was the evil passion to which such men had often secretly given way, a smothered, smouldering, but unextinguished fire, which burst out at last and destroyed them. I have known of relapse into the deadly accustomed sin on the bed of death.

Since then death has enough of trial in itself for the grace of God to master, since those trials are aggravated by all unconquered evil in our whole life, since a good death is the object of our life, and such as we are in life, such we shall almost surely be in death, and what we are in death, such we

c

shall certainly be in all eternity, what remains but
that we make all our life a preparation for eternity?

Heathen wisdom saw a gleam of this. "Who
closes best his last day?" one was asked [f]. "He
who ever set before him, that the last day of life
was imminent." Not without inspiration of God
was that counsel, "In all thy works remember thy
last end, and thou shalt never do amiss [g]."

It was a good old-fashioned practice, morning by
morning, to think of the four last things, death,
judgement, heaven, hell, and to pray to live that day
as one would wish to have lived when the last day
came. We cannot imagine to ourselves that any
given day will be our last. It was said of old, "No
one is so old, as not to think that he shall live yet
one year more [b]." Vitality is strong within us, and
it would be unreal to try to make this a motive for
action. So, as to lying down in one's bed, as though
one should not wake. The human mind gets accustomed to the thought, and may easily enact it
unreally. But, although, humanly speaking, our
anticipations are true; although the cases of sudden
death are rare, compared with the multitude of those
who do not die suddenly; although God mercifully,
for the most part, gives us intimations of our death
(for those who know that they bear about them a
disease which ends in an instant do not in this sense
die a sudden death), yet every day is a part of our
death, and enters into it. For death, which sums
up all, gathers into one the results of each of our
days; and each day as we live well or ill, through

[f] Musonius in S. Maxim. Serm. 36.   [g] Ecclus. vii. 36.
[h] Cic. de Senect. c. 7.

the grace of God or our own fault, is the earnest of many like days beyond. It is a stern nakedness of truth, stern only because it is so true; "He is not worthy to be called a Christian, who lives in that state, wherein he would fear to die." For nothing makes death fearful, except the fear of all fears, lest we be separated from Christ.

You, my sons, naturally cannot think death near. You think mostly that you have many years before you. Youth often sinks down in the grave before age. Yet, humanly speaking, you are right. May you live those many years to the glory of God, and gain a full reward! Yet the question for each is, not how many days I shall live. They were not more holy before the flood. Those centuries of life brought no nearer to God those to whom the flood was not a mere temporal punishment. The years of the oldest, nay, of Methuselah, when past, are but a point, but the twinkling of an eye, except for what they bear in them, good or bad. The question is, not what we have in store, but what is our to-day. It is not the physical, but the moral aspect of to-day, upon which our eternity hangs. It is not the question, How *long* we shall live, but *how* we live. Your past has been the parent of the present; your present will be the parent of the future. As you lived when younger, such, unless there has come some turning to God, or some turning away from Him, is your life now. Age matures the fruit of youth; it does not change its nature. The apples of Sodom, fresh, blooming, rich in colour, have enlarged to their gigantic size, but have, therewith, become dust at the core. The sapling which a boy's weakness could bend at will, cannot, some years later, be riven by a giant's strength. So is it in things of nature, the pictures of ourselves. So is it with free-will. Look at the two extremities of free-will, as it is enfreed and Deiform through grace, or enslaved and imbruted by sin, you can scarce trace its first balancings, before grace had perfected it or sin had deadened it, so that those who know nothing of the secret history of the supernatural life deny its existence.

To-day is ever "the day of salvation." Thou art more in thine own power now, than thou wouldest be to-morrow. God appeals to you anew, "I have set before you life and death. Cast away from you all your transgressions whereby ye have transgressed, and make you a new heart and a new spirit. For why will ye die? For I have no pleasure in the death of him that dieth, saith the Lord God; wherefore turn and live ye." Turn, and the Death of Jesus shall be your life; for He died that we might live; He died to redeem our forfeited life, to hallow our regenerate life, to live in us; to be our life; to be our victory in death. Turn to Him. Look up to His bleeding Hands; His thorn-crowned sacred Head; His meek Eye of love. Thank Him, bless Him; fear for yourself while you bless Him, and bless Him while you fear; He will make a holy reverent awe sweeter than all earthly joy; He will be thy strength in life, thy fearlessness in death, thy joy in eternity. So shall we ever be with the Lord, evermore thanking and blessing Him, and, of His personal mercies to us, most perhaps for that first prevailing thought of reverent fear, "Am I fit to meet Jesus thus?"

SERMON II[a].

WHY DID DIVES LOSE HIS SOUL?

S. LUKE xvi. 25.

" But Abraham said; Son, thou in thy life-time receivedst
thy good things, and likewise Lazarus evil things :
but now he is comforted, and thou art tormented."

IT has become a sort of sacred Proverb, "No man
passeth from delights to delights"—from delights
of the senses to delights of the spirit; from delights
in things temporal to delights in things eternal;
from delights in the creature to delights in the
Creator; from pleasures of time and sense to the
pleasures at the Right Hand of God for evermore;
from joys in things *out of* God, to "enter into the joy
of our Lord," *in* God. And therefore God has so
mercifully sprinkled the destructive sweetness of this
life with healthful bitternesses[b]. He afflicts those
who are at ease with sorrow within or without.
Fence themselves with comforts how they will, they
cannot fence out the invisible messengers of God.
God bereaves, pierces their souls, sends manifold
sickness, disappoints the soul of what it is set upon,
strikes it through and through with the darts of
conscience, wearies it with satiety, draws off the veil

[a] Preached at All Saints, Margaret Street, Ashwednesday,
1865.   [b] S. Aug. Conf. iii. 1.

from their pleasures, and shews one end of all, corruption, and the worm creeping in and out of the sightless eyeholes.

Then come mostly the distress and weariness of the last sickness, and that almost-sacrament of death, hallowed, as an instrument of mercy and a channel of grace, by the precious Death of Jesus. So we may hope for souls, whom we could not endure to think of as lost, while yet we dare not incur the risk, from which they shrank not.

And therefore, since a life of worldly pleasure is so perilous, God has given us this sacred season of Lent, not that we may take up a few good practices, a little self-discipline or mortification, to be laid aside at Easter until the next Lent, just as people exchange the black of their mourning for all their former gay dresses, till Death again strikes one near to them. Lent has its lasting lessons, as well as its own deeper humiliation. Our Passover [c] is a season, not of going back, but of passing on, of inworking into life by His grace, what, by that grace we have learned of humility or penitence, or prayer, or simplicity, or self-sacrificing love.

And so our Lord has sent us to-day a strict preacher; not only the austere Baptist, in his raiment of hair-cloth, "Behold the axe is laid to the root of the tree;" not His own words of Divine love, nor the fiery flame of Paul's glowing soul, nor the deep tenderness of the beloved disciple, nor Peter's zeal for his Master's glory, nor the royal Penitent. He sends us one of ourselves; one, respectable, in man's sight blameless, whom all spoke

[c] S. Bern. Serm. in die Pasch. n. 14.

well of, just, upright, honest, such as are thousands
in this city from North to South, from East to West;
one who, if among us, would be respected, imitated,
followed, flattered, sought, sued; whose lot would
be envied, but—alas for that "but" at the end,
from which God in His Mercy preserve us all!—
damned. It is common to wish that we could see
some one from that bourne, whence no traveller returns, to tell us of its dread secrets, and whether
God is, after all, so strict a Judge, as He says in
His Word. The voices which are said to have come
from the other side the grave, have not been encouraging to sin; the sights, which have been seen,
are terrible. But now, our Dear Lord opens with
His own Lips one secret of that dread prison-house,
and shews us a lost soul. Let us ask him then,
"Why wert thou damned?" Our Lord will provide, that he should answer truly. "Didst thou
seduce others to sin? didst thou take away life, or
defile thy neighbour's bed?" He answers, "my
Judge does not pronounce any thing of this of me;
He has condemned me, but not for any of this."
"Didst thou then any of those things, to which
we owned just now, "the curse of God to be dueᵈ?"
Didst thou "pervert the judgement of the stranger,
the fatherless and widow;" or "smite thy neighbour
secretly," or "take reward to slay the innocent," or
wert thou "fornicator, slanderer, drunkard, extor-
tioner?" "Neither did my Judge pronounce me
guilty of these." "Was it then for something, of
which it were a shame to speak?" "My Judge said
it not of me." "Damned, but not for any of these

ᵈ Commination Service.

things, which men call crimes or vices! For what then?" O, if we could hear the horrible anguish of that remorseful cry, "I had all my good things in my life and I had not mercy upon Lazarus."

We should lose the force of our Blessed Lord's teaching, if we imagine things which He has not said. He has told us elsewhere His judgement on those other sins; and alas! many rich, once made members of Christ, are guilty of them. One, who should live like Dives, would be in proximate peril of very many sins. Luxurious society has very many sins; high feeding leads to wanton living. Aggravated, deepened sin will issue in deeper damnation. But had our Lord meant this to be the instruction of this history, He would have told us. He tells us not, that Dives forgat God altogether, or that he did not pacify his conscience by some good desires now and then. He tells us not, that He did not say his prayers, or that he did not go to the synagogue services—perhaps he was a regular Church-goer, set a good example, as men say; he *may* even have used the Pharisee's voluntary fasting, and given to God with exact scrupulosity the tithe of all which he possessed; he is not blamed for any outward neglect, though plainly his heart could not have been right with God; else he had not lost his soul. But outwardly, his may have been a respectable, decorous, Pharisee religion. One only sin has been thought to be hinted at in that especial punishment of the tongue, the favourite sin of our Christian world, backbiting. Perhaps he had not refinement enough for a new sin, which I hear of in our fastidious times, "am-

biguous words." Any how, it is likely enough,
that he spoke amiss. "Because loquacity," says
S. Gregory[e], "is wont to abound at feasts," (in our
days, he might have said, is their chief zest) "he,
who is said to have feasted amiss here, is related to
burn in hell most grievously in his tongue. Scripture says, 'The people sat down to eat and to drink
and rose up to play.' But before the body is moved
to play, the tongue is moved to jokes and idle
words."

Still more alarming is the thought, that Dives
lived, not only a life of negative, superficial respectability, but that he did some good things, and was
rewarded for them. You know how our Lord says
of those who do good for the praise of men, "Verily
I say unto you, they have their reward." They have
it to themselves, the word means[f], wholly here; and
so, when they come to die, there is no more for
them to have. S. Gregory thinks that our Lord
means the same by the use of the like word[g] here.
"If[h]," he says, "ye are of those who in this
world have received any outward good, ye ought
to fear greatly that very outward good, lest it should
be given you in recompense for some act of your's;
lest the Judge, Who requites you here with outward goods, repel you from the reward of the inward good; lest the honour and riches here be, not
an aid to virtues but the remuneration for toil. For
when it is said, 'Thou in thy life time receivedst
thy good things,' it is indicated that that rich man
had some good, for which in this life he was to re-

---

[e] Serm. 40. in Ev. n. 5.   [f] ἀπέχουσι S. Matt. vi. 2. 5. 16.
    [g] ἀπέλαβες.   [h] l. c. n. 6.

ceive good. And again, when it is said of Lazarus, that he 'received evil things,' it is shewn that. Lazarus too had some evil which was to be cleansed. But the fire of want purged the evil things of Lazarus; and the happiness of a fleeting life re-munerated the good things of the rich man. Poverty afflicted and cleansed the one : abundance remu-; nerated and rejected the other. Ye then, whoever are well off in this world, fear exceedingly for your-selves, when ye remember that ye have done good-things, lest the prosperity allowed you be the re-muneration for those same good things. And when ye see any poor do some blameworthy things, de-spise them not, despond not of them ; for perhaps what is very slightly amiss, the furnace of poverty cleanses. For yourselves by all means fear exceed-; ingly, in that, even after some things ill-done, a prosperous life hath followed. But for them, weigh carefully, that poverty, set over them as a mistress, excruciates their life, until it have brought it right."

But since our Lord does not ascribe any ill to Dives, save that which was inseparable from his life, and since he had probably some natural good in him, what was there in his life so offensive to Al-mighty God, that his soul was lost, and that he was for ever separated from the sight of God ?

It was not simply his hard-heartedness to Laza-rus; else our Lord would have dwelt on this alone. Priest and Levite passed by on the other side from the place, where lay the wounded Samaritan. Our Lord has taught us that the unmerciful shall not ob-tain mercy ; but this is not all. Else He would not have set before us all the rest. The unmercifulness comes as an incident in his life, perhaps an inseparable incident. But it is not the centre of his life. A shilling or two, given grudgingly to get rid of the sight of Lazarus, would not have changed his doom, unless God in His mercy had used even this grudging alms to change himself.

Our Lord tells us three things only of him directly; "He was clothed in purple and fine linen;" a gorgeous, certainly, and beautiful dress, such as the rich only wore, yet not above his station, as men say. It was a token of pride, all fine dressing is. "Some," says St. Gregory [i] very simply yet truly, "think the adornment of very fine and costly garments to be no sin. Had it been no fault, the word of God would not express so carefully, that the rich man who is in tortures in hell, had been clothed in purple and fine linen.—For the facts themselves attest, that no one gets choice dress save for vainglory alone, that he may seem more distinguished than others; in that no one cares about being dressed in costly attire, where he cannot be seen by others." Then, "he fared sumptuously every day." Again, there is no imputation of excess either in meat or drink. Our Lord does not say, that he was a gluttonous man or a drunkard, or that he verged on excess, without actually falling into it. Our Lord uses a very mild word[j], which, in itself, conveys no blame. He used it also in the parable of the other rich man, who "said to his soul, Soul, thou hast much good, laid up in store for many years; take thine ease, eat, drink and be merry [k]."

[i] l. c. n. 3.   [j] εὐφραινόμενος   [k] εὐφραίνου S. Luke xii. 19.

And of that feast of holy joy [m], wherewith the good Father welcomed back the returning prodigal, and, in reference to this, the eldest son, who led a respectable life in his father's house, upbraided his father, "Thou never gavest me a kid to make merry [n] with my friends." He made "good cheer," and that "splendidly" "magnificently [o]," (so the words mean.) There is not one word about excess, about having persons at his table, notorious for their immorality, (gallantry, the world calls it.) He kept a well-appointed table, and was known for the magnificence of his entertainments. Had he lived in these days, the world would have been told the next morning; "Dives gave a splendid entertainment at his elegant mansion in such a square, and, among the distinguished company, were such and such of the fashionable world." And some of the younger of you, perhaps, would have wished that they had been there; and mothers would have bethought themselves how they could obtain tickets for Lady Dives' next assembly. Nor again is it said, that he got his riches in any wrong way, or that he was extravagant with them, or was in debt to his tradesmen, or so delayed his payments, as to cause distress or inconvenience to any of them. He was rich, and he lived up to his income. That is all. Nor again is there any aggravation as to his neglect of Lazarus. Our Lord does not say that Lazarus even begged of him; it only says that he "was laid [p]," as a cripple doubtless, at the gate of his Court yard [q],

---

[m] εὐφρανθῶμεν, S. Luke xv. 23, εὐφραίνεσθαι, ib. 24, εὐφρανθῆναι ib. 32.   [n] εὐφρανθῶ, ib. 29.   [o] λαμπρῶς

[p] ἐβέβλητο·   [q] πυλῶνα.

and "desired to be filled with the fragments which fell from the rich man's table," such as the dogs ate then, and eat now, and which the poor did not get then, as now too they very seldom get them. Much plenty, much waste, much forgetfulness of God's poor! But we hear of no harsh refusal. Dives was pre-occupied probably with the conversation with his rich friends, and scarcely noticed or did not notice Lazarus, or thought that he exercised charity enough in allowing him to lie there. "Others, doubtless, would take care of him," he thought, if he thought at all; "it was a shocking, loathsome sight for *him* to go near. It would spoil his feast and his appetite." And, compared to our habits, it *was* so far a charity, which we should not exercise. Servants or the police would have been bidden to remove such an object. It would have been a memorable deed of charity, had he, before entering in to his feast, paused for a moment, to direct that Lazarus should be taken to the workhouse. Probably he would have cared little, whither he was removed, so that he lay not *there*. Dives, if he thought at all, was right, that others would relieve Lazarus; he had the charity of the dogs, and must have been fed somehow, perhaps, by the poor, who gave him of *their* bread.

And so, at last, the end came. Whether God saw that space of repentance would only bring deeper guilt upon him, and so cut him off suddenly, or whether he wasted that last respite, he died as he had lived. Perhaps in these days, we should, some of us, have read at our breakfast-table, the next morning, "We regret to announce that Dives was taken ill in the midst of a splendid and select circle, remained insensible, and died at an early hour this morning." And then, among us, would have followed the account of the great wealth which he left, and who inherited it, and how his entertainments would be missed in fashionable society; and then, in a few days, his splendid funeral, and the mourning carriages, and the number of the nobility who sent their empty carriages as a tribute of respect to his hospitality, and his magnificent tomb at his family seat, and its flattering inscription.

And people would have said a word or two of the sudden death of Dives, or moralised a little on the instability of human things. I doubt whether any now would have spoken of him, with a truth which they would not understand, as "*poor* Dives." One thing alone people would have shut their eyes to, "Where is he now?" Our Lord lifts up the veil, and tells us, "in torments," "tormented in this flame." Alas, Dives, who would be of thy party now?

What was it then in this life, with so little obvious blame, a life led so fearlessly by so many tens or hundreds of thousands among us, a life led by such multitudes in this and in every city without one misgiving, which was so offensive to God, that Dives is among the damned? Our Lord spoke this, be it history or parable, chiefly for us Christians. His words have been recited among us above these 1800 years. It is a mere negative life, a life in which no great harm was done, nothing but what was inseparable from the life itself; and yet he is damned!

One might say, that his whole life was contrary
to the three central graces, faith hope and charity.
He was living concentrated on self, apart from God
and from any real love of man, indulgent to self,
hard-hearted to misery.

Or, again, one might say, that it is wholly contrary to the Cross of Christ. "God predestinated us,"
S. Paul says. To what? To eternal life? This is
the end of all. But to what first? "God predestinated us to to be conformed to the image of His
Son[r]." What image? Well! Be it the image of His
holiness, the image of His glory. Are there then
no scars on that glorious Form, brighter than the
sun or than all created light, irradiant with His
Godhead? If we would reign with Him, S. Paul
tells us[s], that "we must first suffer with Him."
If we would be conformed to the likeness of His
glory, we must first be conformed to the likeness of
His suffering. "'Too delicate art thou, my brother,
if thou willest both here to rejoice with the world,
and hereafter to reign with Christ." Is the portion
which God gave to His Well-beloved Son, one from
which to shrink? Rather, God says that it is part of
His eternal love, that in that boundless eternity
God fore-knew and fore-ordained all those sufferings, crosses, sorrows, each in its own measure and
its own weight, that thereby we may be conformed
to the Son of His Love, Who bare the Cross for us,
that, thereafter, when He had made us members of
Himself, He might bear our's in us. We hear much,
now, of the believer being identified with Christ,

[r] Rom. viii. 29.   [s] 2 Tim. ii. 12.
[t] S. Jer. Ep. 14: ad Heliod. n. 10. p. 36. Vall.

so that men deny the atonement, on the ground that "[u] if Christ is one with the believer, He cannot be regarded strictly as a victim who takes [took] his place." Blessed be His Infinite love, that first He identified Himself with us by being "[v] made sin for us," that we might be identified with Him, by being "made the righteousness of God in Him." Blessed be His Divine compassion, that first He bare our sins and guilt and punishment, that He might give us of His Spirit, His grace, His holiness; that He took our evils, in order to give us His good. But was Jesus then Incarnate, did God become Man, did He pay that dear Price of all His Precious Blood, did He bear the weight of His Father's displeasure against sin, and was He made "sin" and "a curse," that He might merit for us the grace of living unsacrificing lives, keeping ourselves, as we think, from gross vices, wearing a fair reputation before men, honest, just in our dealings, but doing nothing good? Was our Redeemer crowned with thorns, that we might be refined sensualists? Did He come down from heaven, that we might forget heaven and Him, steeped in all which we can get of this life's fleeting pleasures of sense? Ask Him, Who was crucified for love of you. "[w] If any man *will* to come after me, let him deny himself and take up His cross daily and follow Me." Our Lord makes our coming after Him an act of our own free-will. "If any man *wills* to come." He invites us lovingly; "[x] Come unto Me, ye that labour and are heavy laden, and I will give you rest." He tells us

---

[u] Jowett on the Atonement. On the Epp. ii. 562.

[v] 2 Cor. v. 21.   [w] S. Luke ix. 23.   [x] S. Matth. xi. 28.

His Will for us, "ʸ That where I am, there may My servant be." He loves us to choose Him, with our free God-given love. But one thing He does not withhold from us; if we *do* will to follow Him, our only Good, we must bear our little crosses on the narrow road, which He tracked for us on His Blood-stained way to Calvary. They are heavy tones of wounded love with which He says, "ᶻ He that taketh not his cross and followeth after Me, is not worthy of ME." Not worthy of Him! O what words! When we are all so unworthy, when all is of His worthiness, to be disowned as unworthy, by Him Who so loved us and Who longed to give us of His worthiness!

Or ask the beloved Disciple, who drank in his wisdom and his love on Jesus' breast. "ᵃ If any man love the world, the love of the Father is not in him." Or ask that heart of fire, who always carried about in the body the doing-to-death of Jesus, that the life of Jesus might be made manifest in his body; who died daily; who was co-crucified with Christ; whose life in the flesh was Christ living in him; were these only the marks of thine Apostolate, the badge of thy high office? Not so, he says, "ᵇ They who are Christ's have crucified the flesh with the affections and desires." "ᶜ Be ye fellow-imitators of me, and mark those who so walk, as ye have us for an ensample. For many walk, of whom I have often spoken to you, and now also speak weeping, that they are the enemies of the Cross of Christ." What? Did they blaspheme? did they persecute? did they

ʸ S. John xii. 26.   ᶻ S. Matt. x. 38.   ᵃ 1 S. John ii. 15.
ᵇ Gal. v. 24.   ᶜ Phil. iii. 17-18.

contradict? did they deny? Not in words, but in
life. "[d] Whose end is destruction, whose God is
their belly, and their glory is in their shame, whose
mind is on earthly things." What a climax is this!
One might have thought perhaps that some deeper
sins lay in the words, "Their glory is in their shame."
But he brings us back, as the sum and substance of
all, to the way of life of Dives. " Whose mind is on
earthly things." And then, that we may not mistake, he mounts up, where his own way of life, and
hope and love and soul were gone, and were aloft
with Jesus: he summons us thither with himself to
Jesus. " *Their* mind is on earthly things," but
"[e] our [Christians'] conversation is in heaven."

But St. Paul ever speaks burning words. Ask
then that calm writer, who speaks by the Holy Ghost
in words of such still practical wisdom. Still the
same solemn voice, "[f] Whoso will be a friend of the
world is an enemy of God." There remain but two,
to fill up the sacred choir of the Apostles. Ask them.
It is not of any special sin, (however near such sin
may lie to this continual ease,) that St. Peter and St.
Jude speak, when they give us one comprehensive
description of ungodliness, "[g] following their own desires" in their unbridled undisciplined life.

To Christians it were enough condemnation of
this life, that it is the very contradictory of the Cross
of Christ. This comprises all evil, as to be a fol-
lower of Him, our Redeemer, is the sum of all good
and grace.

But look again in detail. What grace is there

[d] Phil. iii. 19.   [e] Ib. 20.   [f] S. James iv. 4.
[g] 2 Pet. iii. 3. S. Jude 10.

room for, in this life of frivolity, of self-indulgence, of sense, of self? I must not, I suppose, name repentance. It has a harsh austere sound in delicate ears. David says of himself, "[h] Every night make I my bed to swim; and I water my couch with my tears," What a penitence! It would spoil the eyes, and ruin all one's looks. Besides, these persons are to live wholly blameless lives! I wonder how they can say the Psalms on Sundays, (for it becomes respectable Christians to do so,) or call themselves "miserable sinners," unless they mean that Adam was so; or how they can tell God that "the remembrance of their sins is grievous unto them, and the burden of them is intolerable." I suppose that they mean, it is so to their neighbours, and ought to be to them, if they were such "as other men are." *They* have no need of repentance. *They* have never committed, in their youth, sins which the thought of God brings to their mind. Truly I believe that the thought of God does not bring their sins to their mind; for they never think of Him, if they can help it, except that His Providence somehow has made over to them a portion of His possessions on this earth, for which, since it came to them in the way of nature or of lawful industry, they need not thank Him.

But if, perchance, they should need repentance; if human frailty should have its way in this life of sense; if its code of morality should admit of sins, not less deadly, perhaps not less gross, because compatible with public decorum and respectability, what room could there be for repentance in such a life as

[h] Ps. vi. 6.

this? Listen to the indignant irony of a writer on penitence, who lived not long after S. John. "[i]Does it then become us to put up prayers for our sins in purple and Tyrian colours?—Let him seek out the most delicate baths in sequestered spots in gardens or near the sea: let him add to his expenditure; let him get together fatlings of monstrous growth: let him refine old wines, and when any one shall ask, 'On whom dost thou lavish these things?' let him say, 'I have sinned against God, and am in danger of perishing everlastingly; and therefore am I anxious, and I pine away and excruciate myself, that I may reconcile unto myself that God, Whom I have offended by my sins.'"

Well! granted then, that men have no greater overt sins, than can be wiped out by the daily, "Forgive us our trespasses:" granted, that they can go to heaven without repentance, or repent enough for such sins as they have, without sorrow, or that sorrow may be expressed by a mere wish that they had not done the wrong thing,—What have they? Where is life? Where is grace? Where is spirituality? Where is the presence of Christ in them, of which it is said, "[k]Know ye not your own selves, how that Jesus Christ is in you, except ye be reprobates?" "Where is "[l]holiness, without which no man shall see the Lord?"

To Dives one had better speak Chinese (for Chinese is at least a language of nature, and there must be heathen likenesses of Dives without the aggravations of his guilt); no language of earth would

[i] Tertul. de Pœnit. c. 11. p. 368. Oxf. Tr.
[k] 2 Cor. xiii. 5.   [l] Heb. xii. 14.

be more unknown to Dives, than the language of
God the Holy Ghost. How should they know of
the supernatural, whose whole life is carnal? or of
Heaven, whose whole thought is of earth? or of
eternity, whose whole business is to kill time? or of
God, who think only of Him, as of One Whom it is
respectable to own, and to think or say good things
of Him now and then, and Who is to minister to
their comfort, and provide somehow that they should
prolong in heaven a life, like that of earth without
its disagreeables.

But is then this life so surely free from deadly
sin? Is not, rather, the whole of it one deadly sin?
Of old, sloth used to be counted a deadly sin, and,
perhaps, of all the deadly sins the most difficult to
recover from, because it is so negative, so unawakening, like sleeping on the snow. Most lives
of sin have some pause, some break, some remorse,
some intervals of repentance. God may, by some
mightier power of grace, find, at last, an access to
the soul; the soul may receive it, burst its bonds, be
converted and live. The life of sloth, or rather the
death of sloth, is the more *one* sin, because the whole
being itself is sin. The soul escapes seeing individual
sins, by keeping within a certain outward decorum.
It does not commit sins, which would disgrace it to
itself or in the eyes of the world: it is too proud to
be mean, or to commit open disorders, or to risk loss
of reputation, or to fall into humiliating irregulari-
ties, which might, by God's grace perhaps, be the
occasion of saving it by humbling it. It practises
a heathen probity, costless courtesies, the hollow
mimicry of Christian graces, natural virtues; and

then it asks, with the rich young man who went away sorrowful from Christ "what lack I yet?" Nay it is blind, as *that* rich man was not, for it leaves Christ without being sorrowful; and thinks well of itself, because it is respected by the world which is like it; it applauds itself for its regularity in a life without a rule except self-will, without an occupation except idleness; nay which makes a strenuous occupation of indolence, which counts pleasure to be the state of life "to which it has pleased God to call" it; which esteems an universal negligence, save of its comforts or luxury or adornments, the duties of its calling; which counts self-enjoyment, the end for which God the Father created it, God the Son redeemed it, God the Holy Ghost sanctified it. Not to do gross evil is the sum and substance of its good. But where then is the yoke of Christ, so easy because He bears it for us? Where is "the body of sin" which we bear about us, and from which S. Paul longed to be freed? Where is the body, which S. Paul had to maltreat? Where is the broad road which leadeth to destruction, if this life, so destitute of all restraint, of all violence to self; which such multitudes throng, because it is so easy, so smooth, so toilless; whose victories, if it had any, require no struggle on the part of man, no grace of God, no prayer for grace, no self-subdual, if such a life as this is "the narrow?" Where is Christ's wo to the rich, on this ground only, "because they have received their consolation?" Where is the impossibility of serving two masters, God and Mammon, if love of wealth, of pleasure, of comfort, may possess a man, have dominion over him, occupy

his day-thoughts, fill his day-dreams, and he be
counted to love God, and be a servant of God
and not a servant of Mammon? Which is the
Master, He, Who is half remembered in some distracted words (prayer one could not call them without mockery) in the morning, or in some sleepy
thoughts at night, with a little extra-attendance now
and then, on a Sunday, to set the conscience at its
ease, and maintain decorum and propriety? Or is
it he, who fills the imagination, occupies the memory, masters the thoughts, enslaves the will, binds
the affections?

Nor let any one think, that he or she is less like
Dives, because they have not the means of the very
rich of Palestine, or the Dives' of this land, or because the world does not know of them as Dives',
and they do not make any shew in the pomps and
vanities of this world, and enjoy those vanities in a
quiet way. The characteristic of Dives was selfish
and vain enjoyment of his means in the continual
round of worldly pleasure, to the destruction of the
love of the poor, and so, God says, of the love of
God Himself. It was not the amount of the consumption upon himself, but its exclusiveness, which
shut out the love of God and damned him. The
sinfulness of sin does not depend on the greater or
less opportunity of sinning. There may be less of
sin, because more temptation, in the selfish profusion
of the millionaire than in the selfish comforts of one
of moderate means. It is not the splendour of nobles,
sorely as one knows that very many forget Lazarus,
sorely as one may fear for their salvation: it is not
their hereditary adherence to the customs handed

down to them from their forefathers, which, to one
who is accustomed to the thought of eternity, is so
frightful in revisiting this great Babylon.   It is the
growth of luxuries and comforts, as indicated in the
shops, the lesser equipages, the dress, the jewelry,
the trinkets, the baubles, the varied suits of ap-
parel.   It is, that luxuries have become comforts,
and comforts have become necessities; nay, that the
middle class (I mean, such as, I suppose, are most
of us) seems to have confused necessity, luxury,
comfort, in one reckless following of self-will.   And
mean-while Lazarus, where is he?   I saw out of
many streets one or two shops (honour be to them)
where there were "charity blankets" to be had,
amid every thing all around, to tempt to expenditure on self.   The rich had need to be bribed to
help the poor by the cheapness of *their* necessaries,
while there was no need to bribe them to expend
on themselves, save the multiplicity of things to
minister to "the lust of the eyes and the pride of
life."   I could scarce believe my eyes, when I saw
close by, as the price of a single dress in a shop-
window, (and in no shop of the fashionable of this
world) what would furnish a meal to 7000 poor[m].
Apart, as I said, from all trinketry, one Christian
lady was to wear as one of her manifold exterior
dresses, what would have removed the gnawings of
hunger of some 7000 members of Christ.

Our use of the word "charity" has deceived us.

[m] In Oxford Street. The price was £60. £60 would, of course,
provide 14,400 penny loaves. Hungry children before day-break
besiege a soup kitchen, where that sum would, at 2d., provide
7000 real meals.

People have deceived themselves as to their fundamental relation to God as their Creator. They account themselves lords, not stewards of God's gifts
to them. They hold of themselves, as if their broad
lands or their comfortable incomes were their own,
to be disposed of at their own arbitrary will, until
the day shall come, when six feet of earth, the coffin
the shroud and the worm, shall suffice them. God
wills that 'our charity,' as well as all our acts towards Him, should be with our own-free will; but
charity, as well as purity, is an absolute command
of God, which men neglect at peril of their souls.
It is a command which you must obey, at peril of
having the sentence pronounced upon you, "Depart, ye cursed, unto everlasting fire." It is a command, which you must obey, as you would not be rebels against the sovereignty of God, and be punished
as rebels against Him. It is a command which you
must obey, not as if you were doing some great
thing, not as if it were an act of generosity; but in
humility, as owning your allegiance to your God.
You do not, I suppose, think it a great virtue to
pay your income-tax honestly. It is simply, not to
lie and steal. Charity is a blessed income-tax due
to our God, in proportion to our means. It belongs to our condition of life. You speak of dress,
equipages, appearance, furniture, as suited to your
condition of life. Perhaps some of you have been
answering me in your minds, "We must dress,
spend, have this or that elegancy, such or such a
table, according to our condition of life." And I
say to you, that there is a condition of life, ante-
cedent to all these, the due to Almighty God, your

Sovereign Lord, "the King of kings and Lord of lords." And as you must, perforce, discharge your dues to the state, antecedently to your expenditure on your condition, so, as creatures of God, as members of Christ, you have another due upon you, antecedently and in proportion to your expenditure on self, your due to Almighty God, of which not the tax-gatherer but the poor man is the collector; of your payment of which God, year by year, takes account; which, if paid, He will reward a hundred fold; the holding back whereof He will punish, as contempt of Himself and of His love and of the Sufferings of Jesus for you, in Hell.

"It is no almsgiving to give a little out of much." Those guinea subscriptions out of large incomes are mockery of God; that "mite," which one hears of from time to time, is hideous hypocrisy, claiming the praises given to her who gave her all, for what costs nothing.

Dives had this excuse, that it was not an extreme necessity which he neglected. Lazarus was fed by others; yet Dives is in hell. But we know of Lazarus starving and *not* fed; kept out of our sight, often shrinking from it, his cries unheard by us, but heard of God. We know of chronic distress among our artizans; men of the same blood as ourselves, against whom famine tries habitually its strength, so that it is said that "nothing can starve them." The weavers of your gay clothing starve, while you make a shew of their toil. The women, who fit your dresses, perish untimely (some hard by) by their wasting toil. It is a known class of women, which ekes out its scanty wages by occasional deadly, degrading, sin. Rachel weeps for her children; and now, by a worse lot, *is* "comforted when they are not;" for it is better to see them stretched out in death, than to hear the cries of their unstilled hunger. And you, which robe are you weaving for yourselves? Are you arraying Christ in the robes wherewith you clothe His poor, that, at the aweful Day, your Judge may say, "With this have ye clad Me; I see you, not in the defilement of your sins, but clothed in the robe of My righteousness; receive the robe of glory, which I have dyed for you with My Own most Precious Blood?" If not, what remains for you but the robe of everlasting fire, to wreathe round you, your inseparable dress for ever?

One only choice have you, to sacrifice your selfishness, your pride, your love of perpetual comfort, your love of shew, your purple and fine linen, and selfish cheer, for the love of Christ; or, hereafter, yourselves to be the outcasts, whom ye here despise, outcasts from the despised love of God, cast out into outer darkness, the darkness of the lightless lurid fire of Hell.

God give us grace, this Lent, to consider our ways; that, if we have learned something of self-sacrifice, we may learn more in that blessed school of giving love for Love, sacrifices hallowed by His Blessed Sacrifice; or else that first grace to shew mercy, in proportion to our means, that we may not be shut out from His Mercy and His Presence for ever!

SERMON III.

Acts xxvi. 27, 28.

*" King Agrippa, believest thou the prophets? I know
that thou believest.   Then Agrippa said unto Paul,
Almost thou persuadest me to be a Christian."*

O BOLD, noble, self-forgetful avowal of truth, honourable in the sight of men! O base, cowardly, self-
regarding, withholding of the truth, shameful in the
sight of God! As man to man, king Agrippa's
answer to the Apostle was sympathising, gentle,
well-nigh humble, acquitting the prisoner before
him. As man towards his God, his answer was
proud, supercilious, disdainful of enquiry, rejecting
and condemning the wisdom of the All-Wise. As
words of human nature, they must have cost him
an effort, almost beyond our nature, incurring
public contempt, amid circumstances the most trying, sooner than speak untruth. As relates to Divine grace, they were, under courteous terms, a
rude repulse of God, slighting and putting aside
the evident truth of God.

Unhopeful was the way, in which king Agrippa
came to hear the message from his God. The be-

ginning was the herald of the close. From his birth and education, he knew well the subjects on which the Apostle preached. S. Paul, throughout his defence, appealed to him, as thoroughly acquainted with them. Not the Apostle's own defence, but Agrippa's soul, was the aim of the Apostle's fervid words. Agrippa's own knowledge and belief laid him open to the shafts of truth. At this mark S. Paul shot appeal after appeal. He begins by engaging the king's attention. "I know thee to be expert in all questions and customs which are among the Jews." He continues by appealing to the king's hopes, "I stand and am judged for the hope of the promise, made of God unto our fathers," —"for which hope's sake, king Agrippa, I am accused of the Jews."

King Agrippa knew and believed the prophets. He knew and believed their prophecies of the Christ. He knew and believed "the promise" of a Redeemer, "made of God unto their fathers." He knew, and, it would seem, shared the hope, "to which *our* twelve tribes" (S. Paul says, associating the king with himself) "instantly serving God day and night, hope to come." He had heard too of the Resurrection of Christ, although, it would seem, he regarded that great Mystery as a thing impossible. S. Paul appeals to him; "Why should it seem a thing impossible to you, that God should raise the dead?" Agrippa had too, it seems, heard of S. Paul's sudden conversion. For of this, as well as of his Lord's Resurrection, S. Paul says, just before his last appeal to the king, "The king knoweth of these things, before whom also I speak freely; for I am persuaded that none of these things are hidden from him; for this thing was not done in a corner."

S. Paul accordingly, throughout his appeal to the king, refers to his own experience. S. Paul too had once been of that strictest sect of his religion, which now was persecuting himself; he too had once, with all his fiery zeal, "persecuted that way unto the death," and thought that, in so doing, he "did God service." But Jesus, in glory, had appeared to him, and had spoken to him. Jesus had at once given him proof of His Resurrection, of His power, and of His tender love, as well for S. Paul's own soul, as for those whom he was persecuting. Jesus had appealed to *him*, "Saul, Saul, why persecutest thou Me?" and he had listened to the appeal. Jesus had called; he had obeyed. The voices of the Prophets were now God's voice to Agrippa. He believed *them*. "If he believed them, (it is our Lord's own argument[a]) he should have believed Christ; for they wrote of Christ."

Who knows but that Agrippa too might have obeyed, that his "almost" might have been "altogether" a Christian, that he might have exchanged his petty earthly dignity for some high place near the throne of God, the first of that princely band of royal Martyrs, had he not placed himself in circumstances unfavourable to the reception of truth from God?

Agrippa believed in the prophets. He must have heard, in some measure, how manifoldly their words were fulfilled in our Lord. He could not then but suspect, that Jesus *might* be the Christ. How then

[a] S. John v. 46.

does he come to hear the Apostle deliver what, he must have known, *might* be a message from his God?

He came, as a judge of Him Who shall be his Judge. "I also would hear the man myself." Outwardly, he seemed to be judging the Apostle; in deed and in truth, he was judging Christ. He was pronouncing on the power of God, and the wisdom of God, and the goodness of God. On His Power, whether it was possible for Him to raise the dead; on His Wisdom, Who chose thus to reveal Himself and give this evidence of His revelation; on His Goodness, Who required His creatures to believe in Him, Whom He had "[b] declared to be" His "Son through the Resurrection from the dead."

In the prime of life, having had his ambition gratified, step by step, yet still with a rule inferior to his father's, he came, in company with one who to his face had spoken of his own religion as superstition[c]. He came, in order to enable him to give to the Roman Emperor, on whom his worldly honour or disgrace depended, an account of Paul the prisoner, which might seem acceptable and reasonable in the eyes of his master; and that master, Nero. Doubtless, Agrippa meant to act kindly and justly by the Apostle. Besides curiosity, he willed doubtless to give a more dispassionate account of him than his persecutors among the Pharisees and Sadducees.

He came, associated with his sister Bernice, a shame to her sex, of whose sin he was thought to be partaker[d], to hear the messenger of the All-Holy God. He came, in great pomp, to hear of Him,

[b] Rom. i. 4.   [c] Acts xxv. 19.   [d] Jos. Ant. xx. 7. 3.

Who, being God, humbled Himself to become Man.
He came, surrounded with flatterers, courtiers of
himself and despisers of his God, to avow (if he
would avow the truth), that his God was crucified.
"ᵉChrist crucified, unto the Jews a stumblingblock,
and unto the Greeks foolishness."

Thus, fenced around and guarded from the access
of the truth, Agrippa heard the Apostle of truth, as
a Civil judge, impartially. He bore him witness,
which might do credit to a Christian judge, if he
had to stem the tide of popular clamour and popular
injustice. "ᶠThis man doeth nothing worthy of
death or of bonds." "This man might have been
set at liberty, if he had not appealed unto Cæsar."
As man towards man, he was unimpeachable. But
his soul, in what state was it? Straight to his soul
had sped that last appeal of the Apostle; "King
Agrippa, believest thou the prophets?" The Apostle had saved him from all hesitation as to the answer; "I know that thou believest." King Agrippa
(as is the way with such as he) neither assented, nor
dissented. He would not own in the presence of the
heathen, that he believed thus much. He was ready
to own, that he "almost" believed more. O costly,
costless, "almost!" "Costly!" for it must have cost
him some shame to say thus much in the presence of
the scoffing Festus! Costly! for he sacrificed something of this world's credit, and gained nothing for
the world to come. Costless! for they were words
only. They cost him no passing pleasure, no honour,
no self-indulgence. All went on as before. He had
come into the presence of the Light; it had shone

ᵉ 1 Cor. i. 23. ᶠ Acts xxvi. 31, 32.

upon him ; God had sought entrance into his heart;
he had parleyed, but had refused Him; he had heard
of turning from darkness to light, from the power of
Satan unto God, and he had turned away from the
light to darkness.   He and his sinful sister, "and
the governor and chief captain and principal men
of the city," swept away out of the presence of the
Apostle ; and the night of unbelief of error and
of sin closed around and upon them.   Doubtless
Agrippa often, when alone, heard within him the
echo of the Apostle's words, "King Agrippa, believest thou the prophets?"   Doubtless, in his dreams
he often saw the Apostle's look of love, as he said,
"I would to God that thou wert both almost and
altogether, such as I am, except these bonds."   Perhaps, when, in his seventy years of life, he felt its
vanity, he would sometimes wish, that he could
have hearkened to the Apostle's voice, or that it had
not been so hard a thing to be "altogether a Christian."   But when the direct voice of God is not
obeyed, those after-echoes of that voice are seldom
listened to.   Agrippa lived on for the full period of
man's threescore years and ten, an irreverent patron
of the Jews' religion; he lived and died his own idol,
courting the populace by shews, which God's written
and unwritten law forbids; courting an Anti-Christian Emperor, who persecuted the Christians, and
made two glorious martyrs, S. Peter and S. Paul.
Once he thought himself "almost persuaded to be a
Christian;" he died, an irreligious Jew.

  To have been, once in his life "almost persuaded
to be a Christian," was not to "be all but a Christian."   All which was done, was on the part of God.

E

All which failed, was, from himself. It was to have had the truth of the Gospel brought home to his soul, and to have refused it. It was, to have been overstreamed with the light of the Gospel, and to have closed his eyes against it. It was, to have heard the words of God borne in upon him, and to have deafened his ears to them. It was, to have been "almost" overpowered by the grace of God, and to have resisted it, rejected it, baffled it, quenched it. It was, to have been face to face with God, to have been drawn and invited by His love, and to have said, "I will have none of it."

So far from its being any gain to a soul, to have been or to be, "almost a Christian," far better, if it stop there, never to have heard the name of Christ. " ᵍ It shall be more tolerable in the Day of Judgement for Sodom and Gomorrah, than for that city." It betokens no effort on the part of the soul itself. It betokens this only, that God has visited the soul with light so clear, or with terrors so aweful, or with persuasiveness so loving, or with drawings so all-but-irresistible, that the soul was almost scared or convinced, or persuaded, or dragged " by cords of love" into submission to its Maker, and it would not. God addresses each soul, as He knows best, where the access to each is. Felix was shaken through and through with terror; around Agrippa's soul He shed the full clear light of truth. But then the corrupt will, which would not be persuaded to submit itself to its Creator, stands the more deliberately, malignantly, opposed to the will of God. It availed not, in the time of the flood, if any had been per-

ᵍ S. Matt. x. 15.

suaded to come to the door of the Ark. All who
were not in the Ark, when the flood came, perished.
It availed not to Lot's wife, that she had been almost persuaded to quit the whole land which God
had doomed. She became a monument of the wrath
of God, more marked than the undistinguished heap
who perished in the overthrow. It availed not to
that other Herod, that in many things he listened
to S. John Baptist, "ʰand heard him gladly," since,
in the end, he killed him. It availed not to Pilate,
that again and again, he acquitted our Lord, his
Judge, and was dragged unwillingly by his own
evil conscience to do what the Jews, whom he had
wronged, demanded of him. When, at the last, he
condemned his God, he the more condemned himself, because he before had acquitted Him. It
availed not to Simon Magus, to have half believed,
nor to Saul to have half obeyed, nor to Balaam to
have half listened, nor to Judas, to have followed
Christ. Nor will it, our Lord says, in the Day of
Judgement avail those who so far believed in Him,
that they could say, "ⁱLord, Lord, have we not
prophesied in Thy Name, and in Thy Name cast
out devils, and in Thy Name done many wonderful
works?" And then He saith, "I will profess unto
them, I never knew you; depart from Me, ye that
work iniquity." Christ will say that He never knew
them, even when, without love, they had light to
speak holy words of Him, and faith to do miracles,
and seemed so opposed to Satan, that they could
cast devils out of the bodies of men, while he dwelt
in their own souls. The words which they spake

ʰ S. Mark vi. 20.   ⁱ S. Matt. vii. 22, 23.

E 2

were by His Wisdom, the works which they did
were by His Power; what they did and spake was
in His Name; but He will say, "I never knew
you" since, amid this light, and faith, and knowledge, they were also doing deeds which Christ
hates. Yea rather, as it is thought, that there is
no deeper damnation than that of Judas, who was
so nigh our Lord, so it is also thought, that those
priests who shall perish, will incur a deeper damnation, both because they drew others with them to
Hell, and because they sinned against more continual light.

Whatever light a man has, that very light, if he
come not wholly to Christ, is his condemnation.
The greater the light, the deeper the damnation.
"This," saith our Lord, "is *the* condemnation[k], that
light is come into the world, and men loved darkness rather than light, because their deeds were
evil." He saith not, "This is condemnation," but,
" this is *the* condemnation." This is *the* ground and
source of the condemnation, that the light came unto
them, and they loved their sins better than God, and
refused the light, that they might abide undisturbed
in their sins. "[1] All had sinned." God forgives the
past, however black it be; He will make the defiled,
clean; the leprous, whole; spots so deep, that it
might rather seem they would whole seas incarnadine, He will make white as wool; if only henceforth
men will come to Him, love Him, serve Him. "This
is *the* condemnation," that, when men may be forgiven, when men know that they may be forgiven,
they will not part with their sins, that they may

k S. John iii. 19.   l Rom. iii. 23.

have forgiveness, and God for their own God. They choose their sins, and reject their God.

So again saith our Lord to the Pharisees, who boasted of their light, " Are we blind also ? "   " [m]If ye were blind, ye should not have sin; but now ye say, We see, therefore your sin remaineth." Had the Pharisees been indeed blind, their ignorance of Christ had had its excuse with the All-Merciful. Pure, helpless ignorance and blindness, i. e., ignorance and blindness which a man never could have helped, will condemn no one at the last day. But now they said, " we see;" they had certain sight and insight, although they abused it to condemn Christ, and they perished.

Once more, increase of light, if rejected, increases condemnation. " If I had not come and spoken to them," saith our Lord[n], " they had not had sin, but now they have no cloke for their sin." Before Christ came, they believed in Him as " He who should come;" they believed in Him imperfectly, according to their prejudices; still, they believed in Him. Christ came, not as they looked for Him, to exalt their nation, to free them from the Romans, to be a great earthly, as well as spiritual, sovereign. He disappointed their hopes, yet they could not answer His proofs; they could not deny His miracles. They had their choice, to receive more truth which they disliked, or to reject Him Who is the Truth. Some, like Nicodemus and Joseph of Arimathea, received Him. To others He stood in their way; they hated His reproofs; they hated alike His strictness and what they thought His laxity, His love for sinners;

[m] S. John ix. 41.   [n] Ib. xv. 22.

they hated Him, because they hated His humility
and His authority, and His weakening of their authority.   In the end, our Blessed Lord says, "°they
have both seen and hated both Me and My Father."
The presence of the Light, unveiled, called into conscious existence, developed, intensified what was evil
in them.   They had not, comparatively, had sin;
they had not been condemned in that depth of condemnation, had not Christ brought them light and
they rejected it.

We thank God daily (and it is right and our
bounden duty to thank Him) for "the means of grace
and for the hope of glory."   We have many of us
been taught to thank Him in our childhood, that we
were born in a Christian land, where God, the true
God, Alone is worshipped and adored.   But better,
far better, were it to have been born, where God is
unknown, and stocks and stones are worshipped, or
aught more brutish and senseless than stocks and
stones, than, amid the light which we have, for
which we thank God, of which we boast, to sin
against that light, and be but "almost persuaded
to be a Christian."

Who then, you will ask, are these?   My brethren,
the question is of the more aweful moment, because
it seems as though the greater part of those who
will perish, will be of this sort.   It has been said,
and our Lord's words seem to bear out the saying,
"pAlmost all who are damned, are damned believing
themselves to be saved; all those who are cast away
at the last Day, when they hear their sentence,

° S. John xiv. 9.
p Massillon Serm. sur le salut fin. Œuvres i. p. 482.

will be surprised at their condemnation, the Gospel saith, '[q]When saw we Thee an hungred?' because they all expected the inheritance of the just."

Who then, you ask, are these almost "persuaded to be a Christian?" I will ask you, in turn, Who or what is a Christian? You will say readily, "He who believes in Christ, who loves Christ, hopes in Him, and obeys Him; and that, with all his mind and soul and strength, owning no other Lord, but only Christ."

Then I must say to you, whoso wilfully falls short of this, in faith, or love, or obedience, is *not* a Christian, is hanging on only to Christianity; and whoso would be a Christian, if to be a Christian did not cost him this or that, whoso is held back by this or that (be it what it may) from surrendering his whole understanding, or faith, or will, or obedience and himself in any one of these, may be "almost persuaded to be a Christian," but is none. What he admires or respects in Christ our God and His Gospel, by that, through the grace of God enlightening him, he is drawn, and "almost persuaded to be a Christian." Whatever that thing is, which holds him back from that complete self-surrender, that it is, which hinders him from being "altogether" a Christian.

The hindrance may be in faith or life, from the world or the flesh.

In faith, thou mayest be "almost persuaded to be a Christian," but as yet art none, if thou wilfully withhold thy belief from any doctrine which God has revealed; if thou blind thyself, so as not

[q] S. Matt. xxv. 37.

to believe that God has revealed it; if thou turn
away thine eyes, lest thou shouldest be forced to
see, that He has revealed it; if thou palm genera-
lities on thyself, sooner than look God's truth in the
face; if thou thinkest that thou mayest dispense
with it, mayest bend it to thy mind, needest not
be so precise about it, mayest take what thou likest,
and leave what mislikes thee. Truth is one; faith
is one. If thou pare off from any word of Christ,
thou receivest not Christ, but a phantom of thine
own; thou art not conformed in thy mind to Christ,
but wouldest conform Christ to thee. "'If any man,".
(they are almost the closing words of God's revelation) "if any man shall take away from the words
of the book of this prophecy, God shall take away
his part out of the book of life." "If thou wilt be
a Christian, be altogether a Christian," was the
mournful saying of a learned rationalist [s] to a Jew,
owning what he himself was not, owning what it
would be far better to be, but what he had not
yielded his own mind to be.

My brethren, the world will tempt you in this
way, if it have not already tempted you. The world
is the enemy of the Gospel, in faith as well as in
life. Tolerant of every form of error, it is intolerant
of the exclusive claim of truth. It bears with all
"opinions;" it hates faith. Its effort, now, is to
merge all faith in "opinions," as though all truth
were, alike, mere " opinion," and there were no certain truth. And then it pares off, at its will, what
mislikes it. And so the world is full of phantoms

[r] Rev. xxii. 19.   [s] Gesenius. He could not understand why
the Jew should wish to be a Christian.

of Christianity, in which nothing is to shock our unillumined understanding, nothing is to disturb our prejudices, natural or acquired, general or individual. Since then, the proverb tells us, "as many minds, so many meanings," men, if they admit any other principle except that of submission to God's revelation, must have as many Christianities, as there are caprices of human taste and human will. And so there are afloat hundreds of Christianities. You have Christianity without Judaism, Christianity without facts, Christianity without doctrines, Christianity without any thing supernatural, Christianity, which shall only be an "idea;" Christianity with fallible Apostles, fallible Prophets, (alas! that one must give utterance to the blasphemy) a fallible Christ! The blasphemy shocks you. And yet, if thou venturest to lay aside any thing, which Christ has said, because it mislikes you; if you say, Christ cannot have meant this or that, which yet His words plainly do mean, how thin and flimsy is the veil, by which thou hidest from thyself, that thou in this disclaimest His authority, and art but "almost a Christian!"

In life, there are more ways in which a person may be almost persuaded to be a Christian, and yet not be a Christian, because there are more varied ways of self-deceit.

Mind well, my brethren. Before, the question was not of plain, naked, hardened unbelief and blasphemy, but of a subtle unbelief, which eats out the heart of faith, and yet leaves an outward shew of belief. So here, it is not the question as to open profligates, drunkards, adulterers, fornicators, extortioners. These have their own condemnation; but it may be, by God's grace, they may repent the soonest. These too, if they have not sinned away grace and hardened themselves beyond its reach, may, by some powerful access of grace, have anew the choice whether they will be Christians, almost or altogether, whether by a thorough conversion they will be wholly God's, or whether, they will allow themselves to be swept back to the depths of hell.

But, for the most part, those who are almost persuaded to be Christians, have much, often very much, in common with Christians; only this is mostly nature, temperament, feeling, not grace, or if it be grace, it is grace admitted only for a time, to be thrust or jostled out afterwards. Now, in this vast reign of self-deceit, it is important to see and acknowledge, that just what men allege in their excuse, the very ground of their hope, is the ground of their condemnation.

What more common than for a man to hope well for himself, because he wishes to turn to God hereafter: as S. Augustine, in his heathen state, prayed honestly to God; "'Give me continence, *only not yet?*" He saw the beauty of continence; he saw the necessity of belonging to God, and that, without purity, he could not belong to God; but he could not resolve to part with his master-sin. He was not a Christian; he knew that he was none; and prayed that he might be such hereafter, and his prayers were not then heard. If thou desirest to turn to God hereafter, then thou bearest witness against thyself, that thou art not His, *now*. His grace has visited

ᵗ S. Aug. Conf. viii. n. 17. Oxf. Tr.

thee, else thou couldest not have had the wish at
all. Every wish to belong to God, from the faintest
velleity to serve God alone to that last constraining grace, to which the soul yields itself in thankful submission, is of the grace of God. Every faintest wish, hadst thou attended to it, not turned away
from it, might have been ripened to that overpowering grace, which masters each remaining resistance
of the soul. But then, if thou hearkenedst not, thou
resistedst light, thou stifledst grace, thou didst put
away thy God. God, at each time, calls thee, not to
repent hereafter, or some years hence or, to-morrow,
but to-day. "To-day if ye will hear His Voice, harden
not your hearts." What folly then to flatter thyself
that thou hast not given up God formally, that thou
hast not parted with all purpose of serving Him,
when thy very wish convicts thee of having despised
the grace of God, of having been called to be altogether a Christian, and having put God off to some
unknown time! Nay, if when thoughts of death
and judgement come across thee, thou still quietest
the fears which God awakens in thee, with thoughts
of a future repentance, thou art, up to this moment,
stifling the grace of God. If thou buildest on these
hopes, thou buildest on thine own contempt of the
grace of God, Who calleth thee to repentance. But
by these same hopes thou ownest, that thou art not
altogether a Christian now; and, since thou canst
not partly belong to Christ, partly to the evil one,
that thou dost not belong to Christ at all. Thou art
none of His.

Again, no man has all temptations. Compared to
the very bad, the young may think themselves, at

least, passing good. They have not had time to become altogether bad. Nay, they have many fine fresh feelings, warm hearts, generous purposes; zeal, at least, against what is base, or (perhaps) for the good of others and against evil. They have what, penetrated and transfigured by the grace of God, may shine for ever in the kingdom of their Father. These very things, if you look at them and build upon them, will lead to the most fatal self-deceits. Your trial does not lie in *them*. These things too will become corrupted and debased hereafter, if you flatter yourselves as to them, and neglect your real trial. You are tempted to think, " I shall do well enough, because I do not sin in this or that way; " as if Christian holiness were, not to have all vices, or as though Christ had died for you and God the Holy Ghost were given you to dwell in you, that you might not have vices, of which your finer nature is ashamed, which, out of mere generous feeling, you would scorn or hate !

The main trial of each of you, my brethren, lies in one single thing, your master-passion. It has not had time, or has, I trust, not been so yielded to, that it should have infected your whole souls yet. In most alas ! that ruling passion is love of some pleasure of sense ; in others, it is pride ; in others, vanity ; in others, ambition ; in others, love of self ; in others, envy of others. These, of their own nature, run into one another, and some are different forms of the same tyrant-passion. I have mentioned the more, that you may recognise the more readily your own.

Now, whereas the greatest peril of each of you is,

lest he be yielding to his master-passion, and letting it gain dominion over him, the arch-deceit of Satan is to persuade you, that it is all well with you, because you are only yielding to that one. When you take account of yourselves, or when conscience smites you for having again yielded to your master-sin, he would persuade you to look away from it, and would suggest to you, that you are kind-hearted, or gentle, or noble-minded, generous, soon-forgiving, or the like. As if one, sick of consumption, were to think well of himself, because his heart was sound; or one dying of fever were to hope for life, because he had no atrophy!

No, my brethren, in that one trial lies your everlasting doom, your place for ever amidst God's creation, among those who have, by God's grace, chosen God, and become altogether Christians, or among those who have rejected Him and been rejected by Him; your place around the Throne of God, or in Hell-fire. If, by God's grace, you conquer in that one trial, God will give you larger grace, and completer victories and closer union with Himself, until every thing within you is subdued to the love of Christ, and He reigns the undisputed Lord of your whole heart. If you neglect or give way to that one, the sin, which you cherish, will bring in with it the sins which you as yet detest; the cancer which you burn not out, will spread to what is yet sound; the passion which you excuse, because you see in yourselves other natural good, will infect and corrupt that partial good, until it also shall become full of evil. By that one passion Satan holds you. In Baptism, ye "renounced the devil and," not some only, but, "all his works." If thou wilfully choose any one work of his, thou mayest be almost persuaded, at some time when God offers you larger grace, but thou art not yet persuaded to be a Christian.

It may be, that already, strengthening corrupt nature against thyself, thou hast developed some passion into præter-natural energy against thyself. Thou canst not then mistake it, unless thou have come to justify it against God.

Is thy temperament easy, so that thou hast no strength to resist the stronger wills of others, but art persuaded to evil, which, of thyself, thou wouldest not choose, and fallest in with their evil ways, unable even by silence to detach thyself from evil, with which thou art surrounded? Fear of the world and of man's opinion is thy bane. Fear of the world is stronger in thee than the love of God. Break off from society which is too strong for thy better self. This weakness is it, which hinders thee from being altogether a Christian.

Hast thou, in earlier days, allowed thy imagination to be corrupted, so that thoughts which thou knowest to be forbidden thee, come to thee, and thou takest pleasure in them and dwellest on them, or invitest them to thee, even although thou wouldest not do the sins to which they relate? Thou must turn from them wholly, however they beset thee; else thou canst not be altogether a Christian.

Or didst thou allow some wrong habit to grow over thee, which, although it may not injure others, thou didst afterwards, when it had gained strength, learn to be deadly sin? Hast thou again and again resolved against it, and still fallest into it? Thou must by God's grace, renounce it for ever: else thou canst not be a Christian.

Or dost thou allow sloth to creep over thee, so that it has made thee well-nigh cease to pray, even morning and evening, and thou puttest off the thought of God, wilt not rouse thy soul to things above what thou seest, actest in thy daily life, as if God were not, turnest away, or holdest sluggishly back, if God give thee some gleam of prayer? Jew, Turk, Heathen will arise in the Day of Judgement to condemn thee. Canst thou think thyself a Christian?

Or despisest thou truth, when it suiteth thee, in exaggeration, to give life to thy conversation, or to avoid some scrape or some passing shame, or to exalt thyself? Dost thou act untruth, palming off as thine what is not thine? Deceit, in act or word, direct or indirect, in ways habitual to those in thy station or thine own, is lying; and "ᵛ liars," thou knowest, "shall have their part in the lake of fire." Thou canst not lie and be a Christian.

Or does vanity and love of personal appearance or the wish to vie with those of larger means, tempt thee to contract debts which thou canst not pay, and knowest not how thou ever wilt pay? "Owe no man any thing," saith God ᵂ, "but to love one another." Such debts are fraud, and are as much theft, as the more naked thefts of poorer vanity. "The curse of God," God Himself saith ˣ, "shall enter into the house of the thief." Called by this name, thou couldest not say, that such an one as thou art is a Christian.

ᵛ Rev. xxi. 8.　　ᵂ Rom. xiii. 8.　　ˣ Zech. v. 4.

Or dost thou, in levity and wantonness of spirit, by look or word or touch, risk injuring another's soul, or encourage them in sin, or jest at seriousness? To do aught which may injure another's soul, is to be, as far as in thee lies, a murderer of souls; murder more lasting far, than the death of the body; and, ye know that "[w] no murderer hath eternal life abiding in him." Christ died to save men's souls, how canst thou belong to Christ, if out of wantonness thou destroyest those souls for whom Christ died?

Whatever it be of these or other sins, as pride, anger, covetousness, which thou wilfully and habitually choosest, thou must give up thy sin or thou givest up God; thou must in will and deed, renounce thy sin, or thou renouncest Christ.

Do these seem to you hard sayings? Seemeth it to you a hard thing, that any one of these things can hinder thee from being owned in God's sight, as a Christian? Is it then a hard thing, that God made thee to be wholly His, that Christ redeemed thee wholly, and bought, at so dear a price, His own Precious Blood, thy whole self; or that God the Holy Ghost wills to dwell in thee, and fill thee with Himself? Is it a hard thing, that, God Who created thee, redeemed thee, sanctified thee, hath set His love upon thee, and will not have from thee less than thy whole self? God loveth with no half-love. Thou wouldest not, thyself, have any half-love. Let God or thyself be thy measure to thyself. If God has dealt with thee by halves, if Christ half-died for thee, if God, Who is love, half-loveth thee, if Satan

[w] 1 S. John iii. 15.

or the world half-created thee, then requite God with His own, then do thou halve with God; then half love God, half the world; then be half a Christian. But since God loveth thee with an infinite love, since, in the bosom of that love, He everlastingly beheld thee, ere He created thee, and in that love He brought thee out of nothingness, to be the object of His love, to feel, taste, know, His "love which passeth knowledge;" since He "emptied Himself," and became Man for thee, lived, suffered, was despised, mocked, scourged, crucified for love of thee; yea, since Christ now liveth to make intercession for thee, then give Him love for love, give Him a whole undivided love for His Infinity of love.

Then, when you have tried it, you will know how sweet, peaceful, joyous, a thing it is, wholly, without reserve, to have surrendered yourself to the loving will of God. As a half-Christian, you have neither the miserable, feverish, joys of the world, nor the solid, peaceful, joy in God. Only entire self-surrender, only full obedience has joy in God. The more you pare down your obedience, the more irksome it will be to you; the more you would lighten the cross to yourself, the heavier it will be to you. For the little which you do bear, you bear alone. Christ's yoke is easy, because He beareth it with us. He places Himself beneath it, so that it should not press upon us. But He beareth no half-yoke; He dwelleth in no divided heart. He sheddeth His peace in the souls in which He dwells, not on those who will not that He should reign over them.

Take Him at His word, my brother. If, on ex-

F

perience you find Him a hard Master, *then* refuse
His service. No one ever renounced His service,
who knew it. "These fourscore and six years am
I His servant," said the aged martyr[x], "and He
never did me any wrong; how then should I blaspheme my King, who saved me?" But think not
that you can know any thing of it, while you give
but a half-service. You have ever the irksomeness
of beginning, and never the joy of progress; you
know of God as a Master, Whom you ought to
obey; you cannot know Him as a Father, Who
loveth you and cherisheth you: you know of Him
as a Lord, forbidding you what the flesh would
have; you cannot know Him, as replacing what He
forbids you, by the abundance of His consolations,
of assured peace, of brightening hopes, by the foretaste of eternal bliss. You have heard of Him as
one whom you ought to fear; you know of Him as
a Judge Who casts the wicked into Hell, and may
so cast you; you can know nothing of His love;
for He poureth not His love into the "broken cis-
terns" of a divided heart.

You have tried this world, and it has failed you;
the more deeply you would try it, the more deeply
it must fail you, because it is not God, and nothing
short of God can satisfy the soul, which God made
in His own image, to be united with Himself. All
pleasure of this world is but a feverish draught,
irritating the thirst, which it cannot quench, muddier
and fouler, the deeper any one drinks it. If as yet
you know not its unsatisfactoriness, it is that as
yet you have not drunk the dregs. The degree in

[x] S. Polycarp in Eus. H. E. iv. 15.

which you do not know their unsatisfactoriness, is just that degree in which you do not know themselves. The degree in which you do not know the joy of being God's, is just that degree in which you are not God's.

You could not doubt now, which lot to choose, that of Paul the prisoner, like his Master, "despised and rejected of men," his chains, his privations, his bonds and afflictions, or that of the king who heard, pitied, acquitted, neglected him. Not for all his pomp, his wealth, that unsatisfying satisfaction of his pleasures and his ambition; not, if they were multiplied a thousand thousand fold, would you choose his lot. Why? Because of one thing, which the king did not then think of, which he put far out of his sight, but which parted him from all,— his grave. The grave takes off the mask. Now, as you read his history, and all is past, you would, that he had hearkened to the Apostle's voice, and become altogether such as *he* was. Waste not your sympathy. There is one, to whose everlasting bliss it should be turned, thine own. Not Paul only, in his fervent words, but king Agrippa, from his grave, preacheth to thee, "when *thou* art called, be not almost; be altogether a Christian."

God calleth thee by every gleam of joy, which thou ever hadst in doing His Will; He calleth thee through every pang, which thou ever hadst, after any sin which shocked thee. He calleth thee by thy hopes and by thy fears, by thy love of knowledge, thine understanding, thine affections, through the very largeness of thy capacities and thy desires. He saith to thee, I made thee not for

these passing things; for I made thee eternal. I
made thee not for created things; for not in theirs,
but in Mine own image and likeness did I make
thee.   I made thee to be partaker of My eternity;
I redeemed thee to enter into My joy.   Nothing
but I Who am infinite, can satisfy an eternal being.
In Me alone can ye never be wearied; for in My
Infinity shall ye ever find new Beauty, fresh Wisdom, entrancing Love, boundless knowledge, overstreaming delights, thrilling, uncloying, unsating
satisfyingness of joy.   When My Love, My Wisdom, My Knowledge, My Goodness, My Joy, come
to an end, then will thine too: for I have called
you to enter into My joy, and all I have shall be
thine.

SERMON IV[a].

BALAAM—HALF-CONVERSION UNCONVERSION.

Num. xxiii. 10.

"Let me die the death of the righteous, and let my last end be like his."

How often did our young hearts ache, as we heard these words! So true, so full of knowledge, so enlightened, such devout aspiration, and yet so lifeless, so powerless over him who uttered them! Strange melancholy picture of faith without love, light without life, checks obeyed and then disregarded; half-obedience ending in final impenitence and apostacy. Yet, sadly strange as it is, Balaam is the mirror, wherein very many Christians, and those not of the worst sort, may see themselves.

Balaam was half-converted; and so he was not converted at all. He would be half-friends with God, and half-friends with the world, and so he became wholly a slave to the world and an enemy to God. He would not wholly part with his one besetting sin, and so it mastered him and destroyed him. He would not serve God more than he thought he need, and so he ended in deadly opposition to God, disserving God as greatly as he could, and seduc-

---

[a] Preached at Christ Church, Broadway, Westminster.

ing others from His service, and, so soon as he had finished his work of evil, losing his life and his soul. He is one of those terrible monuments of evil, which God has preserved, in mercy to us, out of the mass of human sin, writing on them with the finger of God; "Flee hence; for this way lies the death of the soul."

Balaam was half-converted. He stood on the threshold of the Old Testament, as Simon Magus on the outskirts of the Gospel. Both, before their half-conversion, used magical arts; both, for a time, believed, and made an outward confession of faith; to both God said, that their inward self was separate from Himself; to Balaam, "Thy way is perverse before Me," to Simon, "Thy heart is not right with God." Both were assailed by their old sins, covetousness and ambition; both yielded and perished. Neither willed altogether to part with God; but both, in the end, parted with Him wholly. Simon, when the Apostle pronounced him accursed, prayed the Apostle to intercede with the Lord for him; he became the father of misbelievers, not willing wholly to part with the Gospel, but he decked out his own misbeliefs with some words and phrases from it; and died by the Hand of God in open opposition to it.

Balaam was, Scripture tells us, at one time "[b] a soothsayer." He used unlawful arts to know the future. But, like Jethro, so far, or Rahab in Jericho, he had heard how God had delivered Israel from Egypt, and came to own Him as the One God. He even came to know His Name, "He IS," (for he

[b] Jos. xiii. 22.

uses it) and the prophecy of Jacob as to Judah, for he repeats the self-same words[c]. He must have known of the life after death, and of rewards and punishments to come, and that this good or evil to come depended upon a man's good or evil, his righteousness or unrighteousness, in this life. For he desires not a quiet, painless end, without bodily suffering. His thought is of his soul. His eye is, for the time, full upon the close of his life. He desires not length of days, nor honour, nor, as Christians have, an honoured grave (as in that neighbouring Abbey[d]), nor a prosperous close. He looks on death itself, as death, as the winding up, the "afterwards" of every thing in life; and, looking at it, he desires one thing only, "the death of the righteous." But he who, when all of this life should be over, longed so wistfully for "the death of the righteous," must have known, that something very terrible awaited the soul of the wicked, which he shrank from; that some happy lot awaited the soul of the righteous, which he longed for. He expressed what must be our longings; our heart's wish finds its utterance in his words, when we hear them.

This he knew probably by the direct teaching of God. At least, when Balak's messengers came to him, he bade them confidently await God's answer on the morrow, as one who was accustomed to learn God's will in visions of the night. "[e]Lodge here this night, and I will bring you word again, as the Lord shall speak unto me." And God, Whom he thus owned, he owned with a term of affection, as

[c] Num. xxiv. 9.   [d] Westminster Abbey.   [e] Nu. xxii. 8.

his own God. "ʿIf Balak would give me his house
full of silver and gold, I cannot go beyond the word
of the Lord *my God.*" He knew of the Lord too, as
One Whom, in the letter at least, he dared not disobey. Unless the Lord gave him leave to go, he
dared not go; what the Lord bade him say, he dared
not transgress in any thing, little or great.

Yet with this knowledge of God, he was content
to remain aloof from the people of God. He would
have a religion of his own, at least for himself. He
was, he tells us, in "ᵍthe mountains of the East in
Aram," when Balak sent for him. He knew that
God, Who had bidden Abraham leave that same
country, was now bringing up His people ʰ, after
their four centuries of sojourn in Egypt, back to the
land which He had promised to Abraham to give
them, but he chose to abide where he was. God
Who willed that he should be His instrument, to
shew in the face of Moab His spiritual might, accepted his imperfect obedience, and gave him the
wish of his heart; He gave him religious distinction.
He gave him an aweful power of blessing and cursing, and must have taught him, in some measure,
who were the objects of His own favour or displeasure, since his blessings or curses were fulfilled.
Balak speaks as knowing this. "ⁱI wot that he
whom thou blessest is blessed, and he whom thou
cursest is cursed."

Such was Balaam's outward lot. He was out of
the fold, and the wolf found him. It was the old
temptation; the temptation by which Adam fell, the

ᶠ Nu. xxii. 18.   ᵍ Ib. xxiii. 7.   ʰ Ib. xxiii. 22, xxiv. 8.
ⁱ Ib. xxii. 6.

temptation by which, in every grievous sin, every child of Adam falls; from whom will he receive his wages, from God or from Satan? Which will he choose? Will he see what his soul longs for, at God's Hand, in God's way, or will he take it, against God's will, in his own way, from Satan? The gift, which lay before Balaam on God's part, was that he should be a great prophet. As it is, God revealed a future to him, which even unbelief has been forced to own to be true prophecy. Satan tempted him through Balak to seek for worldly, not spiritual, glory, to seek it through his own arts and enchantments, not from God. Balak's messengers came "[k] with the rewards of divination in their hands," and with Balak's words, "Curse me this people; for they are too mighty for me: peradventure I shall prevail, that we may smite them, and I may drive them out of the land." Then began that half-hearted struggle, which, I fear, too many of you know, my brethren, which, but for some special mercy of God always ends in people's blinding their consciences, and doing what they protested to themselves they would not do, directly disobeying God. Balaam knew, that he ought not to curse Israel; he knew, that he ought not to wish that they should be driven out. For he himself testifies that God was bringing them in; he knew of God's blessings to them. Yet he professes that he will enquire; he will wait to see what God will tell him. Outwardly he is reverent towards God; inwardly, he is rebellious. To pretend to enquire about God's will, when we know it, is to will not to do it. Had he

[k] Ib. xxii. 7.

spoken out on God's side, he might have freed himself from the temptation at once, and been saved. O what fierce storms of temptation, a bold, "I may not, I cannot, God forbid!" would have saved him, and would save hundreds of thousands of us. "How should I do this great wickedness and sin against God?" Our proverbs tell us, "to hesitate is to be lost."

Satan's emissaries read the assent of the heart in the faint denial of the lips. Balaam answers on the morrow; "Get you into your land; for the Lord hath refused to give me leave to go with you." Satan's agents understand well such answers. They can put them into other words, "I would, if I could." So then the temptation is redoubled. Balaam had shewed his weak side, his vanity and worldliness. Balak sees that his refusal is a half-consent, sends him princes, "[1]more and more honourable than they," he entreats him with deference, "Be not, I pray thee, hindered from coming" (in other words, "let not thy God hinder thee," only he veils the ungodliness of his meaning) "for I will honour thee with very great honour, and whatsoever thou shalt say unto me, I will do." Balaam again hesitates, professes, "I cannot go beyond the word of the Lord my God," but asks *them* also to wait, that he may see what the Lord would say to him *more*." O *that* "more!" How many thousands on thousands of souls has that "more" ruined. To wish to know "more," when he had once clearly known God's will, is to wish to know "less;" it is to wish not to know what he clearly knows. "That which is called con-

[1] Nu. xxii. 15—17.

sidering our duty in a particular case," said a very thoughtful observer of human nature[m], "is very often nothing but endeavouring to explain it away." "Second thoughts are wisest," said the Heathen proverb. True! against human passion; but "first thoughts are most honest," against man's self-deceit.

This time God let him go; but with the caution, "[n] And that word only which I shall say unto thee, that thou shall do." God changes his trial, as He so often does, when men persist in willing what He had forbidden them. He will not keep them by force, against their wills. He lets them place themselves in circumstances, more perilous to virtue or honesty or chastity; He allows them to bring themselves into trials, which He would have spared them, had they obeyed His first word. Then came that miracle, which stands, alone of its kind, in the Bible, yet which has a special fittingness here. God willed to use Balaam as His instrument, and so He shewed him, how all things stood at His command; how the tongue which Balaam wished to use against His people, was in His power, and "[o]the dumb ass, speaking with man's voice, forbade the madness of the prophet."

Have any of you thought this a strange miracle, my brethren? What is not strange in this mysterious world of ours? But which is strangest, the miracle through the ass, or the miracle through Balaam? To me, that through Balaam seems far the stranger! Less strange is it by far, yea, if one may reverently so speak, a less miracle it seems to me,

---

[m] Bp. Butler, Serm. vii. "On the character of Balaam." p. 115.

[n] Nu. xxii. 20.   [o] 2 S. Pet. ii. 15.

that God, at Whose command all things stand, should employ the organs of the dumb ass to awaken the blinded prophet, than that the prophet, bent on his covetousness, should, "o'ermastered by His high behest," bless the people whom he willed to curse. Yea, far greater than any miracles on unresisting nature, are the miracles of grace on the resisting will of man.   More marvellous far, that passing miracle, whereby the covetous prophet forewent his price; or that, whereby the profane wilful Saul was for the time subdued, and he, who came to Samuel to seek God's servant to destroy him, passed the night in praising God; or the passing penitence of Ahab who had "sold himself to work wickedness."

But O! how much more marvellous those miracles of grace, when Saul the persecutor was transformed into Paul the Apostle, who "[p] preached the faith which once he destroyed;" or a whole heathen city, one fourth of the size of this great Babylon[q], repented at the preaching of Jonah, and turned from their evil way; or the robber on the Cross owned in the marred Form, which he had just before blasphemed, his Lord, the King of that world whither he was going.   More marvellous now each miracle of transforming grace, whereby "not bodies but souls are raised" from the dead; when the unchaste body becomes again the temple of the Holy Ghost, or the stone-cold heart gushes forth into tears of penitence, or when the sweet winning grace of Jesus attunes the rebel tongue to sing His praise.   Greater miracles ye may know of, if you will, in your own souls,

[p] Gal. i. 23.   [q] Preached when London was estimated at 2,400,000. Nineveh was 600,000. See on Jonah iv. ult. p. 287.

than this, which for a while held in obedience the wavering will of Balaam. For as he came near the place of his trial, covetousness was prevailing with him; else the Searcher of hearts would not have said to him through the Angel, "[r] I went out to withstand thee, because thy way is perverse before Me."

So checked, Balaam, as you know, went well through that trial, on which he entered with God's permission. His heart was wrong still; for twice he went to "seek for enchantments," hoping, in whatever way, to win permission from God to do his own evil will. In vain the king of Moab went out to his utmost border to greet him with honour (alas! how the foolish heart of many of us would have been turned with far less honour from the great of this world); in vain he honoured him and promised him greater honours. God's inward might prevailed; and that, most signally at the last, when Balak brought him to a mountain, desecrated by the most hideous idolatry of lust. There, amid those loathsome idols, through whose influence Balak hoped to prevail, Balaam sought no more to enchantments[s], and the Spirit of God came mightily upon him, and he uttered those wondrous prophecies, which, to this day, are a witness to us, how God revealed Himself to man. Balaam, for the time, heeded not the king's anger, the loss of the worldly honour which he longed for, nor the taunt, "[t] The Lord hath kept thee back from honour." The glory of God was at issue on the strife with rebel man. He preserved His unwilling half-hearted instrument. Balaam returned towards his place.

[r] Nu. xxii. 32. [s] Ib. xxiv. 1, 2. [t] Ib. 11.

Alas! our poor human nature! Never, if we have in any degree trusted in our own strength, are we in greater peril, than when we have just gained a victory. How many seeming victories has security turned into defeat! *How* Balaam fell into the snare, Scripture tells us not. It tells us of the victory of God, when Balak would wrest from God's Omnipotence the curse upon His people. It tells us not, how God's worthless instrument, who "[u]loved the wages of unrighteousness," lighted on the devilish device to seduce the people of God. The death-blow to good comes often, now too, in the moment of seeming but half-hearted victory. God ceases at last to strive with man. It had required miracles, visions, inspirations, to hold Balaam's covetousness in check; when they ceased, Balaam ran greedily after his own bad way, as a matter of course. How many fall by no greater temptation, than they had withstood before! They had worn out God's grace at last, and, left to themselves, they venture again into the temptation and fall. Like Samson, they know not that God has departed from them. It may be that the memory of those rites of Baal-Peor, amid which he had pronounced the words of God, flashed on his corrupt soul and suggested that devilishness. It was on the hill of Peor[v], that Balak took him for the last time to curse Israel. It was through the idolatry of Baal-Peor, that he seduced Israel[w]. It may be that, like Simon Magus or Judas, he wished to make "[x] a gain of godliness," and that, failing to gain from Moses the rewards which he had forfeited

[u] 2 Pet. ii. 15.   [v] Nu. xxiii. 28.   [w] Ib. xxxi. 16.
[x] 1 Tim. vi. 6.

from Balak, he sought again that eminence from the princes of Midian through that Satanic inventiveness of seduction. If Jesus could have willed to become an earthly king, Judas would not have betrayed him. He could have remained faithful, not to Jesus, but to his own worldly interests. If S. Peter could have sold the Holy Ghost to Simon, Simon would have traded within the Church. Could Balaam have obtained his idol, mammon, from the true God, he would not have seduced His people. But there is one way to salvation; many roads to hell. So God tells us, *why* Balaam was lost, through his covetousness, not *how* he came to make his miserable bargain. We find Balaam, after the success of his blasted counsel, perishing in the bad preeminence for which he had sold his soul. He died among the princes, whose rank he coveted. " ʸ They slew the kings of Midian, besides the rest of them that were slain; Balaam also, the son of Peor, they slew with the sword."

God shews us types of different sorts of bad characters, that we may see in them our own peril. The world is full of Balaams. Alas that the Church also, and every religious body, is full of Balaams. Nay, my brethren, unless I had thought that here too (though I could not know it,) there would be those who had begun Balaam's course of sin, it would have been plainly unprofitable to speak to you of his miserable history.

What those direct warnings or inspirations of God were to Balaam, *that* God's Voice in His word and in our consciences is to us. That Voice of God is as

ʸ Nu. xxxi. 8, Jos. xiii. 22.

plain to us, so long as we will, in every part of our
duty to God and man, as those direct commands were
to Balaam. God says, as plainly to us, as He did to
him, "This thou shalt do; this shalt thou *not* do."
We boast ourselves of being an enlightened age; we
pride ourselves on our spiritual light; people look
back with satisfaction on ages which they think
"dark" or benighted. We are, then, by our own
confession, so far in Balaam's condition. No one
doubts that he has full light. Light is all around
us. We hear God's word; we have it read to us;
most of us know much of it; people even abuse their
knowledge of it, by using its words in a profane
way, as if it were a common book. We have it in
our houses, in our heads; would it were in our
hearts also! Without this knowledge, we might
have alas! countless sins; we could not have Balaam's. The special sin of Balaam, was, that he
indulged and fed with his heart's-blood one darling
passion (covetousness), and that, not daring or wishing to go against the direct command of God, he
tried in every way he could, to evade it. He knew
that he was not of the same mind with God. So, not
choosing, what is the first duty of a creature, to become of the same mind with God by obeying Him,
nor yet, what is the part of Satan, directly to disobey Him, he tried to get God to be of *his* mind.
So he made the sort of bargain in his own mind with
God: "If God continues to forbid me this, I cannot
go against Him. But if I can get my own way, I
will." And so, all along, through God's continual
checks or inspirations, he did keep his purpose; he
did say the words which God put into his mouth;

and he did not say what Balak urged him to say, and what would have brought him honour. Nay more, for the time he threw his whole mind into what he said. He was not merely a passive organ of God. You see, by his words, that (though not his heart) his whole mind is in it. He was in a high office; king and princes stood hanging on his words; all hung in suspense on that "*tranc'd, yet open gaze," when, "deep in heaven," the visions of futurity met his eye. Whether, for the time, it satisfied his ambition, or whether he was borne away by the high thoughts, with which God inspired him, he is reckless of the king's displeasure; he delights that he "heard the words of God," and "saw the vision of the Almighty, falling into a trance and having his eyes open." Nay, at the last, he seems to have pleasure in speaking of the fall of human greatness,

> The giant forms of empires on their way
>   To ruin: one by one
>   They tower and they are gone.

He beholds God's sentence fall on Moab, Edom, Amalek: he sees God's people itself, carried captive by Assyria; Assyria, in turn, and, with it, his own home in Mesopotamia, afflicted by Western Empires, and then those empires themselves in their turn, perishing.

> True Prophetic light
> Flashed o'er him, high and bright,
> Flashed once, and died away, and left his darkened thought.

He sees, relates, triumphs, or sorrows, over the vain

* The Christian Year. Second Sunday after Easter.

pageant of earthly things; then turns to his own petty villainy of ambition, and perishes.

> He hears th' Almighty's word,
> He sees the angel's sword,
> Yet low upon the earth his heart and treasure lie.

We can all *now* speak well about the things of God. So did Balaam. Our minds can hardly do other, than go along with the things we say. The manifold goodness of God is so unspeakable, the love of God the Holy Ghost is so amazing, Christians can hardly but find some good words to say of it. Balaam did more; he spoke well; he felt well; he thought well; nay, amid strong temptation, he refused to act amiss; he bore courageous witness as to his duty, the duty of a creature to its God; and this, in the face of an unbelieving mocking, multitude. Why, many would think themselves half-saints; they would be accounted benefactors, patrons of Almighty God, if they did and sacrificed half of what Balaam did and sacrificed. What was wanting then? Where was the difference between Balaam on the top of Peor and Elijah on Mount Carmel, since each stood alone, on the side of God, against a rebel multitude? Words, feelings, thoughts, understanding, deeds, active duty, courageous service, nay some self-denial, were on the side of God. What was wanting? That which alone would give value to all, the heart and will. And so Balaam acted his part, compared to the standard of these days, well. But all was an unsubstantial pageant; for his hour he fulfilled the office of prophet, which was assigned to him; he ended, the Apostate. Knowledge, feelings, sense of his relation to

God, partial obedience, ended only in stamping the Apostate. His soul was the darker, because it had had light, and rejected it; his passing service branded him a deserter.

Mistake me not, my brethren. God is so very good, that He gathers up the very fragments of a decayed life. He is so anxious for our salvation, for whom Jesus died, that it seems as though He would take any thing, which alas! we cast to Him. It is, as if *we* were the masters, He, our servant, for love of us; that His eyes are upon us, to watch whether we will give any thing to Him; and, while we are sating ourselves with the pleasures and good things which He gives us, He gathers up the crumbs which fall from our table. No condescension is too great for Jesus, Who vouchsafed to die for us. He knocks again and again at the door of our hearts, often as we may have rudely closed them against Him, and turned away and drowned His Voice in senselessness and sin, that we might not hear it. "[a]He waits, that He may be gracious unto us; He abides on high," out of our sight, not yet coming to judgement, "that He may have mercy upon us."

But I am speaking now, not of the blessed mercy and forbearance of Jesus, but of ourselves. One ending all this goodness must have, our entire conversion or, God forbid! our final impenitence. "[b]The goodness of God leadeth thee to repentance." God accepts every thing as an instalment, so to say; as an earnest, that thou willest to repent, that thou willest to become His. But while thy soul keeps back one thing, while thou art contriving, in one thing,

[a] Is. xxx. 18. [b] Rom. ii. 4.

G 2

to cheat thy conscience, and hold back part of the price,—all is but Balaam-service; thou art as yet none of His.

Conscience speaks plainly at first. The sin of Balaam is, not to go straight against it, but to try to cheat it, elude it, make it speak something else than what it says. "Thou shalt not steal," says conscience. "It is not stealing, it is borrowing," says the Balaam-soul, "I will repay it." "But thou never wilt nor canst," says conscience. "Fortune may favour me; I will try but this once." "But if thou failest, thou wilt have stolen. To use unallowed, what is another's, is to steal." Like Balaam, such will strongly what God forbids; like Balaam, they cozen themselves, that they will not do what would displease God; like Balaam, they do it, ruin thousands, and end miserably. Or again, it makes false rules of right to itself. "Every body does' it." "It is the way of trade." "We cannot live without it." As if a sin were less a sin, because it is committed by thousands, or as if God could not protect those who keep His laws! *Then*, were the Amorites free from guilt, when "their iniquity was full" and every one did it. *Then* would the complete corruption of a Christian nation be the complete excuse of every Christian for casting off the law of Christ.

Or again, the Balaam-soul says, "True, God has said, 'Thou shalt not commit adultery;' God forbid that I should so sin! But God has not forbidden this or that way of dressing, this or that way of speaking, this or that meeting or intimacy, or connection." If thou wert as diligent in learning what

God forbids, as thou art in cozening thy soul as to what God, as thou thinkest, does not forbid, thou wouldest find that what thou excusest is forbidden to the very letter.

Or, the soul admits the passion into itself, and says, like Balaam, "I will not go to extremities, I will stop short of what God plainly forbids." So Satan lures people on, in lesser acts of the same kind of sin, and then turns round on the unhappy soul, and says, "What good to stop short now? You have done as bad." And so he would at one time teach the soul to hide from itself, that the beginning of a sin has, as our Lord says, the nature of that sin or that it offends God: then he acts the philosopher, and tells the soul, " c All are equally sins, therefore all are equal sins."

Conscience is not thine own voice. It speaks not at thy will, but against it. It is God's voice within thee, approving, checking, upbraiding, condemning. Unchangeable, in itself, as the law of God which it enforces, it will speak plainly at times, though thou sin against it, though thou elude it, though thou stifle it; at least, until thou have sinned away grace, and God has abandoned thee. But beware, as you value your salvation, how you tamper with it; how,

---

c S. Augustine had to refute the Stoic doctrine that "all sins are equal," in a letter to the Donatist Nectarius. Ep. civ. n. 14, 15. Opp. ii. 294, 295. S. Jerome wrote against it in his dialogue against the Pelagians (n. 19 Opp. ii. 700) and against Jovinian (l. ii. n. 3. Opp. ii. 371, 372.) Elsewhere he says, " as many (plerique) think, and chiefly the Stoics." (in Ezek. L. iii. c. x. 9. Opp. v. 98.) The strange error had not then died out; as, in some practical forms, it exists still, and is no uncommon plea for sinning more deeply than before.

Balaam-like, you persuade yourselves that God *may* not disapprove what thou knowest, what He has told thee, that He hates. It is the special peril of a refined age, like this, to refine away its conscience, its duty, its faith. It would not have the weariness of fighting with its conscience. This is unbearably painful, and it would have easy ways. It takes the shortest, easiest, directest, road to hell, by corrupting its guide. It saves itself all remorse, save that which is endless, hopeless, incurable. If ignorance suits it, it will be ignorant, and ignorance is to be its plea to God. If subtlety will serve its turn better, it will "lose its light by having too much light," dazzling itself with false meteor-glares, that it may not see the light of God. It invents plans of salvation of its own. It will act the Theologian. It will tell God that He cannot mean, what He says He does mean; that He cannot have revealed what He has revealed. It would flatter God, that He may connive at its sin. Reversing the excuses of the slothful servant of the Parable, it would tell God, "Thou art *not* a hard master, Thou canst not have meant this; Thou art too good to put such restraints upon Thy creatures, whom Thou hast made with such and such appetites and passions." And so it deposes conscience within, and God without it, and sets, in the place of God, a dumb idol, its own creation; worshipping, as it thinks, its Maker, on condition that He shall not interfere with its sin. Then with its false god it makes itself a false conscience, blinded, corrupted, not ruling its desires, but ruled by them, and says to it, "Guide me blindfold, for thee will I trust; thou wilt give me, undisturbed, what I ask." And his blinded conscience guides him unhesitating, unquestioning, unerring, to the pit of hell.

And now, brethren, if any thought have come to you, of the peril of fostering one heart's sin, or of longing to see that the one sin, on which thy mind is set, *could* be right, or to make terms with God, "Leave me this one sin, and in the rest I will serve Thee," and to wheedle Him, as it were, into consenting to it; if thou hast seen in Balaam to-night any danger of self-deceit—to think this and not to act upon it, would be another form of Balaam's sin, to please himself with the good thoughts which God gave him, to go along with them,—and to disobey them. Dare, my brother, to look into thyself; dare to see what that is in you, which still holds thee back from God; what thou darest not say out in this congregation of thy fellow-sinners, what thy young unbribed, unseared conscience told thee was wrong; and, by God's grace, cast it from thee. Will it be a pang? Yes, till thou have done it; and then by the mercy of God, succeeded by what joy, when the imprisoned soul shall again feel free; and the heart shall again speak to God as its Father, and Jesus shall be again thy very own, He thine, and thou His, and the Holy Ghost shall pour light and peace into thy soul. A few Lents more, and thou wilt see, in the light of God, that every check of conscience was God's merciful Hand, holding thee back from the abyss; every call to give up thy darling fostered sin was the fruit of thy Saviour's intercession, the price of Jesus' Blood. Thou wilt see it, if thou have obeyed, in what amazement

of transporting, transfiguring fulness of Divine joy
and love; if thou have disobeyed to the end, in
what horrible agony of endless suffering. From
which may God in His mercy save us, for His Dear
Son Jesus' sake!

SERMON V[a].

THE LOSSES OF THE SAVED.

1 Cor. iii. 11—15.

" Other foundation can no man lay than that is laid, which is Jesus Christ. Now if any man build upon this foundation gold, silver, precious stones, wood, hay, stubble ; every man's work shall be made manifest : for the day shall declare it, because it shall be revealed by fire ; and the fire shall try every man's work of what sort it is. If any man's work abide which he hath builded thereupon, he shall receive a reward. If any man's work shall be burned, he shall suffer loss : but he himself shall be saved ; yet so as by fire."

You all, I doubt not, hope in some way by the mercy of our God, to be saved at last. The mercy of God is so all but-exhaustless; He has such a marvellous variety of contrivances in the rich resources of His grace and His Providence, to win His rebels to Himself; and the thought of being shut out for ever from His love in the hateful and hating society of Hell, is so horrible, no wonder that you do not imagine of yourselves what is beyond all horror, horrible. God

[a] Preached at Great St. Mary's, Cambridge. Lent, 1866.

grant that your hopes may, all, be true! And yet, or rather because I long that they may prove true, I must say to you faithfully; entire fearlessness of falling into Hell is no good sign. As far as it springs in any from that loving faith in God, which cannot imagine parting from Him Who loved it, or from a meditative contemplation of the Infinite love of the Redemption, or of His past mercies to ourselves, that He Who loved His own will love them to the end, such hopes, if the soul, by God's grace, keep itself from preferring God's creatures to Himself and rejecting God for them, such hopes, if they draw the soul to God, are doubtless inspired by God. But hopes amid carelessness or worldliness, or amid occasional deadly, only half-repented sin, they are not helps, they are hindrances to salvation, because they are hindrances to earnestness, and to that reverend awe, amid which by God's grace we are, the Apostle bids us, to work out our own salvation.

But be it, as we wish and long for; be it, that these uncertain and delusive hopes will not, by the mercy of God, wreck the salvation of any one; that all of us (God grant it!) not through but in despite of those hopes, shall be saved; that God will one day shiver the soul's false brittle hopes and give it true repentance, firm faith, penitent love, well-grounded hope, what then? In one sense, all will be right; for the lowest place in heaven were as much above the desert of us sinners, as heaven, yea, as infinite space is above this spot of earth. It will be, by the mercy of God, infinite eternal gain; for it will be the gain of the infinite everlasting love of God. But it will also be infinite, eternal loss; for it will

be a loss of that measure of the capacity of the infinite love of God, which the soul might have gained,
but would not.

This is what the Apostle speaks of, the losses of
the saved. It is, in one way, a more aweful subject
to us, than even Hell. We may; we trust in God's
mercy, and I hope, rightly, escape from Hell. From
this loss there is no escape, except by casting off our
inured slothfulness, by becoming new men through
the grace of God, by exchanging lukewarmness for
burning love, slavery to the world for freedom in
God, ambition of this world's glory and man's fleeting breath of praise, for ambition of the service of
God and the praise of God; the dull routine of an
unspiritual careless life, for a " pressing onward towards the mark of the high calling of God in Christ
Jesus."

A late conversion after a wasted life will, if God
vouchsafes it, save the soul from Hell, through the
Blood of Jesus. Unless God Who is not bound by
any laws of His creature time, should, together with
His converting grace, pour love into the soul, sur-
passing all His ordinary measures and promises of
grace, it will *not* regain for the soul the lost measure of its capacity of the love of God. This loss is
the more aweful, because it is irreparable.

Certainly what Scripture says of the saved has a
very special awe of its own, because, here, we are in
the province, not of God's mercy but of His All-holy
Justice. It is by His infinite undeserved mercy in
Christ Jesus, that we are saved at all. When we
have been saved, the reward is according to our
works. The " penny " of everlasting life is given

freely to all, who to the end reject not God; nay who,
having rejected Him, do at the last yield up their
rebellion to his mercy, and embrace it. The two
or the five talents denote the eminence of glory, by
which He rewards the diligent use of the gifts, dis-
tributed by God to each, in proportion to his capacity to receive them.

"They," says S. Gregory [b], "who do not labour
equally in the vineyard, all equally receive the penny.
There are indeed with the Father many mansions,
and yet the unequal labourers receive the same
penny; because all will have one beatitude of joy,
although all will not have one sublimity of life."
All will have the beatific vision of our God; all will
have access to the ever-unfolding treasures of His
Infinite Wisdom; all will be inundated with the
transporting fulness of His love. But all will not
be able alike to contain it. There will be narrow,
stunted capacities of souls there, as there are narrow,
often self-stunted intellects here.

What then I wish you to dwell upon with me
this evening, is not the horrible risk of hell, which
a careless or worldly ambitious life involves. True
as this is, perhaps the very good which is in you,
may indispose you to think of it. Though not, as
you yourselves feel, fit for heaven, where "[c] nothing
defiled can enter," you are not yet, by God's mercy,
fit for Hell.

But what I would ask you to think of with me,
are 1) the certain dreadful sufferings of the Day of
Judgement to some who shall be saved; 2) the certain irremediable loss, which some, who shall be

----

[b] Lib. iv. in Job n. 70.   [c] Rev. xxi. 27.

saved, shall learn in that day that they have brought
upon themselves.

Of the Day, of which S. Paul speaks, there is no
doubt. It is the Day of the Judgement of God,
whether it be the particular judgement upon each of
us, when we part out of this life, or whether it be
that General Judgement of all, which shall gather
into one, and exhibit before men and Angels all the
teaching of all those special judgements, showing
to all, that the Judge of all doeth right in all which
He doeth.

Of that Day, Holy Scripture most commonly speaks,
adding some word of awe or terror. But S. Paul also
calls it "The Day." "[d] He is able to keep that
which I have committed unto Him unto That Day."
"[e]There is laid up for me the crown of righteousness, which the Lord, the righteous Judge, shall
give me at that Day." He prays for Onesiphorus,
"[f]The Lord grant that he may find mercy of the
Lord in that Day." It is "*the* Day;" because upon
it hangs our eternity, our eternal doom, the measure
(if by God's mercy we are saved) of our eternal
bliss. Time and change will be no more; growth
belongs to this our trial-time. Thenceforth our mansion in the heavenly Court will be determined; our
place among our Angelic fellow-citizens in bliss will
have been assigned us. We shall have been fixed
in our unchangeable proportion of bliss.

Now the special characteristic of this description
of the Day of Judgement, is, that it relates to the
saved, to those who have builded upon the "Foundation, which is laid, which is Jesus Christ." There is

[d] 1 Tim. i. 12.   [e] Ib. iv. 8.   [f] Ib. i. 18.

indeed a special reference to such of us, as have had or shall have the office of teachers committed to us. But this does not hinder that larger sense, in which we all have to raise a building for God, wherein He will be pleased to dwell; our own souls. And the principle, both ways, is one and the same; that we may be so building on Him, the true Foundation, as to be saved, and yet may, through our own fault and our own free choice, suffer, in that Day of trial, pain unspeakable, and incur endless irremediable loss.

And *this* pain and loss will not come to us through sins which separate men from Christ. For he speaks of those who build these light worthless materials upon that " One Foundation which is Christ." Nay those who build them can persuade themselves, all along, that they are building *upon* Christ, *to* Christ, until the scorching fire of the Day of Judgement shall undeceive them.

Day by day, and year by year, men will have gone on, laying tier after tier of this their spiritual building, which, on account of their real belief in Christ and their trust in Him, they thought enduring. They built on and on; whether they had, from time to time, misgivings, is not said. I can hardly think that God left them without such visitations. But if they had, they stifled them. For they builded on unto the end. But it was " like a dream, when one awaketh." Only they awoke in the Day of their judgement; and the fire was around their habitation: all that they had builded perished to the Foundation, and they themselves escaped, so as by fire, scorched, half-consumed, yet saved.

And yet they must all the while have been earnest in their way; perhaps they were praised, and the praise blinded them the more. Some of them may be had in reputation until now; they may "have left names behind them." Men speak highly of "posthumous fame:" they have toiled for it: they talk of it as the ambition of noble souls. O if the departed still know of what passes on this our earth, what a hideous scornful mockery must that posthumous fame be, when the temple, whose inscription it is, has collapsed in ashes amid the fires of the Judgement Day. And all is perished.

A life-long labour perished! It is piteous, even when we hear of it in this life, when the temporal end, for which a man has toiled all his life, crashes at last. But remediless! And for eternity! It is too terrible; only our God tells it us, that it may not be true to us.

Plainly, there must have been self-deceit about it. For, not without a man's own will and his own fault, would God have allowed such an one to remain so deceived to the end. Yet one cannot name "self-deceit" without bringing the case painfully near to us all, because the reign of self-deceit, at least its range, is so universal. "g The heart," says the Holy Ghost, "is deceitful above all things, and incurable. Who can know it?" "I, the Lord, search the heart, I try the reins, and that to give to every man according to his ways, according to the fruit of his doings." God here too connects the individuality of His judgement and His retribution according to works, with the deceitfulness of the human heart and its

g Jer. xvii. 9, 10.

unsearchableness except by Himself. The idea of
an unerring judgement implies the drawing off some
veil which was on the conscience, a revelation of
the soul to itself. To pronounce sentence is the
issue of the judgement, not its process. To judge
a whole life implies unveiling the whole life. Probably, scarcely the very bad (unless God reveal it
to them for the sake of others) believe that they
deserve or shall incur Hell. Certainly, no one of
the saved would have any thought beforehand, what
place in His Presence God would assign to him.
Probably the Day of Judgement will shew both the
value of things, which seemed valueless but were
done out of pure love of God, and the valuelessness
of things, about which we took the greatest pains,
to which we consecrated most years, for which we
were most praised, because what was human most
crept in there. Probably then, we are all of us far
more concerned in the things, which are to be
burned up, than we at all like to think of. Yet
better think *now*, than know for the first time *then*.

What then are things which shall not be burned,
gold, silver, costly stones? Now thus much is plain at
first sight. First, they represent something costly;
secondly, something very pure. Gold, which is to be
used for the temple of God, must needs be well
purified; the costly stones, if employed there, must
needs have been severed from all which was not as
precious as they. Apart then from any symbolical
meaning which either of them may have elsewhere
in Holy Scripture, (as the fire of love,) one thing is
plainly common to them all, perfect purity. They are
of different values, the one of incomparably greater

value than another, but all agree in this, that they are pure. Martyrdom; suffering for Christ; Evangelising; renunciation of the world for Christ and His poverty and Cross; Virginity; to spend and be spent; to give one's goods to feed the poor; all done for Christ, from the cup of cold water to the Martyr's chariot of fire, have their several values: but, on this one condition, that they be, each one, undertaken, done, lived in, suffered, purely for the love of God. What else can we even imagine that God will reward? To get on in this world, to have wife and children, to lay up for old age, to provide for a family, to be kind to those who love us, to be good or perhaps not bad neighbours, to use worldly courtesy, to speak well of those who speak well of you—all things right or lawful in their way; but what have they to do with eternal reward? Simply, in themselves, nothing. They begin in this world and they end in this world. "They *have* their reward." Their object was some end of this world; it was gained; God, in the bounty of His Providence, gave it. Why should we look hereafter for a second reward from God, for doing what our own natural dispositions prompted us to do, which we did for ends quite apart from God, and which we should have done, had we never thought of Him? True, all these things, nay things necessary to our existence, as eating and drinking, may, if done to a supernatural end, the glory of God, have a supernatural value in God's sight and have their eternal reward. It is a sort of sacred proverb, "It has great grace to do ordinary things extraordinarily well." It is part of the love of our God, because the greater part of our

H

life is spent in very ordinary things, and yet in each
one of these ordinary things, we may please God,
and gain greater grace and larger capaciousness for
His endless Infinite love.

But then all our lives alike may be natural or supernatural. For all may be directed to our supernatural end, God; or to some natural end, an end
of this world; all may be done with a view to pleasing God, or for ourselves or the world around us; all
may be done well, to the utmost of our ability, by
Divine grace, or all things secular may be done
with our best natural ability, for their natural end;
while spiritual things are done in a perfunctory way,
to satisfy our consciences, or, as we think, to save
our souls.

And as the outward acts must be in many, nay,
even in the majority of cases the self-same, while the
soul of the acts, which gives them their real value
for eternity, is their relation to God, or the absence
of such relation, then there is in them most large
scope for self-deceit. What so common as to have
mixed motives for our actions, or rather what so rare
as to have any one motive for any one action, unless
indeed it be a lower one? Thus one might help a
poor man, out of human compassion, or because he
expected it of one, or to get rid of his importunity,
or in condescension, or because it was right, or because others did, or it would be expected of one, or
for fear of Hell, or to satisfy conscience, or out of
Divine love, or because his hands are Christ's Hands,
to receive our alms, or to have his prayers, or to make
up for a sin or self-indulgence, or because he, by his
thanksgiving, would glorify God, or because God the

Holy Ghost put it into one's heart and one dared not turn away. Now since the range of motive is so large, the range of self-deceit must needs be large also. For although conscience may tell us at the time, " you did *that* for such or such a secondary or poor motive," no one likes to remember it, much less to count up all the like acts which we did from this or some other lower motive. The world praises us, and it is hard to think the world wrong, when it is kind and pleasant, all the more, because it is not its wont. Self-love suggests to us the memory of the act which was good, and forgets the motives; and that, all the more readily, because we sometimes act out of better motives, which self-love takes care to remember. Then too it keeps out of sight the mountains of daily self-indulgence, which throw a cold damp shade over these insulated acts of charity springing out of God's grace.

But the Day of Judgement must clear up all this. It not only is to "[h]bring to light the hidden things of darkness;" it will also "make manifest the counsels of the hearts," and then, as shall be the issue of that unveiling, " shall every man have praise of God."

And since nothing can receive praise from God, which is not, more or less directly, more or less purely, done for God, whether as speaking in men's consciences by His natural and eternal law, or by whispers and solicitations of His grace (even when He is Himself unknown, as in the heathen world), or by His sensible drawings, or by habitual grace, or sense of duty, or by God-given instinct and generous impulse, then the Day of Judgement will, I

[h] 1 Cor. iv. 5.

fear, to very many of the saved, who now stand well with themselves, be a terrible discovery, how very little, in their whole lives, they have really done for love of God.

And this, I believe, to be what the Apostle means by those things which shall be burned up. Things they are of different degrees of lightness, by which different minds imposed upon themselves, as though they were of value when they were of none. But the most plausible will not leave a rack behind, more than the most openly worthless. Nay, it may be, that the most plausible, and seemingly the most solid, may have the most endurance of pain, both because the loss will be the more unexpected, and because there may be more of things offensive to God, not levity, but vanity or self-conceit, self-opinion or pride. For caprice has at least nothing systematic in it; but pride, vanity, self-will, self-pleasing are alas! powerful springs of action, which put themselves forth under an almost infinite variety of disguises, and are sure to be most busy there, where they are least suspected.

Nothing but a continued active habit of directing our actions to God, such as results from offering them to God, morning by morning, for the day, and then renewing that direction often through the day, by some brief prayer as, "For Thee, O Lord;" or continuous prayer for grace, will rescue some fragments of our acts from the unclean contact of those spiritual harpies, our besetting faults. And if this has not been so, and self-examination has been superficial, and has not been directed to our motives, then, what a terrible unveiling of ourselves to ourselves will the Day of Judgement be! God has in His mercy at times lifted up the veil beforehand, and shewn those who had wished to serve Him, how much of what they thought to be grace was mere natural activity. But to see first in the Day of Judgement, that life had been one great mistake; that so very little or nothing had been done purely for the love of God; that, of that little, something had been afterwards taken from God and given to the world, in some seeking for human praise; that, amid the wood, hay, stubble, of a whole life-time, there had been but a grain here and there of what was pure (oh, that it were but a little gold-dust or some chip of a costly stone) it would be a misery, to which all miseries of this life concentrated in one would be nothing.

And yet I have mentioned but the light side of the misery. For I have said nothing of the Look of Him, our Judge Who died for us, and of the sight of His Thorn-scarred Brow, and the Wounded Hands and Feet, which our sins rove wide asunder, and by which we would not let the wounds of our souls be healed. I have said nothing of the blackness of the ingratitude, seen for the first time as a whole, side by side with that Aweful Countenance of Holy, reproachful Love. I have said nothing of the horrible sight of all our blacker ingratitude, in rude repulses of grace, in obstinate pertinacity of sin, in the insolent mockery of those courteous dismissals of God, which procrastination of stricter ways or of clearly perceived duties, or of turning to God altogether, involve; wherein the soul in fact says to

God, "when I have a more convenient season, I will call for Thee, my Creator." No one, who can even imagine something of what God is, what the love of Jesus, what the blackness of the ingrati- tude of his own sin, but must feel sure that the sight would be so piercing, that soul and body would, in this life, part asunder through the intensity of the agony.

God has not revealed how long the Judgement shall last to each. It may be, that the whole evil of every act shall be shewn to us in one concen- trated gaze (as life is shewn at times to those drowning), or it may be that the evil or imperfection of each deed will be shewn to us, one after the other, each burning in more deeply the lesson of the other, in a way, which would, in this life, be unendurable. Origen's thought is not improbable, that under these materials, which are consumed more quickly or more slowly, God meant to teach us, as to the shorter or longer endurance of suffer- ing, ensuing on greater or lesser sin. "[i] The nature of sin is like the material, consumed by the fire, built, the Apostle Paul saith, by sinners, who, on the foundation of Christ, build wood, hay, stubble. Wherein it is manifestly shewn, that some sins are so light, that they may be compared to stubble, wherein the fire, when approached, cannot abide long. Others are like hay, which too the fire con- sumes without difficulty, yet lingers there some- what longer than in the stubble. Others are com- pared to wood, in which, in proportion to the crimes, the fire finds a great and lasting aliment. So then

[i] in Lev. Hom. xiv. n. 3. T. ii. p. 259. de la Rue.

each sin, according to its quality or quantity, pays its just due of punishment."

"He himself shall escape, yet so as by fire." To see his work perish in the fire, then, will not be his only suffering. Whatever that fire be, he himself will be saved, even after the loss of all, by himself passing through it. "It is said," says St. Augustine[k], "'he himself shall be saved' yet so as by fire. And because it is said, 'shall be saved,' that fire is despised. Yet although they be saved by fire, more grievous will be that fire, than whatsoever man can suffer in this life. And ye know what bad men have suffered here, and can suffer; as much as the good can suffer. For what has not a malefactor, robber, adulterer, wicked, sacrilegious man endured by the law, which the Martyr hath not endured in the confession of Christ? The evils here then are much lighter; and yet see how men do whatever you bid them, sooner than endure them. How much better do what God commands, not to suffer those heavier sufferings." Yet if the soul be saved, those sufferings too will have an end. Sufferings, of which Scripture so speaks, are not likely to be short. They are to burn out the dross of a life. They are to teach the soul the sinfulness of its sins for all eternity. They are to teach it to accept as the boundless love of God towards it, to be among the last in the kingdom of heaven, as the highest place, which God in His Righteousness could give it.

But what if there be, as some fathers have thought, suspense in that day? What if the soul sees its imagined goods vanish one by one, in that aweful

[k] in Ps. xxxvii. 2. 3.

fire, and know not the issue? What if it have to doubt, whether it have builded on the Foundation at all? What if this doubt endure, God knows how long, when minutes of our time shall seem an interminable existence? Human-thought can conceive nothing terrible enough for that Day, which God has pronounced so terrible. Yet the terrors too will have an end. The losses will, in all eternity, have no end. The graces, purchased by the Blood of Jesus, have been refused, wasted, and cannot then be recalled. God did all He could do, without forcing the soul's free-will, and it was cast aside for human praise or self-conceit and vanity. We shall know then, why there can be no second trial-time. Here we know only that there is none. As we sow, so shall we reap. "[1] Look to yourselves, that we lose not those things which we have wrought, but that we receive a full reward."

Ye are young still; ye have open, generous hearts; you would not simply escape Hell. You would fulfil the end for which God created, endowed, redeemed, called, justified you, for which He made each of you just that self which He has made you. Look then well, what is the end of what you do. Is it simply some form of self? or is it, God? Are you living mere natural lives, or are you stirring up the gift which is in you, the grace of God, which was lodged in you, when you were made members of Christ, the fruit of *His* Presence within you Whose temples ye were made, God the Holy Ghost? It may be that the body of the life which you are leading is, in the main, in the right direction; that you

[1] 2 S. John 8.

would not knowingly do what would separate you from God. God be thanked, if, thus far, you have remained or have returned under His sheltering care. But look to the soul of thine acts. See, if thy first fresh thought is, "So God wills;" "How shall I best please Him?" "Can I do this better for Him?" or whether you are living a mere listless, soulless round of mechanical employments, amusements, perhaps, in their turn, but with no effort to concentrate thyself on the will of God for thee, the end for which Jesus bought thee at so dear a Price, for which God the Holy Ghost is so prodigal of His gifts and calls.

I have not spoken of that dread hopeless place, which is the sinner's doom, except to hope that you all will, by God's mercy, escape it. Even of this it is no good token to be secure. For many alas! as are on that broad road, few think it of themselves, and *they* least fear it, for whom it is most to be feared. I have been speaking only of sufferings which, in the Day of Judgement overtake very many of those, who were perhaps never severed from Christ.

And of these, the suffering is the least evil. For to wake up to the sight that one had loved our Good Lord with only half a heart, and so had less power of love to love Him, would be worse than the pains of Hell, if any there could love Him.

In presence of death, now brought present to us[m], give one earnest gaze at the Judgement Day; see its blazing fires burn up all which is not in some way

---

[m] The Master of Trinity, Dr. Whewell, had just died suddenly by a fall from his horse; his death was widely felt.

done for God, and ask whether thou wouldest wish to be that scorched stunted soul, which should have the least possible capacity of the love and the knowledge and the wisdom of God throughout eternity. If not, choose God with the will of thy soul, as He has chosen thee. Pray Him to seal thy choice; and all dull things in life will have fresh joys, everything will give you fresh occasion of shewing Him your love, every thing will be to you a fresh channel of love, a fresh ground of thanksgiving. And you yourselves, though you would not know it nor believe it, while your defects grew but more visible to you, and you wondered, day by day, more at the monstrousness of our ingratitude to the tender love of our Father and our Redeemer, would, day by day, ripen in that love, which will seem to you so poor; day by day will add a ray to that eternal crown of glory, for which God formed and re-formed you; day by day will, by God's grace, enlarge you to receive more and yet more of that Infinite Love which made you, redeemed you, seeks you, for His own love.

EVE.—THE COURSE OF TEMPTATION.

GENESIS iii. 4, 5·

"And the serpent said unto the woman, Ye shall not surely die: for God doth know that in the day ye eat thereof, then your eyes shall be opened, and ye shall be as gods, knowing good and evil."

EVE's temptation and fall is the forerunner and counterpart of the falls of the sons and daughters of Eve, especially of those who are relatively in her condition, innocence as yet not sharply tried, the relative innocence of youth, before its first great fall. Her central temptation was, to seek against the Will of God, in a way of her own, forbidden by God, a good which God willed to give her in His way. So much is this an image of us, that a school has been found, which teaches, that Eve's act was a stage in human progress, "the first bold venture of reason, the first beginning of moral being, the happiest event of human history [b];" "the eternal myth of man, whereby he becomes man [c];" "the freewilled

---

[a] Preached at S. Mary's, Oxford. Lent, 1870.

[b] Schiller üb. d. erste Menschengesellschaft nach d. leitfaden d. Mosaisch. Urkunde. Werke, x. 389, ed. 1838, in Delitzsch *ad loc.*   [c] Hegel, Philos. d. Gesch., p. 333, ib.

human spirit, bursting through the bands of instinct and the narrow home of animal peace, to soar unhindered to the hot struggle for hallowing [d]." "The narrator would shew, how man found his way out of moral ignorance and unindependence, and attained to moral knowledge and self-dependence, but therewith took on himself greater duties, than he had before to fulfil [e]." As if a debasing slavery to evil were a necessary condition of the knowledge of the difference of good and evil; as if previous estrangement from God were the essential preparation for being His friend; as if a ghastly independence of the All-wise were the necessary pathway to matured wisdom; as if the subjugation of our spirits to the natures which we have in common with the beasts which perish, were the indispensable stepping-stone and threshold to "the glorious liberty of the sons of God," and disobedience to our Creator were essential to the perfection of beings created in His "image and likeness;" as if lawlessness were true liberty, wandering amid error the condition of the attainment of truth, abuse of our God-given faculties the essential practice of their use, unreason the handmaid of reason, moral darkness the one only vestibule to the true Light, the Light in which God dwells, the Light which He Is! But for sin, the Incarnation might have been without the horribleness of the Passion; we might have been as God, yea, God-united, engodded; and God might have been as one of us, without our being first as the Evil One or as the brutes. Heaven might have been, without those

---

[d] Einhorn (a Rabbi) Princip. d. Mosaismus, i. 65, ib.

[e] Knobel, *ad loc.*

everlasting cursings and blasphemies; the reign of
Divine love, without that dark realm of hate; the
ever self-unfolding communication of the satisfying
fulness which God has and is, without that eternal
impotent rejection of God which would that He
were not.

But God willed, for our endless well-being, to be
loved with our full free-will. He would not (even
if it does not involve a contradiction) be loved without our free choice. He willed to condescend to ex-
pose Himself (so to speak) to the free choice or contempt of His creatures. He empowered them, by
His grace, to choose Him; He even made it a violence to their engraced nature, not to choose Him.
But He subjected Himself to the vile indignity that
He Who Alone Is, Who hath and is all Good, the
perpetual Fountain of all Perfection as of being,
should be rejected by us, who have no being save
from Him, who have from Himself the power of
rejecting Him, rather than not bestow on us the
unspeakable dignity, freely to choose Him.

And so, since that ever-to-be-repeated choice is of
such infinite moment, God gives us the history, not
of the moving temptation only and the fall, but of
the order of Satan's wiles and Eve's tampering with
her tempter.

Satan prepares for the fall by exaggerating the
prohibition. He would convey hard thoughts of
God, without directly touching on the prohibition
itself. "Can it then be," he asks, "that the Deity [f]
(he omits the special name of God) hath forbidden

---

[f] אלהים. The special name, by which God revealed Himself to
man, יהוה, is omitted in this dialogue.

you to eat of any ^g tree of the garden?" Much as he
might say now, "Has the Deity forbidden all progress? Has He put bars to the intelligence which He
has created, and fettered the free scope and use of the
reason which He has made a created image of His
own?" Or, "Does God indeed mean to forbid us
the enjoyment of the appetites which He has given
us?" As though to restrain a mighty stream within a prescribed channel, that it waste not itself and
change not the fair bright face of nature around it
into a foul morass, were to dam its course! Satan
would not directly impinge on the commandment
itself; as now too he never begins at once with
suggesting the overt breach of some chief commandment. He knows well, "No one at once becomes
all bad ^h." But he would familiarize the mind to, or
lodge in it the thought, "the Deity *could* be hard."
It was the beginning of the fall, to hold intercourse
with one who had such thoughts, and had suggested
them. The idea, although set aside as a fact, was
lodged in the soul, which held parlance with him
who had suggested it. Not to reject the first in-
sinuation of evil, is virtually to consent to it.

Eve's answer agrees in two ways with our wont,
when giving way. It seems most likely that she
added of her own to God's command. For in this
state of original righteousness, the command "not"
to "eat of the fruit of the tree," and "not" to
"touch it," would alike be positive commands. Neither was wrong in itself, except in so far as it violated a command of God. Nature was whole *then.*

g The force of לא תאכלו מכל.
h "Nemo repente fuit turpissimus."

There was no temptation to contravene it. Allegiance to its Creator was its only trial. When God forbids *us* to do anything, for fear that the first step should lead to the next, it is that the first is easier to *us*, is a less wound to conscience than the other. So the thought or imagination of sin, such as is forbidden in the "thou shalt not covet," lies nearer to us than the violation of the seventh or eighth commandment. But in the state of man's innocency, when nature was not yet disordered, there was no stronger temptation to eat, than to touch, what was forbidden. There was no occasion to place a fence round a further law, when to break either would have been the same offence, the breach of a positive law of God. Had God forbidden to touch the fruit, to touch it had been to do what God forbade. Eve's answer, then, fair as the words sound, betrays that Satan's poison had begun to work in her soul. She made out, that God had forbidden more than He had; the very suggestion which Satan had just now, more broadly, made to her. "Of the trees in the garden we may eat, and of the fruit of the tree which is in the midst of the garden God hath said, Ye shall not eat of it and ye shall not touch it."

Then follows the other token of giving way. She adds, "Lest ye die." Not the sin itself, not the loyalty to her God, not the ingratitude in disobeying Him Who had so bountifully endowed her and surrounded her with all things fair and beautiful, not the thought of that daily converse with God, and His being with them as a Friend, not the dread of the severance of that relation of love with Infinite love, which God Is, is foremost in her mind; but the penal consequences to themselves of the breach of the commandment, "Lest ye die." True, God had said, "In the day that thou eatest thereof, thou shalt die." True also, that the dread of hell is often, in our now fallen nature, the first beginning of a conversion to God. True also, that, as it involves an eternal severance from and loss of God, the fear of it may rightly quicken the converted soul in its exceeding dread of that which is the true severance from God, sin. But in our unfallen nature it was already a leaning to a fall, that the penal consequences of sin were put forward, rather than the offence against God. It is not, "My God hath forbidden it, therefore I cannot do it, and sin against Him Who made me and daily continueth these peaceful blessings to me;" but, "Ye shall not eat thereof, neither shall ye touch it, *lest ye die.*" She speaks of God as an austere Master, and forgets all His love.

Satan saw his advantage and seized it. Eve, thinking of the penalty to herself, not of her allegiance to her God, laid herself open to and invited the bold lie, "Ye shall assuredly not die." Nay, it was impossible that they should die. It was in contradiction with other certain truth, with the very name of that, the eating of which He forbade, "the tree of the knowledge of good and evil." "For the Deity doth know, that in the day ye eat thereof, ye shall be as the Deity Himself, (i. e. thus far, in this point of knowing good and evil, which, Satan suggests, God had grudged His creature) "knowing good and evil." If, then, the knowledge of good and evil was to be the result of eating the fruit, then death

could not anyhow be the immediate consequence of
the act; else there would be no room or scope for
those immediate effects, of which God spake by the
very name. No, it could not be. There was a long
future before them; a future, in which they should
exchange their holy simplicity, or rather (as she
would think) engraft upon it a knowledge, in its
degree, like to that of God Himself Who forbade it,
the knowledge of good and evil. But therewith he
insinuated also that God withheld that knowledge,
not in mercy, but grudgingly. He Who made man
in His likeness, willed not (Satan would have it)
that he should be altogether like Him. He held back
something, which would be good for His creature.

Eve had lost sight of the thought of her allegiance
and loving relation to God, in the thought of the
penal consequences. The contradiction was plausible in itself, so soon as it was out of her mind, *Who*
had said it. It had, as have most of Satan's lies,
a mixture of truth, which gave colour and gained
entrance to the lie, which it disguised. So far they
were to become like to God, that they should "know
good and evil." But how? By losing their Divine
likeness to God, Who had made them "very good,"
and united them to Himself by His grace; knowing evil, not, as He does, objectively, as something
wholly alien from Himself and excluding Himself,
but by *becoming* evil. Just as now Satan offers freedom by breaking God's law, and substitutes real
slavery, the gradual weakening and almost destruction of free-will, the slavery to evil habits, for the
glorious liberty of one-mindedness with God.

Then followed the typical course of sin. She

looked, she considered, she weighed; but it was the one side only, the side of temptation. "She saw that the tree was good for food, and that it was a desire to the eyes, and a tree to be desired to make one wise, and she took of the fruit thereof and did eat." Holy Scripture probably veils the fiery consequences of that eating, and tells us only how Satan's promise was fulfilled. "Their eyes were opened, and," as the fruit of the tree of knowledge, "they knew" —what? "that they were naked." "They had become like God," but severed from Him. They knew good and evil. But instead of knowing evil afar, from the free height of good, they now know good only from the deep abyss of evil, wherein they had fallen. "Their eyes were opened." "[i] Had they been blind before? They had been blind only to the mere sight of sense. They saw that they were naked, and saw it not; for they saw themselves in God, saw all in Him, referred all to Him; nought of sense occupied their minds; in all they saw, they looked beyond to God; a mantle was over all, and that mantle was the glory of God." The flesh was fallen away from the might of the spirit; the spirit from the life in God. Broken was the band between the spirit and God; broken, the band of the spirit and the flesh. This alone remained, that having lost that robe of original righteousness, with which God created them, they felt shame; that having sinned against their conscience, they did no violence to the conscience which testified against their sin.

God has retained in us such likeness to Himself, even amid our self-made unlikeness, such traces of

[i] Delitzsch, *ad loc.*

His image even amid our defacing of it, such secret
unintelligent longing for Himself, even while we are
wandering far from Him among His creatures, that,
if we will not seek Himself, we must seek some perverted likeness of Himself. The soul must, with
the will, if faithful, or, without the will, if unfaithful, still she must, in her blindness, dimly own her
Creator. If she turn from Him, she must still seek,
without Him, what she findeth not pure or un-
tainted, till she return to Him. "In her very sins
she seeks but a sort of likeness to God, in a proud
and perverted, and therefore slavish, freedom[k]." She
could not, at first at least, be deceived but by "a
false and shadowy beauty[l]." Pride, ambition, false
tenderness, curiosity, sloth, prodigality, covetousness, anger, alien as they are from God, what seek
they but to be as God? So S. Augustine traces out
the deep thought. "[m]Pride doth imitate exaltedness,
whereas Thou Alone art God, exalted over all.
Ambition, what seeks it, but honours and glory?
whereas Thou Alone art to be honoured above all,
and glorious for evermore.—The tendernesses of the
wanton would fain be counted love; yet is nothing
more tender than Thy charity, nor is ought loved
more healthfully than *that*, Thy truth, bright and
beautiful above all. Curiosity makes semblance of
a desire of knowledge, whereas Thou supremely
knowest all.—Yea, sloth would fain to be at rest;
but what stable rest besides the Lord? Luxury
affects to be called plenty and abundance; but Thou
art the fulness and never-failing plenteousness of

[k] S. Aug. de Trin., xi. 8.   [l] Id. Conf., ii. n. 12.
[m] Ib., n. 13. The original is fuller.

incorruptible pleasures. Prodigality presents a shadow of liberality; but Thou art the most overflowing Giver of all good. Covetousness would possess many things; and Thou possessest all things. Anger seeks revenge; who revenges more justly than Thou? Grief pines away for things lost, the delight of its desires, because it would have nothing taken away from it, as nothing can from Thee."

Wonderful nobility and community with Himself, in which God created us! Marvellous circumscription of our being by Him from Whom we evermore derive it, that even in sinning, rebelling against God, turning away from Him to His creatures, and turning them away from their rightful use, we yet cannot wholly emancipate ourselves from Him, we must seek some distorted likeness of Him, the more hideous, because it is distorted from so Infinite a Good.

But then look at the magnificent counterpart. Sin is an aweful, in itself an irremediable, mistake. It is to miss our real, our only, our everlasting Good, for which our God in His love created us. It is to have taken a fiery draught which burns through all our veins, for "the rivers of pleasure at His Right Hand." It is to have taken our enemy for our god, slavery for freedom, a flickering meteor, an exhalation dancing around morasses, for the true light; it is to have lost for eternity that, for which God in His Infinite love created us. But then, if we have chased the ever-retreating shadow, the substance is there; if we have mistaken the glass for the pearl, the counterfeit for the royal image, the lie for the truth, still the counterfeit is the pledge to us

of the existence of the glorious original; the for-
gery, of the true God-stamped image; Satan's lie,
of God's truth. God, Who made us for Himself,
made nothing in us, for which He provided not, the
full contentment; and that, not hereafter only, but
now. Long we for freedom? He will make us,
"free indeed." He will give us freedom, which they
who have it, know to be real. Long we for knowledge? He has spread wide open for us the boundless variety of His creation, but above all, He gives
us a real knowledge of Himself: He opens to us His
own being and the mysteries of His love, where our
only darkness is from the excess of His light. Long
we for love? *Here*, too, pure love has an intensity
of joy, an image of heaven; so that it has been truly
said in a measure, that "love is heaven and heaven
is love;" and we scarcely turn from sin to God, but
He sends a thrill of love into the soul, the faintest
touch of which is above all creation. And beyond,

> " The heart that loveth knoweth well
> What Jesus 'tis to love."

In many things (would God I could think it was
still in all, my sons) ye must be in that first stage,
in which your temptation is to a forbidden fruit, as
yet untasted. In whatever degree it has not been,
ye know that the first stage is, to think that there
can be anything good, besides or against the expressed mind or will of God. The next is to question, "Can God indeed have meant to forbid this?"
"Hath God indeed said?"—Can God indeed have
meant to lay such and such restrictions on His
creature? To what end should He have placed the

tree of knowledge in the midst of the garden, unless He meant us to eat thereof? The soul dares not at once openly rebel against the known will of God. If it *will* not be of the same mind with God, it must set itself to persuade itself that God is of the same mind with it. It is a necessity of our being, until we are lost, to be in harmony with Him Who is the end of our being, God. It is not all, fear of punishment; still less, slavish fear. It is holy dread to burst the band of union with God. Self-deceit is the soul's screen to hide from its eyes its severance from God. It dares not look its deed in the face, and do it. It snaps the bond of love, but looks away. The heathen persuaded themselves of old, that the gods were the patrons of their sins. "Shall I not do, what the great Jove did? I did it gladly[u]." They consecrated their sins to their desecrating gods. The worst sins were, in nature-religions, the most consecrated. *They* said, "The gods meant this or that." In Christianity, men say more modestly, "Must not the God of nature have meant it?" After habituation to sin, the self-excuse is boldly laid aside; the inured profligate says boldly, "God did mean,"—what God in the most express terms forbade.

And so, as to faith. Hath God indeed said, that on this very day[o] Almighty God took our poor human flesh to be united co-eternally with His Godhead, and that, in the humility of the Virgin's womb? Has God indeed said, that He Who, in our human time, was two days old, was Almighty God? or that

[u] Terence.
[o] March 25, the Feast of the Annunciation of the B. V. M.

God Himself, in our Flesh, was crucified? Or has He indeed vouchsafed to tell us, how He Himself exists in His Co-eternal Love, Father, Son, and Holy Ghost? Or has God indeed said, that He has set Himself as our free choice, freely by His grace to choose Him, or freely, despising His grace, to reject Him, to be (oh, misery of miseries!) eternally miserable by eternally rejecting *Him*, Whom the soul knows to be the end and centre of its being?

Indurated unbelief decrees peremptorily, "There is no God," or "human nature is God," or "we have no freewill or no immortality, but are like the beasts which perish." But unbelief ever begins, "Hath God indeed said?" meaning, "We cannot or will not think that He hath said it;" and quickly there follows that further thought, "He ought not to have said it, or so to have circumscribed the judgement of His creature."

Then follows, or is almost one with it, "Assuredly thou shalt not die." For God plainly cannot punish what He has not forbidden, or count it to be a rejection of His declared truth, to deny what His creatures have ruled for Him, that He cannot have meant to reveal. Only Almighty God and we are somehow to change places. We are to be His critics and judges, not He our Judge; we are to rule for Him, what He shall reveal to us. We are (which it comes to) to make our God, instead of having as our God, Him before Whom the Seraphim with their burning love veil their faces, from Whom the highest Intelligences are content ever to receive something of His exhaustless Fulness; Him, in Whose tender love we reposed in our childhood; Who never failed us; Him

Who made us; and to depend on Whom was our peace, and the full contentment of our joy.

Such were the foreruners of the fall. Then followed the, alas! so often-repeated history. "She saw," "she took," "she ate," "she gave to eat." She had got rid of the fear of God. Why should He, how could He, punish so disproportionably an act so slight? She had seen His bountifulness; she had not seen its withdrawal. The seducing spirit who spake with her had disobeyed and had not died. All other fruits in the garden had been harmless: the fruit of the tree of life had, by God's appointment, some mysterious influence for good; why should not the fruit of the tree of knowledge? She had not *our* experience, to which everything speaks of the death of the body; the sun shone on no new-made graves then; no parent's loss foretold the death of the child. She would "rather believe that God could forgive the sin," that He could threaten what He would not fulfil, "than endure not to know, what this thing was, which He had forbidden," or *why* He had forbidden to eat thereof. Satan cannot persuade *us*, against our daily experience of human mortality, that we shall not die the death of the body. But it is the self-same argument, by which he prepares our fall;" ye shall not die eternally." God threatens "the worm which shall never perish," "the inextinguishable fire." God is disbelieved; His creature's lie is believed.

Secure, then, from harm (as she thought), *she saw.* She looked what it could be. Alas, if one were to name in one word, the parent of sin, the ante-dater of all other temptations, the destroyer of purity of soul, the corrupter of the senses, the disputer with God the Holy Ghost for the possession of His temple, the soul,—earlier, mightier than all passion but *that* which gives it its food and nourishment, and strengthens its mastery, it is,—ye know, my sons, what I mean—(Oh, how Satan repeats his hellish triumph over Eve, when he has awakened it)—*Curiosity.* Victory were, by God's grace, comparatively easy, were it not that the devil's porter [p], curiosity, opened the gates, and brought in those beasts of hell which lay waste the soul. They who have not, in boyhood, indulged curiosity, are blessedly exempt from a whole embattled army of trials which it lets in on the poisoned soul. The baleful·poison of the tree of knowledge has not spoiled the imagination, stirred up passions by nature happily asleep, created longings which belong not to its age, nor taken the will captive, when innocence would still start back from completed guilt.

> "Curiousness, first cause of all our ill,
> Is yet the plague which most torments us still."

Sins within the soul sometimes wound more gravely, they are more perilous, they can, in the nature of things, be more indefinitely multiplied than outward sins, though the outward sins of the same kind are seldom wanting. "Every man is tempted, being drawn forth and enticed by his own sin; then lust, having" by union with the will "conceived, bringeth forth sin; but sin being perfected, bringeth forth death [q]."

Eve saw that the fruit had its threefold attractions. She had seen it before, but without the desire to eat;

[p] S. Thos. Aq. in Gen.   [q] S. James i. 14.

now she gazed outwardly at the lusciousness of its look, the invitingness of its beauty; and inwardly she saw all those tempting properties, of which the serpent had told her, the promised knowledge; and, gazing on these, she (as we have learned from her) forgot all besides. All other delights which God had spread so bountifully around her, the delights of every sense, when the senses, too, were pure, and everything of earth was transparent with the beauty of heaven; her innocent love for him, from whose being her own was derived; her immediate relation to God her Creator; her intercourse with God as a Friend—all was forgotten in that long, curious, empassioned gaze. "Why gazest thou," says S. Bernard[r], "so intently on thy death? Why love to gaze on what thou mayest not eat? Sayest thou, 'I stretch my gaze, not my hand; to see is not forbidden me, only to eat.' Fault though it be not, it is fault's index. For whilst thou art intent on one thing, the serpent secretly glides into thy heart, speaks blandly to thee, holds thy reason by his blandishments, thy fear by his lies, saying, 'Thou shalt in no wise die.' He augments thy anxiety, while he stimulates appetite; he sharpens curiosity, while he suggests cupidity; at length he offers what was prohibited, and robs of what was allowed; he offers an apple, and steals away paradise; thou drinkest deep the poison, thyself to perish and to be the mother of the perishing!"

"She ate and she gave to her husband with her, and he did eat." O horrible aggravation of sin, with its almost impossibility of perishing alone. Eve was

[r] De gradib. humilit., c. 10. n. 30, Opp. p. 578.

emancipated from the yoke of the prohibition which she had never felt until she rebelled against it; she was proud of her liberty, her progress, her independence; she was all in all in herself; she had eaten and she had not died; no remonstrance of God pleaded against her, no sentence of God had condemned her, the echoes of the "in the day that thou eatest thereof, thou shalt surely die," had faded away. God's threatenings were not so real. Intoxicated with her impunity, with a whole wide future of successive triumphs before her, with proud hope of her self-acquired likeness to God, she sought to associate her husband in this her new career, the partner of that glorious course which she had opened to him. "He ate." The fall of humanity was completed; the robe of righteousness was gone; Adam had become her partner again, but in shame. Dreadful fascination of sin! It is a miracle of mercy, if a sinner escape spreading the feverish infection of the leprosy of his sin.

Such is the oft-repeated history; such the sad wailing note of warning, floating down, but too often unheeded, from the closed gates of our lost paradise. "If thou wouldest avoid completed sin, flee from beginnings;" tamper not with it; let Christ's Cross, the seal on thy brow, fortify thee against imaginings; trust not thyself to rule for thyself, that God may not have meant what, as His Word is true, He has plainly said. Remember the closing words of God's revelation to man: "[s] If any one shall take away from the sayings of the book of this prophecy, God shall take away his portion from the book of life."

[s] Rev. xxii. 19.

Such was the fall. In the mystery of to-day is the restoration. "In very truth," says S. Augustine[t], "we too confess that had the Lord willed in such wise to become man, as not to be born of a woman, this had been easy to His Majesty. For as He could be born of a woman without the man, so could He be born, not even through a woman (as was Adam). But this He did, that in neither sex His creature man might despair. If being man, as He was to be, He had not been born of a woman, women might despair of themselves, remembering their first sin, that the first man was deceived through a woman, and they might think that they had no hope whatever in Christ. He came then as man, but born of a woman, as though saying to them, 'That ye may know that the creature of God is not evil, but sinful pleasure perverted it; lo, I am born of a woman. I do not then condemn the creature which I made, but the sins which I made not. Let each sex behold its glory, let each confess its iniquity, and each hope for salvation.' The poisoned draught was given by a woman to man for his deceiving; let salvation be given to man to drink through a woman for his salvation. Let woman compensate for the sin, that by her man was deceived, through conceiving Christ. Thence also women first announced to the Apostles the risen God. The woman announced death to her husband in Paradise; woman, too, announced to men salvation in the Church. The Apostles were to announce to the nations the Resurrection of Christ; women announced it to the Apostles."

[t] Serm. ad pop. li. n. 3, Opp. v. 284.

And not only so, but as our Blessed Lord over-came for us, in fact and in ensample, the threefold temptation of Adam, the eating the forbidden fruit in the " Command these stones, that they become bread ;" the vainglory, " Ye shall be as God," in the " Cast thyself down ;" the covetousness, "Knowing good and evil," in " The kingdoms of the earth and the glory of them [u];" so He vouchsafed to His Mother, at the vestibule of the Incarnation, to reverse the temptations and disobedience of Eve. The vainglory of Eve was reversed in the God-given humility of Mary, when she was willing, if such should be God's Will, to become the scorn of man ; the disobedience of Eve by the obedience of Mary ; the faithlessness of Eve by the faith of Mary. In the well-known words of the Father [v], " With a fitness, Mary the Virgin is found obedient, saying, ' Behold Thy hand-maid, O Lord, be it unto me according to thy word ;' but Eve was disobedient, for she obeyed not, while she was yet a virgin.—As she, becoming disobedient, became the cause of death both to herself and the whole human race, so also Mary, having the pre-destined Man, and being yet a Virgin, being obe-dient, became to herself and to the whole human race the cause of salvation. The knot of Eve's disobedi-ence received the unloosing through the obedience of Mary ; for what Eve, a virgin, bound by incredulity, that Mary, a virgin, unloosed by faith." Eve dis-believed through vainglory, longing to be as God, and lost her place in the creation ; Mary, through humility, blindly believed God's word by Gabriel,

[u] S. Greg. Hom. 16. in Evang.
[v] S. Iren. iii. 22. 4. See more fully in p. 295, 296. Oxf. Tr.

and was placed above all simply created beings, or all possible creations, in a nearness of love and glory which cannot be imagined, as Theotokos, the Mother of God.

She [w] was the Mother of our Redeemer, and so from her, as the fountain of His human Birth came all which He did, and was, and is to us. She, being the Mother of Him Who is our Life, became the Mother of Life; she was the Gate of Paradise, because she bore Him Who restored to us our lost Paradise; she was "the gate of Heaven," because He, born of her, "opened the kingdom of heaven to all believers;" she was "the all-undefiled Mother of holiness;" because "the Holy One born of her was called the Son of God;" she was "the light-clad Mother of Light," because He Who indwelt her and was born of her, "was the true Light which lighteth every man that cometh into the world."

Such is the contrast, my sons, which this day suggests, of faith and faithlessness, of self-elation and humility, of receiving all things from God, or trying to wring them from Him: of dependence on God, or a would-be independence of Him. Eve willed to receive from Satan what God for the time gave in measure only, and sank our race in depths which we see around us, which we feel, alas! in ourselves, the bondage of this death; and although she herself was saved, her name is a by-word. Mary willed blindly to receive whatever God should give, whatever He should appoint. And where is she?

[w] I repeated here words of my Eirenicon, Vol. ii. p. 27. On the relation of these and the like titles in the Fathers to the Incarnation, see Ib.

What has been, cannot cease to be. She, who was the Mother of God-Man here, must be His Mother still. Little were it to be Queen of Angels. *The* special bliss must be the special love of the human Mother and the Divine Son.

Men tell you much of the grandeur of progress, the glory of independence, the bursting of trammels, the laying aside of antiquated notions, the being lords over yourselves. God grant that you may be lords over yourselves by being subject to the Infinite. God give you to burst every trammel which binds you! For His service is perfect freedom. God give you true progress, progress in God to the Infinite Wisdom in God! It is not the question what ye shall seek, but from whom ye shall seek it; from him from whom Eve sought it, who can give you but a lying semblance of the Gifts of God, or from Him Who Alone hath true Knowledge, true Wisdom, true Light, true Riches, true Love?

Choose really, truly, fixedly, to whom you will belong, whose you will be, whom ye will have; and may He direct and fix your choice, Who will be the everlasting Portion and Joy of those who choose Him.

SERMON VII.

MAN'S SELF-DECEIT AND GOD'S OMNISCIENCE.

S. Matt. vi. 22. 23.

" The light of the body is the eye; if therefore thine eye be single, thy whole body shall be full of light. But if thine eye be evil, thy whole body shall be full of darkness. If therefore the light which is in thee be darkness, how great is that darkness !"

Look all the world through, who well-nigh is not persuaded that he is in the right? I speak not of hereditary error, such as that of the Heathen, broken in upon by no light of truth: nor even of such Christians, as abide ignorantly, through some invincible prejudice, in the errors in which they have been educated. These, though they may sit in darkness and the shadow of death, are not responsible for darkness which they did not gather round themselves, or for any degrees of light, which did not shine in upon them. "[a] The times of ignorance God winked at." He imputed not unto them ignorance, contracted through fault of their distant forefathers, not their own. Their trial lay in what they still saw, in the witness of Himself which God still left and gave in His book of nature, or as to the secret motions and

[a] Acts xvii. 30.

voices of His grace, heard by them alone in their conscience. He "over-looked," took no notice of what was the fruit of involuntary ignorance. This alone He "winked at." They had their own trial, though different from ours: they have each been brought into the judgement of God, but for what they knew or might have known, not for what they could not know. "God overlooked ignorance," S. Paul says. He does not say that He overlooked wilful sin. The most degraded types of humanity, the wildest savagery, had its own trial of knowledge too; but it was, so far as they willed, not "to retain God in their knowledge," not for the moral degradation, into which they had been plunged, below the condition even of fallen man. An hereditary cannibal might not be responsible for his cannibalism. Some forbearance towards an enemy, some touch of mercy, suggested by the Omnipresent, ever-operating Spirit of God, may be accepted for him, for the sake of the unknown Redeemer Who died for the sins of the whole world. Cannibalism cannot be so offensive in the sight of God, as the horrible barbarities which we have lately heard of in the un-Christian, anti-Christian warfare of men, who bear, and glory in, the Name of Christ. What are called our "neglected" or "outcast population," the "young Arabs" of our streets, may not be so far from the kingdom of God, as those who so call them; those, whose neglect occasions them to be what they are, our decent, orderly, selfish (whoever they are) irreligious rich.

Self-deceit plainly must be self-wrought. Its nature and offensiveness are, that men, in some or in

K

many ways, darken their own conscience by shutting out the light of God.   There must be the more
scope for it, the greater the light, with which any are
surrounded.   Whatever crimes, violations of man's
better nature, brutalities, brutishness, there may be
among Heathen nations, there is the less scope for
self-deceit.   Among them, it can only find room,
where men stifle the inward workings of the Holy
Spirit, the unknown God. *Our* boast is of our light.
Therefore the largest reign of self-deceit must be
among ourselves : therefore each one of us may the
more apprehend that he suffers by it. So large and
pervading is its reign, that whoso has not learned and
shaken off some of its dominion, may be morally certain that he is yet under it, perhaps its slave.

Self-deceit is almost as varied as the human mind.
For it is the working of nature, to exempt itself
from the uncomfortable operations of God's Holy
Spirit upon it ; a false conscience, dexterously framed
to overlay and stifle the voice of the true.   It is the
outcome and result of repeated lies, which the soul
tells to itself; first .timidly whispered, then said
hesitatingly, then with less and less misgiving, or
amid or after intervals of misgiving, until at last
they are told to itself with effrontery, resenting all
contradiction.   It is as varied, as human finiteness
admits of, forming as many combinations, as those
startling varieties of numbers which baffle all calcu-
lation.   Its subject-matter is, whatsoever the soul,
from self-love, or passion, or pride, or ambition, or
conceit, or covetousness, or anger, or envy, or
rivalry, or sloth, wishes not to see.   It will take
for its armour, the word of God, or human opinion,

or popular maxims, or spiritual guidance, which it has itself taught and guided to misguide itself; the multitude of evil-doers, or misapplied sayings of saints; or the idolatry of human intellect and imaginary progress; the saying of a self-confident master, or its own self-confidence. It will darken itself by mists of its own creation wherein it envelopes itself, or by the enlightenment of the age, or by inspirations, as it deems, of God; by its own good or its neighbour's evil, nay the vehemence of its own evil; if by any means it may hide itself from the strictness of God's law or the clearness of His word, or from judgement to come.

Look at the variety of pleas, by which the poor Jews cozened themselves, not to receive our Lord; that they knew His human birth[b], or that He was not born[c], where prophecy declared that He should be, and where He was, born; that no prophet, (which was untrue) came out of Galilee[d]; that, working miracles on earth, He gave no sign from heaven[e], and that yet He said, "'I am the Bread which came down from heaven;'" "the Bread which I will give is My Flesh which I will give for the life of the world;" or that working such miracles, that He bare record[g] of Himself; that none of the rulers believed on Him[h]; or that the Christ should abide for ever, and Jesus said that He should be lifted up, i. e., by what death He should die[i]; or that He Whose teaching God the Father authenticated by miracles, which,

[b] S. Matt. xiii. 55-57. [c] S. John vii. 42. [d] Ib. vii. 41, 52.
[e] S. Matt. xii. 38, xvi. 1. sqq. S. John vi. 30-32.
[f] Ib. 41, 42, 52. [g] Ib. viii. 13. [h] Ib. vii. 48.
[i] Ib. xii. 32-34.

according to their own belief also could not be wrought, except God were with Him [k], broke the law of His Father, [l] because by miracles or teaching of mercy He enlarged the law of His servant Moses; [m] because He, being, a man, made Himself God; [n] because He declared that He, the Son of Man, had power on earth to forgive sins; and not only broke the sabbath, but said also that God was His Father, [o] making Himself equal with God; or because (which that law no where forbade) [p] He showed His love for publicans and sinners by eating with them, as though He connived [q] at the sin which He condemned, in winning gently from it those for whom He came to die; or, as though He could not read the heart of the penitent Magdalene, because they could not read it: or again they turned their own sins against Him, that He allowed His disciples to neglect " [r] the traditions of the elders," whereby they themselves transgressed and taught others to transgress the commandment of God; or because, (this at least they put forward to themselves and among themselves) temporal ruin might come upon themselves and their people through (they could hardly but think) a mistaken jealousy of the Romans [s]. They feared the loss of temporal things more than of eternal, and so (as many as repented not) lost both. Such were the outward pleas, but what were the inward grounds? That [t] they loved the praise of man, more than the praise of God; that they received [u] honour

---

[k] S. John iii. 2.   [l] S. Matt. xix. 7. Ib. xii. 10-14.
S. John ix. 16, 29.   [m] Ib. x. 33.   [n] S. Matt. ix. 2-6.
[o] S. John v. 18.   [p] S. Matt. ix. 10. sqq.   [q] Ib. xi. 19.
[r] Ib. xv. 1. sqq.   [s] S. John xi. 48. [t] Ib. xii. 43. [u] Ib. v. 44.

one of another and sought not the honour which cometh of God only;[v] because they were not of God and had not the love of God in them; because, as even Pilate, a heathen and a bystander could see, he [w] *knew* that for envy they had delivered Him; because they were [x] an evil and adulterous generation; because they closed their eyes, [y] and were blind .leaders of the blind; because they were hypocrites[z]; because they taught to keep God's commandments and did them not[a]; because they did all their works to be seen of men[b]; because they did the [c] lesser matters of the law and made much of them and omitted the greater; took heed to the outside, and were unclean within[d]; because Jesus spake against them, and they feared the diminution of their credit with the people.

What a world of unconscious motive! Outwardly, and what they doubtless said to themselves and to each other, there was zeal for the truth of God and for the right faith in Him, and for the law which He had given by His servant Moses. The truths, for which they professed themselves to be zealous, for which they were blindly jealous, were fundamental. They related to the Being of our Creator, or to our relation to Him as His creatures. God Himself had proclaimed the Unity of His Being. "Hear, O Israel, the Lord our God is One Lord[e]." It was the first of the commandments, given amid so much awe, "Thou shalt have no other gods before Me." True was it which they said, "No one, who is not God,

[v] Ib. viii. 47. v. 42.   [w] S. Matt. xxvii. 18.   [x] Ib. xii. 39, xvi. 4.
[y] Ib. xiii. 15. xv. 14.   [z] Ib. xxiii. 13.   [a] Ib. 2-4.
[b] Ib. 5.   [c] Ib. 23.   [d] Ib. 25-28.   [e] Deut. vi. 4.

could without blasphemy make Himself equal with God." It will be the very central sin of Anti-Christ. True, again, that God had set forth as His own attribute, "forgiving iniquity and transgression and sin [f]." True was the denial implied in their question, which we hear now so often repeated, " Who can forgive sins, but God only [g] ?"

And what was within? Mainly this. Love of· what every one loves, unless his own conscience have taught him its worthlessness, and even after he has in some degree learned it, the praise of his fellow-beings; longing to be had in honour, and, consequently, passion against Him Who diminished it. This was their central sin. Up to a certain point, their character was good. Our Lord pictures one as saying (He does not imply, untruly), " I am not as other men are, extortioners, unjust, adulterers or even as this Publican." He allows their self-denial, their exactness. S. Paul speaks of his life, as one strict and, " [h] touching the righteousness which is in the law, blameless." " [i] After the straitest," most exact, " sect of our religion I lived, a Pharisee."

But it all helped only the more to blind themselves. Dwelling on its own good and others' ill, it could not see its own ill, or others' good. The habit of censoriousness, formed by habitual judgement of others' misdeeds, incapacitated it from seeing good. Blindness, which could not see humility in the Publican, nor penitence in the Magdalene! Censoriousness, which, when become universal, ventured upon the All-holy! Why allowed He this? Why did He

[f] Ex. xxxiv. 7.   [g] S. Mark ii. 7. S. Luke v. 21.
[h] Phil. iii. 6.   [i] Acts xxvi. 5.

that? Until, at last in the Name of God, they committed Deicide ; they gloried in their religion, and made murder of the Just One, an act of religion.

But observe the process, by which they blinded themselves. For now too it is a very common one. It was a false application of truth. This is the parent of almost every heresy, by which people have hidden from their own eyes or from others the truth of God. Dwelling upon one set of truths, or of texts which establish them, against another, men deny, in the Name of God, the truths of God. What a host of errors are dissipated by that explanation of the Athanasian Creed, "Equal to the Father, as touching His Godhead, and inferior to the Father as touching His Manhood !" Yet what is essential to the verity of His Human Nature, is still alleged to contradict the Verity of His Divine [k]. God cannot pray to Himself. Therefore He, our High Priest, could not pray for us, as Man, if He is prayed to by us, as God, He could not, being God, have said, as Man, " My God, My God, why hast Thou forsaken Me ? or " Father, if it be possible, let this cup pass from Me." And so on. "He that believeth shall be saved ; " therefore "Baptism in the Name of the Trinity " is useless. The heavens were to receive Jesus "until the time of the restitution of all things [l]," therefore, although He made Himself supernaturally present to S. Paul [m], He cannot, in fulfilment of His own words, " This is My Body," make Himself supernaturally present on our altars. God Alone for-

---

[k] Essays and Reviews. "On the interpretation of Scripture," pp. 354, 355. [l] Acts iii. 21.

[m] Acts ix. 5. 17. 27. xxii. 14. xxvi. 16. 1 Cor. ix. 1. xv. 8.

giveth sin; therefore He cannot, by virtue of His words, "[n] Whosesoever sins ye remit, they are remitted unto them," empower man, as He did Nathan, to absolve from sin in His Name. "Christ was once offered to bear the sins of many;" and since He ever, at the Right Hand of God, as our Great High Priest, presenteth within the veil that Sacrifice which He once offered, such pleading, in our belief too, cannot interfere with the oneness of that one Meritorious Sacrifice offered on the Cross; but if it is taught that the priests are appointed by Him to make, by virtue of the Real Presence, a continual oblation of His death and merits for the whole human race,—this *does* interfere.

So, 1400 years ago, it was said to a heretic Emperor, "[o] Remember that there is no one heretic, who doth not say falsely, that what he blasphemously says, he sets forth according to the Scriptures— One, while he understandeth not, 'I and the Father are one,' hath neither God the Father nor God the Son. Another, through his frantic women, maintaineth another Comforter. Others hate the law, because the letter killeth, and the devil is the prince of this world. All speak the Scriptures without the meaning of Scripture, and, without faith, put forth a faith. For Scriptures are not in reading, but in understanding; not in prevaricating, but in charity." "All heretics," says another [p] who was for thirty years engaged in their conversion, "receive the Scriptures as an authority; to themselves they seem to follow them, whereas they do follow their own

[n] S. John xx. 22, 23.   [o] S. Hil. ad Const. ii. 9.
[p] S. Aug. Ep. 120 ad Conent. n. 13.

érrors, and are heretics, not because they despise the Scriptures, but because they understand them not." "The devil, the author of heresies," says S. Athanasius[q], "because of the ill-savour which attaches to evil, borrows Scripture language, as a cloak whereby to sow the ground with his own poison, and to seduce the simple." Self-deceit has to veil from itself its contradiction of truth; else it would be, not self-deceit but open rebellion. What marvel that *he* should employ Scripture as a bait for our willingness to be deceived, when he dared to hold it out to Him, the All-Holy? Each holds himself to be exempt from self-deceit. Yet each holds all, who contradict him, to be deceived; nay it has been assumed as a maxim, that those are most deceived who hold an hereditary faith. We hear much of doctrinal prejudices; we hear nothing of antidoctrinal prejudices: unless it be that firm believers (as we all do) trust, that those invincible prejudices are, in God's sight too, invincible, and will be looked on as an excuse in the great Day for having in ignorance rejected His truth. We hear much of supposed traditional error, we hear nothing of the possibility of self-originated error. Nay, because there have been large discoveries in things of time and sense, it has become a rule with some, that in those too which God has directly revealed, what is new is true; what is old, is false. Or again men have taken this or that half-understood or un-understood truth of revelation, and have said, "I cannot believe that God taught this or that; therefore I will not believe" what, in despite of their unbelief, is God's Word.

[q] Orat. i. c. Arian. § 8. p. 188. Oxf. Tr.

And so the Church of Christ is rent; God's truth
rejected; charity wounded; humility lost; the purposes of His love defeated; His tender care of us
set at nought; His grace baffled; His Holy Spirit
cast out; the Fall renewed; the recovery forfeited;
the Blood of Jesus wasted, because men will not
look, face to face, at what they are doing, and fall,
hoodwinked, self-confident, seeing the less because
they think that they see, into Satan's snares. "[r] If
ye were blind," our Blessed Lord said to those who
rejected Him, "ye should have no sin; but now
ye say, 'we see,' therefore your sin remaineth."
"[s] Because they thought they saw, they sought not
the Physician; they remained in their sins." He
who was blind from his birth saw both in mind and
body. Had these been blinded through necessity
of nature, the disease of unbelief had been pardon-
able. Now they saw the miracles, but were not
drawn to God Who gave them: they made themselves out to be instructed in the law, to be understanding in the Scripture: therefore they had no
plea for disowning Him "[t] of Whom Moses and the
prophets did write."

The self-deceit as to faith is limited, at least in
individuals. It is a monotonous, caw-caw, repeti-
tion of the same lie or sophism or false inference to
a person's self, the same setting Scripture at vari-
ance with Scripture, or the over-ruling of its plain
meaning by the same alleged impossibility, or by
the Jewish, "How can these things be?" under
which the human intellect shelters itself from the
truth which it wills not to receive.

[r] S. John ix. 41.   [s] S. Aug.   [t] S. John i. 45. add S. Luke xxiv. 44.

Self-deceit as to life is well-nigh boundless. One heresy is enough for most people, at least one central heresy. The mind lies asleep beneath its " [u] refuge of lies," and the light seldom anew penetrates or disturbs its recesses.

Self-deceit as to life has need to be more active, more unremitting, more wary, because the occasions for blinding one's self occur daily, and in each separate act the true conscience, until it is cauterised, will, by God's grace and the inspiration of His Spirit, rebel against the false, which silences it. How many thousand thousand acts and enacted thoughts of pride, or self-conceit, or self-complacency, or satire, or cunning, or censoriousness, or obstinacy, or hardness, or voluptuousness, have gone to stamp upon the countenance which was formed in the image of God that unmistakeable expression, which nothing but a strong battle, by the grace of God, will mitigate or efface. And, meanwhile, no one is less conscious of it than the poor victim. And why? Because he is ignorant of himself, because he has never seen himself, because he has wished only to see one half of himself, and to hide from himself that part of himself, which, if he saw, he must, by the grace of God, change.

This is the first great element and motive of practical self-deceit. It is unnatural, not to be at peace with ourselves. Our end is everlasting peace with God. Now we may be at peace in two ways. In healthful peace, because, by God's grace, we are on our way towards that ever-blessed everlasting peace; because "[v] the fruit of the Spirit is love, joy,

[u] Is. xxviii. 17.   [v] Gal. v. 22.

peace." We count not our stumblings, our bruises, if we know that, with the strain of every nerve, we are pressing onward to our everlasting home. We count not the buffeting of the billows, the reeling of our bark, or its being half-submerged by the waves, if, drenched by the seas, staggered, quivering, stunned, reeling, it still disengages itself, and rises upward. Or, men seek a peace by the absence of all struggle. This is, of course, a short road to peace, and we all like short roads. The problem is to satisfy ourselves, that all is right, and somehow to keep out of sight what is wrong.

Self-deceit is as manifold as human hearts. Each heart has its own way of tricking itself. The broadest way is to mistake nature for grace. A pious and distinguished preacher, among the revivers of piety in the last century [w], left it as the discovery of his last illness, "how much activity, which seems to us to be of grace, is of nature." What a discovery at the close of a long life of activity! Yet blessed, that God revealed it to the soul in this life! It is the source of all self-complacency. God has given to each of us some natural graces. One is kindhearted; another liberal; another strict; another tender; another eager; another laborious; another patient; another persevering, and so on. Now the first temptation in life is, to dwell on these good natural qualities, and mirror ourselves in them, and look away from the rest. If we look steadily at them, they fill up our horizon. We have uncomfortable feelings, that these are not our whole selves. But they are pleasant to our friends, or to those

[w] Cecil.

around us. Our little narrow circle dwells with pleasure upon them. Every gift of God is so beautiful.
We reverse the Apostle's rule [x], rest on our lees, remember "the things which are behind," and forget
"those which are before." What is good in us is
pleasant to our friends; their love makes them dwell
upon it to us; our self-love makes us dwell upon it
exclusively. They wished to encourage us in progress in good; we used it to stand still. But without
very searching self-examination, or some great terror,
or sight of death and nearness to eternity, or penetrating sorrow, or whatever forces upon us the stern
reality of life, what has been our over-weening or
exclusive estimate of ourselves, remains such. The
prophet pictures us, "[y] Ephraim is a cake (on the
coals) not turned." The fire which should have
penetrated it, spoils it: the one side, black and
burned: the other damp, clammy, lukewarm: the
whole marred; only not hopelessly, because the miracles of the grace of God can yet, unlike material
substances, unmake and remake us.

Yet we are, after all, such poor things, that we
can hardly cheat ourselves wholly by realities or by
unsought praise. Imagination helps us much. Few,
I suppose, have been, in youth, exempt from all
day-dreaming. Yet here we are in the very land of
unrealities. We develope our own supposed good
qualities, so undisturbed by difficulties or by any
of the rough realities of life. Temptations, sloth,
thwartings, self-sacrifice and the need of it, trials
of temper, the seductiveness of things pleasurable,
every thing which, in the world of actual being, be-

[x] Phil. iii. 13.   [y] Hos. vii. 8.

sets evèn real excellences, is out of sight. We do not need even the grace of God (though we do not, of course, tell ourselves so, for this would make our unrealities unreal to ourselves); all is smooth as the ice, without any risk of falling; all is rose-colour, without fear of showers.

Yet pure imaginations, destructive as they are to humility, enervating, the counterfeit of reality, and shutting out all reality the more, like a bright mist, because they are its counterfeit, will not yet do the work. They exhibit us always on our favourite side of ourselves. Still we are conscious, more or less, that they are dreams. Their unreality is our protection. They picture to us what we hope we should be and do : they develope what we most like in ourselves, as we hope it would, in such circumstances, be developed ; they help to blind us, because they conceal from us the fact, that every quality in us is secretly influenced by every other ; that no good in us could be perfectly unfolded, unless we were ourselves perfected. But we know that the beautiful selves, which we picture to ourselves, have not yet been realised.

God is such an intense reality, that there can be perhaps no complete self-deceit, except in the name of God and of religion. If men would shut out God from His own creation, it can only be in the name of God, as the poor Jews crucified their and our Lord in His Name ; and He forewarned His disciples; "^zWhosoever killeth you, shall think that he doeth God service." If men plead for their sins or justify them, they can but do it in the name

^z S. John xvi. 2.

of God. "God made me so," is the last excuse of those who become like the brutes which perish. More dexterous even than the Heathen, who first made gods for themselves, like themselves, and then copied the gods whom they had created in their own likeness, these make the True God responsible for our abuse of His creation. Owning, that He made us, and ignoring that we, by every abuse of our free-will, have been forging fetters for ourselves, ignoring also that witness of proverbial wisdom, " custom is a second nature," they confound the nature which God formed, with the second nature which they have deformed. Refusing to use the freedom, with which God anew enfreed them, they enslave the nature formed in the image of God to the lower nature which we have in common with the brutes, and impute to God the slavery into which they "[a] sold themselves." Yet this is simply to deny God in the name of God.

The deeper abuse is, to turn the gifts of God against Himself, and make His calls to His service a reason why we should not serve Him. Yet what else is all that tranquillising ourselves, because God has given us good and warm feelings, appreciations of His Holiness;

> "[b] Brightest transports, choicest prayers,
> Which bloom their hour and fade:"

or zeal, (though we too often make it like Jehu's), zeal, which is too often against our fellow-sinners rather than against our common sin; or perception of the beauty of goodness, which yet, like the Phari-

---

[a] See 1 Kings xxi. 20. 25, 2 Kings xvii. 17. Rom. vii. 14.

[b] Lyra Apostolica, n. lxviii.

sees, we do not, or soon tire of doing; conception of
humility, which we practise not, or which, if we
practise it as humility, becomes and betokens the
more real pride ; charity, which we make costless or
perform vicariously; submission to God's Will when
we cannot help it, and magnifying our own submis-
siveness; sense of God's presence, which was His
gift, and which we soon forget; some devotions at
Communion, which does not leaven our day; acts
done for God, which we afterwards offer behind our
backs to the world ; sorrow for great sin, which,
when absolved, we forget in the joy of God's forgiveness; exactness in God's service, which yet we
empty of its soul?   O where is the bound of God's
goodness or of our own boast of it, while we waste
it; which leaves next to nothing against the Great
Day, unless it be the burden of our God-robbing
ingratitude and continual self-glorification?

Yet these too, dwell on their bright side as we
will, have their own limit.   Mirror them as we will,
forget what we will, occupy our thoughts how we
will with them, uneasy thoughts, that this is not our
whole self, will still come over us.   We are our own
witnesses.   The most inordinate self-love and self-
esteem needs some prop out of itself to support it.
And so, because by God's mercy, we cannot wholly
blind ourselves, we get the world, or our friends or
our spiritual advisers, to finish the work by throw-
ing dust in our eyes, through its courteous, unreal
or cowardly praise, which seeing that we want it,
people are afraid not to give us.   The love of praise
is an instinct in youth; it is the natural longing for
approbation from those who can estimate them better

than themselves; it becomes a diseased appetite, as youth ripens into manhood. No absurdity is too absurd for it. It resorts to acts, which boyhood, with its keen, natural, sense of the ridiculous, jests at. It will depreciate itself, that people may contradict it; it will act the humble, in order to be made proud; it will fear that it did ill or failed, in order to be assured that it did well. It will own its infirmities, to be assured that they are not so great as it thinks. It will own a partial truth, hoping to be comforted by partial untruth, which its self-love makes entire; it makes estimates of itself which it would be startled and shocked, if any one held to be real, and dresses up its case, in order to ask advice which it does not want and will not take, unless (which is its only object) that advice confirms itself in its delusions of self-esteem. It is restless, because it suspects something to be wrong; but it wants, not a cure but an anodyne. It has as many antics as a mountebank, and is about as serious, except in its one object, the only one which it will not own, of being deceived. For if it would honestly recall its contrivances, it could not probably remember one case, in which, in any grave matter, it asked, with any thought of taking an opinion adverse to its views, although perhaps it may, in lesser things, to establish to itself its docility and its truthfulness;— the qualities, which, whatever besides it has, it eminently does not possess.

Yet, after all, this anodyne will not suffice, else people would not have recourse to it so often. Conscience wants to be laid asleep. Yet, until it is cauterised, it will wake up again. So we have another resource. Whoever wishes to unlearn pride, will look steadily at his own defects and at the graces of others. We mostly reverse this. We are conscious to ourselves of that hidden skeleton in our house, which we like not to think of, and which we will not face. But then, if others have the like, it makes matters even. At least, we are no worse than others, perhaps better. It would seem impossible, that, under the Gospel, which is such a law of love, there could be so much evil-speaking, against the express command of God, unless, in some strong way, it ministered to self-love. People do not break God's commandments out of mere wantonness. But to depress others, elevates self. Yet this too it does with an instinctive limitation. The Pharisee thanked God, that he was not as others; and then he specified some sins, which we may believe that he had not. He kept at least from any extreme violation of the 7th and 8th commandments; he paid tithes most exactly : he fasted more than was required. But what a mass of unknown sins he left unnoticed ! The sight of the Publican awakens in him the thought of common sins of the publicans. But look at the catalogue of heathen sins, of which S. Paul implies that Jews also were guilty ; " covetousness, maliciousness, envy, murder, strife, deceit, malignity, secret maligning, open slandering, insolence, contemptuousness, arrogance, disobedience to parents, faithlessness, unlovingness, unmercifulness—what a range of hateful sins, of which he says nothing! And of these, envy led that class of religionists, of which he was the representative, not to murder only, but to Deicide. And

yet, his comparison with the Publican laid all consciousness of any of these asleep; by dwelling on the
publican's faults, he made himself secure, and by
security fell into far worse. And is he not the very
pattern of our ordinary morality? Nay one might
almost say, " would to God he were ! " Our own
once-favourite satirist, as part of human nature, held
up to scorn those who

> "c Compound for sins they are inclined to,
> By damning those they have no mind to."

We dwell on, speak of, censure, backbite, rail at,
ridicule the sins or faults of others, (I cannot but
hugely suspect), in order amid the dust and din to
hide our own from ourselves. For few are quite
gratuitously malicious. The Pharisee was silent
about envy, hatred, malice, pride. For at least we
have so much knowledge or instinctive dread of
ridicule, that, very seldom, I suppose, would a con-
ceited man denounce conceit; the ambitious, ambition; the niggardly, niggardliness; the luxurious,
luxury; the slanderer, slanders. Any more than
one, seamed with small-pox, would point out, how
another was marked with it, or one with a cast in
his eyes, would speak slightingly of another's squint.
We have sufficient consciousness of our own infirmity, to avoid all mention of it, even in others,
and thereby bear witness that we are hiding our
eyes from it, and excusing it to ourselves by all this
accusation of others.

What a realm of self-deceit is all self-excuse! In
most of it, more or less, we lie too. But the self-

c Butler's Hudibras.
L 2

deceit is still the same. We instinctively fasten on
some point, which we think or which may be exag-
gerated or mistaken; and under cover of it, untruth-
fully to ourselves, deny the whole.

There is yet a graver form of self-deceit in this
self-excuse. There is scarcely a sin, to which people do not become inured, so as scarcely to think
of it as an evil, because they are so often guilty
of it. They have an instinctive sense, for instance,
in childhood, that something is unbefitting; they
would not like their parents or friends to know of it.
They hide it. The fine bloom of innocence is gradu-
ally rubbed off; it is done to-day, because it was
done yesterday. "Had I but known of confession,"
some have said in later life, "I should have been
saved all this misery: " forgetting, that if they violated instinct, they might have broken through any
other hedge; and laying the blame on circumstances,
rather than on themselves. Nothing is so blinding
as sin. Man must be at peace, and if his true conscience condemns him, he has, if he will continue in
sin, no help, as it were, for it. He must make himself a false conscience, to protect himself from the
reproaches of the true. Is it not so? Remember the
earliest consciences you had, from the grace of Baptism, from early teaching, when your souls were
fresh from their Maker's Hands. If things have
gone ill with you, think of the first bad book you
ever read, how you would have been ashamed to
have been found with it, how you would have shrunk
to be discovered in making the Bible an occasion of
knowing evil, or in searching in a Police-report,
to find something wherewith to taint your imagina-

tion. Think what you would have thought of the first
act of sin, before you had accustomed yourself to the
thought; what you would have thought of it, in one
you loved tenderly! Man turns away from his conscience, hides himself from its voice, stifles it with
other thoughts, forgets it, lies to it, buries it. Things,
which one would have once been startled at, become
every-day-things, necessities.

. And yet how strict we can be, in things to which
we are not inclined, nay think well of ourselves because we are so strict. *Then*, we can see the beauty
of God's law, the wrong of injustice, the misery of
grinding the poor, the hatefulness of selfishness, the
selfishness of self-indulgence, the majesty of truth,
the magnificence of self-denial. We can see clearly,
speak fervidly, judge precisely in all things which
concern another. How is it, when our own interests
or passions are concerned? Then, the condition of
the world around us shews, that all things become
confused, embroiled, entangled. Evil becomes good,
and darkness light. The eye sees through a false
medium, and all is discoloured to it. And how great
is that darkness!

But to what end? The Psalmist tells us the result as to all this self-flattery. " [d] He flattereth
himself in his own eyes"—this is what we do more
or less gravely; but to what end? literally " to find
out the iniquity, to hate it." The end of all this
self-concealment is God's searching out, punishing,
the sin, when there is no remedy, but the sinner, at
last, incapable of turning, fixed in evil, remains the
object of the everlasting displeasure of God. David

[d] Ps. xxxvi. 2. .

says of himself; "^eI said, I will confess my transgressions unto the Lord; and Thou, Thou forgavest the iniquity of my sin." If one lulls one's conscience as to sin, and makes all smooth to one's self, there is no repentance, no confession to God, no forgiveness. In the Day of Judgement God lays bare, what we had so smoothed over, what we had disguised so dexterously, yet which was ever present to the mind of God. The Great Day will but lay open God's everpresent judgement.

"^fThou, God, seest me." To what end then even of this world, to lie to ourselves, when God, all the while, reads us true? To what end to tell ourselves that we have good motives, when God, in His unchanging Light, sees that we have bad or indifferent? To what end to persuade ourselves that we cannot help what we can, when God sees our neglect, or dismissal, or despite to His Grace? Why imagine that we are liberal to the poor, when God sees our profusion on ourselves, our comforts, our luxuries? To what end to tell ourselves, that God is our end, when God, of Whom we speak so freely, knows that our good repute, our self-esteem, are our own idol? Picture we ourselves to ourselves, as we shall stand, bared of this body and of all whereby we cozen ourselves or get ourselves cozened by others, before Him Who is the Truth. We cannot imagine ourselves, penetrated through and through by that Divine light, and not feel instinctively that we shall see ourselves other than we ever saw before. Secret things of our hearts will be illumined, not only to others but to our own eyes. What must

^e Ps. xxxii. 6.   ^f Gen. xvi. 13.

be without or against our will then, when there is
no remedy, why should we not do now, when, by
God's grace, the sight may heal us?

"Thou, God, seest me." "ᵍThe eyes of the Lord
are in every place, beholding the evil and the good."
The eyes of the Lord are there; because God is
there. It has often been felt, how one penetrating
human glance will silence the rising excuse, or the
half-false, unconsidered, expression. The soul, which
felt itself read through, dared not lie to itself in the
presence of that keen human intelligence. But now
the Sight, in which we live, to which we lie open,
Who sees our thoughts before they are formed into
words, ʰwhich understandeth the thoughts long before; ⁱa discerner of the thoughts and intents of the
heart, does not behold us, as we are obliged to picture
it (if we do picture it) afar off, in Heaven. We lie
down, act, think, speak, alas! sin, and cozen ourselves, in the midst of It. We lie to ourselves, encompassed, shone through, by that all-seeing Light.
God is Omniscient, being also Omnipresent. He
not only sees each word, thought, act, of each creature which He hath made, with that indivisible
knowledge, which appertains to the simplicity of
His Being. He sees each, as present with each.
In darkness, He is Light around us. If any thing
will ever disentangle us from the folds of this all-
embracing self-deceit, it will be the consciousness
of this still more closely-enfolding Presence of our
God. We cannot picture it to ourselves, but we
can know it. It is essential to the simple Being
of God, Who is " wholly every where, but the

ᵍ Pr. xv. 3.　　　ʰ Ps. cxxxix. 2.　　　ⁱ Heb. iv. 12.

whole of Him no where." It is the simplest truth
of faith.

Act then, as knowing it to be real. "[k]In Him we
live and move and are." Nearer to us than the air
we breathe, the people who meet us, to whom we
are inclined to wear a mask, nearer to our heart
than that thick veil which we fain would draw between us and them, is our God.

Speak we to Him, as intimately present to us;
Who knows and loves us better than we can know
or love ourselves; Who listens to our heart; Who is
the Fount of every holy thought;[1] Who is not One
in one place, and otherwise in another, but the self-
same; [m]Who knoweth, not with any variety of knowledge, but unchangeably Eternal; [n]Who so cares
for every one of us, as if He cared for him alone;
and so for all, as if they were but one;[o] Him, "the
Truth which is Eternity, and Love which is Truth,
and Eternity which is love;" which possesseth all
things, which giveth Himself to be possessed by us,
but Who "[p] vouchsafes not to be possessed together
with a lie:" [q] Him Who is present to all consciences:
to the good, as a Father; to the evil as a Judge.
Speak to Him; unfold thyself to Him; desire that
He should unfold thee to thyself; go out of thyself
to God; commune with Him: desire that He Who
readeth thine inmost soul should read thee to thyself, and as thou art faithful to Him, He will lay
open to thee all the dark corners of thy heart, that
He may fill them with His light and love.

Once thou must know thyself. Once, that All-

[k] Acts xvii. 28.　　[l] S. Aug. Conf. xii. 7.　　[m] Ib. xi. ult.
[n] Ib. iii. 11.　　[o] Ib. viii. 16.　　[p] Ib. x. 41.　　[q] Ib. 73.

searching Eye will reveal to thee thy whole self; all, which thou ever hiddest from thyself; all, which thou didst never see, because thou hadst closed thine eyes to thy real self, and wouldest not admit His light. To what end to hide now, when it may be for thy salvation to see it, what thou must see, when the sight would but make thee shrink terrified from the ever-blessed Presence of God, and shudder back into the outer darkness; when conscience, then first clear and awakened, would anticipate the Judge's sentence, "Depart, ye cursed?"

God, Who is Light and love, has "[r]brought us out of darkness into His marvellous light," and has made us all "[s]children of light and of the day;" "we are not of the night nor of darkness." He, the true Light, came a Light into the world, to be our light. Ye would not abide in darkness, from which Christ came to free us. Light leadeth not to darkness, nor darkness to light. In the Lord we are light; without the Lord, we are darkness. He giveth us His Light here; yea, He is our Light, that hereafter in His Light we may see light, even that Uncreated Light, which is seen by the light of the heart here, and there in it's irradiating satisfying brightness. "[t]Wouldest thou see that light? Cleanse the eye whereby it is seen: 'Blessed are the pure in heart, for they shall see God.'"

[r] 1 S. Pet. ii. 9.   [s] 1 Thess. **v. 5.**
[t] S. Aug. in Ps. 26. En. 2. n. 15.

SERMON VIII[a].

OUR PHARISAISM.

St. Luke xviii. 11.

The Pharisee stood and prayed thus with himself, God I thank Thee that I am not as other men are.

There is, perhaps, scarce a character in Holy Scripture which men more detest, than this Pharisee. I suppose, much on the principle that we loathe the ape, because he is so hideous a likeness of ourselves. For if we detested or despised him, as being in any way our inferior, as having unamiablenesses, which we have not, we should have arrived at out-Pharisee-ing the Pharisee, like him in all except the religious side of his character, in that we do not thank God that we are (as we think) not like him.

And yet, for the nineteenth century, he is a very respectable religionist. One might, if one dared follow one's own impulses, wish that we had more of them. Any how, the wives of our people would be safe; for he was no adulterer. We should have fewer of those commercial crises, which bring calamity on so many innocent people, and shew the hollowness of our national claim to honesty (Pharisees in this,

---

[a] Preached at S. Paul's Knightsbridge. Ashwednesday, 1868.

in all but his truthfulness); for he was "not unjust."
Our poor would be better off, and we should have
more shepherds in this vast wilderness of souls; for
he paid tithes of all which he possessed : a double
tithe, you will recollect, one for God's Priests, the
other for the poor, and another tithe every third
year for the poor; 4s. 8d. in the pound he any how
gave to God, nor, as our wont is, underrating our
property for the poor's rate, but a good 4s. 8d. in the
pound on the average of the three years. "I give
tithes of all which I possess." Then, in the country,
the poor had the corners of his fields, and were preferred to the pigs, as his gleaners. Then he was
regular at synagogue-worship; he set a good example
(as I doubt not, he told himself), and the chief seats
which he chose, would not vie with our old-fashioned
Churches in London or our family-pews in the
country. He used too some sort of self-denial; for
he fasted twice in the week, going herein beyond
what the law required of him. He had a zeal towards God, such as it was; for he "compassed sea
and land to make one proselyte." He liked religious conversation: for he liked people to call him
"Rabbi, Rabbi," that is, Teacher. One who would
be like him must any how "promote religious knowledge," as we speak. The Pharisees used impatient
words against the ignorant poor, when these preferred Jesus to them; but they did, at least what
they could to teach them, as far as they knew themselves. Well! we have almost a model Christian of
the nineteenth century; very exact in his religious
duties, doing for the poor in his temporal wants what
God's law commanded, providing for religious in-

struction, leading a regular moral life, strict in his dealings, not exacting, giving nearly one fourth of his income to God. Why! name such an one on the Exchange[b], or any other great resort of those abounding in wealth, I fear that a good many would think him mad. I remember when the chief plea · why a singular person should be formally pronounced mad, incapable of managing his property, was that he gave a good deal to God; and those of us, who held him to be right[c], were thought almost beside ourselves, in a very dangerous proximity to madness. I fear that if any one, in one of our public marts of commerce, were to say, "As you would keep God's law, you must give one tenth of your income, of your gains to God," if people could not get rid of the saying by counting him a mad-man, they would think him a most inconvenient preacher. Well then, I said rightly that, humanly speaking, we might wish for a good many more such Pharisees among us, to mend the condition of our poor; and, for the sake of the tone of our upper-class morality, it would indeed be a godsend, if there were none worse. He was well-satisfied with himself; he did very many things which were good; he kept himself from much which was bad; he could not have done the good or avoided the evil without God's grace. He had the light of the Mosaic law, and al-

[b] Some observatious, made since this sermon was delivered, occasion me to add that I did not imagine that I could be supposed to be reflecting on any class of persons. I used the term only, as a sort of proverb for wealth.

[c] As witnesses, cited to prove his sanity at a previous period. It was some thirty years ago. He had neither wife, nor child, nor any one dependent upon him.

though he had lost all the teaching of its manifold
continual sacrifices, he acted up to the light at least
of those precepts, which he selected out of it. Many
Pharisees were hypocrites, our Lord tells us. He
does not say so of *him*. We have only to take his
character, as our Lord gives it. What then was
wanting to him? Was that loveless contempt of the
Publican the whole defect? Again, our Lord does
not say that he was wrong, as to what the Publican
had been. He did not know that he was a penitent.
It was of the grace of God, that he had not been,
what the Publican had been (for it is of God's grace
that we are kept from any sin), and in his dry unloving way he thanked God for it. He was right
about him, as he was about the poor sinner, whom
he would not have Jesus to allow to touch Him.
He knew "[d] who and what manner of woman " she
was : our Lord said that "her sins were many."

It was not the one or the other grace, which he
wanted to have deepened. It was not, as people
think of themselves, that he needed to be somewhat
humbler, that this or that censorious speech had
better have been unsaid, or was wrong. It was not
merely that vein of boastfulness, that he paraded,
somewhat ungracefully, any good which by nature or
grace there was in him. All these had their spring
in one central underlying evil, which poisoned all.
He had missed and neglected that which was at the
centre of God's revelation by Moses, the knowledge
of sin. He had attended at their public worship,
and thought well of himself for doing it; he had
seen the continual offerings for sin ; perhaps he

[d] S. Luke vii. 39.

knew in a way that we are all sinners; if he were
among us, no doubt he would say at least weekly,
"we have erred and strayed from Thy ways, like lost
sheep;" for he too said in David's words, " ᵉ I have
gone astray like a sheep which was lost;" and he
would not have meant altogether to have made such
a confession in the name of others; though what
he would have meant, it is difficult to say. Perhaps he would have repeated them, as some do the
words, " the remembrance of them is grievous unto
us, the burden of them is intolerable," and think
them a strong way of speaking. Perhaps he thought
of what he himself would have been or might have
been, if God had not saved him; for which, as we
know, he thanked God. " God, I thank Thee, that
I am not as other men are." He would have been
a respectable Heathen; as a Socinian or a Deist,
he would have been pointed out as a pattern of
morality, to show that we have no need of Jesus
or a Redeemer; he would have been a triumph for
human nature, ignorant as it is, that all good in
it, in Judaism or Heathenism too, as well as in
the Gospel, is of the grace of God. But he was
not a religious Jew: he had the form of godliness
without its power. He was deficient, not as to the
branches, but as to the root and sap of his religiousness. He had missed, through pride, the
whole teaching of the religion of Moses, by which
it fixed men's eyes and their faith upon the Redeemer Who was to come; and, having missed it
through his own fault, he returned home from his
exemplary Sabbath-worship, unjustified; the sins, to

ᵉ Ps. cxix. 176.

which he had, through sin, blinded himself, so as
not to ask for forgiveness, were unforgiven. Worse
still! He returned home, more out of favour with
God than he came. He came to worship : he gained, not the favour of God, but His displeasure.
Yet he had merits of his own. Not without the
grace of God, nor without some violence upon
corrupt nature, had he kept himself from gross injury to his neighbour, as to his wife or property.
(Would God, one may say again, from what one
hears of the world, we had more such Pharisees,
or, at least none worse than this Pharisee!) Not
without God's grace is any one kept from any sin,
or does any, the least good. Not without God's
grace was he exact in what he did of duty, or in
keeping from what he kept from of sin. But Satan, through this boastful self-idolising, destroyed
this idol, which at much cost and pains he had
made : he lost the grace and the fruits of grace, of
which he boasted. He had some good deeds : the
publican came, loaded with his sins ; he very probably had all the sins, from which the Pharisee
thanked God, that he had kept himself. Yet the
Pharisee, who was rich, went empty away, severed
from the grace of God, unjustified. He came, ex-
alting himself to heaven ; he returned, thrust down
to hell. The Publican, bowed down by his manifold sins to the verge of hell, returned a citizen of
heaven.

What then was it, which turned this, in itself, real
gain to loss, and the real loss to gain ; which made
the Pharisee, with his real good deeds, a dwelling-
place of Satan, and the Publican, with his real evil

deeds, a fellow-citizen of angels, their peer, their joy?

It much concerns us to know. For our Lord points out this Pharisee-righteousness as a righteousness, with which we might be tempted to take up, with which we might deem ourselves secure of heaven, and, in this our security, might miss it. " [f] I say unto you, That except your righteousness shall exceed the righteousness of the Scribes and Pharisees, ye shall in no case enter into the kingdom of Heaven."

Now, in this, we need not doubt that our Lord is speaking, not of the " whited sepulchres, " the hypocrites among the Pharisees, not of their worst, but of their best, while they remained such. For our Lord had been speaking of a real but partial obedience to the law; He goes on to speak of limitations, whereby men made God's commandments easier to flesh and blood. It is then a real righteousness in its degree, of which He is speaking; a real, strict righteousness, such as St. Paul had, who " [g] after the straitest sect of his religion, lived a Pharisee;" a righteousness, in which men placed a hedge around the law, doing something more than the letter of the law commanded, and avoiding something more than the letter of the law forbad; a righteousness, such as Paul had, when he lived, "touching the righteousness which is in the law, blameless [h]," which he once esteemed as "gain," but which, when he came to know Jesus, he accounted loss [i].

They were obviously two primal Christian graces,

[f] St. Matt. v. 20.   [g] Acts xxvi. 5.
[h] Phil. iii. 6.   [i] Ib. 7.

which the Pharisee lacked, humility and love : his
lack of humility engendered his unlovingness. For
"true righteousness compassionates its fellow-sinner ;
false righteousness disdains him." But what is the
special source of the Pharisee's pride ? For, however little we may know of ourselves, we know that
pride is the centre of every spiritual sin ; that not
only envy, jealousy, censoriousness, evil-speaking,
soreness at contempt from others, ambition, heresy,
unbelief, misbelief, unsubmissiveness, but even sins,
which seem most without our wills, in which we
seem most passive, anger and impatience, spring
from pride.

The form of his pride was, what is mostly spoken
of with so little blame; it is mostly so little offensive; it sits so easily; it is so good-natured, at
least to its equals; it makes no special claims, except to remain undisturbed; it will allow to every
one else (so that it be not impinged upon) what it
claims for itself; it is so smooth, amiable and comfortable with itself, and too indolent and self-occupied
to discompose others, unless trod upon.

The Pharisee's central failure was, what is the
central failure of this day too, what this solemn season was intended, among others sins, to remedy,
self-complacency. Only the self-complacency of the
Pharisee had a touch of religion in it; he thanked
God for what he had not of evil, or had of good.
The good which he had not, and the evil which he
had, were out of his sight. True, his thanks to God
were praise of himself; he was on very good terms
with God : he gave to God what he thought God
wanted of him. God had made him what he was,

M

and he thanked God for it.   What lacked he yet?
Why should he suspect that he lacked any thing?
Would God (one must think, again and again), that
our Christian self-complacency were half as religious!   Yet what wanted he?   What want we, if
we are like him?   Alas, well nigh every thing.
For he returned, that which the Publican came, a
sinner unjustified.   He acquitted himself; he was
condemned by his Saviour and his Judge.   He had
no knowledge either of himself or his God; he had
no love for his neighbour or his God.   Self was his
centre and his god.   It was as if God existed for
him, to do him good, to make him such that he
could make himself what he was; not that he
existed for God, to become like unto God.

This was and is the practical fruit of self-complacency.   He and we too often dwell on any good we
think we have ; worse still! good, often, of nature
rather than of grace; for grace is the most humbling
thing in the world.   Such acts are easily repeated;
they cost *us* individually little, whatever they might
cost others whose temptations are different ; and may
give evidence of their valuelessness by their uncost;
we tacitly lay good store by them; we mirror ourselves in them.   And then, alas! for all besides, the
picture, which we thus form of ourselves, fills our
canvass.   The mirror of our mind reflects to us what
we present to it; and all which we purposely leave
behind, that great hideous humpback of unknown,
unthought-of, unenquired-for sin, grows, day by day,
the more deformed, makes us the more deformed in
the sight of God and His holy Angels, because, in
our ignorance of it, we are continually aggravating

it. Some good we must well-nigh all do. For nature, though "far gone from original righteousness," is not yet wholly corrupt. Some good we must do because nature itself requires it; our peace of mind, requires it; we must have at least something, wherewith to cozen ourselves; some fig-leaves, to hide us from ourselves; something we can look at and not loathe ourselves; something which may take our eyes off from ourselves. The remnants of Paradise, or some unwasted residue of Baptismal grace, serve our turn. Natural kindliness, (it may be the basis of much grace) will supply a large fund; natural activity is almost inexhaustible; it occupies so much room with its seeming service; it stands so well with our fellow-men; it has always something new, wherewith to occupy us and take our eyes off from that distressing sight, our real selves. Then, what a mist will ascend out of the round of daily duties, duties which, if done exactly to God out of the grace of God for the love of God, might gain large grace and bring us nearer God! What a statue-like resemblance they bear to real good; only lifeless, because not enlivened by the life-giving Spirit of God. Sunday-service will serve to make up the measure of the six days' self-deceit. It is the natural atmosphere of Pharisaism. We have to look well to our week-day services too. All, which might breathe on us gales from heaven, may come charged with the perfumes of our self-conceit. Alas for poor human nature, that it can satisfy itself with mere barren negations! Yet this was a characteristic of the Pharisee, "God, I thank Thee, that I am not as other men are." Not to do things dishonourable; not to do things mean; to shrink from a falsehood as

M 2

impairing self-respect, what a dignity they give us in
our eyes! Then to employ the poor in ministering to
our luxuries, or give a coin now and then to Lazarus,
or the annual guinea to a few religious or charitable objects,—every one praises our liberality. Who
can deny then that what we have, as our's, the Queen
of virtues, the daughter of the great King, to present
us, as welcome denizens of the heavenly court? Or
if we see the need of more positive love, there are the
domestic charities. We are eminently, people say, a
domestic nation. We, at our best, idolize one another; we magnify our petty offices to one another;
we mirror ourselves in each other; we gratify our
own or each other's selfishness, and call it love.
What a petty round of costless nothings is, even in
some so-called religious tales, the ideal of Christian
excellence! It would seem as if self-sacrifice, if it
impinged on the smooth surface of domestic life, were
the only enemy we had to dread. A nation of Poly-
theists! If any of us escape from falling down before
our national idol Mammon, then we have as many
idols, as we have individual good qualities; we each
have our household gods, in which we worship ourselves. We boast ourselves of our national charities
or charitableness, monuments mostly of departed charity, scarce held in being by our unsacrificing gifts.
Our charity forsooth! Were an Angel, evil or good,
to go round these miles of human habitations, the
centre of our legislation, the would-be focus of our
intelligence, the heart of our material prosperity, the
treasure-house of our wealth, thence to report to the
Judgement-seat of God, what we have done, what
left undone, could we, without heart-sickening dread,

imagine their report? Could we boast *then* ? And
yet it is not an Angel's report, but our Judge Himself, Who sees, one by one, the oppressing of each
hireling in his wages, to cheapen our luxuries ; the
scanty wages, which our selfish extravagance alone
admits of, eked out by the sins of the mothers, to
sustain the children who cry to them for bread and
they have it not. He, their God and their Father
and our Judge, He Who has promised to hear their
cry, He, Whose Heart of love listens to every throb-
bing of every human heart, what if He asks us,
"What do ye more for these My members, what do ye
more for Me in them, than if I had never died for
you ? " If we counted, not the little which we give,
but the much which we retain for our luxuries or
comforts, while His members are a hungered and by
us unfed, naked and by us unclothed, sick and by us
unvisited, wherein could we say that " our righteousness exceeded the righteousness of the Scribes
and Pharisees ? " And if not, wherein is our hope
of Heaven ?

Or turn we to another of our boasted virtues ;
"Any how, we are a domestic people. " You reproached us just now, you may say to me, that we
made an idol of our domesticity. Any how, we are
a moral people.

Of you, who are here this day, it would be horrible
to doubt it. But are we then to be saved alone?
But how is it, that we hear the echoes of those
things, which those in your society must, I suppose,
have witnessed ? What are fathers, brothers, mothers doing, what are all they in higher society
doing, that we can hear of an undress, as if we were

still in Paradise ; of the bareness of dress of savage life, unredeemed by savage simplicity ; of persons, as it were, exposed to view as though the drawing-rooms of our nobility were slave-markets ; in which the young, in the full freshness of opening life, are set for sale to the highest bidder, a coronet or a millionaire (no matter of what character), and so it is thought fair and right, that the purchaser should see what he buys, and make his choice amid the competing wares ? [Are the eyes of our men to be more modest than the persons of our women [k] ?]

There is worse behind. But I forbear, although a Christian's spirit must burn within him, to see this great city wholly given to the idolatry of self, and that none dare speak openly of what is openly done. St. Paul says, "it is a shame to speak of those things which are done of them in secret." Alas ! among us he must have said, "it is a shame to speak of those things which are done of them openly." Shame binds *our* speech, but neither the speech nor the acts of those, who used to furnish our ideal of maidenliness and purity. Yet of this I may speak, as notorious, that, through this prevailing barbaric love of finery and pomp, our young men betake themselves to relations, unhallowed by marriage, against the law of God, because they cannot support the sinful extravagance, to be hallowed forsooth by marriage. St. Paul says, "The married woman careth for the things of the world, how she may please her husband." The world, not the husband, must be the end of these extravagances, of

[k] Not preached. But men have complained of this unbecomingness.

which some dare not even tell their husbands. But
where then is the married love of such? What is
this gorgeous, selfish, pitiless array, but an earnest
and image of the robes of eternal flame?

Such are not you. God forbid! But well I remember the time, when no rank, no brilliancy, no
station was allowed to compensate for moral purity.
A sinful woman saw her own sinfulness reflected to
her conscience by the aspect of the society which
God's Providence formed her to adorn. The mothers of those days prized the, at least, unblameable-
ness of those, to whose houses they introduced their
daughters, more than their station. If mothers in
these days seek the fashionable houses of those,
from whom, if they were poor instead of wealthy,
they would shrink, what do they but connive at
and abet the damnation of those, once Christians in
deed as well as name? What do they but cheer
them on in their way to Hell, and repeat to God
Cain's impious taunt, "Am I my brother's keeper?"

But any how, you will say, our Church-going is
right. We cannot be Pharisees to-day. We are
all as Publicans together, to beat on our breasts, and
cry, "God be merciful to me, a sinner!" God grant
it may last! But of all the Pharisaisms of the day,
our Church-going seems to me the masterpiece.
How so? What does or ought our coming here to
profess? What, but that prayer is the life of our
lives, that we live by every word that proceedeth
out of the mouth of God; that the Sacrament of
our Lord's Body and Blood unites us to Him, that
we long to increase this Life-giving union with
Him? We come, we return; we have gained, we

trust, for our souls a treasure unutterable, that " Christ should dwell in us, and we in Him, that we should be one with Christ and Christ with us."

Do we believe what we say? How then is our belief not our condemnation? Is union with God a selfish thing? Is it something to be appropriated to ourselves? Is the Coal of fire, which not Seraphim, but the Lord and God of the Seraphim, has approached to our lips, not to burn in our hearts? Is it nothing to us, that our brethren starve spiritually, while we keep to ourselves the Bread of life, and here or there only, in this wide-waste wilderness of human souls, one is found to cry out, " Let him that is athirst come and take of the water of life freely?" Whither are these three millions of human beings going[1]? To the Judgement-seat of Christ. But what afterwards? I own, I hope more for the degraded poor than for the self-satisfied rich. At least, they are not Pharisees. God grant that, even

[1] It was calculated after a careful enquiry, by the statistical Committee of the [Bp. of London's] fund, that, " out of three million souls in the metropolis, one million were destitute of all known means of Christian instruction and worship."

In the last four years nearly ⅛ has been added (partly by the Ecclesiastical Commissioners) to the Clergy of London, 147, out of 1127. It is too low an estimate to say that there ought to be nearly three times as many, 3000. The late Bishop of London planned the erection of 50 Churches, besides those in Bethnal Green. They did not provide for the increase of population in London during the period in which they were erected. The present Bishop of London has wisely begun with " Mission Clergy." But " Missions" amid populations of from 4000 to 12000, and those in some places condensed heathen populations, what are they? God give the increase! " Many have answered nobly to our appeals, but the multitude of those who have been deaf to them is far greater." Bp. of London's Charge, p. 70.

in their last hour, they may be as the Publican! But what do we to this end? A certain number of missions here and there (and these sometimes persecuted), a few Scripture-readers or Bible-women, are these our worthy efforts to recover from Satan's jaws the sheep of Christ, and show how we prize the Precious Blood, by Which we boast that we know, more than others, that we have been redeemed? What but this atmosphere of Pharisaism, with which we are encompassed, this yellow fog, mingled of all the faults of Pharisaism, Sadduceeism, Herodianism, which chokes our breathing and obstructs our sight, could make us take up with such a zealless, loveless, lifeless worship of God, Who is Love, as this?

What then is the remedy? The root of the evil is, ignorance of God and of ourselves, ignorance of our relation to God, of His love towards us individually, and of His claims upon us as His creatures, redeemed by the Blood of God. We cannot know ourselves, unless we know God. How should we know what is crooked, if we never measure it by an unbending rule? How should we understand our darkness, if our eyes are never lifted up to, never enlivened by the brightness of Divine light? How should we know our unholiness, if we never contemplate His sinless purity? How could we imagine the foulness of our ingratitude, unless we gaze on His ineffable Goodness which daily overstreams us with its benefits?

Be this, then, our task, this Lent; to unlearn whatever Pharisaism cleaves to us, by contemplation of our God, by knowledge of our relations to Him and of our duty to Him, and by large-hearted love to our fellow-sinners. We may be sure that we all have more or less of the Pharisee clinging to us; for it presses in upon us through all the habits and ways of our times, and if we are not conscious of some Pharisaism, it is the Pharisaism itself which blinds us. Every feeling of self-satisfaction, all dwelling upon ourselves, our doings or our words, is Pharisaism. All self-pleasing, all smoothness, all acceptance of others' praise, except as a token of their love, is Pharisaism. Then only are we unlearning to be Pharisees, when men's praise stings us with its own valuelessness, and men's good opinion makes us dread to be hypocrites, except that we cannot help it; and every thing around us or within us, the good or evil of others, our own seeming good or real evil, our good, because at best it might have been so much less poor and we might have been less ungrateful for it, our evil, because it is so intolerable, should issue in that one cry, "God be merciful to me, a sinner! To the sinner above the Publican, be Thou merciful as to the Publican." I say then are we *beginning* to unlearn it? For, say it though we may from our hearts, we have but a hazy, shadowy gleam of light, with what profound abasement of truth we ought to say it; what a hideous thing we mean, when we call ourselves "sinners." S. Paul had no title for himself, but "chief of sinners." What depth of meaning can we give the word, that it should fit such as we are?

Yet look up to your God; think what it is, that He, the Infinite, the All-Holy, the All-Perfect, should, in the tranquil self-sufficingness of His illimitable bliss, have in all eternity loved thee, and purposed,

in time, to make thee the object of His Eternal
love; that He, needing not aught out of Himself,
vouchsafed to need thee; that He in time created,
redeemed, sanctified thee, to be a little likeness of
His perfections, an image, according to some especial grace, of some special beauty in Himself. To
this end were the drawings of His grace, the loving
severity, if so be, of His chastisements, His abundant Sacraments, His manifold calls and voices and
speakings to thy soul within and without; and all
this, with that individual care and love, as if He
existed but for thee, remembering thee when thou
forgattest Him, watching for thy return; tender, not
to weary thee by His importunities, yet sparing
no solicitations which might win thee, submitting
Himself to all thy rebuffs and rudenesses and dismissals, yet knocking anon at the door of thy heart,
"My child! wilt thou open to Me now? fear Me
not;" all but constraining thee by the might and
attractiveness of His love, yet leaving thee free,
freely to accept Him, as thou wouldest one on this
earth, who offered thee his love! Thou wouldest
love such an one on earth. Where then has been
our loyal affection, where our devotion, where our
self-forgetful gratitude, where our fealty, where our
burning passion, to requite freely that self-emptying
love, which, being contented with that Co-equal
Love which He Is, Father, Son, and Holy Ghost,
would, in God the Son, become such as thou thyself,
lest He should lose thee? Oh, if one had never
done one other sin, if one were full of all other
saint-like virtues, if self had not tinged and tainted
with its horrid defiling leprous touch any good in

us, if there was nothing but this horrible ingrati‐ tude, could we abide ourselves, if He were only one of us? Since He is God, what can we utter with our deepest agonised heart-cry but, "God be merciful to me a sinner?"

Yet, thanks be to His love, He has left us those, in whom to undo our ingratitude, in whom to feed, tend, clothe, shield from cold, from sickness, from pining suffering, from untimely death, Himself, our Lord, our God, our Judge—His poor.

And who could plead so persuasively to you, as those who ask you this day through me [m]? Here is nothing repulsive, no revolting sin-contracted habits, no loathsomeness of misery; no dread, that our gifts (jealous as we are of our own, while so careless as to our God's good gifts) should be wasted. They, who so ask you, are your fellow-Christians, who, in this life, have more of Christ's earthly lot than we; for they are destitute of all things, while we have abun‐ dance of all things. But they ask only for life at your hands. They are husbands who implore you, that their wives and children may not be deprived untimely of their care; they are fathers, mothers, who ask that their children may not be left father‐ less, motherless; that their homes may not be reft of their stay; that their poor hearths may not be dark‐ ened of the sunbeam of a parent's love, or, amid the aweful temptations of this sin-scourged city, may not be deprived of a mother's watchful care. Fa‐ thers say to you who are fathers, mothers, to you mo‐ thers: "You *can* help us. As you would that God

[m] Preached for the Ascot Hospital for convalescent and incur‐ ables.

should hear you in your trouble, hear me; have mercy on my child."

For it is just when the soul is hanging between life and death, when, in God's providence, those whom He has stricken, but has in a degree raised up, will live, if they have food, good air, and tender care, and, if not, will die, that you can help those who minister to preserve their life. For the Foundress of this hospital, in her labours for the desolate poor in the North-East of London, discovered how many died, not through some severe disease, which God allowed to rage among them, but when He had abated it, and nothing was needed but man's charitable care, they perished, because they had it not. And so she conceived the plan of a convalescent Hospital, of which England then had but one; and *that*, not for the very poor. She has laboured, and others have entered into her labours. Silently, unaided except by one individual, without public appeal, she and her Sisters have carried on their devoted work. The conception, the gradual development, and maturing of the plan, the laborious attention to details, upon which the solidity of any plan depends, were wholly her's. May Jesus reward her! One who has seen her well-conceived self-sacrificing labours during the Cholera, said of it; "From what I saw then, I expected something solidly good; but *this* surpasses my expectation." And this was a scientific opinion. Now that the plan has stood the test of time, now that above £10,000 has, with careful economy, been spent upon the work itself[n], others are asked to expand a work, which can be

---

[n] i. e., apart from the annual expenditure.

expanded more effectively and with less cost than a
new one could be begun. In the last Cholera year, the
cure of 145 patients from the North-East of London
alone, was completed in that hospital. They can
now receive between 30 and 40 at a time; they ask
to be enabled to minister, according to the original
plan of the Foundress, to 100 at once. I speak of
what I know. I have witnessed the glad enjoyment
of returning health among those who had recently
been prostrated by disease. I have heard the gratitude poured out, after their return, in their poor
habitations of this city. I have known the impres-
sion made by the grace of God, through the unob-
truded devotions; how God has, through them, converted the soul, while He restored the life of the
body.

We have most of us been touched to the quick by
the severe illness of one whom we love. We have
looked on the wasted form of some loved child, when
the fierceness of a disease was over, and the Physician has said, "with watchful care, good food and
(when it can bear it) good air, the child will live."
How did our heart bound with thankful joy, that
God had given us what we needed for them! Or,
we may have had some sharp illness ourselves, and
God may, through all those helps with which He
so abundantly supplies us, have given us new life
and energy, new years, new powers to serve Him.
As God has done to you, as you hope in the the next
trial-time God will do to you, so do. Think, when
one comes to gather your alms, that it is not he
whom you see, but that being, whom you love most
tenderly, and whom, through tender care and nurs-

ing, God restored to you. Think that he whom you love, asks you, "O shew mercy for my sake ; for God gave me back to your love ;" think what it would be, to dread, the next time God shall so visit you ; "I was not merciful then ; perhaps God will not this time show me the mercy which I showed not." Think, above all, of Him your Judge, Whom in these you feed, Whom in these you tend, to Whom in these you exercise His delegated prerogative of giving life, and Who in His heavenly Courts will proclaim, "See what they have done to Me ; see how they have cared for Me !" Be merciful after your power ; and in that Dread Day, on which hangs eternity, may you hear those words, "Come, ye blessed of My Father, inherit the kingdom prepared for you from the foundation of the world. For I was an hungred and ye gave Me meat; I was thirsty and ye gave Me drink, I was sick, and ye had compassion upon Me."

SERMON IX[a].

PERSONAL RESPONSIBILITY OF MAN, AS TO HIS USE OF TIME.

S. John ix. 4.

" I must work the works of Him Who sent Me, while it is day. The night cometh when no man can work."

Whose world are we living in, our own or God's? Who is master of our being, ourselves or God? To whom are we to give account of our being, to ourselves or to God? Questions, all very simple to the understanding, but which we answer practically, in exactly the opposite way to that which we in theory and in words acknowledge. We confess, daily, most of us, to Jesus, "We believe that Thou shalt come to be our Judge." We follow that confession by the imploring cry, "We therefore pray Thee, help Thy servants, whom Thou hast redeemed with Thy precious Blood!" We sum up our prayers for pardon for sins, for mercy, by all He has done, merited, suffered for us, with "In the Day of Judgement, Good Lord, deliver us." We cannot say a Creed without confessing our belief, that He, now

---

[a] Preached at S. Mary's, Oxford, Lent, 1868, as one of a series, "On the responsibilities of man."

our Redeemer, shall hereafter be our Judge. The belief remains on our lips; we hold it in our understanding; does it enter into the texture of our every-day life? Supposing that, by God's grace, we have been kept to-day from anything very notably wrong, does it occur to us that "to-day" will have anything to do with our eternity? Well, it may be startling, that this one day (if there have been nothing in it markedly against the will and grace of God) should have to do with our eternal doom. Look back, then, to yesterday, or to many yesterdays, or to weeks past, always supposing that there have been no marked deadly sin in any of them, nothing which should, unrepented of, separate you from God, and destroy your spiritual life; nothing, in which you shall have taken a marked part against God's law, and have chosen the wages of the Evil one, present pleasure and eternal death. Granted your time of life, the buoyancy natural to it, the recreations, amusements, merriments, lightheartedness, which, in measure, no one would, at your age, wish to interfere with, so they be innocent, is there still nothing, which should, you think, influence your eternal being? But does it then come to this, that, but for those marked sins, of which God says that "[b]they who do those things shall not inherit the kingdom of God," we need have no care, no anxiety, no thought about eternity?

To take the seeming ways of the mass of mankind, one could have no doubt that they think so. Here and there, *one* seems to be aware that lesser acts lead to greater of the same kind; that repeated acts form habits; that custom gains an iron power over

[b] Gal. v. 21.

N

the will, until a man, by misuse of his free-will, almost destroys the freedom of his will, to be recovered only by some strong effort and some mightier accepted grace of God. But, for the most part, if one were to ask any one, why he did any given thing, except just the actual necessary duties of his state of life, without which a person could not live or attain the temporal end which he wished for, the honest answer would, I fear, be, "because I like it." In other words, a man's own will is, with certain great exceptions, the rule and measure of his acts; and, to judge from men's ways of speaking, Almighty God and he have each very good reason to be satisfied with the distribution. Almighty God gets His fair share; perhaps, more than He used to have, or more, may be he thinks, than others give Him. Almighty God has his prayers, morning and evening; some prayers (I fear for the most part not very many) in the Chapel-service; then on the Sunday, God has anyhow twice in the day his bodily presence (wherever or however occupied his mind may be, for, I fear, a notable part of the time), a poor man has a shilling every now and then; in the week-day, he gives a certain number of hours (very few, I fear, unless ambition has its share in the arrangement) to the cultivation of his mind. For the rest, who disputes his right to it? It seems as if the impious flattery of the Roman poet, when the weather cleared in the morning for the Imperial spectacle,—

"With Jove divided empire Cæsar sways,"

were the religion of Christians, and that over ourselves at least we hold a partnership of jurisdiction with Almighty God. Of course, to make this not Atheistic, it must be put in the form, that Almighty God has waived His absolute right over us; that for this His unlimited dominion over us He has substituted a sort of feudal sovereignty, in which we, holding this His earth or our portion of it and our time in it, as a sort of feof from Him, are bound to render Him certain limited services, to withhold ourselves from doing Him certain very limited despites, and that, these being either discharged or deferred (well is it, if the payment of God's dues is not deferred to some unknown period beyond our power, at the supposed end of life), then over all the rest we are to be seized as lords, and it is resented as a very unreasonable and unjustified, and almost monstrous, demand, if any one put in any claim, on the part of God, as to any portion of this wide heritage which we hold of Him.

Of course, we have no intention to be Atheists. We speak respectfully of God, as far as we know of Him. He is the Great First Cause of all things, Who made our first father, Adam, some 6,000 years ago. He made this earth which we inhabit, whether with any distinct thought of us, geologists leave as a question in abeyance. He upholds us all somehow in being; whether by unvarying laws which He made at some time heretofore, people do not define to themselves. He is very great, and when people are in trouble, they betake themselves to Him. People can with difficulty, or cannot altogether, escape the idea of judgement. But then by whose rule? Tacitly or avowedly, men mean their own. From the "I am no worse than my neighbours," by

which the poor man satisfies his conscience amid the
thought of death and judgement, to the "God cannot
punish what belongs to the nature which He made,"
of the self-justifying dissoluteness of the rich; they
mean, in fact, "we will not," (or to speak respectfully,) "we shall not, we will not have it, that we
shall be judged, otherwise than we will."

"Responsibility!" the word is almost clean gone
out of our common language, except that we speak
of the "responsible minister of the Crown," in the
sense that the Sovereign has to give no account of
her acts to man; and a "responsible" person or firm,
is one which can discharge his or its monied obli-
gations; and we can understand that *that* responsibility must be complete to the very last farthing.
How is it, that we can so discern our relations to
this world, and, in the midst of the light of the Gospel, cannot discern our relations to Almighty God?

And yet this would-be quasi-independence of God,
if it were true, what a miserable lowering of our
whole being it would be! For what would it amount
to? Simply to this, That as to a large range of our
being, we were beneath the notice or care or thought
of Almighty God; that what we did or did not do
was too insignificant for Him to heed; that He left
us to battle (for battle we must, if not with sin, with
misery in this stormy world), and set no more store
by us, than we do on the uptorn weed, cast on our
shores by an angry sea, unless indeed men make use
of its decay and corruption to manure their fields.
Wonderful dignity of man's would-be independence,
to attain, in his own idea, to this, that he is held of
too little account by God's Infinite Wisdom to be re-

garded by Him; too mean, for Infinite Love to love him; too puny, for God's Infinite Majesty to stoop to elevate him; too limited, for Divine Intellect to communicate Itself to him, to enlarge him; too worthless, for Divine Greatness to heed, whether It have or have not his service or his love. Miserable as it is false, and proving itself false by the misery to which it would abandon us!

The true dignity of our nature lies in that relation to Almighty God, which involves the minutest responsibility. We, all of us, think or have thought something more highly of ourselves, to find ourselves an object of interest to one who was our superior in whatever our standard of eminence was, pure intellect, or maturer knowledge, or ripened thought, or even this world's rank; it has added (whatever our standard was) dignity to our estimate of ourselves. If they bestowed individual unpaid-for pains in developing our powers, we not only felt grateful to them, but a certain responsibility in corresponding to their pains.

Faint shadow all, all human love, care, thoughtfulness, of the ever-present all-comprehending love of God, of which it too is (though one of the least) a fruit!

This is the true greatness of man, to belong to God; enfreed by God, to become freely the slave of the love of God. For the inconceivable greatness of man is, to have been made by God for Himself; to have been made by Him, Who Alone is Greatness; Alone, Goodness; Alone, Wisdom; Alone, Majesty; Alone, Infinite Love; nay, Who Alone Is; and Who, being Alone the Source of being, Alone, can bestow true glory and greatness; and the glory and the greatness which He bestows, must be in some created likeness of Himself, since there is no ideal greatness and goodness and glory out of Himself, for which He could form us.

The only adequate object of existence is to exist for God. The only adequate pattern of perfection which to copy, is Almighty God, or God made Man; Man, Who was therefore perfect, because He was also Almighty God. The one unvarying interest *in* this life, or *of* this life, is that God cares for us, that God loves us, that God, Whose Being is ever to communicate Himself, Whose mode of existence within Himself is in a continual communication of Himself the Father to the Son, and the Father and the Son, as One, to the Holy Spirit, Who is the Bond of Both,—created us, to whom to communicate Himself. Our inexpressible perfectibility is, that He wills that we should be little likenesses of Himself; and that, lest we should lose any or all of the perfection which He designed for us, He watches as well as guards us so minutely, is so jealous that nothing out of Him should divide our hearts with Him; that He supplies us with such graces, visits us with inspirations, appeals to us by calls and re-calls and re-re-calls, immerses us in Sacraments, provides a fresh Sacrament anew for us for every fresh fall, will not let us go, lest we should miss the end for which He created us,—Himself. The measure of our greatness is God's care for us, His protection of us against ourselves, His anxiety to preserve us for Himself.

This is the great end of our being, which Almighty God wills that we should win by correspondence to Divine grace, the possession of Himself. God has

willed to make us, not like the Angels to whom He
unveiled His glory at once, and left it to them to
choose or to refuse Him ; to exist, each in that separate order in which He had created them. To us,
whom (it is the common Theological opinion) He
created to fill up their ranks, broken by the fall of
those who fell, He has given an almost immeasurable
power of progress. Progress, the love of which, well
or ill-aimed, is the ruling principle of all but stag-
nant minds, is our perfectibility. We have no choice
but progression or regression. And this progression
is by us here unimaginable. We see indeed something of some of the qualities which gleam through
men's looks or words; we see a supernatural light illumining what is of earth. But what the sum of all
shall be, what relation all shall bear to the sitting on
the right hand or the left of Jesus in His kingdom,
it is reserved for the Day of Judgement to declare.
We know of an especial nearness of those who shall
sit on the twelve thrones, judging the twelve tribes
of Israel. We know of that Virgin-band, who follow
the Lamb whithersoever He goeth. It has been said
of more, I think, than one, that God had revealed,
that he was for his burning love received among the
Seraphim. But, even as it is One in our nature,
Who is for ever personally united with the Godhead, so, above all the highest creatures, whom God
either has or ever will create, in a special dignity
and nearness, one and alone, (even as the Incarnation, God made Man, is one and alone,) must *she*
exist, with whose flesh God the Son willed that His
Flesh should be consubstantial, whose flesh He, in
His own Body deified, whom on earth He willed to

obey as His own Mother. This dignity of unspeakable nearness to Himself, He, plainly, ever predestin-
ed for her, and in one instant He bestowed it on her.
But by what giant progress in graces, by what un-
deviating correspondence to Divine vouchsafements
in time, must that soul have been formed, to whom,
in her fourteenth year (it is thought) was vouchsafed
the choice, which, by Divine grace, she accepted at
the risk of shame and reproach, that of her, ever-
Virgin, should be born the Saviour of the world, her
God! Yet her Son pronounced her more blessed for
her obedience than for her Mother's care of Himself.

This progress, from the lowest scarce-saved soul
to that throne, which is most encompassed by the
effulgence of the Divine, has but one limit, time.
No bound is there to the rich accumulated succes-
sion of Divine graces; no limit to the intensity of
the Divine power of grace, except our grace-acquired,
grace-gifted, capacity to receive it; no term to the
developement of our capaciousness to contain God,
except this, that growth must be in this life, in time.
After this life, if by God's mercy we attain, is the
everlasting fruition of God, in that degree, to which
by Divine grace we have been enlarged in this life.
But growth is no more. Ever-enlarging knowledge
of the Infinite Wisdom of God there will doubtless
be; ever-unfolding will be the treasures of Divine
love. But as, here, we are men, not Angels; and as
Angels are not Archangels, nor Archangels Cherubim
or Seraphim, or Thrones, or Dominions, or Powers,
and as each Angel is thought to have his own special perfection and beauty, so we shall each, in all
eternity, remain that special soul, which here we,

by our use of the 'grace of God in time, became. At the great account, we are to receive according to the deeds done in the body, whether good or bad; then are the five or two talents to be bestowed on each, according to our faithfulness in cultivating whatever God has entrusted to us. Paul, glorious as he will be, he to whom to live was Christ, he, by whose mouth Christ spake, he, in whom Christ inworked, whom He empowered mightily, will be evermore that glorious spirit which, by God's ever-inworking Spirit, he became, (whom may we, though afar, behold, and joy in his joy in Christ!); but he will be evermore that, which through his zeal and sufferings and love of Christ he in time became, and no other. John, too, will be there, with all that love which he drank in when he lay on Jesus' bosom, which he drew, hour by hour, from the love of Jesus Who loved him, and still more perhaps from that martyrdom of threescore years and ten, during which his soul was parched with thirst to behold again his Lord and his God, Whom he loved. Yet is he the same John, who, through that long privation of the sight of Him Whom his soul loved, was formed for the eternal love of God and Jesus. There is Peter, with his soul of fire, through whom Jesus first admitted both Jews and Gentiles into His blessed fold; his soul on fire with all that love, which the look of Jesus kindled in him when fallen; love, augmented all his life long by his penitent remembrance of the occasion of that love, by his loving joy in partaking of the sufferings of Christ and his loving faithfulness in feeding His Master's sheep, anew committed to his care. Yet is he the same, which by all that fiery zeal and love, penetrated through and through by the Spirit of God, he became.

This, then, is the measure of the value of time, the possession of God, the greater or lesser possession of Him, Who is all Goodness, all Wisdom, all Beauty, all Sweetness, " the Fountain of all knowledge, the Fountain of eternal light, the Torrent of pleasure," the all-sufficing Beatitude of all creation, yea, of all possible creations. For He may be possessed in an all-but-infinite variety of degrees, infinite to us, who have no measure by which to measure them; degrees, as far removed from us as the furthest star, whose light has visited this earth, is in space; yet all infinitely below the infinity of our God. But in this all-but-infinite range of beatitudes, there is a growth almost unbounded, so that even if we have chosen God Alone for our Portion, we might still, by His grace, rise as much above what we are, as Heaven is above earth. For there are no limits to the might of the grace of God, except those which we ourselves put to it. There is no limit to the height, Alps over Alps arising, to which each formerly-attained height seemed like a dead plain, except our lingering in the plain of the devoted cities, when an Angel's hands are leading us on, yea, when the Lord of the Angels bears us up by His pierced Hands, bids us tread safely on the lion who would devour us, and beats down Satan under our feet.

Did you ever see any one perfect? The blessed Saints of God knew, that *they* were not. The graces, which God most worked in them, seemed to them the most imperfect, because in them the film was most cleared from their eyes, and, though through

a glass darkly, they saw something of the perfection of God. Everything which is in earnest, is
striving toward perfection; everyone who is in earnest, finds that it is not here, that here are but the
germs; the flower and fruit will, we trust, through
the Blood of Jesus, unfold in eternity. Yet such
as is the germ here, (well, if there be no canker!),
such will the flower be in eternity.

We all seem to ourselves to have energies, which
are never completed here. We all seem to have a
work to do, of which, at best, some fragments only
are wrought out here. Year by year, all life long,
we have to lay aside aspirations which we once had;
works, for the glory of God, we have to leave undone
for ever, the pyramid, which we would build for God,
narrows as life goes on; well is it for him whose
building has least wood, hay, stubble in it, or is
broken off the least unsatisfactorily!

But these things, though evidences of the value
of time, do, except as far as they are ensouled by
the love of God, and the pure purpose of serving
God in them, belong to time only. The eternal loss
or gain of that power of loving God, which God, in
His eternal love, desired that we should attain, is
for eternity.

Sloth, then, as a deadly sin, is a far more comprehensive, terrible, almost irreparable evil, than most
of us have been apt to think of. Sloth, as mere
idleness or want of exertion, is, in your seed-time
of life, a greater disqualification to serve God hereafter, than you can now be aware of. No one is
aware of the value of anything which he is wasting,
while he is wasting it. The almost irreparable loss

opens our eyes. Powers of mind, which are not developed in the due period of their development, are probably stunted for life. Habits of accurate thought, which are not formed then, are probably lost for life. Each period of life has its own appointed work; and it is rarely allowed to any one, to make present time do the work of the present and the past at once.

Idleness is also, as you know, proverbially called "the mother of all vices." It is Satan's own enclosure, his own special country, where he hunts and ensnares souls. Not relaxation, but relaxedness is a peril of souls. Relaxation, which is to fit for dutiful exertion afterwards, may be used to the glory of God, in thankfulness for the exuberant buoyant strength, which it vents, as well as the repairs of the daily decays of nature, which the Apostle instanced as a thing to be done to His glory, or as we may lay us down to rest in Jesus. It is well known how a Saint[c], when asked what he should do, if he knew that our Lord would come that night to judge, said that he should finish what he had then begun; for he had begun it for the glory of God, and for Him he should finish it. Yet what he so meant to finish was an ordinary game, certainly more used in his country than in ours by such as would lead lives devoted to God. It is not, then, what seems to some of us, even an undue measure of relaxation, which we should dread for you. We may dread that the habits of boyhood may be prolonged unduly into manhood. But this is scarce an evil. Be what you will, so that you retain the

[c] S. Charles Borromeo.

innocence and piety which belong to boyhood. Genuine gladness of heart is well-pleasing to our Good Father, Who giveth us all things richly to enjoy, Who has decked His creation with gladness, the ray of Whose light transmutes the dullest things of earth into a radiance of almost heaven-born joy.

Think not, it is joyousness of soul which loyal duty to your God could interfere with. How should it, since "love, joy, peace," are first-fruits of His out-poured, indwelling Spirit? It would transmute, engolden joy, not damp or quench it. How should rebellion against God spice joy? What joy is there in unseemly jest, or coarse ribaldry, or half-uttered, half-hinted filthiness, or insolence to the Name of God or to His Word?

But the deepest fear for you, the deepest fear for us all, the all-comprehensive fear, is, not as to the waste of portions of time, but one universal waste of all. Much of life must pass in nothings. Waste seems to be a great law of this our world below. God scatters a profusion of His choicest gifts, and nothing seems to come of it. Sleep and its attendant offices mostly take one-third of our lives. Then there is in other ways the daily re-cruiting of nature's daily decays. Then the inter-course with others; what fruit brings it? We have employments, which we cannot call directly wrong; but what comes of them? The strongest brain cannot be ever at work (the worse for us, if it could), and we must perforce relax. What good is there in it all, even if we escape sin? If we are intellec-tual, our brains become little encyclopædias of a variegated knowledge. We forget far more than we remember; and what we do remember, what use can we make of the greatest portion of it? Solomon, whose wisdom the Queen of Sheba came from the ends of the earth to hear, sums up his own experience: "ᵉOf making many books there is no end, and greedy study is weariness of the flesh." What a life of fiery zeal it was, which Elijah summed up: "ᶠIt is enough; now, O Lord, take away my life; for I am not better than my fathers!" Truly, if no more came of it all than we see, life were one waste. To see evils, and to be powerless to remedy them; to see men steering a goodly vessel, with precious merchandise, straight upon the rocks, and counting it good service; to call, and there is none to answer; to labour, and the winds are contrary; what would this life be, if one counted the body of this life only, but labouring for the wind?

But where, then, is the soul of this life? This it is, which made me speak of the risk of one universal waste of time. For since, to us individually, time is that portion of days (few or more) which we live here on earth; and since the only adequate end of this life is to gain Him Who made us for His boundless bliss and love; and since He wills to communicate Himself to us in eternity in an almost infinite variety of degrees, according to our capacity to receive Him; and since our capacity to receive Him will vary endlessly, according to our use of His grace here, the power of love which we have acquired, the conformity to His bleseed Image, the God-inworked likeness to God; then all of time, all of life is lost, in which a man does not lead the supernatural life of grace, does not grow in the capacity of loving God.

ᵉ Eccles. xii. 12.   ᶠ 1 Kgs. xix. 4.

This is the soul of every outward act, of every word, of every thought. It matters little, what the body may be. It matters nothing, whether it be the most menial act performed on this earth, or the highest intellectual achievement, whereby a God-gifted intellect unlocked some secret of God's creation. This is the body still, to be transfigured by the grace of God. The sun which illumines and gladdens this our orb has no more, if so much, relation to God, as the poor worm, which is trampled upon and dies. Even the meanest thing done to God, is of countless price; any, the most magnificent work, done for any end out of God, is absolutely worthless.

This, then, is the one secret of life, this its one undying interest; this alone gives unity to life, this alone makes life not objectless; this is abid-ing reality amid a world of shadows; this endures, while all around perishes,—to live to God. It may be, so thou art not living in sin, thou wouldest not have to change one outward act, certainly not one outward employment. The body would remain the same, at least in its great outlines. The studies, if they are right now, would be right still; the re-creations, if they be innocent now, would continue still. Not the outward things would be changed, but thou. For such as a man's love is, such is he. And him thou lovest, for whom thou doest what-soever thou doest. If thou doest them for ambi-tion, for pride, for vainglory, for vanity, for human opinion or praise, these are thy gods; they are thy reward. "Verily, I say unto you, they have their reward;" they have it, our Lord says, wholly to themselves [d]; they have it, not again to have it;

---

[d] ἀπέχουσι.

they have it to themselves in time, not again to
have it in eternity.

Dost thou them for God? God, ere thou hast
done them, has laid up thy purpose among His
treasures. When by His grace, thou hast done
them to Him, thy act is stored up for thee, to be
rewarded in the Great Day.

Is God too little for thee? Is He too low an
object for thy ambition? Is His Wisdom too narrow for thee to covet? Is His love not fiery enough
to kindle thy soul? God has made thee individually, to be the object of His love. He created
thee, when He might have created millions of beings less unworthy of His love. He created thee,
with the whole good-will of His Infinite love resting on thee alone. He redeemed thee, as if there
were no other to die for. He imparts Himself to
thee as individually, as if He were not the sustenance of Angels, the Life of all which lives. What
craves that Almighty Heart of love, but that thou
shouldest return Him love for love, that thou shouldest, in all eternity, have larger outpourings of His
love? This, then, is the measure of the value of
time, eternity of infinite love, proportioned to the
love thou bestowest here upon thy God. Empassioned love here does everything as would please
the object of its love. Thou wakest, morning by
morning, with the love of God overstreaming thee.
Give thyself for the day, thy thoughts, thy words,
thy acts to His love; to speak words or to leave
them unspoken, to do acts or to leave them undone,
as thou thinkest in thy truest heart, that thy God,
Who loves thee, in His love for thee, wills for
thee. Thou lovest thyself only with a finite love;

God loves thee with an infinite love. We love ourselves with a blind love; God loves thee with an infallible love. Oh! it will give such a deep interest to life's dullest monotony, to do those monotonous things to thy best, according to the mind of God. No time will be heavy to thee, which shall upbear thy soul to God; no employment will be dull to thee, in which thou mayest approve thyself to God (nay, the duller, the more interesting, because in it there is less of self, and so, more safety that it is done to God). It will be a joy to thee to repress the half-spoken unseemly word; for thou wilt have gained the larger capacity of love of God. The men of this world would think it a token of madness, if anyone had strewed along his path the glorious lustre of precious stones, such as are pictured in the heavenly Jerusalem,—diamonds, pearls, carbuncles, rubies, amethysts,—and he, neglecting these, were to treasure up shreds of hay and straw? But now they are not precious stones of any passing lustre, to which, if so thou dost, thou preferrest the dry hay and stubble of this parched, perishing life. They are priceless pearls of purest beauty which thou mayest gather, not to form any created coronet, but whereby thou shalt thyself shine with the Divine Glory, the beatific Presence of the love of thy God. Remember Him now; remember Him in these His redeemed, now restored to His love [d], and He Who will not remember thy sins will remember thy love, and will repay thee with Himself, thine own beatitude for ever, thine own God, to be thine own for ever.

[d] For a penitentiary.

*" This My son was dead and is alive again: he was
lost and is found."*

THE tenderness of this parable (which must have
spoken to every sinner's heart since our Lord uttered it,) comes enhanced to us (if one may so say
reverently) because it was our Lord's defence of His
conduct towards sinners. Classes, most loathed by
the sanctimonious among the Jews, the publicans,
hated for their extortions and oppressions, and a
coarse populace, dregs of society, whom all recognised as "bad characters," who lived in the breach
of every law of God and man, whom common contempt called "sinners," had been drawn to Him by
the hidden magnet of His compassionate love. They.
"[b] were continually (S. Luke says) coming near,
close to Him;" and He received them tenderly [c] to
Himself as His familiar friends, in whom His soul
delighted; and they shared His meal. He made
no difference between Himself and them, receiving,

---

[a] Preached at Christ Church, at a College service.
[b] ἦσαν αὐτῷ ἐγγίζοντες. S. Luke xv. 1.   [c] προσδέχεται.

with them, from• His Father the common 'sustenance of our human nature. What a sight! Only we can picture what they were; not, what He! We have seen faces, marked by low cunning or sensuality or ferocity, or hardened by griping avarice or by the scowl of habitual hate. In the midst of them, one calm, holy, Divine Countenance, radiant with super-human love, tells them by Its very look, what He said to the chosen twelve; "ᵈ Ye are My friends." For He was the "ᵉ Friend of publicans and sinners." We can think how those dark countenances may have caught some softening relaxing tinge from His Divine love, as even a heavy cloud may gain a roseate hue from this world's setting sun. Scribes and Pharisees growled their condemnation of such conduct. Our Lord gives, as His only answer, the three parables, each with its own trait of individual love for sinners and persevering diligence in seeking and finding them. But the lost sheep and the coin are pictures of us; the prodigal son is our own selves. It is the perseverance of human ingratitude, overwhelmed and overpowered at last by the perseverance of Divine loving-kindness.

See the ingratitude. It is our own. The prodigal son had every thing good with his Good Father. What the Father says to the elder son, was, in the nature of things, true of the younger son also, before he left his home. "All Mine is thine." God shares His creation with us. His are all the things around us, because He created them; our's by His grant of their use. Ourselves He attempers so, mind and body, the faculties of both, in such

ᵈ S. John xv. 14. 15.   ᵉ S. Matt. xi. 19. S. Luke vii. 34.

adapted proportion, that it might have spoiled each one of us, had He given us aught besides. Nay, when He says, "All Mine is thine," He excepts not Himself. He communicates Himself, as far as each can receive Him. "I," He teaches us to say⁣, "am my Beloved's, and my Beloved is mine." The very strength, talents, intellect, wit, which any of us have abused against Him, to break His laws, were, in the way of nature, upheld in us by Him, at the very time that we were breaking them. Else we should perish. He upholds our strength, while we sin against Him, lest we should not have, whereby to turn to Him, and again become His.

The son (it is the temptation of our youth) is not satisfied with his Good Father's gifts, unless he be allowed to hold them independent of Him. He had all with his Father; he asks, to have them to himself. "Father, give me the portion of substance, which falleth to me." He asks, in words, what every longing for independence, every dislike of restraint, every wish to be free from that service which is "perfect freedom," enacts in deeds. "I would be absolute lord, have at my own disposal, deal with, use, spend, employ, direct, as I like, what Thou hast given me to hold of Thee. May I not use time, talents, gifts, powers of mind and body, as I will, without a galling restraint?" So some said of old, "ᵍOur lips are our own: who is lord over us?" "Why should I not utter that irreverent speech, or that ambiguous or licentious word, or speak lightly of sin, or do that nameless deed, which my nature suggests?" "Give me," for my own use, "that por-

ᶠ Cant. vi. 3. vii. 10.   ᵍ Ps. xii.4.

tion of goods which falleth to me." God so respect-
eth our free-will, with which He created us, freely
to love Him, that He leaves us to take our evil
choice, if so be, through the misery of our choice,
we may be driven back, sooner or later, to choose
Him, the Fountain of all good, our God and our All.

Our better instinct shrinks from displeasing Him
in His felt Presence. People could not commit some
deed of sin or shame, in the sight of some picture
of Jesus, looking, as it were, on them. So the prodigal's next step was to forget his Father. "He
removed far away from his home to a far country."
[h] Not by space, but by affections, are we with God,
or far from God." "The far country is forgetfulness of God." Severed he was from God, in Whom
he "lived and moved and was;" severed by will
from Him, from Whom he had had his being; he
interposed those boiling surges of his passions and
pleasures between himself and his country, an exile
from his home, self-banished from his Father and
his God.

And being severed from God and His grace, what
could he do but waste the gifts, which he no longer
held of the Good Giver? "He wasted his substance." What substance? All which he had from
his Good Father; that substance, which his Father
had apportioned to him; gifts of nature, of the world,
of grace; natural endowments, good qualities and dispositions; health and strength; his best and freshest
existence; fine gifts of memory, reasoning powers;
the delicate bloom of his innocent years; the snow-
white purity of soul, the presence of God the Holy

[h] S. Jer. Ep. xxi. 5. 7.

Ghost within him, the consciousness of his sonship to God, even that freedom of will, which he abused by leaving his Father (for this too becomes so enslaved, that men at last deny that they ever had it): his past, his present, and (as far as in him then lay) his future—they who are physicians of mind or body, and have observed the effects of a course of sin on each, know something of what that means, "he wasted his substance in riotous living." May you, my sons, never know it fully!

His Good Father meanwhile held His peace, knowing well that He should not be heeded; yet left not His son uncared for. "I, poor wretch," S. Augustine says of his own prodigal but heathen youth[i], "foamed like a troubled sea, following the rushing of my own tide, forsaking Thee and exceeding all Thy limits; yet I escaped not Thy scourges. For what mortal can? For Thou wert ever with me, mercifully rigorous, and besprinkling with bitter alloy all my unlawful pleasures, that I might seek pleasures without alloy. But where to find such, I could not discover, save in Thee, O Lord, Who teachest by sorrow, and woundest us to heal, and slayest us, lest we die from Thee."

When he had spent all, there arose a mighty famine, and he began to be in want. "[k]For whoso departeth from the word of God, hungereth; whoso departeth from the Fountain, thirsteth; whoso departeth from the Riches, lacketh; whoso departeth from Wisdom, is dulled; whoso departeth from virtue, is dissolved. Truly then did he begin to be in want, because he had forsaken the treasures of the

[i] Conf. ii. n. 4.   [k] S. Ambr. in S. Luc. L. vii. n. 215. ad loc.

Wisdom and knowledge of God and the depth of heavenly riches. He began to be in want and to suffer hunger; for nothing sufficeth to prodigal pleasure."

"He began to be in want." Some turn to God on the first trouble, with which He punishes their evil choice, the evil of their ways. Not so the most; not so those, by whom Jesus was surrounded, whom He was picturing. Man, when in a wrong way, apart from God, must, upon some check of suffering, either return or plunge deeper. And mostly they plunge deeper, dulling or stifling their sorrow with fresh sources of sorrow. Since the soul, being made by God for Himself, cannot be satisfied by aught out of God, the more it would satisfy itself, the more sensible must its famine be, the more desperate its unremedying remedies. The poor prodigal felt his want, but went his way, went further from his God, joining, cleaving to a citizen of that alien country, some one, perhaps, more hardened or experienced in sin, who could teach him, how in some more desperate way to still his insatiable cravings. This too, in God's mercy, failed; and then, in the extremity of his misery, he remembered his once happy home, the innocence of his childhood, the peace of his unsullied years, how even those, who served his Father for hire, had enough and to spare, and *he*, once a son, once sharing all with his Father, was perishing. "He came to himself." He had, all this while, been away from himself. There is no sight which one, separate from God, so dreads to see, as himself. The inmost secret of all that "energetic idleness," of which the heathen poet speaks, is to escape some vacant moment, in which the sinner may be alone with himself, may have to face himself.

Then followed those characteristics of true repentance, instantaneous decision and action, "I will arise and go to my Father." "And he arose and went to his Father." Delay is fatal to repentance. "¹Make no tarrying," says the son of Sirach, "to turn unto the Lord, and put not off from day to day; for suddenly shall the wrath of the Lord come forth, and in thy security thou shalt be destroyed." "ᵐ He Who hath promised forgiveness to the penitent, hath promised no morrow to the procrastinator." To say, "I will repent to-morrow," only means, "I will not repent to-day." "To-day" is ever "the day of salvation." To-morrow's sun will shine,—one to-morrow's sun will shine upon our graves; but who has promised to-morrow's grace?

Then there was the re-awakened memory, that *He*, against Whom he had sinned, was his Father. Misery was the occasion of his repentance; misery awoke him to himself; but to escape from misery was not the one object of his repentance. Foremost stands out, not the thought of his decay, not, that he was (though he was) a wreck of himself, but his Father. "Father, I have sinned against heaven and before Thee." He was still a son, though he had cast away every gift which belonged to him as a son.

¹ Eccls. v. 7.   ᵐ S. Aug. "God hath promised thee forgiveness: the morrow no one hath promised thee." Id. in Ps. ci. Serm. 1. n. 10. Opp. iv. 1098; also Serm. xxxvii. [87. Ben.] p. 229. Oxf. Tr. S. Greg. in Evang. Hom. i. 12. 6. "He Who hath promised pardon to the penitent, hath not promised a morrow to the sinner."

One only longing he had, to be again in his Father's house, which he had so thanklessly deserted; to be in his Father's Presence in any condition whatever, though but as a hired servant. This too he asked as a favour; for he was below them; they had, as servants, been faithful.

Then his confession was without excuses. Like David's, it is only "I have sinned," "Against Thee, Thee only, have I sinned."

Yet even then, he was a great way off. Might not his resolution or his purpose fail him? Might not his old habits, to which he had sold himself, draw him back? Might not some occasion of sin surprise him, some sudden passion storm him, some despair numb him, and he lie down and die? His Good Father anticipated all this: He saw him, saw His inmost soul, and met him.

What a meeting of the All-Good, and that, until just now, almost-all-évil. No mitigating good has been told us of him: nothing but selfishness and selfish sin; for sin is very selfish; nothing, whereby any one might deem himself shut out, as being a greater sinner. Not one gleam of good, until his repentance. Yet the Father reproaches him not. He asks not, "Where hast thou been? what hast thou done? why so long, so far away? where is all which I gave thee? why hast thou changed thy glory into shame?" Nay, He anticipates the confession; He will not let him speak, until He has shewn him His love. He folds him in His arms, lest the son should cast himself at His Feet. He upholds him: He kisses his son's profaned and passion-stained lips. His son could not even carry out his purpose of saying,

"Make me as one of thy hired servants." For his Father had already received him as His son. He owned his unworthiness of his Father's love, of having such a Father; and the Father only met his confession with tokens of honour. He sees the sins, only to ignore them : the nakedness, only to hide it under the goodliest robe; perhaps He meets the son's thought of being a hired servant by the gift of the shoes on his feet and the signet-ring. The feast in his honour was more; it was love and joy in the restored communion of the Father and the son. The self-righteous brother's detailed reproaches the Father owned in the single words; "He *was* dead," "he *was* lost," and these too, only to efface them by the words, "he *is* alive again," "he *is* found." Whatever had been in the past was annihilated now by the present. "God," it has been magnificently said[a], "is a God of the present."

But, although the restoration was complete, the peril had been extreme. Our Lord Who came to die for our sins, to save us from their guilt and power and penalty, does not, even in His mercy, conceal their blackness. We should not know what gratitude we owe. The son had been "lost!" He had been "dead." God tells us of those "[o] *dead* in trespasses and sins." "[p] She, who liveth in pleasure, is dead, while she liveth." The life of the body is the soul; the life of the soul is God. He had lost God: he was dead. Bring home to yourselves the picture of that living death, which the Prophet speaks of as befalling rebels against God, how they are living

"[n] Deus præsentiarum est." [o] Eph. ii. 1. 5. Col. ii. 13.
[p] 1 Tim. v. 6.

corpses; "their flesh moulders away, while they stand on their feet; their eyes moulder in their sockets, and their tongues in their mouth^q." Picture to yourselves one such, standing in this Church, those horrible black worms, creeping in and out of the sightless holes. Your flesh would creep, your young blood would curdle at the sight. Alas! if there is but *one* in this Church, whose soul is dead in deadly sin, a dead soul, putrefying through its sin, is, (if we could see it within the fair outward beauty of a young healthful frame,) O how intolerably more aweful! For the body decays, sown in corruption and dishonour, to be raised in incorruption and glory: but a dead soul,—who shall give it life?

Yes! *One* can give it life. One can say to the soul, though bound with its grave-clothes, and the heavy mass of sin burying it, motionless to all life and good, and itself decaying or decayed; One *can* say, One *does* say to the dead soul, "Lazarus, come forth." His word is still being performed daily; "^r The hour is coming and now is, when the dead shall hear the voice of the Son of God; and they that hear shall live." He still watches, like a Father, over His lost child: He marks its wandering: He, within and without, solicits its return: He still meets it, when a great way off, by His inward encouraging grace: He still says, "Thy sins be forgiven thee:" He still falls on its neck and gives it the kiss of peace: He still restores the lost robe of righteousness and anew espouses the soul, "^s as a chaste virgin" unto Himself, and the heavenly courts re-

^q Zech. xiv. 12.   ^r S. John v. 25.   ^s 2 Cor. xi. 2.

echo with jubilees of joy, the triumph of their king
" The dead is alive again; *My* lost son is found."

My sons, may God, in His mercy, preserve you,
each one, from falling ! If any, alas! have fallen and
is dead through sin, He, your Saviour your God and
your Salvation Who became Man, is at this moment,
waiting to receive you; He longs for your return
more than you can to be restored; for He Who bare
our sins in the Agony in the Garden and on the
Cross, knows, more than any in heaven or earth can
know, this intolerable weight from which He would
free you. "ᵗ Why will ye die ? I have no pleasure
in the death of him that dieth, saith the Lord God;
wherefore turn and live ye." To Him with the Father and the Holy Ghost &c.

ᵗ Ezek. xviii. 31, 32.

SERMON XI.

THE PRODIGAL SON.

S. Luke xv. 17. 20.

"And when he came to himself, he said, I will arise and go to my Father.—And he arose and came to his Father."

The prodigal son had run the ordinary course of sin. He had wasted his Father's first best gifts, the spotlessness of innocence, his snow-white purity, his first freshness of soul, his dowry of nature and of grace. As far as in him lay, he had "wasted all in riotous living." Misery alone had not recalled him. He had gone from bad to worse, labouring to drown his sense of misery in fresh sources of misery. These too failing him, God brought by His grace the thought of His own Fatherly relation to his soul. He remembered that he had a Father, though deserted, forgotten, seemingly lost to him. His Father put it into his heart to return to Him. "I will arise and go to my Father." He had lived a reckless heathen life. One thing he did *not* do. When God put the thought to return to Him into his heart, he did not delay. He did not put off to an unknown future his purpose to return. He said not, "I will return to-morrow,"

when these trammels have less power over me, when
my sin solicits me less. He said "I will arise and go
to my Father," and as soon as he had pronounced
the words of penitence, which he would say, "He
arose and went."

This is the condition and characteristic of all true
repentance, of all noble enterprise, of all devoted purpose—instantaneous obedience to the calls of grace.
By this was formed the goodly company of the prophets: by this the fishermen and the publican became the converters of the world; by this the fierce
persecutor of the Church came "not to be behind the
very chiefest Apostles." " I was not disobedient to
the heavenly vision." He said, "Lord, what wilt
Thou have me to do?" and did it. By this the lowly
Virgin became Theotokos, "the Mother of God."
" Be it unto me according to thy word!"

Direct disobedience has been converted and saved:
we hear of no conversion of one who promised future
obedience. The son, who said, "I go not," afterwards " repented and went." Of him it is said, that
he " did the will of his Father." We hear no future of him, who said "I go, Sir," "I *will* go," and
went not. "To-day," we repeat daily in the Psalms,
" if ye will hear His voice, harden not your hearts."
"[a]Behold *now* is the accepted time," S. Paul applies
to us the words of the prophets, " behold *now* is the
day of salvation."

Jesus, when He wept over Jerusalem, said so
mournfully: "[b] If thou hadst known, at least in this
thy day, the things which belong unto thy peace."
"He looks on it with compassion," says a thoughtful

[a] 2 Cor. vi. 2.   [b] S. Luke xix. 44.

preacher [c], "not because it was to be destroyed by the Romans; not because it was on the eve of the most utter ruin; not because her children were, like Cain, to be wanderers on the earth; not because the Holy One was soon to be condemned to death therein, a death the most shameful and most cruel; but because she 'had not known the day of salvation' given to her, in which the Lord brought her peace. This drew forth the tears of the Son of God. He ascribed the reprobation of the Jews, not to the hateful Deicide which they were going to perpetrate on His Own Person, but to the voluntary blindness which hindered their knowing the time of the visitation of the Lord:—'because thou knewest not the time of thy visitation.'"

What is then the danger of delay, what is its offensiveness, that God warns us, that if we neglect His grace *to-day*, the to-morrow to which we procrastinate may not be a day of grace to us?

It is *not*, that God would not hear us, if we were to choose *then*, what we delay to choose *now*. It *is*, that our delay shows that we have not the love of God *now*, and that we do not wish to have it.

What is it which God desires of the sinner? That "he should be converted and live." What then is the opposite to conversion? It is a terrible word, because God is our only Good, our Hope, our All; but it is, you know, "*a*version." If we are not turned *to* God, we are turned away from Him. It is a terrible word, because it is *so* outspoken, *so* true; and God is *so* good. Yet God tells us plainly, what we are do-

[c] Bourdaloue, Sur le Retardement de la Pénitence, Œuvres i. 447.

ing. He says, not only, "thou hast cast My words behind thee;" "they cast Thy Law behind their backs," but "Thou hast cast ME behind thy back:" "they have turned to Me the back and not the face!" an act, which has become a proverb for marked contumely.

But is it not so true? is there any thought, which men so try to get rid of, unless they are obeying Him, as the thought of God? For it is the thought of a Master Who is disobeyed, a Father Who is disho-noured; a Benefactor to Whom we are ungrateful; an Almighty, Who is defied; an Indweller Who is chaced away; a Judge, Who can punish. It speaks of engagements broken, duties violated, conscience silenced; not to speak of disgraceful thoughts, words, deeds, upon which the name of God falls, like the light upon a dark cloud, intensifying its blackness. There is an impatient dislike of the serious mention of God, if any be given to unlawful pleasure, or frivolity, or dissipation. Such have a distaste for it.

Yet there is no half-way, no middle term. God is the Centre of our being. He must be, because He is our Creator; we, His creatures. He made us for Himself, to find our endless uncloying bliss in Him. His commandments are a transcript of a portion of His Infinite holiness, of His Being. He gives them to us, to conform us in our little way to Himself, that we may be holy, as He, our God, is Holy; merciful, as He, our Father in Heaven, is merciful; loving, as He, our God, is Love. If we turn from His commandments, we turn from Himself, Whom, in a

d Ps. l. 17.　e Neh. ix. 26.　f 1 Kgs. xiv. 9. Ezek. xxiii. 35.　g Jer. ii. 27, xxxii. 33.

degree, His Eternal law expresses, Whose image and likeness, in which He created us, He wills through them to re-create in us. And so turning from Him, we become more alien from Him. We learnt in our boyish days, "The same to will, the same to nill, is the condition of friendship." "[h]Alienated from God through wicked works;" at "[i]enmity with God;" "[k]haters of God," are but gradations of the rebel soul's hostility to God. We cannot love *Him*, Whose law over us we hate.

But delay of repentance has this special characteristic, that it is continually hearing, and dismissing to a more convenient season, the grace of God, the pleading of His Spirit in the soul. It is not like a sudden fall, through the fierce stress of passion, yielded to but repented of. It is a chronic state, an ever-renewed "not yet." The grace of God, whether through the pious teaching in childhood, or better habits formerly, or some remembered impressions of good, continually solicits it. God wills, in His ever-present love, to have that soul as His own. And the soul responds, with that sluggish, listless, "not yet." It knows something, how necessary God is to the soul, or it dreads at least the consequences of being parted from Him for ever. It wills not to be parted from Him wholly, nor yet, on His own terms to have Him. And so it would compromise with God; "the present for me, the future,"—when pleasure shall have lost its zest, or passion its violence, or circumstances shall change, or marriage shall remove temptation, or the buoyancy of youth be over,—" the future for Thee. Now, I cannot endure restraint; religion puts

[h] Col. i. 21.   [i] Rom. viii. 7.   [k] Ib. i. 30, &c.

on such strait-laced ways, in this or that person : 1 would be free; my thoughts, my words, my acts, must be at my own disposal. Hereafter I will be stayed; I will live a decent life of religion hereafter; but now I would be free. To-day for me; to-morrow, O my God, for Thee."

I will not ask now, "Is then slavery to sin the only freedom? Are not the blessed Spirits around the Eternal Throne in their entranced adoring contemplation of the Beatific vision, or Seraphim in their burning love, or Cherubim in their God-given wisdom, free, evermore in their unconstrained love choosing freely each new manifestation of His Love? Was not Paul as free, when, God-impelled, he sped his fiery course from East to West to carry to benighted hearts the light of the glorious Gospel, as when, 'full of threatenings and slaughters,' he 'compelled men to blaspheme?' Is the law of life more galling than the yoke of sin? Is love a bondage? Is mastery over self less ennobling than slavery to one's lower appetites?" But granting that Christian obedience is, although free, still the enfreed service of the soul, what means the delay of this service? What is it, but to abuse the love of God against Himself? to live in the prolonged impenitence of a continual delay, because God is long-suffering? to put aside His grace, because He is so gracious? to prefer sin to His Goodness, because He is so good? to bind the chains of sin tighter, by a daily or weekly habit of what offends God's aweful purity, because God is Almighty to break them? If God were to say, as in the parable, "This night thy soul shall be required of thee;" were He to say, "Repent to-day, for there shall be

no room for repentance to-morrow;" we all think,
what diligence we should use in setting our houses
in order; how we should repent, and protest our
sorrow for our sins, and beseech God for pardon, in
whatever way we might. We cannot imagine defer-
ring repentance, if God were to say, "Repent this
day, or thy soul will be lost for ever."

Would we be in earnest, if God were to be thus severe, and shall we be less earnest, because God deals
so tenderly and lovingly with us? Shall we be evil,
because God is so infinitely good? Shall we keep
the door of our hearts tight-closed, because Jesus,
Who stands without, knocks so gently? *Who* knocks?
He Whose Hands still bear the prints of those rack-
ing nails, which fastened Him not so tightly to the
Tree, as His love for us; He Whose Brow still wears
the marks of that crown of thorns, which pierced
Him not so sharply as did our sins.

> O love that passeth knowledge,
>   So patiently to wait!
> Oh sin that hath no equal,
>   So fast to bar the gate!

It must be "to-day" once. To-morrow, and to-
morrow, and to-morrow, and each to-morrow's morrow, were they prolonged to "the last syllable of
recorded time," must each in their turn become "to-
day." The past is gone; the future is not our's: one
time alone is our's, not "to-day" even, but this
moment, as it passes. If thou wilt turn to God at
all, it must be in some "*now.*" We cozen ourselves with this ever-coming, never-come, "to-morrow," because it is *not* now. We think that it will
be easier to turn to God then, because it does not

involve present, instant decision. We do not like
to be brought to a stand, "Wilt thou choose God
or no?" But it must be so. Were men (which you,
with the generous warm hearts of youth, could not
now think of,) to put repentance off till the last dregs
of life, when the last sand of life is ebbing out, and
there is nothing left to offer to God on the bed of
death, it must still be, *now.*

But in no yet future *now* will the grace of God,
now stifled or dismissed, be more powerful: your
own wills will be weakened by continual failure;
the iron fetters of habitual sin, which each act of sin
rivets the more tightly, will not be burst by any
less resolute effort, in any "hereafter."

Apart from the universal uncertainty of life, (and
he whose restoration from the gate of death now fills
a nation's heart with joy[1], is of an age, when fewer in
proportion drop out of sight, I believe, than, my sons,
at your's) I would trust any uncertainty rather than
the uncertainty of the procrastinating human will.
It is uncertain, how long God will think fit to solicit
you with His despised grace. Nay! there may be an
aweful mercy in leaving the obstinate soul unsoli-
cited by grace, lest the repelled grace should add
to the account against you. To-day, the time is certain, the grace is certain, your will may be certain.
In that morrow's morrow, to which you would procrastinate, all is uncertain. It is but a "perhaps."
Perhaps you may turn to God, perhaps you may not.
But what follows? Perhaps you may save your soul:
perhaps, and more probably, you will lose it. Would

[1] Written when the restoration of the Prince of Wales, was
recent.

you stake your eternity, the sight of God, or the loss of God, endless joy or endless woe, upon the chance of such a "perhaps?" The hour of the dying Robber's repentance by the Cross of Jesus was not his last hour. It was his first.

Once more God submits Himself to your's, His creature's, choice. Jesus, Who still intercedes for you, implores you from Heaven, not to waste in yourselves the Price of His Blood, the travail of His soul. One, still held fast by his sins, saw under the picture of the Crucifixion, the simple lines,

> "This have I done for thee;
> What doest thou for Me?"

"What indeed?" he cried; "nothing!" and forthwith he turned to God with a whole-hearted repentance. Thou canst not see Him now; but the Eye of Jesus in His Love still rests on thee. His Voice still calls to thee, "There is no peace in sin. Wilt thou not come to Me? Come to Me, to Me, and be at rest. Come to Me, and I will give you all which thou canst contain of Mine own boundless joy, of My infinite love."

SERMON XII[a].

REPENTANCE, FROM LOVE OF GOD, LIFE-LONG.

S. Luke xxii. 61, 62.

*And the Lord turned, and looked upon Peter. And
Peter remembered the word of the Lord, how He had
said unto him, Before the cock crow, thou shalt deny
Me thrice. And Peter went out, and wept bitterly.*

Rich in its harvest of souls, beyond all other seasons, is this our season of Lent. How should it not
be, by God's goodness, when it brings before us our
own sins, and leads us on, step by step, to the Cross
of Jesus? But many are called, few chosen; many
begin, few persevere; many begin, again and again,
in this season of Lent; but Easter, our Passover,
instead of being a time of passing and pressing on,
in haste, with our loins girded up to serve God, is
too often a time of falling back.

And therefore now, towards the close of this our
season of Lent, when we are just on the threshold
of our dear Lord's Passion, in which we see most
vividly the black ingratitude and hatefulness of our
sins, and the deep lustre of His forgiving love, it
has been assigned to me to speak to you of that
mark of true loving repentance, that it is life-long.

[a] Preached at S. Mary's, Oxford. Lent, 1857.

In other words, true sorrow for sin, out of love for Jesus, does not pass away. The more we hope that we are the objects of the love of Jesus, the more we hope that He has forgiven our sins and renewed us by His Spirit and loves us, the more we must sorrow, if we love, that we ever sinned against His Infinite Love.

Of such life-long repentance for forgiven sin, an Apostle, yea, the very chief Apostle, is our pattern.

S. Peter's was an aweful fall, a fall from which men rarely recover. It was a fall against the strongest previous light, in the presence of the Light Himself. In the very sight of Jesus, he denied Jesus. Even Pilate, although he condemned Jesus, was awed by Him. Pilate half believed. He would have believed, if he could have loved. Those who accused Jesus were put to shame; His judges were confounded, because striving to bring false witness against the Holy One and the Just, they failed.

Peter saw this; he saw his Master's majestic silence, and His judges crouching and quailing, even amid their malignant hate, as owning already against their will Him, Who " should come to be their judge." Peter had received the fullest knowledge, and that, by revelation of God. Our Lord had sealed the truth of his inward inspiration when He said, " Flesh and blood hath not revealed it unto thee, but My Father which is in heaven [b]." He had confessed our Lord to be God and Man. "Thou," the Son of Man, " art the Son of the living God;" and on this he had received the promises. He had beheld death at a distance, and, foremost of

[b] S. Matt. xvi. 17.

·all, had said, " Lord, I will go with Thee to prison
and to death." Foremost in profession, he was alone
in denial. He had owned his Lord to be the Son of
God, now he denied being His disciple, or even that
he knew Him.

Forewarned, but unshaken in his self-confidence,
he fell. His Lord Himself had warned him before his
fall; he ventured into peril: amid his peril, and fallen
already, he was warned by the sign which his Lord
had given him. He took no heed, continued in peril,
and fell worse than before. Falls always prepare for
further falls. As is the case in the body too, it is
more difficult to recover, than not to fall. Innocence
is a great safeguard. However near a man may have
been to falling, it is something to have been saved,
by God's mercy, from the entire fall. Shame, which
aids to withhold from a fall, withholds from repentance. It was harder for Peter to confess our Lord,
when he had once denied Him. He had to contradict himself. And so, the more the truth was brought
home to him, "Thou art a Galilæan,—thy speech be-
wrayeth thee," the more desperately he denied it.
Several seem to have accused him at once; and he,
•driven into a corner, turned, as men do, the more desperately against them, and, with perjury and impre-
cation on himself, denied his Lord. "Then began
Peter to curse and to swear, saying, I know not the
Man." "The cock crew." "The Lord turned and
looked upon Peter." That look brought him back to
himself and to Jesus. That "look lived in him," during all the years of his Apostolate. He died to himself, that he might live to Jesus; and living to Jesus,
in the end he died for Jesus.

Peter's was a very great sin. At first sight, it seems as great a sin as Judas'. Judas sold his Lord; Peter denied Him. It *was* a very great sin; but it was the sin of presumption, not of malice. It was not directed against his Master, as was Judas'. But of all a Christian's sins, it was one of the worst. Our Lord Himself has said, "cWhoso shall be ashamed of Me and of My words in this adulterous and sinful generation, of him shall the Son of Man be ashamed when He cometh in His own glory and His Father's and of the holy angels;" and, "d Whosoever shall deny Me before men, him will I also deny before My Father in heaven." St. Peter trusted himself more than his Lord. For his Lord had said to him, "e Thou canst not follow Me *now*, but thou shalt follow Me *afterwards*." He promised him for the future, while He deterred him for the present. Peter would outrun his Master's call. He saw what he wished to do for his Master; he weighed not what he *could* do. He would die for his Master, before his Master had yet died to redeem *him*. The Passion of Christ is the fountain of grace, of strength, of endurance, of every blessing. Before that fountain was opened, Peter would do, in his own strength, what his Lord had promised him that he should do, but only in his Redeemer's. And so he could not but fall. Jesus allowed him to fall (as now, too, He almost always allows the self-confident to fall); and so He revealed himself to himself, that thenceforth he might build upon the Rock, not upon himself.

Yet Peter's fall was the fall of self-confident love. Had he not loved, he would not have adventured

c S. Luke ix. 26.   d S. Matt. x. 33.   e S. John xiii. 36.

into the High Priest's palace at all. "He went in to
see the end." He went to see what would become
of his Master Whom he loved. Perhaps he thought
that, when the chief priests saw Him face to face,
and heard His words, they could not venture to condemn Him. Or he may have gone in, with that sort
of uncertain hope which people have, that what they
dread will not happen, although they know not *how*
it should not; only they cannot bring themselves to
think that what they fear so exceedingly, will be.
And so his faith, which rested not blindly on his
Lord, failed when his hopes failed. He had trusted
in his own hopes, that he would in some way be
spared the trial; not in his Master, to be borne
through it, and over it. And so, when his hopes
failed, his faith and his love also failed. Had he not
had love, he would not have ventured into danger;
had he had that "perfect love" which "casteth out
fear," he would not have been betrayed into the great
sin of denying the Lord, through fear of a little maid,
lest he should be called to fulfil his loving boast,
"Lord, I will follow Thee to prison and to death."

Peter, then, was not like souls who fall into sin,
because, for love of the pleasure of the sin, they
venture as near it as they dare. He was led into
the near occasion of sin by a self-trusting love of
his Master. He was like those over-confident souls,
who think that, to do some good, they may venture
into peril, which proves too strong for them. They
seldom return without the feeling of a wound. They
either have not done what they ought, or they have
done what they ought not. They have either failed
to do anything for Christ at all; or they feel that

they have displeased Him in some unloving, un-
humble way of doing it; or they have even been
ashamed of Christ, and consented to what they should
not. For we may deny our Lord, without doing
it directly towards Himself. He says to S. Peter,
"Thou shalt deny Me thrice." Yet S. Peter (God
forbid!) did not say anything against our Lord; he
denied of himself, that he was Christ's disciple. So,
then, for a man, in thought or word or act, to deny
that he is Christ's disciple, is to deny Christ. Alas!
among those who are thought to be Christians, and
who think themselves such, how manifold are such
denials! And yet, had our good Lord then left
S. Peter, he must have perished. "[f] Lord, to whom
shall we go?" S. Peter had said: "Thou hast the
words of eternal life." And he had gone away from
Him, of Whom he had owned that He Alone had life
eternal!

Yet thus, too, Jesus looked on Peter, as He does so
often on us, by some sudden check of conscience, or
upbraiding of His tenderness, or thrilling sorrow, or
burning shame, that we have not been faithful to Him,
our loving Saviour. Only his gracious look on S.
Peter had this gift also, that it at once brought home
to him his sin, and sealed his forgiveness. It could
not be otherwise. It was He, the Redeemer, the Fountain of Mercy, "with Whom is plenteous redemption [g]." *His* Eye, which pierced His disciple's soul
and drew the water out of what had just been as a
rock of flint, could not but have beamed with Divine
tenderness, which healed while it wounded. O could
we but see that Eye, as it rests on each one of us,

[f] S. John vi. 68.   [g] Ps. cxxx. 7.

amid our sins, or negligences, or unfaithfulnesses!
How could we bear, ourselves to have deserved that
reproachful, displeased look? how could we enough,
out of our shame and misery, adore His mercy, which
vouchsafed to look on such as us!

Yet *therefore* is that full, brief history of Peter's
repentance the more instructive, because he was forgiven. "He went out, and wept bitterly."

Doubtless he then no longer "[h] feared those who
could only kill the body." If he still had fear, one
only fear had he; the fear of sin, and of displeasing
his Good Lord. He went out from the scene of his
sin, from the occasion of his sin, from the temptation
to his sin. This is the first step to earnest repentance. In one act, he confessed his presumption, he
owned his weakness, he corrected his fault, he placed
himself out of temptation. True penitence is ever
humble, and distrustful of self, while it trusts in
Jesus. "Whoso remains in a slippery place, must
think lightly of his fall[i]." Whoso remains in what
has been to him an occasion of sin, has no true repentance. If thou wouldest truly repent, flee the
places, and haunts, the occasions, the opportunities
of thy sin.

This was Peter's first decisive act. He removed
from risk of sin; he removed into loneliness. Loneliness is the place of repentance. If God touches thy
soul, quit others, at least for a time, and sorrow to
Him apart. Sorrow for sin, out of love for Jesus,
must be apart from the world, and alone with Jesus.
Let Him Who gave thee thy sorrow, alone be the
witness of it. Those are true tears which He alone

[h] S. Matt. x. 28.   [i] S. Bern., Serm. Pasch. i. § 17, p. 905.

witnesses, which are shed apart to Him. Peter went out from the sight of men. He knew that his Saviour's Eye still rested on him, as his Saviour's look lived in his heart.

He "wept bitterly," and yet he knew himself forgiven. This is another mark of true repentance. He sorrowed for forgiven sin. Repentance cannot be real, unless it remove from occasions of sin; it cannot be deep, unless it continue when its sin is (as it hopes) forgiven.

This is the characteristic difference between true and surface repentance. True repentance is life-long. So far from ending with forgiveness, one might rather say that it then begins. While the soul fears that it is unforgiven, its penitence is a penitence of fear. It dreads Hell; it dreads the wrath of God, and, at best, it dreads being shut out for ever from His Presence. Its object is chiefly itself. The penitence of forgiven sin is a penitence of love. True, it is still displeased with itself; it must mourn its lost graces, its soils and stains and scars; its crippled powers; its dwarfed stature; its weakness towards good; its distance from its God; else it would not be penitence. It must know and feel that it has undergone a great loss through its sin; that it is but the wreck of what it might have been, had it not so sinned. It must long—if not to be replaced where it might have been, in that nearness to God for which He made it—yet to have as much of His love, as, through His undeserved mercy, it can any how obtain. Yet it is ever chiefly taken up with the thought of God and the love of God. "Against Thee, Thee only, have I sinned."

Such has been the character of those great models
of Scripture penitents, David, and S. Peter, and S.
Paul. They were penitents for forgiven sin; and
their penitence lasted all their life long. God saw
David's penitence in those two words, (as David
spake them j,) " I have sinned against the Lord."
Who can tell or imagine the agony of David's soul,
as Nathan rehearsed to him God's goodness to him,
the yet larger abundance of goods which He had had
in store for him, had he asked of his God what he
gained through such sin, *his* own ingratitude and
God's displeasure? But in that brief space of grief,
David's heart was pierced through and through; his
penitence was begun, expressed, accepted. The confession, "I have sinned against the Lord," was met
by the authoritative words, "The Lord also hath put
away thy sin." God Himself declared that He had
"put away the sin," and it was not. But David's
penitence then began to flow. He who had been
forgiven by God, was taught by the Spirit of God to
utter that deep Psalm of penitence, which has ever
since expressed the inmost longings of penitent souls:
"Have mercy upon me, O God, after Thy great
goodness." God's voice had pardoned him, yet he
longed to be washed more and more from his wickedness. O doubtless that "more and more," "wash
me more and more from my wickedness," echoed on
from David's lips, as it has on theirs whom God has
taught, through him, the words of penitence, until
the last "more and more" yielded up the soul,
wholly purified by its Saviour's Blood, "in Whom,
not. seen, he believed." It must have lasted on, for

‏ j חטאתי ליהוה ‏

he says, long after he had been forgiven, "My sin is ever before me."

S. Paul's sin, in persecuting Christians and compelling them to blaspheme, had been forgiven, as if it had never been. He was wholly a new man. He was out of Christ when he sinned. When he believed in Christ and was baptized, he was re-born in Christ, and became a new man. Yet on account of this sin, as to which Ananias bade him "[k] be baptized, and wash away thy sins, calling on the name of the Lord," he to whom God bare witness, "[l]he is a chosen vessel unto Me," so remembered his sin that he counted himself "[m]the chief of sinners;" "[n]less than the least of all saints," i. e. lower than the lowest Christian, who, before he was in Christ, had not so sinned; "[o]not worthy to be called an Apostle."

Morning after morning, cock-crowing after cock-crowing, S. Peter wept his fall. Some lentile-broth, of the daily value of a farthing[p], was, for his whole life long, the penitential food of *him*, by whose hands God wrought special miracles, by whose shadow passing by He healed the sick; through whom He first admitted both Jews and Gentiles into the Church; to whom, first in dignity among the other Apostles, He gave the keys of the kingdom of heaven.

No one who has the heart of a man left, can know (as far as *man* can know) what sin is, and what God is, and what He is to us, and not repent, his whole life through, for forgiven sin. One deadly sin is an infinite evil. Adam's one sin brought death into the world, and cost the Blood of the Redeemer. To

[k] Acts xxii. 16. [l] Ib. ix. 15. [m] 1 Tim. i. 15. [n] Eph. iii. 8.
[o] 1 Cor. xv. 9. [p] S. Greg. Naz. Orat. xiv. de Paup. Cur. § 4.

choose wilfully one deadly sin is, to choose Satan for
God, to part with God, to renounce God, to be separated from God, to be alien from God for ever. Measure the depth of sin by what you will—the infinite price of the Blood of God the Son, or by the
endless pains of Hell,—each is infinite. Infinite in
value is the precious death of Christ; infinite in their
duration are the pains of Hell. Infinite, too, is the
love of God, against which the sinner sins.

Now if it were human love only, had we only
deeply pierced a heart like our own, had we been
ungrateful, unmerciful, unfaithful, cruel to a tender
heart bound up in one with our own, and they had
forgiven us, could we forget it? Would not their
very look remind us? would not their loving gentle-
ness reproach us? would not their very forgiving
tenderness almost choke us? Were the Good Father
of the prodigal son, who had rebelled against him,
wasted his substance with harlots, forsaken him, held
his love cheap,—were that good Father a man only,
could the restored son forget it? would not his "best
robe," and his "ring," and the peace and abundance
of his home, remind him of the swine husks, and his
rags, and his misery, and starvation?

And yet these, and all the tenderest affections,
are just the images under which God shadows out
to us His eternal love. Nay, He tells us that a
forbearance, which man could not use, He uses.
He calls us children, though we rebel; He calls us
friends, though we betray Him; He betroths our
souls, and we forsake Him for vile, passing, sordid,
brutish, disgusting pleasures. And He, what doth
He? what saith He? "q Thou hast played the harlot

q Jer. iii. 1.

with many lovers, yet return again to Me, saith the Lord?" And what, if we return? "[r]I will betroth thee unto Me for ever; yea, I will betroth thee unto Me in righteousness, and in judgement, and in loving-kindness, and in tender mercies. I will even betroth thee unto Me in faithfulness." He "abhors not our polluted and loathsome mouth[s]," but admits us to the kiss of peace; us, "the ruined, wretched, excessive sinners." He not only receives us back again, but He receives us as if we had ever served Him. He upbraids us not. Nay, He tells us how, in the Day of Judgement, He will, if we " repent, and bring forth fruits meet for repentance," own us as though we had ever served Him, forget our past sins amid our tardy and lingering service, and welcome us, "miserable sinners," with His "Well done, good and faithful servant."

But shall *we* forget it? Surely his Lord's forgiving love is now, and will be for ever, part of S. Peter's joy. Surely he cannot thank his Lord enough in all eternity for that gracious look of love amid his sin. Surely all His redeemed, yea, each one of us, if by His grace and mercy we attain, shall love Him above all things, and be amazed above all things, and ever go forth out of ourselves in wondering and adoring love, that, such as we were, He loved us, called us, gave us repentance, and faith, and love, forgave us, sanctified us, loved us unto the end.

. But then, my sons, it is unnatural, ungrateful, unloving, as well as perilous to our souls, to forget what we have been, to lay aside our repentance, while we are in the body.

---

[r] Hos. ii. 19, 20.   [s] Bp. Andrewes' Devotions.

It is perilous to our souls. For, if we forget our sins, we shall most likely, before we are aware, again fall into them. "'Be not secure about forgiven sin, to add sin to sin." Sin which is but skinned over, bursts out again. It looks to thee dead, and thou thinkest thyself dead to it. If thou relax thy grasp, thou wilt find it but a seeming death. Well is it, if it spring not up again, and, ere thou art aware, slay thee!

But, were it ever so safe to forget forgiven sin, it is not loving, nor humble, nor reverent, nor grateful, nor happy. One who so forgets it, it is too likely, never had any true repentance at all. The bitterness of repentance passes away; repentance itself deepens, when its bitterness is gone. Love replaces fear, not sorrow. We may even have reason to fear pride and wounded self-respect in that very bitterness. Yet it may be right that repentance should have bitterness. Peter "went out, and wept bitterly." "ᵘ It is an evil thing and bitter to have offended the Lord thy God." It is a bitter thing to have lost innocence or purity; to be what God Himself cannot unmake; to have done what God can forgive, but what God's Omnipotence cannot cause to be undone; to have forfeited that to which God called you; to have to begin again; to have done what God must hate, else He would not be God.

But bitterness is not a chief part of repentance. It is rather a part of the punishment which God has annexed to sin than any ingredient of repentance. There will be bitterness enough in Hell, where there

ᵗ Ecclus. v. 5.   ᵘ Jer. ii. 19.

is no grace, no repentance. It is a bitter thing to
discover, for what filth and wretchedness, what a
thing of nothing, what a passing, unsatisfying, degrading pleasure, the soul has parted with God, lost
His favour and grace, destroyed and damned itself,
forfeited Heaven, brought itself down to Hell. It
is a bitter thing for the soul, to see how it has ruined
itself, to have its sins, heaps upon heaps, brought
before its eyes, another, and another, and another,
a whole, endless array of sins, marshalled wherever
it looks. They stand like so many spectres before
it. They shriek in his ears, "Yes, you did me, and
me, and me." The past lies stand up and say, "You
did tell us, and for what? Because you could not
endure a little shame; yet by us you offended God."
Thefts arise and say, "Yes, you did us, and for what
vanities? To trick thyself out with some petty
finery, or improve thy food, or get some petty self-
indulgence for thy taste. It is all gone, but we remain, and by us you offended God." What a hideous band oaths are. The sinner sees them putting
on the angry looks with which he uttered them,
and mocking him with them, and taunting him,
"We did thee no seeming, passing good, yet by us,
thou didst offend God!" Then follow the wrong
jests, the profane jokes, the words which did shock
modesty, or did laugh at innocence, and would make
it ashamed of God's gift of purity, and destroy itself.
These, too, repeat the jibes, and ask the soul, "What
was your gain through us? Through us thou didst
murder innocence and purity and loveliness, which
God had made, in which Christ delighted, which the
Holy Ghost hallowed." Then throng around the soul

Q 2

thoughts and words and acts of vanity, and pride, and conceit, and say to it, "With us thou didst trick thyself out; in us thou didst vaunt thyself and hug thyself and didst hunt for the empty breath of praise, or flattery, or idle compliment, and didst idolize thyself, and seek to outdo others, and didst forget thy God; and what were we? what were we worth?" I have not spoken, my sons, of a yet fouler brood, of which Scripture says, "it is a shame to speak of those things which are done of men in secret." Yet all the foulest sins of the heathen are done now by those who call themselves Christians. Adultery, fornication, uncleanness, lasciviousness, sins done with no eye upon the sinners but the Eye of God and of the holy angels, and of the devils who tempted them and clapped their hands in malicious exultation; or sins which helped to drag others too to the pit; sins of sight, of thought, of memory, of touch. If these have once been admitted by the soul, they come mostly heaps upon heaps, heaps upon heaps, one dragging on another, and that another, until what at first was a mere temptation from without, becomes a habit, seems to be a necessity, and the soul feeds on its daily poison, instead of its "daily Bread." Yet any one such sin is enough to plunge the soul in Hell.

It *is* a bitter thing to have forfeited for such emptinesses or such foulnesses, the grace and love of God. Think what God is, All-good, the Fountain of all Good, all Beauty, all Loveliness, all Wisdom; Who hath in Him all which could be desired, enjoyed, loved. And what was the worth of thy sin, for which thou didst exchange thy God, and sell thy soul to Satan? A misery, when thou hadst done it. Horror, self-reproach, bitterness, self-hatred, the gnawing of conscience, touched by the grace of God, may be great helps towards a deep, self-abasing repentance. With this grace, they may lead to strictness, watchfulness, diligence, in avoiding the borders of sin, "self-revenge[v]," humility in one's self and towards others, and, in its time, zeal against that desolating monster, sin, and adoring amazement at the love and long-suffering of its Redeemer, which so long endured its ingratitude. Without the grace of God, they lead the sinner to still deeper sin: they have made suicides as well as saints. They exist in Hell.

True repentance is a loving sorrow which mourns, for the love of God, that it has offended God. This sorrow ought to live on; yea, it deepens, as God's goodness to the soul deepens. To part with it would be to part with love. For it springs from the Fountain of God's love and tenderness; it was wakened by the tender, reproachful look of Jesus; it was quickened by the Holy Spirit, Who melted the hardness of self-hatred into the subdued sorrow of penitent love.

Deceive not yourselves, my sons, allow not yourselves to be deceived by any one who would tell you that repentance is a bitter, hard, distasteful, irksome way. "It is an evil and bitter thing to have offended the Lord thy God," thy Redeemer, thy Lover, thy tender Father. It is an aweful sight to behold thy sins. But thou hast not thy choice, whether thou wilt see them at all. Thou *must* see them, either here, to lay them all at the Feet of Jesus,

[v] 2 Cor. vii. 11.

that He may cleanse thee from them; or in the Day
of Judgement, never to part with thee, but to drag
thee down to Hell, and torment thee with their hateful sight for ever, deathless as thyself and as God.

It is a bitter thing to know how thou hast sinned;
but repentance is full of sweetness. It flows from
thy Redeemer's wide-open Side, pierced for love of
thee; the Blood, which in thy sins thou despisedst,
yea, (horrible,) didst trample on, gushes out anew
to bedew thee, "cleanse thee," mark thee again with
His sacred Cross, which in thy baptismal innocence
He put on thee, though now it is the Cross of Blood.
He Who was prodigal of His Blood for love of thee,
is careful of thy tears, which thou sheddest in penitent sorrow, for love of Him. Angels watch over
thee, and rejoice over thee. True, loving penitence
has the blessing of well-nigh all those beatitudes
whose wondrous fulness has so often amazed us. It
wreathes in one the "Blessed are they that mourn,"
"Blessed are the poor in spirit," "Blessed are the
meek," "Blessed are they that do hunger and thirst
after righteousness;" and it holds them over thee
for thy future crown and diadem; yea, and that other
blessing which thou mightest have thought for ever
forfeited, "Blessed are the pure in heart,"—this, too,
though as yet fainter and dimmer and higher, still
hangs over thee; for He has said, " What God has
cleansed, that call not thou common," even thyself,
cleansed by His Sacred Blood.

My sons, you *would* have this lot; you *would* escape Hell; you *would* gain Heaven. Be not scared
back from repentance. They have not tasted repentance with the edge of their lips, who speak of

it as bitter. Bitter it is to have sinned; bitter to
have undone thyself; bitter to have been ungrateful to such great love. But this is past. It is that
thou mayest not add bitterness to bitterness, that
God calls thee to repentance. Bitter it is to be
haunted by the memory of thy sins. If thou wouldest not be dogged by them, face them; look at them;
abjure them; repent them; and they will haunt thee
thus no more, or a hearty "Lord have mercy" will
set thee at peace from them. Bitter is sin, bitter is
its every fruit; but not bitter is the heart's true sorrow for sin. This is full of sweetness; for it is full
of the love of Jesus, and pours it over the wounded
soul. Gnawing remorse, or loving, sweet, soothing
sorrow! One thou must have, if thou hast sinned.
Remorse, the foretaste of the sharp, fiery fangs of
the undying worm; or loving sorrow, the herald of
the never-ending joys of forgiven love.

Would you learn this loving sorrow? It is the
gift of God. Do this, then. I will tell you only
simple things. There are harder things for hardy
souls. But these shall be simple, easy, what will
hinder no work, over-tax no feebleness, wear no
health.

Loving penitence is a great, precious gift of God.
Ask it, then, of Him. "Ask, and ye shall receive."
The Church often puts it into our mouths. Again
and again we ask Him not only to forgive us our
sins, but to "give us true repentance," to "give us
hearts to love and dread Him." Make the most
of these prayers; be very careful to use *them*. Ask
Him earnestly, continuously. He has pledged His
own truth to you, that He will give it you.

· ·But then do not act contrary to your prayers. It would be to act contrary to your prayers, in thought, word, or deed, to make light of sin. To. make light of sin is to make light of Hell-fire, and of the Blood of Jesus. For sin cost the life of Jesus, and unrepented sin, with the sinner, is the fuel of Hell-fire. ·

Now sins were often done in buoyancy of spirits, amid jollity and gaiety of heart. And people who will not make a mock·of ·sin, will let themselves go over in thought the pleasant scenes which surrounded it. Go not back in thought to anything connected with your sin. Shun the whole coast of sin. Its breath is death. Think you that S. Peter could ever speak of the coldness of the night of his Lord's Passion, and of his warming himself by the fire in the High Priest's palace? So neither do you, if you would preserve loving penitence, ever go back in thought to things, though sinless, if connected with thy sin. Think not that you may dwell safely, in thought, on the words of flattery or of love, and keep your soul away from the sin which followed. Before thou art aware, thou wilt have lost the fineness of thy sorrow for thy sin. ·

Avoid levity. Levity is not cheerfulness.· It is mostly the veil of a heart-ache, if it spring not from mere emptiness ; and it ends in· a heart-ache.

One more, very solemn thing. Do not put away, as gloomy, any personal fear, even of being lost, or of death. If it comes often, God has some work for it to do in your soul. He sends it, or (which is one) He lets it come. He sends the fear into your soul, that you may have no cause to fear. He sends you fear, to take .away real fear. Let it have its way ;

only cast yourself, with it, at the Feet of Jesus, and He will hush you more tenderly than your mother could.

These are only things which you are not to do. I have only as yet told you one thing to do; to pray earnestly for this loving sorrow.

- The dread of Hell brought you, probably, to repentance. Shrink not from thinking of Hell. No one, probably, who thought much of it, ever fell into it. A poor woman who had its fires, day and night, before her eyes, and despaired of her salvation, and lost, for the time, the power to pray, was asked, in order to shew to herself that she was penitent, "Would you still commit a sin?" "No one *could* commit sin," was the answer, "with the sight of that place before her, as I have now." Think, morning by morning, of the four last things, Death, Judgement, Heaven, Hell, and that thou art one day nearer to thine everlasting abode. And by God's mercy, thine everlasting abode will be with Jesus.

But think of thy sins with the love of Jesus. Do not think only even of the great truths of faith, that a ransom has been paid for us sinners, that we are justified by faith; but think of Jesus, speak to Jesus, pour out thy soul to Jesus, as thine own Redeemer, thy Friend, thy God, thy All. Live much by His Cross: the atoning drops will fall upon thee. Twine thyself round it with Magdalene. Look up to His forgiving Eye, and say to Him, "Lord, I *did* crucify Thee; I drove those hard nails into Thee; my sins twisted those thorns around Thee; yea, by my sins I have crucified Thee again; worse yet, I despised Thy Blood shed for me. Yet despise me not, O

Lord, despise me not; but wash me, cleanse me, keep me, like the penitent thief, by Thee."

Then, day by day, take all slights and unkindnesses and crosses, all pains and sufferings of body or spirit, as from thy Saviour's chastening Hand. What are we, that we should think much of slights, who deserve to "[w]rise to shame and everlasting contempt?" Humility and penitent love will grow together, if we take all good from God, as deserving it not, all evil with a " we indeed justly."

But if thou shouldest cling to our Lord as present to thy mind on the Cross, how much more when He comes to be present to thee, to give His Body and Blood to be " verily and indeed received by" thee; when He comes, as we pray, to "cleanse thy sinful body by His Body, and to wash thy soul in His most precious Blood." Here chiefly tell Him; "Lord, I am not worthy, I am not worthy that Thou shouldest come under my roof; yet Thou Who didst not disdain to lie with the brute cattle, Who despisedst not the harlot coming to Thee and touching Thee, despise not me, but take away my sin, the utter sinner[x]."
Then, when thou hast received His Holy Body and His Life-giving Blood, cry to Him with a yet deeper heart's cry, " O Lord God, Lamb of God, that takest away the sins of the world, have mercy upon me."

Once more. As God has shewn mercy upon thy soul, have mercy upon others. He who said to S. Peter, " When thou art converted, strengthen thy brethren," says it, in our little measure, to each of us. Only let it be in humility, and in allowed ways. At least, pray for sinners who forget God, with thyself.

[w] Dan. xii. 2.   [x] Bp. Andrewes' Devotions.

I spoke of life-long penitence; I might have better said, a "life-short" penitence. Short, at the longest, were the life of man. Too little to requite the love of God were the love and service of a whole life. More or less of thy time of service has already been cut short by thy service of sin. Short as life is, a life-long service and devotion were something precious. For it is a whole, all which a creature could offer to its Creator. But when the first, best years have been wasted in thoughtlessness or sin; when thou hast already spoiled thine offering, and hast no whole burnt-offering to make to Him; when thou hast, if not the dregs and refuse, yet only the impaired residue of thy life to offer, then to speak of a "life-long" offering of any sort seems almost a mockery. Yet it means,—offer to God the whole which thou canst, and God will accept that whole, though it be but a short fragment of this poor, short span of our life. Only, since thou canst no longer give Him all, let thy heart sorrow to Him till thou see Him, that thou hast so wasted His gifts, and now canst only offer Him what is so little, so poor, so marred by thy sin. God does not ask of thee suffering. He asks of thee only sorrow, that thou didst displease Him, sorrow for this brief time, into which He will infuse calmness, and peace, and rest. By loving grief for sin, He will soothe all other grief; He will, amid thy sorrow, give thee many a thrill of joy, more transporting far than this world's highest, purest joys; He will gather thy tears and turn them into pearls in the Heavenly crown which He prepareth for thee; and when thou beholdest His forgiving Countenance, how wilt thou wonder that thy few tears of penitence should have "quenched for thee the fires of hell;" that thy brief mourning should so be comforted; that thy few brief sighs should be turned into endless Halleluias; that thy passing sorrow, stamped and hallowed by thy Saviour's Blood, should be thy passport to thy Lord's own joy!

y Tert. de Pœnit., c. xii. p. 349, Oxf. Tr.   See p. 766, note m.

SERMON XIII.

DAVID IN HIS SIN AND HIS PENITENCE.

PSALM li. 4.

" Against Thee, Thee only, have I sinned."

A BLOOD-STAINED saint! Surely, among all the mysteries of nature or of revelation there is but one, impenetrably, unfathomably, dark; of which reason has no solution, in which faith itself can see no light, except by looking beyond it to its God. And yet it surrounds us, presses upon us, is in us, of us; well is it if, by the grace of our God, it masters us not! All those mysteries, of which men have spoken so boldly, are light and light-giving. The mysteries as to God, what are they but the unfolding to us of something of His Being, Which it shall be the bliss of Heaven to behold? There, the darkness is but the dazzling effulgence of His light. " [b] Thou clothest Thyself with light as with a garment." All which we see is light. It is the light itself which, in this life, shrouds as yet the glories of His Deity. Mysteries as to God are but glimpses from His ineffable light. All from God is light; all which is darkness is from ourselves,

[a] Preached at Great S. Mary's, Cambridge. Lent, 1864.
[b] Ps. civ. 2.

The one dreadful, unfathomable mystery is, sin.
God created beings out of His Infinite love, that they
might be for ever increasingly blessed in His love.
He created all good, in grace. He offered Himself
to their love; to the heavenly spirits, unveiled; to
Adam, known, believed, but unseen. He willed to
be chosen by the free-will of each. We know the
result. His creatures could behold the All-Perfect,
face to face, and could say, " I will not have Thee."
This choice is sin. This choice every deadly sin has
more or less consciously repeated. The creature re-
jects the Infinite Good, which is God, for something
out of God. Satan chose to be first in hell, rather
than be all-but-first in heaven.

But since sin is this unutterable mystery, no wonder that we sinners misjudge well-nigh every thing
connected with it. We weigh with unjust balances.
The subjects of men's apologies have been those
characters in Holy Scripture whom God rejected.
The objects of their censure have been those whom
God approved.

Strangely have Nathan's words been fulfilled, century after century: " Thou hast given great occasion
to the enemies of the Lord to blaspheme." The
heathen taunted us of old, " Lo how these Christians
follow innocency, extol faith, venerate religion, teach
chastity, whose princes appear to have committed
homicides and adulteries. David himself, of whose
line ye say Christ chose to be born, sang of his homicides and adulteries. What can the disciples be,
who have these for their masters [c] !" Modern blasphemy delights to blacken " the man after God's

[c] In S. Ambros. *Apol. David* ii. c. 3.

own heart." It *was* a terrific fall, terrible as well as piteous. In his youth, noble, chivalrous, generous, dauntless, tender to his relentless persecutor, " a heart of fire," to whom the love of Jonathan was wonderful, passing the love of women [d]. He, so tender, so forbearing; he whose heart smote him, that he had a little shamed the enemy who sought his life; who passionately lamented Saul too, as lovely and pleasant; he who so hated wrong, who was so moved for the poor man's ewe-lamb, could this be he who had his own gallant soldier slain? He, so blameless in youth, could he, when life had begun to set, be stained so miserably through the passions of youth? I have said nothing. For I have spoken of nature only.

His inner life we know from his Psalms. What, when we know, that in God he laid him down to sleep [e], to God he woke [f]; God he set always before him [g]; his eyes ever turned toward his God [h]? He knew the nothingness of all fleeting things, even the fullest store which God Himself could bestow in this life; and had chosen no created thing, but his God, for his portion, and the beatific vision of God, beyond the grave, for his inheritance [i], and meantime the sweet familiar intercourse with God, which God, he says, bestows on them that fear Him [k]. His royal cares hindered not his meditating in the law of his God, day and night [l]. He delighted to be humble before God, yet thought not that it was humility. He knew the frailty of nature, and prayed that pre-

[d] 2 Sam. i. 26.　　[e] Ps. iv. 8.　　[f] Ib. iii. 5.　　[g] Ib. xvi. 8.
　　[h] Ib. xxv. 15.　　　　　[i] Ib. xvii. 14, 15. xvi. 5.
　　[k] Ib. xxv. 14.　　　　　[l] Ib. i. 2.

sumptuous sins should not rule over him[m]. He had reverent sympathy with the sufferings of his Redeemer, yet to come; he felt them as his own[n]. All his Psalms bear witness to his one fixed will, that God, and no created thing out of God, should be his deliberate choice.

Yet these too were gifts of ordinary grace. What, when God had chosen him, not like Balaam, as the unwilling instrument of prophecy, but to attune his soul to the secret inspirations of His Spirit, that the Spirit of the Lord should speak by him, and His word be on his tongue[o], and should pour forth by him that wondrous, ever-varying, melody of thoughts from God to God, which have expressed the inmost longings of the soul for nearly 3000 years, which Christian thought could unfold, but has not yet exhausted; for it was God's word through man! God speaks to us in all His word; through David's Psalms we speak in God's own words to God. An inspired writer, and so deeply inspired (O horrible!), for one brief moment an adulterer and a murderer! Surely nothing can weary the condescension of our God, or the overwhelmingness of His grace, or the perseveringness of His love, Who chose to be called the Son of *him* who had so fallen, Who, obliterating what He gave him the grace to repent of, still calls " the man after His own heart" him who " did right in His eyes, save in the matter of Uriah the Hittite[p]." It is an intense mystery of sin, that man should admit so black a spot, where all around was so fair; it is an intenser mystery of God's love, that He

[m] Ib. xix. 13. [n] Espec. Ps. xxii.
[o] 2 Sam. xxiii. 2. [p] 1 Kgs. xv. 5.

should have arrested so black a spot from spreading and overcasting and infecting the whole. Yet now too, those conversant with human souls know something of that aweful ever-watchful malice of Satan; how he delights, if he can, to precipitate a person, if but once, into a sin, foreign from the whole history of his soul before or after, and leave it stained and blighted with a sin foreign to its nature. The self-same cause is probably the occasion in both, false security. David says it of himself: "q I said, I shall never be moved. Thou didst turn Thy face from me and I was troubled." The Apostle says: "r He that thinketh he standeth, let him take heed, lest he fall." To think himself secure is to fall at the next step. David was secure, careless, desired, hoped that it would not prove sin, that Bathsheba might be free. Then he had to give up his passion or his sin. He did not abide in his sin. She came, she went; outwardly he went on as before. Then came the dread of involving her in a disgraced death, and of his own shame. Then the attempt to deceive him whom he had injured, and lastly, the slaying him with the sword of the children of Ammon.

David's was the worse death. To part with the soul is the death of the body; the death of the soul is to part with God. It is to part with the life of grace, the light of grace, the union with God. It is to lose God. David, had he so continued, must have been like Cain, or like him who had the outward likeness of David's act, in that he sold the innocent Blood to His enemies, and " s went to his own place."

q Ps. xxx. 6, 7.　　　r 1 Cor. x. 12.　　　s Acts ii. 25.

R

In one way, the sin was irremediable. It changed David's eternal condition. It is the terrific character of sin, that, though it may be, *as though* it had never been, God has made it to be self-contradictory, that what has been, should not have been. What we have been, *that*, in all eternity, we must have been. God can forgive sin; He can be to us as if we had never sinned; perhaps He could, (although He does not), obliterate the memory of sin in His forgiven ones; He can overwhelm it with the rich exuberance of His grace and love; He can (thanks be to Him) transform ourselves; He can and does re-create us, so that the sin should leave no trace on the soul, save that the soul hates it with perfect hatred, and, through the grace of God, will love, with the whole compass of its being, Him Who forgave it. His redeeming, forgiving love, is our deepest joy here; to love Him Who loved, and, loving, redeemed us, will be a joy of all eternity. God can re-make us. One thing Almighty love cannot undo. He cannot now (since it is self-contradictory) make it, that the great penitent never should have sinned, as he did sin. David, like the blest Robber, the first-fruits of the Redeeming Blood of Jesus, is, through those same merits, glorious with the indwelling glory of God; yet his soul, doubtless one of the highest of much-forgiven penitents, is still a soul, which, by two insulated acts, broke, to the uttermost, God's most sacred laws of purity and of love.

How then was he restored? Grace had been sinned away. He was left to his natural self. He had still those habits of mind, short of grace, which had been formed by grace. He had still the strong sense of

justice, and hatred of the very sins by which he
had fallen, which responded so quickly and so indig-
nantly against cruelty and wrong, when called out
by Nathan's parable. He must have had remorse.
He was a man still; the wreck of a noble, ardent,
generous man. The sight of the accomplice of his
sin, who had been the occasion of his further sin,
must often have recalled to him with agony, *whose*
she once had been. With the news of the war there
must have flashed before his eyes that phantom-form
of his noble mighty one [t], ranked among his [u] thirty-
seven faithful warriors, placed where the battle was
hottest, fighting for him, forsaken by his orders,
hemmed in, faithful unto death to him, the faithless.
Remorse is the fruit of the most condescending love
of our God. Neglected or stifled, it is the last grace
by which God would save the soul; it is the first, by
which God would prepare the soul, which has forfeited grace, to return to Him. Precious, inestimable,
in God's mercy almost inextinguishable grace, which
God is so unwilling to withdraw, because it is the
last hold which keeps His redeemed, while they
are looking over and ready to cast themselves into
the pit of hell. God sitteth within the soul, as its
Judge; His voice speaks, and with power; He turns
the soul in upon itself; the undeadened soul is its
own incorruptible accuser, the witness against itself,
its own executioner. Go where man will, he cannot
leave himself; his guilty conscience is himself. If

---

[t] " I cannot sleep," said an old Arab, who when very young
had slain a man for the sake of the horse which he rode, "I cannot sleep without seeing the grey mare and her rider before me."
Tristram, Land of Moab, pp. 331, 332. [u] 2 Sam. xxiii. 39.

even love is extinct or asleep in the soul, it tells the soul, "Thou hast degraded thyself; thou art become like the beasts that perish; thou art not what thou wert, what thou shouldest be, what thou once longedst to be." If faith, though now an inoperative belief, is not altogether lost, it says, "Thou hast deserved hell;" and the cowering, tormented soul is forced to own, "I have."

But remorse, although a first step to repentance, is not repentance. For remorse centres in a man's self. It dreads the temporal penalty of its sin; it dreads more or less distinctly its deserved doom; it sees in the distance the fires of hell; it writhes at the thought of itself. While it is mere remorse, it does not turn to God. Cain had remorse, and accused God; Esau had remorse for his profane sale of his birthright, and purposed to regain it by fratricide; Ahab had remorse, did some great deeds of humble penitence, but died in his pride and rebellion; Judas had remorse, but hanged himself and went to his own place.

And so God, in His love, sent to David the prophet, the very sight of whom might recall to him the mercies of God in the past, His promises for the future, and the memory of those days of innocent service and bright aspirations, to which the soul, overtaken by sin, looks back with such sorrowful yearning. Nathan was the prophet who had accepted his purpose of building the temple, and when this was deferred, for the blood which had of necessity been shed in war, gave him those promises, which culminated in our Lord[v]. How often now too.

[v] 2 Sam. vii. 1-17.

will the sight of one, known in innocency, strike
through the soul with the piercing—it may be, by
God's grace, converting—thought, "What was I
once? what might I have been? what am I now?"
You know how, by enlisting his better feelings, Nathan predisposed him for grace, and then heaped on
the head of the convicted sinner those coals of fire,
the accumulated forecoming mercies of his God, Who
had daily loaded him with benefits, and would have
given him more than all which his heart could crave,
had he sought it from Him, not against Him. The
heavy stone, which lay on the choked dead heart,
was rolled away; the dead was alive again, the two-
edged sword of God's word, Judgement and Mercy,
had slain him to himself, that he might live to God.
The awakened soul burst out in those two words [w],
"I have sinned against the Lord."

Then was remorse absorbed, transformed, spiritua-
lised into penitent love. The relation of the creature
to its Creator was restored. I! Thou! All else had
vanished before him, as it shall at the Day of Judgement. He who had foretold the good to David's
house, had now foretold its woe. "[x] The sword shall
never depart from thy house." David is as though
he heard it not. One thought filled his soul; one
sight alone he saw. "I have betrayed, been faithless to, have sinned against my God." That thought,
that sight, never departed from him. His first gush
of penitence lived on more vividly in his great penitential Psalm. "Against Thee, Thee only have I
sinned." What? had he not sinned against Uriah?
Yes! Penitence does not extenuate guilt, but it sees

[w] חטאת ליהוה   [x] 2 Sam. xii. 10.

it all, where, in contrast with the All-Perfect Holiness, it looks most terrible, in God. His brave
soldier was dead. Reparation there was none. The
sword of the sons of Ammon had removed to Abraham's bosom the faithful Hittite, adopted into the
one family of God. He does not say *as to* whom he
had sinned, but *to* Whom; to Whom he was amena-
ble, Who is the centre at which all sin is aimed, as
all good is directed towards Him; Whose love the
sword, which slew Uriah, wounded; Who Alone could
condemn him, because He was sinless; against Whom
Alone his own special evil lay, because He was All-
Good. It was nothing to him, although the whole
world, his fellow-sinners, should lessen his sin to
him; that they should make those pleas, so readily
made for the great; that they should not dare to condemn, being themselves self-condemned as sinners.
The whole world, with its praise or blame, its acquit-
tal or its condemnation, is as if it were not, an utter
blank to the soul which, face to face, stands before
its Maker and its God. "Against Thee have I sinned, Who madest me in Thine own image; against
Thee Who, in all eternity, didst love me infinitely,
and didst make me, because Thou lovedst me; against
Thee, Who didst will that I should be a little created
likeness of Thy perfections; not a microcosm, but a
little god upon earth, goddized by the presence of
God. Against Thee, Who all my life long didst tend
me with such individual love, as if in all Thy creation Thou hadst none besides to love; Who didst enlighten, engladden, engrace, inspiritualise me; Who
didst place, yea hide me in Thine own Presence,
and admit me to the secret intercourse of a friend.

Against Thee, such in Thyself, such towards me, I have sinned."

And what is sin? What is it to own that one has sinned? What is it but to own one's self guilty of the basest, blackest, shamefullest ingratitude, which, were it shewn to a fellow-sinner, one could never lift up one's head again? What is it, but to charge our God with want of wisdom or of love, that He forbade us those things, which we did against His All-Holy Will? What is it, but to wish that God were other than He is, less holy, less good, less just, less righteous, less perfect? What is it but to wish to unmake God, as He is, and to make us a god, such as we are, who could take pleasure in our foulnesses, and in us, so foul? "Thou thoughtest," saith God [y], "that I was even such an one as thyself." Wilful sin is to tell God, the only Good, to His Face, "On Thine own terms I will have none of Thee. I prefer this and this and this to Thee."

Bitter it is for a sinner to awaken from his stupor, and to own all this to himself and to his God. And thence all those lying excuses to hide the black spot, if one could, to cover it with our half-transparent hands, and tell God, "It is not there: He was mistaken in calling it sin, we did but follow our nature, such as He made us."

Bitter it is to own that we have parted with God, unfitted ourselves for His Holy Presence, defiled our souls, lied to our consciences, mocked at grace, despised the glorious end of our being, condemned ourselves to everlasting severance from God, exchanged the goodness of our God for Satan's hateful mastery.

[y] Ps. l. 21.

And since it is so hard and bitter a thing to own
this, therefore it is the greatest grace to own without
reserves, without excuses, not hiding, like Adam, our
sin[z], how we have worse than fallen from heaven to
hell; for "better were it, free from sin, to enter hell,
than, defiled by sin, to enter the kingdom of Heaven."
Better were it! for, with God, hell were heaven;
without God, heaven were hell.

And so those words, "I have sinned against the
Lord," had such transforming power. For it was
the grace of God, translating the soul from darkness
to light, from the power of Satan unto God. The
closed heart was opened; the corroding poison was
cast out; the soul was of one mind with God; the
love of God made the memory of sin a channel of
Divine Grace.

But this was the beginning of the renewed life of
the soul, not the end. It issued in a constant longing for a re-creation, a reverent fear springing from
the sense of what it had deserved, an earnest craving
for a more thorough cleansing from every stain or
spot of sin, a thirst for the purging by the atoning
Blood, an unvarying sight of his forgiven sinfulness, spreading far and wide from the core of original sin; a longing to do free noble generous service,
and all, from God to God, from God's re-creating,
renewing, enfreedoming, ennobling grace.

A little of David's soul we see in his acceptance
of God's thickening chastisements, his meek bearing
of Shimei's curses, his accepting them as the voice
of God declaring his deserts, his prompt forgiveness.
It is as if he had heard the words, "Forgive, as thou

[z] Job xxxi. 33.

wouldest be forgiven." It is one offering of himself on each occasion to God, "Burn, cut here, and spare for ever." He was "very wroth" at Ammon's violation of nature; but he was still. *He* had been an adulterer. Absalom fled after his fratricide. David restored him. He charged his captains to deal tenderly with the parricide son, before whom he had fled. He himself had been a murderer. Where was the fiery spirit, which had so resented Nabal's churlishness? The sword, which slew Uriah, had, through God's grace, pierced his own soul. Well might the poor father wish he had died for the unnatural son, whom his own example had taught deadly offences against purity and the life of man, and who, as far as men knew, had died impenitent in his sin, and, if so, had died the second death. The broken and contrite heart cannot crush an offence against itself.

But far more deeply do David's Psalms lay open his inmost soul. For they are the words, which God the Holy Ghost gave him, the " unutterable groanings," which the Holy Spirit embodied in words, which have been the voice of penitents ever since, and shall be, until the number of God's elect shall be accomplished, the vacant thrones in His many mansions shall be filled, and the sounds of penitence shall be transfigured into the jubilee of forgiven love. " Unutterable " were those " groanings," though uttered. We hear the words; we know their meaning; they expressed our poor penitence; but there is a depth of sorrow below, which human heart has perhaps never fathomed, which, when we have learned something of God-given sorrow for sin, is still be-

yond the compass of our souls. The words express
our sorrow; they teach us how to express it to God;
but there is a deep base of mourning sorrow which
our poor voices do not fill. It is the Divine Dove,
teaching the penitent, through the great penitent,
how to moan for sin. It tells us that sorrow for
having displeased our good loving God is, in this
life, inexhaustible. We learn it, as we learn every
grace, by opening our souls to receive from God what
in its whole compass is unattainable.

And this sorrow was not that first stunning crushing sense of sin, which the erring soul has on its first
conversion. The deepest of David's psalms of penitence express the sorrow for forgiven sin. Once he
tells us, how it was with him, while the sense of his
guilt was upon him, ere he confessed it to God.
"While I kept silence, my bones wore away through
my roaring all the day long. For day and night Thy
hand was heavy upon me; my life's sap was changed
into the drought of summer[a]." But those wearying
groanings, those nightly tears, with which, night by
night, he made his bed to swim; that eye-consuming
grief[b]; that suffering within and without, when the
hand of God pressed him down and his own sins passed as it were over his prostrated soul[c]; and he was
"writhed," "bowed[d]," "congealed[e]," "crushed[e],"
"sightless[f]," "strengthless[f]," "fleshless[g]," "scorched[h]," "withered[i]," "heart-stricken[k]," were, when
he was forgiven; he had known his forgiveness from

---

[a] Ps. xxxii. 3, 4.   [b] Ps. vi. 6, 7, 8.   [c] Ps. xxxviii. 2, 4.
[d] Ib. 6.   [e] Ib. 9. Heb.   [f] Ib. 11. Heb.   [g] Ps. cii. 5.
[h] Ps. xxxviii. 8. Heb.; cii. 3.   [i] Ps. vi. 3. Heb.; cii. 4.
[k] Ps. cii. 4.

the voice of God Himself by His Prophet. Yet more. David had been secure once, and had fallen terribly. He never was secure again. He had a reverent fear that he might lose God. He could bear the thought, because God sustained him, and he clung to his God. Still the thought, the prayer was there, "Cast me not, fling me not away from standing in Thy presence." Once, but for God's overwhelming grace, he had been lost for ever. Had the messenger of death been sent then, when Uriah was slain, before even the fulfilled sin had brought its remorse! Like the penitent of the Gospel, after his Father had received him, he still said, "I am no more worthy to be called Thy son." Still he prayed, "For Thy tender mercy's sake, fling me not away." David knew of that place, where there was no remembrance of God [1]. He had known God, as his own God; he knew what it had been to be without God; and he dreaded, as the most intolerable of all agonies, the endless loss of God and of the beatific vision of God, hopeless for ever.

Then David knew the "stain" of sin. O that deep, ingrained, intolerable, ineffaceable stain of sin, which would whole seas incarnadine, which nothing can wash out but the sacred Blood of Christ. Yet this too not at once. The sin is forgiven at once: the eternal penalty is remitted, but its effects remain, "[m] scourges in our sides and thorns in our eyes," which God in His mercy leaves to goad us on to more devoted exertion; spectres of past sins, which haunt us; hateful thoughts, their genuine offspring, ready to storm our momentary consent; a chill cold mist

[1] Ps. vi. 5.   [m] Jos. xxiii. 13.

clinging to us, pressing in upon us and numbing our energies for God, weaknesses, confusion of motives, tongue-tied cowardice in the cause of God. And since evil is only displaced by grace, he prays for a re-creation. "[n] Create in me a new heart." He uses the word, whereby God speaks of the creation of the heaven and the earth. For greater and more joyous is the re-creation of one sinner that repenteth, than of the whole sidereal system. "Wash me mightily from my sin; let a mighty perennial stream of mercy wash away the mightiness of transgression."

But pardon, cleansing, justifying, renewing, sufficed not David; they content not the penitent. Whoso has been upon the brink of Hell, whoso knows that he has deserved to be flung away from God's presence, whoso has known the value of a soul by the peril of his own, would not be saved alone, if indeed any, except in some extremity of long-suffering, could be saved alone.

And so, with that re-creation, he prays for that promptness of heart, ever impulsive, or rather grace-impelled, to princely[o], generous service, which should teach sinners the ways of God, and be saved with a multitude of returning souls.

Such was, in summary, David's penitence, a restful, never-resting sorrow, for the love of God, that it had displeased God; self-mistrustful, God-trusting; ever longing to be cleansed more and more by the Atoning Blood, to be re-created, renewed by the Divine Spirit, ever thirsting for the salvation of sinners, that his fellows in sin might be his fellow-penitents. Strange contrast with our smooth ways of would-be

[n] Ps. li. 10. ברא   [o] Ib. 14. Heb.

repentance, which tells God in an easy way, that it has done what it ought not, and so makes it up with God, "[p] and goeth its way, and straightway forgetteth what manner of man it was." Which then was the right? Judge your own selves. Natural is it, to shrink from the sight of remembered sin. For it has a countenance more terrible than Hell. Natural were it, if to forget it were to efface it. Yet I speak not now of grace or revelation; I ask which was truest to our better nature, to our human feelings? Picture to thyself one who was to thee as thine own soul, who had loved thee, yearned and watched over thee with the love of a tenderest mother, and, I say not, picture thyself (thou couldest not do it), but picture every ingratitude shewn towards her, her children suffering every evil of soul and body at the hands of him, whom, together with them, she had ever tenderly cherished! Suppose such an one fully forgiven, overwhelmed with fresh love. Could he forget what he had done? Could he, in fullest, most undoubting possession of her love, not reproach himself the more, not repent the more? What were the love of the tenderest mother to the tender yearning love of Almighty God? Thy mother bore thee. God, in His eternal love, created thee for Himself, for His love. Thy mother might die for thee, she could not redeem thee; too precious is the price of thy soul [q]. God gave His Son to be incarnate and to die for thee, as much as if in the whole world there had been none beside, for whom to be crucified. God cared for thee day by day; day by day, and hour by hour, thy Saviour interceded; yea at this moment He inter-

[p] S. James i. 24. [q] Ps. xlix. 7, 8.

cedeth for thee. God the Holy Ghost ever warned thee against thy sin, never wearied of knocking at thy heart.

This is He, against Whom we sinners sinned. If our sin ever injured another, was ever committed with another, by word or deed, they were His sons and daughters, against whom we sinned : in them we sinned against Him. It is He Who says, "[r] When ye sin so against the brethren—ye sin against Christ." Men speak of David's sin. Might not the faithful prophet rise up in the midst of this church, and, to any one who had injured another's soul, say more terrifically, "Thou art the man." The murder of the body may be but the passport to heaven. The murder of the soul is Satan's own act, the plunging into Hell. Have we love? Have we fear? Have we hearts, that they should not break at wounding such love, with the crushing weight of such guiltiness?

We have been wiser than God. We found it joyous to dwell on the goodness of our God, and the love of Christ, and the sweet communion through the Spirit, and we thought that the love of Christ would alone constrain men to love Him, and we shrank from contemplating the horrors of hell. And so the unpreached doctrine slipped out of men's practical Creeds, and we are startled to find that the suppressed doctrine was denied, imperilled, though, in God's mercy, not yet forfeited. And we have luke-warm repentance, and easy ways, and tampering with sin, and opiates for the conscience, and stuntedness in spiritual growth, and giant thank-

[r] 1 Cor. viii. 12.

lessness. We have a sensual, debased population, and hard rocky hearts against our brethren's cry and need.

Fear of Hell drives men to repentance; fear of Hell quickens repentance, for it intensifies the love for the Redeemer. Never will men feel the all-but infinite evil and hatefulness of sin, save in sight of Hell and of their Redeemer from Hell. Not for any slight cause did God become Man. Not for any slight cause were those aweful sufferings, which exsuded those drops of Blood, or called forth that loud Cry upon the Cross. God, become Man to die for men, and that unutterable woe, are aweful counterparts.

Let not men deceive you in the Name of God. Trust God with His own creation. Think if there is any way, in which that aweful truth of the eternity of woe could have been taught, in which God has not taught it. Think Who revealed the sinner's hell, Whose lips, full of grace, spoke of its being better never to have been born[s], of the whole body being cast into hell[t]; Who bid us fear Him which is able to destroy both body and soul in hell[u]; Who told us so often of the furnace of fire and the outer darkness where is weeping and gnashing of teeth[v]; Who warned us of losing our souls[w], Who spake of *their* worm and *their* fire, their own special suffering as undying and unextinguishable[x];—and think whether He or man would deceive you.

---

[s] S. Matth. xxvi. 24.   [t] Ib. v. 29, 30; xviii. 8.

[u] Ib. x. 28; S. Luke xii. 4.   [v] S. Matth. xiii. 42, 50, &c. viii. 12, &c.   [w] Ib. xvi. 26. S. Mark viii. 36.

[x] S. Mark ix. 44, 46, 48. cf. Isa. lxvi. 24. See "Litany of our Lord's Warnings," by the Rev. J. Keble.

Men accuse God, while they flatter Him. They call it blasphemy against the love of God to say that He could sentence any to eternal woe. It is against Thee, our Redeemer, that they renew the accusation of Thine enemies on earth, "Thou blasphemest." For Thou didst teach it us. And if Thou, the Truth, the true Love, Eternal Love, deceivedst not, then men who say that Thou taughtest pious frauds for our good, that Thou didst use in ambiguous senses, side by side, the self-same word of "everlasting life" and "everlasting fire," knowing or ignorant that there was no fire which lasts for ever, blaspheme Thee. Forgive them, Lord, Who forgavest Thine executioners.

No, my brother, my son, bow your minds for this little while to the intensity of this dread mystery. Dare to look at Hell, and read there our own deserts, and how God must have loved thy free love and choice of Himself, that, at the risk of losing thee, He endowed thee with that nobility of choice, to choose Himself.

Gaze on the Blood-stained Form, that meek Eye of love, those outstretched racked arms on Calvary; hark to that loud piercing cry of superhuman agony, "My God, My God, why hast Thou forsaken Me?" But that thou mayest understand what man can imagine of that dread Agony, the blackness of sin and of its ingratitude, look down on hell. The thought of both, of Him Who saved thee, and from what He saved thee, will by His grace, be the best preservative against deadly sin.

If thou hast fallen grievously, there thou wilt learn the black hatefulness of thine own deadly sin,

for which God could choose no other lot; there thou
wilt learn the infinity of thy Redeemer's love; there,
to cling closer to His Cross; there, to bear thankfully the little sufferings which He lays upon thee;
there, to dread the slightest incursion of sin; there,
to shake off this apathy which numbs us, that we
know not what is burning love for souls or fiery
zeal or self-sacrificing piety, and pass by on the
other side, while our brother perishes; there thou
wilt learn that it is more than the whole world,
yea than a thousand worlds, to be His instrument
of saving, even if it be but one soul; there wilt
thou learn to ask of Him Who will give it thee,
true repentance, meek reverence, loving faith; and
He Who died to save thee will extinguish for thee
the fires of Hell; and that aweful doom from which
He saved thee will but deepen the depth of the
God-given, God-sustained, God-enabled love, wherewith thou wilt eternally love, eternally praise, Him
Who loved thee, and gave Himself for thee.

SERMON XIV[a].

2 Cor. xii. 7-9.

"There was given to me a thorn in the flesh, a messenger of Satan to buffet me, lest I should be exalted above measure. For this thing I besought the Lord thrice, that it might depart from me. And He said unto me, My grace is sufficient for thee; for My strength is made perfect in weakness."

TRULY there is no bound, no condition, no restriction to the transforming power of the grace of God, except His poor stubborn creature's will to receive it. Temptation, the instrument of our destruction, converted into a channel of Divine grace! Inward shame from shameful temptation, the earnest and worker of glory in God! Satan's malice, attracting for us Divine love! Human weakness, the perfecting of Divine strength! Strange marvels of our fallen but redeemed world! O the wondrous condescension of our God, Who not only dwells in us, the lowest of His creatures, but Who makes that which is the most debased and debasing in us, that which is most contrary to His holiness, most alien from His Will, most rebellious against His Goodness, the means of

[a] Preached at S. Giles', Oxford. Lent, 1860.

our restoration, the receptacle of His Grace, the in-
viter of His Presence! He hallows us through that
which is unholy in us; He makes us the more His
sons through that which is most rebellious in us;
He perfects us through that which is most imperfect
in us. S. Paul, imitating our Lord's threefold prayer
in His Agony, besought the Lord thrice, that the
cup of his temptation might depart from him; and
then, at last, as the Angel appeared from Heaven to
our Lord, strengthening Him, so, on S. Paul's third
prayer, not an Angel, but the Lord of the Angels appeared to him; and His consolation was the refusal
of his prayer; "My grace is sufficient for thee; for
My strength is made perfect in weakness."

But great as God's work is through temptation,
we must the more carefully distinguish the sorts of
temptation. What is temptation to one is no temptation to another; and, conversely, where one is unharmed, another would emperil his soul. A person
may even pass through seemingly greater temptations, and fail and fall miserably in the less, which
are more akin to his weakness or against which he is
less guarded. Temptations are as manifold as the
manifold cravings of our manifold human hearts.
There are temptations of every age, disposition, temperament. There are temptations of the young, of
the middle-aged, of the old; temptations of the prosperous and the courted, temptations of the hapless
and neglected. Riches and poverty; exuberant spirits
and depression; health and sickness; independence
and dependence; intellect and dullness; beauty and
deformity; occupation and leisure; every condition of
life, every circumstance in every condition, every in-

cident, every action word or thought, has its temptations; because temptation is the means whereby God perfects us, and fits us, His fallen creatures, to be the companions and peers of those who never fell, living links in the vast circle of adoring, obedient love. And, as a rule, the greater the advantage, which any has in the eyes of man, the greater the trial and the peril.

Yet these are not the temptations which we have practically to distinguish. For to every temptation, which God appoints, He annexes its own accompanying grace. Different temptations are to be met, in their own different ways; but the one broad separating line, which we have to regard, is this, Are the temptations of our own seeking or of God's permitting? In the one, God tries *us;* in the other, *we* tempt God.

Now, as to all temptations, which are voluntary, there is but one rule of salvation, "Avoid them as you would avoid Hell." To remain wilfully in a near occasion of sin, is to trifle with God and your own salvation. Temptations, incidental to any condition to which God calls you, and in which He wills you to abide, may be instruments of grace, salvation, glory. Temptations, from which you might lawfully escape and do not, are self-sought instruments of damnation. Joseph, a slave, could not escape the temptations which God permitted from a wicked mistress. Even thus he avoided daily the occasion of temptation, and fled it, when it found him; and he stands out as the great monument of God's grace, in unsullied purity. David, a monarch, placed himself in peril, and he too is a monument of the grace of

God, but, through what intense suffering in those nearest to his affections, through what inward anguish of soul, through what tears for his meat, ashes for his bread, through what nightly groans for his rest, was he restored; his sin a lasting source of blasphemy against Him, Whom he had chosen as his Portion for ever!

Temptations, which once were of our own will, may *now* be without it or against it. Nay, this is the most common history of all temptation. The young abuse their imaginations, allow themselves in thoughts of sin, indulge curiosity, read bad books, hear words suggestive of sin; and so strengthen against themselves passions, which, in God's good purpose towards them, they need never have known. Nay this is the history of almost every besetting passion, whether it be bodily or mental, coarse or, as men speak, refined, sins of the flesh or of the mind, ambition, vanity, love of praise, pride, or whatever it is, the trial of the full-grown man or woman has most of its aggravations from the indulged imaginings of the child. But whether the trial were, in the origin, self-sought, self-fed, self-strengthened against ourselves, still, if it come against you without your will now, God does not count against you repented sin. He in His Mercy, regards that as involuntary, which, although the fruit of your own former evil will and your former sin, you do not will, do not feed wilfully, *now.* Nay, He but pities us the more, because we have maimed ourselves, and have aggravated our trials.

But we dare not speak or think of the might which Jesus will give to us and be to us against tempta-

tion, without first looking well, in what temptations
He will *not* help us, in what temptations He does not
help men. For we might deceive ourselves either
to some dangerous fall, or to one universal fall, if
we think that Jesus does help us or will help us,
where He does not or will not, where His own Divine mercy forbids Him to help us.

He does not help those who are living for this
world. With a great part of temptations, and of
yielding or not yielding to them, Jesus has nothing
to do, unless in the way of general Providence. The
victories which Jesus gives are victories of the omnipotency of Divine grace. If men sin not, out of
some worldly motive, if fear of shame or of loss of
character, alone keep them from sin, these are but
the victories of human motives over human temptations. It is a gain that a sin against the love of
God has not been committed; it may be a great
mercy of God, that the actual sin has been checked.
But the grace of God has nothing to do with it. A
life, filled up with such victories, would be a life of
seeming goodness, empty of the grace of God. Motives, which may be lawful auxiliaries to the tottering soul, will, if they stand alone, leave the soul all
human. Or again, if men surmount one temptation
by another, if they displace temptations to self-
indulgence by covetousness, sloth by ambition, or
conquer anger by pride, this is but casting out one
devil by another, and often by the worst of the
two. In this way, men plume themselves upon victory, while their whole life is defeat. They see
what they conquer; they see the sins of others which
they have not; they see not, whereby they are con-

quered. For it is their own sin, to which they have blinded themselves. The life of those who live for the world, can hardly be called a life of temptation. Satan does not trouble himself to tempt his slaves. It is not a life of temptation, but a death of subdual.

But these think not of temptation, nor know of Divine grace. Yet neither mayest thou hope for Divine grace, if thou seekest for temptation or remainest in the near occasion of it, or consentest to the first steps towards it. God has promised you that He will not suffer you to be tempted above that ye are able; to *this*, He has pledged His own faithfulness. But observe the promise. It is not, if you willingly abide in temptation; it is not, if you, in any way, are yourselves party to the temptation; it is not, if you are careless about it. God promises, that the enemy shall not have power against you. He does not promise you, if you put yourself in his power. He promises to you, as to Lot, a way of escape; He does not promise you, that if you stay in the midst of the conflagration of your passions, you shall not be consumed by them.

Nay, aweful as is that form of mercy, it is alike mercy and justice to you, that Christ will not give you grace, if you tempt Him by placing yourself in the near danger of sin, and in what is to *you* temptation. Terrible as it is to fall, at the least an eternal loss, a step towards the loss of the soul for eternity, it may be even more destructive to the soul, if God did not leave it for the time to its fall. To fall is risk of death; to abide, dallying with sin, brings on a death-sleep, from which humanly there is no awakening. To abide wilfully in the neighbourhood of sin, comes either from pride or from secret love for the sin. Pride is the sin of the apostate spirit, and is itself death to the soul. That subtle affection for sin, which, moth-life, is ever playing around it, is dazzled by it, allured, fascinated by it, concentrates the soul on the sin, and alienates it from God, even more effectually than a life broken between falls and repentances. Sin, in itself, has something so loathsome, so remorseful, so dissatisfying, that, till the conscience itself is seared, it sends the sinner back to God, hating himself and his sin. The imagination of sin, the dallying with it, the indulgence of the senses, short of what the soul *must* own to itself to be a grave fall, steeps and drugs the soul more thoroughly in sin, immerses it in a thicker and more blinding mist, interpenetrates more the whole moral texture of the soul with evil, than, at an earlier stage, does the actual sin itself. It is one of those slow, accumulating poisons which awaken little or no suspicion, which leave little or no visible trace, which destroy no one function of the frame, but pervade all, taint all, waste all, until, without any seen cause, death comes. And therefore God, at times, allows the tempter a mightier power, and the soul is awakened to bitter repentance and life, through the fall, for which it had prepared itself, by which Satan prepared its death. Wondrous, rare, but always unexpected mercy of our God, never vouchsafed to those who sin presuming on God's mercy, seldom vouchsafed to repeated sin, awakening the soul from the hopeless inurements in sin by the blasting touch and the grasp of the evil one. Yet fearful must be that tampering with sin, for which Almighty mercy has no other cure, than a forfeiture of grace, which at the best, after a life-long repentance of forgiven love, changes His rebel, but restored creature's place around the eternal Throne, and places him among those, whom His grace has failed to preserve but whom it has restored. But understand me well, my brethren. For there is no way so narrow and so large as this of temptation; so narrow, in that there are thousands of ways of self-temptation, and every self-temptation is a form of death; so large and so safe, while a man is but in the way of temptations which God appoints to him, and uses the defences against them, the whole armour of God, with which God provides him. It is in itself, death to the soul to tamper with sin; it is in itself, a still deeper death to enact sin. God may, by a miracle of mercy, open a man's eyes to the sinfulness of his own heart, by abandoning him to the fall, for which he had prepared himself. But to think that it matters not, whether a man sins deeper because he has sinned already; to think that he may as well complete an act of sin, because he has begun; to think, when the soul or body are fretted by temptation, that he had better give rest from their wearying cravings by some degree of yielding to it; these are but so many devices of the Evil one to inure the soul to habitual sin. At times, or at first, a slight consent to sin is all which Satan requires. If he obtains this, he withdraws the temptation. He has gained one step, and, in his deep dreadful game for the human soul, he has learned too much experience in these thousands of years, to risk by a heedless precipitancy the advantage which he has won. To try to get rid of temptation, whether in imagination, or thought or word or deed, by any the slightest consent to sin, is to offend God, and give advantage to Satan against the soul, which he will not fail to use another time.

But further, as in all God's dealings with us He acts in a Divine order and through means, and willeth to unite our poor human wills with His Divine, so, when we are so far in the order of His appointments as not to bring temptation on ourselves, He still requires us to use all human means for its removal. Not only must you avoid all proximate occasions of sin, remove yourselves from those who would entice you to sin, from societies which favour sin, but you must take special heed, that you feed not your own ruling passion. For as, to put yourself in a near occasion of sin from without, is to tempt God, so, and not less, is it, to strengthen, or not, as far as in you lies, to weaken that within, which tempts you. Whether you, by your own free will, allow the inward impulse to sin to become strong, so that a slight temptation from without masters you, or whether you place yourself where strong temptation from without kindles what, without it, would be a very bearable temptation from within, you alike tempt God. God is ready to work for you miracles of grace. He longs more to give you strong, victorious, grace, than you can long to receive it; but He will not, for your own soul's sake, work those miracles, otherwise than according to His own Divine Wisdom. Our Lord, when, for us, He vouchsafed to be tempted by the Evil One, taught you this. He Who had been, above nature, sustained without food for those forty days and forty nights, would not put forth His miraculous power, uncalled for; teaching us that to look for an unneeded miracle, is to tempt the Lord our God. But all grace is miraculous, yea, the very highest miracle, as much higher than what are ordinarily known as miracles, as the moral is higher than the physical world. To ask God, then, for grace, is to ask for a miracle of His Almighty love. To ask Him for this grace, not to strengthen nature but to supersede it, not in order to empower us to that which without that grace we could not do, but to dispense us with doing what is in our own power; to ask Him for a mightier overpowering grace which may carry us over temptations without any cost of our own, instead of using His grace to do that which should diminish or weaken those temptations to us; all this is to tempt God. This niggard service, by which men would indulge themselves as much as they dare, and then leave it to God to carry them supernaturally over temptations whose strength is derived from their self-indulgence, is contrary to all generous and noble love, as well as all faith and the whole order of God. It is to "keep back" from God, as much "of the price," as we can retain (as we think) without deadly sin, and then to expect Him to accept it, as though it were the whole, and to do for us, without our cost, what, with His grace, we should have done ourselves. To speak plainly. If thy temptation, or the temptation of thy time of life, is to fleshly sins, then to pamper the flesh, to feed high, not to use fasting or abstinence, not to keep under the body and bring it into subjection, is to expect God to work a miracle for thee, which may save thee from the effects of thy self-indulgence. Heathen wisdom knew better than this. The heathen proverb, my sons, ("sine Cerere et Baccho"—you remember it,) bears witness to the Apostolic wisdom alike in our weekly day of abstinence and in the abstinence of Lent.

If, again, thy temptation is to vanity, then all this trickery of dress, wherewith our women caricature the extravagances of a neighbouring nation, and make themselves (if they knew it) the laughing stock of those whose admiration they would draw—what mockery of God it is, amid every thing which can minister to vanity, to pray God for humility; amid exposure of person, of which Heathen Rome would have been ashamed, to pray for modesty ! To do what you would fain hide or to desire to hide what you are, and to pray for truthfulness; to speak well of self, and to pray against vain-glory; to heap up luxury and comfort around you, and to pray for charity to the poor; to foster ambition, and to pray for humility; to indulge in expense beyond your means, and to pray for honesty; to distract yourselves amid all the pleasures of the world, and to pray for some love of God and heaven; to occupy and throng your thoughts with cares, not of God's allotting, but of your own seeking, and to pray not to be worldly; this would be, not mockery of God only; but such evident hypocrisy, that men dare not do it. Reason itself tells men, that it is a contradiction, to cut off nothing which leads to sin, to indulge in all things which favour sin, to lay the soul open on all sides to the assaults of sin, and yet to pray God to deliver it; and so they who *will* do these things, either settle down in a heathen morality, or justify themselves against God, as if He had made them what they have unmade themselves, and condemning God they damn themselves.

In these things, then, men tempt God, Whom they blaspheme while they lay the blame on Him, as though He had made them unequal to conquer the temptations which they foment against themselves, with which they surround themselves, against which they take no heed. God has promised you that ye "shall not be tempted above that ye are able." He has not promised you, that ye shall not tempt yourselves above that ye are able, or that, if you so tempt yourselves, ye shall not fall. But you do tempt yourselves above that ye are able, if, within, you strengthen your own temptations; if you do not in whatever way you lawfully may, weaken your own temptations; if you let yourselves be carried down the current, without looking what are *your* temptations; if, by unwatchfulness, you admit them within, leaving your soul open to them for them to come in and out, as they will. You do tempt yourselves above that ye are able, if you thrust yourselves into callings, into which God does not call you, and which favour your ruling passions; which foster vices which you have, or require virtues which you have not; if you place yourselves in any near occasion of sin, or under circumstances in which, whether others stand or fall, you have before fallen.

But while all temptation, of our own seeking or our own allowing, is full of peril, and in drawing it to yourselves you draw to you everlasting death, in nothing is the Christian more secure than in temptation for which he has used and does use the means of God's appointment; temptations, which he in no way invites or occasions, but which God permits. For in all conflicts which God hath appointed for you, His Eye, the Eye of "the Captain" of your warfare and "of your salvation," rests with strengthening love upon you; your cause is not so much your own as His, Who created, redeemed, sanctified you, for victory; your enemy is His, Who has vanquished him; your sense of weakness is the condition of His strength; your battle-cry is, "mistrust self, trust God." He Whom you trust is pledged to deliver you. He rejoices in your victories. He fights and conquers in you; "[b]He wrestleth in you; He engageth; He Himself, on the issue of the conflict alike crowneth and is crowned."

Christ is your Victory, for He has conquered your enemy; He has broken the force of your temptation. Christ is your Victory, for He is the Pattern and Reward of your conflicts. Christ is your Victory, for He on the Cross hath merited it for you; He, your everlasting Intercessor, obtained for you the grace to have victory. Christ is your Victory, for He, the Almighty, Who hath conquered death and hell, fighteth in you.

Tamper then not, yourselves, with your enemy, within or without, and then never lose courage, even if you should aforetime have tampered with him. Trust in Christ is assured victory. Christ has conquered your enemy. Satan is lord only over willing slaves; the god he is only of the world which worships him, and seeks from God's blasted creature what the Creator longs to give them aright in the

[b] S. Cyprian Ep. x. (ad Martyr.) n. 2. p. 29. Oxf. Tr.

order of His creation. "ᶜ I beheld Satan," He said,
"like lightning fall from heaven." Christ has broken
his power; He has bound himself, the strong man;
and us, his goods, He has rescued from his grasp.
Whatever power he yet has in the Heathen world,
whatever fearful power he yet may have over his
willing slaves, no power hath he against thee, except so far as God allows it, not to conquer thee but
to give thee occasion of victory, to place in thy
power the opportunity, by His grace, the more to
please Himself.

Christ Himself has endued you with power for
victory. When He made you members of Himself,
He lodged in you an unseen, Divine, power. He
sealed you with His Spirit; He clothed you with
Himself; He imparted to you life, yea, Himself Who
is Life; He clothed you not with golden armour,
but He "ᵈfenced you round with the Trinity." And
how does He now continually refresh His fainting
warriors, not only by created grace, not only by Divine consolations, but by Himself Who is Life, dwelling in us, that we may dwell in Him, inoneing Himself with us, that we may be one with Him! How
shouldest thou be vanquished against thy will, whose
Indweller is God?

This is thine habitual strength, thy habitual grace,
that Christ, if thou wilt, is thine, and thou art His.
But now, over and above, He, in every particular

ᶜ S. Luke x. 18.   ᵈ "Well I know, that I shall tread on thee,
the asp and the basilisk, and shall tread on serpents and scorpions,
fenced round by the Trinity." S. Greg. Naz. Hom. 40. de S.
Bapt. n. 10. p. 697. and again, "Thou hast need—to be with the
Trinity" Ib. n. 16. p. 702.

temptation, mitigates and tempers the temptation down to thy power of resistance, and strengthens thee in proportion to its strength. In Job and in S. Paul He unveils to thee His dealings with His servants. In Job, thou seest the Evil One, wandering to and fro, seeking whom he might devour, yet not allowed to put forth his hand to touch Job's life. "He lets go our enemy, but keeps him in; He looses, but He bridles him." He gave Job into the hand of Satan, but parted not with him out of His own; He gave Satan permission to try; He allowed him no power to overthrow. In S. Paul, thou seest the other side of the picture. We *hear* of Satan's messenger sent to buffet; we *see* Christ strengthening to endure. His thorn was probably that temptation of the young, which to the Apostle, the preacher of the Gospel, by whom Christ spake, in whom Christ lived, who was "crucified with Christ," who "bare about" with him "His marks," whom "neither life nor death could separate from the love of Christ," was the most involuntary, the most against his will, the most hateful and the most humiliating. Yet His Redeemer saw it good for His servant, that he should endure that, which seemed most to separate him from his Lord, to be most alien from the life of the spirit and spiritual contemplation, most unlike what we could imagine the portion of a saint of God. He who failed not His Apostle, He who taught His Apostle that never is He nearer than when He seemeth to be furthest away; never is His "strength" more "perfected" than in His servants' "weakness;" never is He more glorified in His servants than when they are most humbled; He will not fail thee.

Only look up to Him, "the Author and Finisher of thy faith." It is the weakness of these times, that men look so little to Him, Who is their strength; that they live so much in action, and so little in communion with their Redeemer. We are so distracted by the continual whirl of passing things, and so little in sight of that glorious Throne, where Jesus ever sitteth, looking down with love upon us, pitying us, calling us, longing for us, interceding for us, that we may be His for ever! Who would think that we lived in a redeemed world? Who would think that we are members of a Head, thorn-crowned on Calvary, now shining in the radiance of the Godhead, the delight of angels, the Worship of the universe? Who would think, that flesh like our's had once been, on earth, united with the Godhead in the One Person of the Eternal Son; that it is now inseparably united with His Godhead, admired, loved, adored by every order of Angelic being? Could we lie grovelling here, amid petty passions, idle vanities, contemptible ambitions, sordid gains, trivial anxieties and still more trivial successes, wasting jealousies or destructive pleasures, if we looked up, and saw that, amid those glorious orders of Heavenly intelligences, which behold the Face of God and are entranced with the beatific sight of Infinite Love, there is our vacant seat. There, in glory which not S. Paul or S. John could fully behold in the flesh, is that place in thy Father's house for which God created thee, which thy Redeemer died to purchase for thee, which He is in Heaven to prepare for thee, for which, through those effluences of grace which ever stream forth from His

Presence He would prepare thee. Thou wouldest think of an earthly, fading inheritance, to come to thee perhaps when thou shouldest be old, and then to pass away from thee. Why not think of the glories of thine eternal unfading inheritance? You love the praise of man. You could picture to yourself the pleasure of some human praise or flattery. Is the praise of God less sweet? Is His love less transporting? Will the "well done good and faithful servant," be less overpowering, that thou canst find no time nor leisure, to think of it now?

"[e] The destructive sweetness of things temporal is not driven out except by some sweetness of things eternal." Men nauseate love, which shall not sate the blessed through all eternity, the love of God, because they know it not, think not of it, will not know of it. Look to Calvary, or look to the Right Hand of God, and temptation will, by God's grace, lose its power over thee. Behold those Limbs of thy Divine Lord, racked and rent, joint from joint, in anguish for thee. Behold His Divine Eye, dimmed with Blood and death, yet resting in His eternal love on each one of those, for whom He shed that Blood, and so, on thee. Canst thou look on those limbs so torn, and then go and profane thine own? Couldest thou look on that Eye of love, and then go injure a soul for whom He died? Thou couldest not. Or could you gaze steadfastly on that ineffable glory of thy Lord, and think that He wills thee to serve Him, that thou mayest enter into that transcendent brightness, that unspeakable bliss of love, and then turn away to those fierce feverish pleasures, which

[e] S. Aug. de musica vi. 36.

leave thee sickened when they are past? Thou couldest not.

Give then, if but some few minutes morning by morning, to think of thy Saviour; *now* at this time of His approaching Passion, it were best in His great Humility; hereafter if thou art so drawn, in His Glory. Only think of Him; speak to Him; ask Him to draw thee to Himself. Temptation will have lost half its force, as thou learnest to think, not of the things of earth only, but of thy Lord. Be prepared against thy own temptation and pray against it. And when it comes, or when that instinctive notice of its coming, which God mostly sends, just flashes across thee, lift up one thought to thy Redeemer at the Right Hand of God. One, "Lord help me!" and swifter than lightning-flash, His grace will be in thy soul. There are some temptations which can only be overcome by clasping the hands, and crying, "Lord, save me." But whether He at once deliver thee, or whether, for thy greater good, He allow it still to try thee, fear not. It will not hurt thee. I knew once, how a fierce agonizing temptation tormented one for seven nights and six days; day and night and he had no help, except in crying to the Lord his God. Then it vanished, as though it had never been. Not only will it not hurt thee, by God's grace, but it is part of God's eternal purpose of love towards thee. "Each trial has its" own "weight." And He Who "'ordereth all things in number, weight and measure," in His eternal wisdom ordained and weighed and proportioned and fitted each of our's. He know-

<hr>

[f] Wisd. xi. 20.

T 2

eth whereof He made us; He knoweth our weakness; He considereth us, how each temptation will
affect us; how or when we can best resist; how or
when we should be liable to fall. He knows, whether we shall most be moved by some sudden as-
sault, or worn out by long importunity of temptation. He, by Whom "all the hairs of our head are
numbered," has counted every temptation which He
will allow to befal us, has determined every great
or little accident in each, has appointed the order
in which He will allow them to come upon us, the
order in which we may best withstand them, in
which they may best ripen His graces in us, and
issue to His glory and to our's in Him. Each trial
has its own weariness or vexation and distress. But,
by God's grace, they can do us no further harm.
They may press in upon the soul, they may disturb
the imagination, they may disorder the passions;
they may make a wild tumult in our senses. They
cannot, without our deliberate will, extort our consent; without our consent, they cannot make us
traitors to our God. Temptation withstood, however clamorously it may have summoned thy soul
to surrender, is not defeat but victory. Hold fast,
amid the din, to Christ, and He will not let thee
go. Each trial has its distress; but it has also its
reward. Each trial surmounted by the grace of
Christ, is one jewel in the crown, which He wea-
veth for thee. Each trial, in which thou art upheld
by Him, is one step in that ladder from our Bethel
here to His ever-blissful Presence. Each enhanceth
thy everlasting bliss; each expandeth thy capacity
for the love of God; each was devised, permitted,

ordered, by His Infinite Love; each is a special token
of His favour, and draws its virtue from the Cross of
Christ. Only hold thee still in humility to Jesus;
He will comfort thee by the way; He will refresh
thee by His consolations. He will temper each trial
to thee. As night and day alternating bring on the
end of time, so the night of trial and day of consolation lead on to that bright endless day, when thou
shalt see the fruit of thy trials and of thy Saviour's
grace. Thou shalt see how each trial has its counterpart in thine endless joy; thou shalt hear how it
will sweeten the tenderness of thy Saviour's tones
of love, "Well done, good and faithful servant; enter thou into the joy of thy Lord!"

SERMON XV[a].

THE CONFLICT, IN A SUPERFICIAL AGE.

PSALM xxxix. 6, 7.

"*Surely every man walketh in a vain shew: surely they are disquieted in vain: he heapeth up riches, and knoweth not who shall gather them. And now, Lord, what wait I for? my hope is in Thee.*"

Or, to give the full meaning of the words, at the sacrifice of the beauty of the translation—

> In a mere shadowy being doth man walk to and fro:
> For a mere breath do they so tumultuate;
> He heapeth up, and knoweth not who their ingatherer.
> And now, Lord, what have I ever hoped?
> My longing expectation—it is for Thee.

EVERYTHING in this world of trial has a twofold aspect. Everything, although evil, may, through the grace of God, work to man's true end, his salvation, and his life in God. Everything, although good, may, through man's contempt of the grace of God, work to the endless loss of that for which God created him, the blissful sight and possession of God, in the deathless death of separation from the love of God. Things, unfavourable though they be in themselves, may, by God's grace, be used to our salvation; things, favourable though they be in themselves, may, against that grace, be abused to our damna-

[a] Preached at S. Mary's, Oxford. Lent, 1865.

tion. Natural dispositions, good or bad, outward circumstances, dispensations of God's providence, prosperous or adverse, may, and do, turn either to good or evil to us, as by His grace we follow, or by waste of His grace reject, God's purpose to us through them. God's judgements (it has been long observed) have been seasons of intenser evil of those persevering in evil, or of conversion and purification of those who used that grace of God which was offered to all. The concluding trial of the world is summed up to Daniel, "Many shall be purified, and made white, and tried; and the wicked shall do wickedly: and none of the wicked shall understand; and the wise shall understand [b]." The wicked, not understanding, shall do yet more wickedly through the same trial-times, whereby the fearers of God shall gain purity and whiteness of soul, and purging away of dross. Nothing, alas! is more common than to see natural good run to seed, waste, even ally itself to evil; so that the corn-crop, once so full of promise, unnourished by grace, ends, at last, in ears thin, withered, blasted by the east wind, as profitless as the darnel. The natural good becomes a source of self-deceit, in that the soul rests in it, and looks away from or condones its evil; and the result is a beautiful, smooth, unwrinkled surface, chiselled as by a Greek statuary, but as lifeless as his stone. Contrariwise, the hard outstanding natural faults, the rough irritable temper at which people take such offence, may be God's instrument in keeping the soul low, itself to be the last conquest of His grace. What, alas! more common than that a graceful na-

[b] Dan. xii. 10.

tural easiness of disposition is yielding, even to deadly sin? Moses' hasty, fiery temper, although it lost him Canaan, gained him that especial praise of God, Whose grace transformed it into the "exceeding meekness[c]" above all the men upon the face of the earth.

We have all of us this blended natural evil and good in us; some, commonly some *one*, prominent disposition to good, which is the richest ore for Divine grace to sever from the dross, and yield pure and glorious, grace-enkindled, to the glory of God. And we have some *one* chief evil disposition, the "besetting sin," which is the chief instrument within us, whereby Satan would ensnare us to our destruction, and corrupt all our good. And one of these two results must be the end of each, the grace of God penetrating the whole and leavening it, or the evil deceitfulness of Satan corrupting the natural good and making all evil.

This same blending of natural good and evil, which is found in the individual, re-appears in the aggregate of individuals, in the nation or the age. We speak familiarly of "the national character" of all the nations which we know, each with its blended good and evil. (You will readily recall these several characteristics to yourselves). The successive ages in Europe have in such wise had each its own mark impressed upon it, that writers have characterised them, and given to each its name.

And, again, we ourselves, one by one, partake of the character of the age in which we live, as, on the other hand, we each, like so many drops in the huge

[c] Numb. xii. 3, ענו מאד

ocean, contribute to swell it. Over and above our natural character, we are, each of us, moulded in our degree by the character of our age. We are (apart, at present, from grace) other men than we should have been, had we, with these same natural dispositions, lived in any other century than that in which God has placed us. And self-knowledge has this double office to perform, to understand what we are of ourselves, and how we are influenced by that great world around us, of which we are a part. God the Holy Ghost has a distinct office to perform towards us, from that which He would graciously have done for us in any other age, in that He vouchsafes to give us grace, in reference not only to our natural character, but also as that character is directed both to good and evil by the influences around us.

Every age has its own natural good and evil; its good, a help by the grace of God, to good; and its evil, an all-encompassing, ever-recurring temptation to evil, pressing in upon us, thronging us, carrying us off our feet before we are aware, ubiquitous, represented to us by most with whom we have converse, inhaled with almost every breath. Its good is an impulse, by grace helping us onward; its evil a miasma, out of which we cannot escape, poisonous, but, alas! pleasant. Plainly, all the natural circumstances, under or amid which we are placed, will form part of our trial, because they form part of our life: everything in this world, according as we use it, is "a savour of life or a savour of death."

But the most subtle danger of the spirit of the age is analogous to that, incidental to the natural good in the individual, viz. that it should form a character, in which certain natural virtues should be substituted for Divine grace.

It imports us, then, much to know, what are the natural advantages and disadvantages of the age in which we live: its disadvantages, for therein lies one special outward hindrance to our salvation; its advantages, because they are so many helps towards our salvation, if, by His grace, we use them rightly; and it should be a ground of thanksgiving to God that He has so far surrounded us with a healthy atmosphere; and we should the less take them to ourselves or think any good of ourselves for, them; for plainly they are the less anything of ours, inasmuch as they belong to most around us.

Now it *has* advantages for our soul's good, that we do live in a refined, reading, intellectual, active age. Not, as I said, that nature can do the work of grace, or that, without grace, these same things would not turn to evil or be a snare to us, or minister the more fatally to self-deceit, or absorb us out of the atmosphere of grace, or hide from us God and the invisible; nor that some of our trials do not lie in them.

Refinement, of itself, may only blind us the more, because its sins are the more subtle. Its sins are more malignant, more deliberate, more unawakening, more directed against God, more diabolical. A man sins in them more, face to face, against God. Still, in a refined age, sin is not so much obtruded upon us; it does not so much seek us, if we do not seek it. It is veiled, and we need not lift the veil unless we will. We feel that we do violence to our conscience if we lift it. Then, again, shame may keep men from shameful sins. It is much to have shame on the right side. We shall think so, if we think of that "shame of a less shamelessness[d]," which becomes a temptation, when sin is openly and coarsely spoken of.

Again, the world's refinement is based upon Christianity, even though the world knows not of it. Without Christianity it never did exist, and could not exist; for it is based on principles which the Cross first taught; self-denying love, preferring others to self. Yet to act aright, in daily outward things, is a great help towards inward rightness. It is a beautiful body, unensouled indeed as yet by the grace of God, yet ready for Him, in His goodness, to breath into it the breath of life.

Then, again, we should thank God that He has placed us in an intellectual or reading age. For cultivation of mind, although without the grace of God it would only sharpen an instrument for Satan, is in many ways very subservient to grace. First, it is a direct antagonist to the sensualism which is a vice, not so much of our age, as of our English nature, and which is, now more than heretofore, a wide-spread destroyer of soul and body. Our proverbs tell us of the antagonism between intellect and sensuality[e]. We see it in the countenance. That most delicate organ of God, the human brain, is directly injured by self-indulgence. There are marvellous ways in which some sorts of self-indulgence (which some here, alas! must know of) impair fine-

[d] S. Aug. Conf. ii. 7.
[e] " Dainty bits
Make rich the ribs, and bankerout the wits."—*Shaksp.*

ness of intellect, make memory less tenacious, bring a cloud over the understanding, cause a sudden collapse or snap in reasoning, mar the creativeness of intellect. The instrument suddenly gives way, because it has been, thoughout, marred, disordered. (I speak of what I have been told of old by the sufferers.) Grace has so much to do for our poor nature, and we so shrink from its touch or from direct conflict, that it is a great thing to be able to arm our higher nature against our lower, as an auxiliary and servant of grace. It is a poor thing; but the struggle is for our lives, and we must be thankful for any shelter, however mean and homely and unspiritual, which God provides for us, so we can take refuge in it from that storm of sin. Our intellect is a present gift which God has bestowed upon us, which we cannot but value; and it is a good thing for us to know, that sensuality is a deadly foe of our intellects as well as of our souls. For men flatter themselves that repentance will make all right about our souls, (God is so good,) but the injury to intellect is sensible, irreparable.

But this requires thought. Intellectual employments have this advantage, that, even without being directly religious, they raise the soul into a higher, purer, atmosphere. It is a great gain, when young, to elude the enemy, to fill the imagination with pure healthy thoughts, to distract the mind from subjects which would lead to sin. The proverb tells us, that "idleness is the mother of all vices [f]." Occupation, then, at least, cuts off the occasion of a whole brood of sins. It does not bring us within the sphere of

[f] L'oisiveté mère de tous les vices.

grace, but it is an outward and powerful protection against sins, which would carry away youth as with a whirlwind out of it. Experience, I think, will tell most of you, that your busiest times have been the times freest from temptation. We have, then, great reason to thank God for having placed us in an intellectual, or, at least, a reading age.

Intellectual activity is one form only of the activity of our age; and every form of activity, which is not itself evil, is, although not connected with grace, a safety-valve for ourselves. Man's self is his worst foe; and, so far, everything is his friend which tends to take him out of himself. The habit, too, of activity is a preparation for activity in what is good or beneficial to others. We may mistake natural activity in good things for grace, all the more because activity is instinctive to us. Still, since sloth is a deadly sin, it is a great thing that its contradictory, activity, is nature to us. This channel for grace is at least unobstructed, ready to receive the life-giving stream of the grace of God. I have dwelt on this the bright side of our times, first, because it is truthful; then, because thankfulness to our good God requires it; then too, because gloominess is very disedifying, disennobling, paralysing.

But perhaps some of you may think that this which I have said about intellectual activity supersedes the necessity of any warning about that which has been assigned to me to speak of to you to-night, "The Conflict in a Superficial Age." On the contrary, it is the very occasion of that warning. True, discovery has been most active. It has seemed as if God had laid open to us His natural world, had bestowed upon us a new revelation of it, new powers and methods of decyphering it, and as if He meant to unfold to us more and more of the mysteries of His physical creation. We could almost imagine that there would be no limits to our discoveries, save that, being His creation, it is the finite expression of that which is infinite, and that we are discovering only a chain of causes and effects. The first principles lie as much hidden from our sight as ever. Still He *is* unfolding to us marvel upon marvel of His wonderful works. Thanks be to Him for every instance of His marvellous goodness!

But observe, the question is not about the discoverers, but about the "age," i.e. about ourselves, who are the receivers of the knowledge. And *we* may be superficial in two ways, quite compatibly with the brilliancy of the genius which discovers. We may be superficial in our way of appropriating knowledge, which it requires a wondrous combination of God's gifts to discover. Then, too, the nature of that knowledge may tend (of course through our abuse of it) to make us take up with knowledge which is very superficial to *us*, touching only the surface of what concerns our real being and our own souls. Our Lord has said, "[g]What shall it profit a man, if he gain the whole world and lose his own soul?" What then does it profit a man, if he gain the knowledge of the whole world and lose the knowledge of God Who made his soul, and by the knowledge of Whom his soul is to be saved?

Yet these are just the abuses which people are making of that knowledge which, in these days more

[g] S. Mark viii. 36.

than in those before us, God is so manifoldly unfolding to us.   Its very manifoldness tends to make us superficial.   Men pause on nothing, weigh nothing, have an opinion on everything.   We think that we know much, because much is known.   Yet what is all this doing with us, but forming a habit of imagining, that we have an adequate personal knowledge of what we, for ourselves, know nothing ?

The discoveries, also, are wholly as to things without us, God's physical creation.   But of ourselves, the most marvellous mystery of that creation, whose life of grace is the study of angels, whose lower nature only belongs to the world of sense, who were formed in the image of God and re-created in the likeness of God made Man, whose union is with God, whose soul is His dwelling-place, what more do we know of the mysteries of our being, of the laws of our thought, of our supernatural life, of our intercourse with God, or of the manifold ways of God's love and mercy with the soul?   Men have closed almost everything spiritual to themselves, every deeper thought of God, of their own being, because *there* they found insoluble mysteries, and *their* delight was in things which they could master.

I said, in regard to us individually, that one main peril is, lest we rest in that natural good which God endowed us with, lest we be content with the lesser part instead of the whole, with the cultivation of the natural instead of the supernatural, our natural selves unspiritualized, unelevated, untransformed by the grace of God.

This same is the special danger of the spirit of the age, lest it occasion us to take up with natural

beauty instead of holiness, with natural knowledge
of God instead of divine revelation, with a vague
knowledge about God instead of a personal relation to Him and union with Him by His indwelling
Spirit.

Look at the modern tone of morals. I speak not,
of course, of those whom God has called out of the
world, or of those who are daily living near to God,
resting on the merits of Jesus in humility and meekness and self-abnegation. I mean, what is the ideal
of the age? For it is " the age " which we are
speaking of; it is " the age" which we are tempted to
make our standard of the will of God for us.

I think I might without injustice (would to God
it *were* injustice !) sum it up as decorous and amiable.
This would include that outward refinement which I
spoke of; unwillingness to pain one present, a certain kindliness, the avoidance of what would shock
people's idol, public opinion, such as would be vice
in any of its coarser forms, drunkenness or actual
adultery, or flagrant dishonesty. Then, of course,
there must be a general recognition of one's duty, at
least to one's neighbour, and so much of one's duty
to God as is involved in saying some prayer morning
and evening (would God some real heart's-prayer,
even if short, were always said) and going to church
once, perhaps twice, on the Sunday. Men's end is
to be comfortable with themselves, which includes
that it should not go wrong with them hereafter.
With this there must, of course, be a recognition
that we are imperfect creatures, who habitually fail,
although mostly as an anodyne to conscience, " We
are imperfect, and we cannot help it."

- ' But where, then, is anything which involves any real conflict with Satan or with self? What Scripture-description of a life to God, in God, could men even think of as fitting to themselves? I do not ask as to our, in any way, fulfilling it, but only as to our setting it before us as a thing, by God's grace, to be fulfilled. How would the words sound, were one—I will not say in any place of amusement, but—in any domestic circle, to name the words 'perfection,' 'devoutness,' 'self-sacrifice,' 'single-heartedness,' ' sanctity,' ' spirituality,' ' responsibility,' ' collectedness,' ' self-abasement,' ' contrition,' ' humiliation,' ' zeal,' ' meekness,' ' poverty of spirit,' ' hunger and thirst after righteousness,' ' prayer without ceasing,' ' thanksgiving in all things,' ' doing *all* to the glory of God?' I have not spoken of any of the austerer graces, ' self-revenge,' ' self-contempt,' ' self-mortification,' 'co-crucifixion with Christ,' of which S. Paul speaks; nor again of contemplation, meditation on God or on Jesus and His sufferings, communion with God, personal love for God, union with God, and that continually growing; nor yet, once more, of God's being "a jealous God," jealous that the love to Him should not be parted between Him and His creatures. But those words, which express only ordinary Christian graces, some of them the subjects singled out by our Lord for blessing, or which S. Paul speaks of as mere matters of course, so to say, in a Christian life and passes on, would they not sound startlingly to the soul, as if they had belonged to a different being? And truly they do belong to a different being. For men are, unconsciously, living mere natural lives, without effort, without aim, without struggle, without victory, without compass, without lode-star, crossing the perilous sea of this world, where countless souls are shipwrecked, without any consciousness of peril, or any desire except to escape unrespectable sins, such as, they hope, that a moderate share of six deadly sins, pride, covetousness, gluttony, luxury, envy, anger, is not, nor an entire possession by the seventh, sloth, as far as it is spiritual. Christians are leading natural lives, (except as far as habitual grace was, in baptism, bestowed upon them, and is kept feebly alive by listless prayers,) and the Christian's life is supernatural.

But where, then, is the Christian's non-conformity with the world? where his transformation? where his new creation? where his Christ-mindedness? where Christ's life in him? where "the fruit of the travail" of the Redeemer's soul? to what end the indwelling of Christ? wherein is his sonship to God? what is santification? or what means being "a temple of the Holy Ghost," or "[h] walking with God" (which the old patriarchs had before Christ died), or the outpouring of the Spirit in our hearts? The higher, more penetrating requirements of God's law, the consciousness of sin as an offence against the will of God (not as 'vice' only, or a defect in ourselves and an offence against our moral nature), and the supernatural aids of grace as the antagonist of sinfulness and the enabler of men's weakness, have faded out of popular literature together. It is penetrated with an unconscious, simple-hearted Pelagianism, which ignores all deeper truth as to both God and man, because it has lived too much in the outer

[h] Gen. v. 24. vi. 9.

world of sense and its manifold interests, ever to think seriously of its own needs, or of God's ever-ready, ever-inviting grace, or of its own unintermitting relations and duties to God Who made it.

And so, in regard to what calls itself " the theology of the nineteenth century," it corresponds to this aspect of man. To *us*, to whom God has disclosed something of the nature of sin and of His aweful holiness, the centre of the Gospel is His Divine, unspeakable mercy to us, His sinful creatures whom *He* made, whom we unmade, whom He redeemed and re-creates. We can never forget our own special relation to God. We are not, as yet, " like unto the angels;" we are " saved in hope" only; we are not in our home, but in an enemy's land. And therefore awe enters so largely into our relation to God. Our Lord has said to us, "'I will forewarn you, Whom ye shall fear. Fear Him, which, after He hath killed, hath power to cast into hell; yea, I say unto you, Fear Him." What of the new theology ? All which it proposes, which is not mere denial of truth, (hinted by some, avowed by others,) is a more graphic delineation of the outer circumstances which eucompass the sacred history. To know the atmosphere in which David or S. Paul moved, is to shew men more the mind of the Psalmist or the Apostle[k]! Holy Scripture tells us of another haze which has to be broken through, than any supposed to lie on the history of the Jews, that we may see clearly, what mists

[i] S. Luke xii. 5.

[k] "Theology of the Nineteenth Century" in Fraser's Magazine, Feb. 1865, p. 256. I took this the rather as a specimen, having been informed that its writer spoke of it as a sort of manifesto. I was able here only to touch upon a few characteristic points.

of earthliness have to be dispelled by "the Sun of Righteousness." It tells us of another veil[1] than the veil of time; the veil which lies upon the natural un-illumined heart of man, which veil is to be removed, not by the knowledge of some outward history, but by conversion of the heart to God. "When it shall be turned to the Lord, the veil shall be taken away[m]." It tells us of another ground of understanding or not understanding the mind of God,—whether a man have "received the spirit of the world," or "[n] the Spirit of God, to perceive the things freely given us by God;" whether a man have simply his natural powers, (be he, thus far, as highly gifted as God has ever created the keenest intellect of man,) or whether he be illumined by the Spirit of God; whether he would, of himself, know the mind of God and teach Him, (as men make their "moral sense" the interpreter of Divine truth,) or whether he "have" himself "the mind of Christ," being taught of Himself to understand Him.   Pleasant is it to know anything which illustrates even the outward part of the Word of God; useful is it, so far, if by any means the truth of the sacred history be brought more vividly home to one who unhappily believes it not.   Yet the knowledge of the natural can teach only the natural. The unhappy man[o] who learnt to believe the existence of Jesus only from the country which saw His mighty works, unillumined by His Spirit, unconverted by His grace, returned only to blaspheme Him.   Better never to have known of Him!   It was

[1] 2 Cor. iii. 14. 15.   [m] Ib. 16.   [n] 1 Cor. ii. 12.

[o] M. Renan. "For the sake of this, (' to know Christ,') passages even in Renan's work may be read with instruction." (Fraser, p. 263.) Having read Renan, I cannot imagine, which.

the nearness only of the unconverted robber who looked into that meek Face to blaspheme Him. It was the nearness of the rude soldiers who beheld "the Lamb of God Who taketh away the sins of the world" only to increase their own; the nearness of those who "spat in His face and buffeted Him." Better far, not to have heard of the name of Christ than to delineate Him as the enthusiast deteriorating into the conniver at imposture.

The background of the mountains of Judah can throw no light on that sacred Form which went about doing good, suffering, speaking "[p] as never man spake" among them. When those scenes, now hallowed by remembrance of Him to those who love Him, beheld Him present, "the Light of the world," they who "loved darkness rather than light," who were blinded by their imagined sight, hallowed those scenes the more by crucifying Him Who came to enlighten them. They shed the Blood which redeemed the world and sanctifieth it, as the common blood of a malefactor and a deceiver. The knowledge of human errors, which He came to correct, can cast no light upon the Divine truth, which He was, which He came to reveal, which He heard from the Father. He came to shine in the darkness, not to receive light from it.

And what light is He to receive from us? "The more fully it is understood what He was, what He did, what is meant by His life, by His death, by His resurrection, so much the more fully," we are told[q], "will the Church understand the sense in which He was Divine, and the sense in which He was human."

[p] S. John vii. 46.　　　　　　[q] Fraser, p. 263.

This is to be the end of the new meditative study of
our dear Lord's incarnation, life, and death for us
sinners, that we are to know in what sense He, One
God with the Father, "the Word," Who "was with
God" in the beginning, "ʳand was God," and for us
"men and for our salvation" was made Flesh, was
God; in what sense He Who was Perfect Man was
human. The basis of this new theology is to be, to
unlearn our God-given faith; its development is, not
to expand but to destroy what God gave us. The
denial of truth is to be the development of truth.
The statement that future punishment is *not* everlasting is to be the development of the faith that
it *is*. Not-being is to be the development of being;
death, of life.

And what is to be the end of this learning? In
part, the simple words of God, to learn which needs
no research, that "God is love;" that He, Who is
the source and pattern of all perfection, is "a moral
Being." O wonderful discovery of what every child
can read in every page of the Bible! that God is
holy, just, faithful, true, and alone good. And then,
that He "is a righteous Judge, Who will deal with
us according to truth." Strange Gospel for fallen
man! "Enter not into judgement with Thy servant, O Lord, for in Thy sight shall no man living
be justified." "Woe be even to the commendable
life of men, if, laying aside mercy, Thou shouldest
examine itˢ."

This, then, is the central superficialness of this age,
and of what calls itself its theology, that it is so
occupied with things of sense or intellect which do

ʳ S. John i. 1.   ˢ St. Aug. Conf. ix. n. 34, p. 179. Oxf. Tr.

not bear on man's inner nature, that it forgets itself and its relation to God. It treats with God—nay, it would be truer to say, it treats *of* God—not with the tender familiarity of reverential love, but with the calm complacency of one whose rights God is bound to respect, and who is, on the whole, on good terms with God. And therefore it is false and hollow to God and to itself.

These two objects of knowledge, unlike as they are, of God and of ourselves, mutually condition one another. And that, in part, because God has revealed Himself to us, chiefly in reference to ourselves. To "see God as He is," is the reward of eternity: to "know as we are known" is God's gift, when, by His mercy, we shall see Him "face to face." Now we see in a mirror only some reflection of His attributes and His love. But to see them in that mirror, our own inner eye must be cleansed; no breath of self must dim the surface which is to reflect God. The soul, which knows not itself, and has not, by the grace of God, purified itself, will not see clearly the image of God, which it has deformed in itself. "He that hath this hope" of seeing God, S. John saith, "purifieth himself, as He is pure." "We," says S. Paul, " with face which hath been unveiled," (ἀνακεκαλυμμένῳ προσώπῳ) —mind, he says not, with face which sees by any natural discernment of its own, but with face from which the veil, which intercepted the light of Divine truth, has been removed by another, that is by Christ and the Spirit of Christ,—"We, with face unveiled" by Christ in our conversion to God, " beholding in a mirror," no

<hr/>

ᵗ 1 S. John iii. 2, 3.　　　ᵘ 1 Cor. xiii. 12.

lònger any reflection of our natural selves, but "the glory of God," are illumined by that Divine light which we behold; we receive in ourselves some of the effulgence of that glory which we contemplate; we are changed and transformed into that same image of God which we gaze upon; and *that* "from glory to glory," from one degree of glory, to another, from one degree of transfiguring light to another; and *that* still, not of ourselves, but such as He alone can work Who is the Lord of the soul, the Almighty re-Creator, the Spirit of God, "as by the Lord, the Spirit [v]."

This is a "progress" worthy of the name; a progress from one degree of Divine light to another, until the last perfecting on earth, the last sanctifying, illumining grace yields the soul, cleansed by its Redeemer's Blood, made meet for the unmerited gift of God, the eternal beatific vision of Himself. This is true illumining, because the soul is over-streamed by the light of God. This is true freedom, because it is wrought by Him Who makes those whom He frees, "free indeed." "[w] Where the Spirit of the Lord is, there is liberty;" freedom from the darkening power of sin; freedom from ignorance and error and our own dull conceptions; freedom from prejudices, not from the light of the old eternal truths, but from our own short-sighted guesses, and uncertain speculations, and hasty prejudications of that truth which God IS and reveals, that we may be able to receive in unclosed minds the irradiating, transforming light of God.

Such is the goal, such the prize, deiformity; to be

[v] 2 Cor. iii. 18.　　　[w] Ib. 17.

formed *by* God *for* God, into a likeness of the all-good God. But step by step. The first step is the cleansing of the soul. The first condition of the removal of the veil, which over-spread the whole world out of God, is to turn to God. "When they shall turn unto the Lord, the veil shall be taken away." "To depart from evil, that is understanding[x]." Yes, dare to see thyself! Behold thy whole self, such as God will unveil thee to thee, some image of the knowledge at the great day; place thyself under the penetrating light of God; pray Him to exhibit thee to thyself, all which thou ever hast been, all which thou art, all which thou wouldest hide from thyself, under one ray of His Divine light. Do this, having first set God before thee, not as "the Deity," not as a "First Cause," but as "the living God," out of Whose Omnipresence thou canst not move; in Whom thou hast sinned; Whose supporting, enabling strength thou hast abused against Himself to sin; Whose love, every selfish injury of another's soul has wounded in its tenderest depth; to Whose aweful justice thou art absolutely responsible; Whose individual loving-kindness for thee, in every rejection of any known motion of grace thou hast despised; Whose temple in thee, if thou broughtest unclean thoughts into thy soul (much more if there was any sin in act), thou defiledst; to Whom, by any deliberate habit of sin, thou saidst in fact, "I will not have Thee to reign over me." Set God thus before thee, and, by His mercy, the Pharisee-religion of the day will not again be thine.

Nor will God leave thy soul, from which He has

[x] Job xxviii. 28.

cast out the Pharisaism or Pelagianism of the day, a blank. Rather, it will then cease to be a blank. He will take the pen of His Spirit, and write on thy soul His own ineffaceable inscription, "Redeemed by the Blood of God," "Redeemed by the Blood of thine own God." Then will all things take their due place. Then will thine existence cease to be "shadowy," for thou art sealed for eternity by the Blood of Jesus. Thine eternal life is begun. Then will the things of the age cease to be superficial; there will be no mere surface left; for everything will be filled with life, everything will have its endless end, Almighty God. Thou wilt shrink into nothingness before His aweful Majesty, only to be re-created, enlarged, filled by Him Who fills the universe. Then will intellectual activity be empowered to range freely, not aiming, Phaethon-like, to snatch the reins of the horses of fire from its Father's hand, but circling in the God-described orbit round the eternal throne; not less free, but "free indeed," because it shall freely choose the good for which it was chosen, its free-will enfranchised, emancipated, disenthralled by Christ. Fetters are for the rebellious. God's service is "perfect freedom," freedom from one's worst tyrants, one's self, or the craven fear of man's opinion. Then will science range freely, unhurried to rash conclusions; intuitive, because in its measure inspired by Him Who is the Indweller of the soul, Whose enabling Spirit suggests every true thought, natural or supernatural.

O that you could know, O that you may know, how joyous, how glorious, is the liberty of the soul, enfreed by God; how magnificent the dignity is, throughout the common duties of the day, to have God for one's end. Nothing is irksome, nothing oppressive, nothing shallow, nothing heartless. For God ennobles everything, lights up everything, kindles everything with the ray of His love, which is at once Divine light and Divine warmth. Then thou shalt walk, not in a shadowy being, as this life would in itself, at best, be, but up and down with God; in God thou shalt take thy rest; with God shalt thou rise; with God converse; His wisdom shall be thy wisdom, His truth thy light, His love thy joy. And if this be the mirror, what the "face to face?" "And now, Lord, what have I ever longed for? My longing expectation is for Thee."

And now, my sons, go your way to this new world, upon which there stream beams of light from the half-opening portals of heaven. Christ looks on you, His soldiers; Christ looks to see your victories in His strength; Christ at this moment and evermore is interceding for you; Christ, Who will crown His own deeds in you, will Himself be crowned in you, yea, in you for whose salvation He thirsted on the Cross, "He shall see of the travail of His soul, and" (amazing condescension of Jesus) "shall be satisfied [y]." Only [z] as you go, remember, for love of Him, those who, with you, were once made members of Christ; whom man's selfishness and animal passions have degraded; whom Christ has plucked anew, "brands out of the burning;" whom Christ is anew purifying by His Spirit to shine (with us too, as, in His mercy, we trust) with their own brightness, as His redeemed in the kingdom of His Father.

[y] Is. liii. 11.   [z] There was a collection for a Penitentiary.

SERMON XVI[a].

THE GOSPEL, THE POWER OF GOD.

S. LUKE xxiv. 49.

" Behold, I send the promise of My Father upon you: but tarry ye in the city of Jerusalem, until ye be endued with power from on high."

MAN'S power had been weighed in the balance, and had been found wanting. Minds, as acute, as rich, as varied in their gifts, as any which God had created, had done whatever could be done in the way of intellect. The intrinsic beauty of goodness, its fittingness, the moral duty of seeking it for its own sake, and as the end of man, had been taught with all the power of Greek intelligence. The schools of philosophy had decayed. Their lessons had become mostly powerless on those who taught in them. Socrates, Plato, Aristotle, were to use a world-wide influence within their own province, the human intellect. Their instantaneous failure, and three centuries of decay, had shewn that they were not to be the moral teachers, or the regenerators of mankind.

Rome had tried what man could do on the moral side. The stern, unloving warriors, strict with them-

[a] Preached at S. Mary's, Oxford. Lent, 1866.

selves as with others, had stamped on their polity
and their people a rigid morality. It is a marvel
to us, how at least fidelity on the wife's side could
become to such an extent a heathen virtue. Contrast with the miseries and iniquities revealed and
fostered by the English Divorce Court, Roman faithfulness, through which, in a hot climate, divorce was
unknown for two hundred and thirty, some say, for
five hundred and twenty years[b]. But the hard,
icy virtues of the republic, frost-bound by the necessity of discipline, had, under the warm glow of
prosperity, melted into one stream of universal dissoluteness. The failure of a mighty effort leaves the
greater hopelessness. It is a calm historian, who
(about our Lord's birth,) turned away sickened from
his own times, in which, by a rapid but complete
declension, "we can bear," he says, "neither our
vices nor remedies[c]." Another, who could speak
freely of iniquity at which he afterwards connived,
says, "Will the wise ever cease to be angry, if once
he begins? All is full of guilt and vice; more is
committed than can be constrained. A great war of
wickedness is waged; daily the lust for sin is greater,
the shame less. Casting out all regard for aught
good or just, lust fastens where it wills. Guilt is no
longer stealthy; it parades itself. Iniquity is so sent
abroad, has such might in the hearts of all, that innocence is not rare only: it is *not*[d]." A wide-
spread nature-worship, whose centre was the mys-

[b] "230." Plutarch. Comparat. Thesei c. Rom. c. 7. "520" Val.
Max. Hist. v. 6. 1. "521." A. Gell. Noct. Att. xvii. 21.

[c] Liv. Præf. ad Hist. v. fin.

[d] Seneca de Ira, ii. 8. It is thought to have been one of his
earliest works.

tery of reproduced life, consecrated sensuality; the philosophy of Stoics or Epicureans, the most rigid or the most lax, alike justified degrading sin*d*; human nature cast itself willingly into the black pool, to whose edge its gods beckoned it on.

Even Jewish life had decayed. Its most esteemed sect was rigid in externals, in love heartless, in inward life reprobate. Ambition and hatred of their masters had desecrated the prophetic promises of spiritual victories into temporal hopes. An Epicurean sensuality had bound down the hopes of a third class to the things of this life.

It seems as though God had waited, until there could be no hope of the moral regeneration of man from man, to work His own marvellous work. As He employed the poor, the illiterate, "unlearned and ignorant men," "*e*the foolish things of the world, and the weak things of the world, and base things of the world, and things despised, yea, things" accounted as if they "were not"—to confound the wise and the mighty and that which held that it alone *was*, in order "that no flesh should glory in His Presence," so He allowed man's keenest intelligence, and strongest moral power, the instruments which He had Himself formed in the natural order of things, to try their utmost and fail, that the Divinity of Jesus and His revelation might stand out the more clearly, after the recognition of the impotence of what was grand, powerful, beautiful, perfect in its way, but—human.

What was lacking, was not so much understand-

---

d See Döllinger Heidenthum and Judenthum, B. v. c. ii. p. 328.

e 1 Cor. i. 28.

ing, or motives, as power. The unwritten law written
in men's consciences (however, here or there, it was
obscured even in its primal laws) was clear. "'I
see what is better, and approve it; I follow what is
worse," is a confession of human nature, just as our
Lord was coming. Dissoluteness had not yet quite
eaten out among the people the old beliefs in a sort
of heaven and hell, the Elysian fields and Tartarus;
but it was the powerless echo of a mighty truth,
whose dying sounds moved neither heart nor intellect.

Not, then, the inherent might of truth was wanting to the soul; man had already more truth than
he availed himself of. Not persuasive motives;
what man had already, were powerless. Motives
will not enable one paralyzed to move. The Gospel
has constraining motives, stronger than hope and
fear, love for Him Who so loved us. Yet love, too,
has its constraining power to those alive, not to one
dead. And human nature was dead to good, in its
trespasses and sins.

What then was needed, besides all revealed truth,
was "power." Our blessed Lord came to give us
that power, being Himself "the wisdom of God, and
the power of God[g]." He came to give a new beginning to our nature, by Himself taking it. He
took our human weakness, to impart to it His Divine might. The power which He was and had,
He, by His Manhood, lodged in it. Mankind was
redeemed by weakness; it was converted by power.
The power had been hidden in His humiliation, for
the suffering of His atoning Death. The reason for

[f] Ov. Met. vii. 19.   [g] 1 Cor. i. 24.

shrouding it was removed on His resurrection. Then
He Who "was of the seed of David according to the
flesh," was, "according to the Spirit of holiness,"
i. e., according to His holy and Divine Nature,
"defined" or marked out to be "the Son of God
in power by the resurrection of the dead[h]." This
power He laid as the groundwork of the Apostles'
mission; "All power is given to Me in heaven and
in earth. Go ye therefore, and disciple all nations;
I am with you alway, unto the end of the world[i]."
This power, which was His, He bade His Apostles
wait until they should be invested with it. "I send
the promise of My Father upon you; but tarry ye
in the city of Jerusalem, until ye be endowed with
power from on high[k]." And this power was the
indwelling of the Holy Ghost. In Him they were
to be baptized, immersed, flooded. "Ye shall be baptized with the Holy Ghost not many days hence[l]."
"Ye shall receive power, after that the Holy Ghost
is come upon you[m]."

Doubtless this power included the gifts of superhuman works wrought by the Apostles, as S. Peter
speaks of our Lord Himself: "Ye know, how God
anointed Jesus of Nazareth with the Holy Ghost
and *with power:* Who went about doing good, and
healing all that were oppressed with the devil; for
God was with Him[n]."

Its first expression was in the gift of tongues;
but the gift of tongues was only the vehicle of the
Divine power. "[o]We do hear them speak in our
own tongues *the wonderful works* of God." S. Paul,

[h] Rom. i. 3. [i] S. Matt. xxviii. 18—20. [k] S. Luke xxiv. 49.
[l] Acts i. 5. [m] Ib. 8. [n] Ib. x. 38. [o] Ib. i. 11.

in speaking of what "Christ" had "wrought by" him "to the obedience of the Gentiles, by word or deed," distinguishes these two; "in the power of signs and wonders," "in the power of the Holy Spirit [p];" an outward and supernatural power of miracles, and an inward transforming power of the Spirit.

But the outward miracles were the body, not the soul. They were God's glorious works of Divine love attesting His Presence. The rending of the rocks, the earthquake, the fire, were but the forerunners of the Lord; He was not *in* them; God manifested Himself in the still small voice [q]. The mighty works in the Gospel accredited God's messengers, as come from Him; they disposed men's hearts to listen; but the might which converted the heart, was the Gospel itself, spoken in the words of God to hearts which He opened to receive it. The Gospel itself was "the power of God unto salvation [r]." "The preaching of the cross was to them who perish foolishness; but to us who are saved it is the power of God [s]." "My words and my preaching were not in persuasive words of man's wisdom, but in demonstration of the Spirit and of power [t]." It was not "persuasiveness of man," but "demonstration of God;" not demonstration of hu-

---

p Rom. xv. 19.   q 1 Kings xix. 11, 12.   r Rom. i. 16.
    s 1 Cor. i. 18.

t Ib. ii. 4. "The Divine word saith, that what is spoken (although in itself true and most persuasive) is not self-sufficing to reach the human soul, unless some power from God be also given to the speaker, and grace engerminate in what is spoken; this too being, not without God, infused in those who speak profitably."—Orig. c. Cels. vi. 2.

x

man reasoning, but a divine power and energy of heavenly grace. It was an Almighty and ever-present power, working in and through them. "I became a minister of the Gospel," says S. Paul, "according to the gift of the grace of God, which was given to me, according to the inworking of His power[u]." And this power they bore about with them in this our decaying frame, "in earthen vessels, that the transcendingness of the power," they say, "may be of God, and not from us[v]."

Yet they were but great eminent instruments of Divine power. "The Spirit of the Lord spake by" them, "and His word was on" their "tongue[w]." Speaking with Divine power, they brought over the world to God; savages they persuaded to learn wisdom; all the whole order of the world they altered. But they were only triumphant captains in the war of the Lord, under the great Captain of our salvation, chiefs of the Church, lights of the world. They who so bare Christ upon their tongues, who had that seraphic love, doubtless have their thrones with cherubim and seraphim. But the "power" itself they speak of, as the common possession of the Church. For it was one and the same Spirit which, having been given without measure to our Lord, was thenceforth to be poured forth fully upon His Church, giving to the whole Church (when acting as a whole) that inerrancy which He gave to His Apostles; streaming, in its sanctifying powers, upon all its members; in all, supernatural, lifting up the soul above nature, uniting it to God, and restoring His

[u] Eph. iii. 7.   [v] 2 Cor. iv. 7.
[w] 2 Sam. xxiii. 2.

likeness in it. .In the Apostles, above all, were those gifts of the Spirit, which were for the benefit of others. Yet these, too, all but infallibility, continued on in individuals in the Church since; nay, even in its lesser members; for if any one speaks so as to reach a brother's soul, our Lord's words still come true of him; "[x]It is not you that speak, but the Spirit of My Father Who speaketh in you."

. But in the conflict which belongs to all, the Apostles needed the same armoury as we ; we are gifted with that same endowment, whereby they trampled upon Satan, subdued the flesh, despised the world. To them, too, weakness was Divine might. It is one of the few personal revelations to himself which S. Paul records, "My grace sufficeth for thee, for My power is perfected in weakness[y]." "Therefore," he subjoins, "most sweetly will I rather boast in my infirmities, that the power of Christ may reside upon me." Apostles had the same weaknesses as we, save those which any of us entail on ourselves by evil habits; we have, for victory, for eternal life, for glory, for that which is the glory and the joy of eternal life, the love of God, the same helps as they. "The least grace," it is a dogmatic saying[z], "is able to resist any concupiscence, and to gain eternal life."

But S. Paul, who glories in his own weakness, exults in the superabundant might of grace deposited in the Church for each of us by virtue of its union, and ours in it, with Christ, its Head. Inspiration itself (since it must needs use our human words) does not seem to suffice him, as he piles up words upon

[x] S. Matt. x. 20. [y] 2 Cor. xii. 9.
[z] S. Thom. 3. p. q. 62, art. 6, fin. comp. q. 70, art. 4, conc.

x 2

words to utter as he may, that which is unutterable;
the transcendentness of the might of the grace of God
to usward.　It is not to be uttered in words.　As

> "He who loveth, knoweth well
> What Jesus 'tis to love,"

so he who has used grace, knows something of the
power of grace. Its fullest power *that* saint alone can
know, who here below used it most, and whom it
has uplifted nearest to the throne of God.　The Ephe-
sians knew it.　They were a source of unceasing
thanksgiving to S. Paul for "the faith in the Lord
Jesus, which was among them, and the love to all the
saints [a]."　And therefore he prayed for them, that
God would reveal to them by an inward illumining
of the eyes of the heart,—what?　Some fresh truth?
Some larger knowledge of Himself?　No: but what is
the transcendent greatness of the power of His grace
which they knew already.　"That the God of our
Lord Jesus Christ, the Father of glory, would give
you the spirit of wisdom and revelation in the full
knowledge [b] of Him; having the eyes of your heart
enlightened, so that you may know, what is the hope
of His calling, and what the riches of the glory of
His inheritance in the saints"—(this relates to what
eye hath not seen nor ear heard, the glory of those
already perfected, but he adds, as equally an object of
revelation, the might of grace which God puts forth
here below)—"and what the transcending greatness
of His power to usward the believing, according to
the working of the strength of His might, which He
worked in Christ, in that He raised Him from the
dead, and placed Him on His Right Hand in the

[a] Eph. i. 15, 16.　　　　　[b] ἐπιγνώσει, v. 17.

heavenly places, far above all principality and *power* and dominion, and every name which is named, not only in this world but in that which is to come, and hath subjected all things under His feet." And *Him*, Who is thus above all might He has given to be the Source of the might lodged in all of us, who from that time to the end are "the believers." "And Him He gave to be Head over all to the Church, which is His body, the fulness of Him Who filleth all things in all."

He parallels "working" with "working;" the greatness of His power to usward who believe, with the might of His power whereby He raised Christ from the dead. The might of grace operating in us was involved in the might which gave life to the dead Body of Jesus. "According to," he says; as the effect is in the cause. And what might? The might of Him Who is above all might which can be named or conceived. And why should this might, shewed forth in our Lord, redound to us? Because we belong to Him. He is our Head, we are His members; and He vouchsafes to account something to be lacking to Himself, until the last redeemed sinner, the price of His Precious Blood, shall be gathered unto Him, because the Church, i. e. the whole multitude of His redeemed, is, as being the body of Him Who is our Head, the fullness, or filling up, of Him, Who, in His Godhead, filleth all things in all.

We have seen the height, look now at the breadth of this power, how he prays for those of another Church [c], who had the same faith in Jesus, the same love towards all saints, in whom the Gospel had been

[c] Col. i. 4, 6.

not only fruit-bearing but growing since they first heard of it. He prayed unceasingly, that the grace and the knowledge of the will of God should spread through their whole spiritual being, and *that*, with power. "That ye should be filled with the thorough knowledge of His will in *all* wisdom and spiritual understanding, to walk worthily of the Lord to *all* pleasing, fruit-bearing and increasing in *all* good work, empowered in *all* power according to the might of His glory, to *all* endurance and long-suffering with joy[d]." The glory of the might of Christ is manifested in being put forth to strengthen us; the power, wherewith we are empowered, is in conformity with the might of Christ, and universal.

And this he prays even for his most recent converts[e], that "our God would count them worthy of His calling, and fullfil all good pleasure in goodness, and all work of faith in power." And this power, lodged in us, stands opposed to our mute shrinking from exertion. "God did not give us a spirit of cowardice, but of power, and love, and of correction[f]."

This power they had, having been once powerless. The Epistles embody spiritual facts. They appeal to people's souls, what they had been, what God had done for them, what they had become. They had been, for the most part, like others. Heathens, they had lived in heathen sins. They had been dead to all spiritual things, in trespasses and sins[g]; sold under sin[h]; slaves of sin[i]; sin ruled over them by a law to which they were captive[k].

d Col. i. 9—11.   e 2 Thess. i. 11.   f 2 Tim. i. 7.
g Eph. ii. 1, 5; Col. ii. 13.   h Rom. vii. 14.
i Ib. vi. 17, 20.   k Ib. vii. 23, 25.

They *all*, S. Paul says emphatically, "we all," i.e. all alike, Jews and Gentiles, "were occupied in the lusts of our flesh, doing the wills of the flesh and of our minds, and we were, by nature, children of wrath, like the rest[1]." Nay, they had not only their inherent powerlessness. As they had now the powerful inworking of God the Holy Ghost for good, so aforetime they had the inworking of an evil spirit for evil. As the patriarchs walked to and fro with God, so now people "walked according to the course of this world, according to the ruler of the power of the air, the spirit, who now worketh[m]," not in them who had been freed from him but, "in the children of disobedience."

And so S. Paul bids them be tender to the heathen, as having once been what these still were; "shewing all meekness towards all men; for we too were formerly without understanding, disobedient, erring, slaves to divers lusts and passions, passing our whole lives in malice and envy, hateful and hating one another[n]."

Men were amazed, S. Peter attests, at the change, as they are now too at the conversion of one, Christian in name only; and, as they do now also, they calumniated them. "Sufficient is the past time, to have worked out the will of the heathen, by walking, as ye did, in lasciviousnesses, lusts, drunkennesses, revellings, carousals; wherein they are amazed, that you rush not with them into the same slough of profligacy, speaking evil of you[o]."

But from all this Christians had been set free, and free they remained. Their two conditions, their past

[1] Eph. ii. 3.   [m] Ib. 2.   [n] Tit. iii. 3.   [o] 1 Pet. iv. 3, 4.

and their present, were as different as darkness and
light, death and life, utter slavery and perfect freedom, prostrate weakness and superhuman strength,
degradation below man and elevation above man.
And between those two states there had been an act.
Were there no history besides the Epistles, these
would be records of the marvellous transformation
of countless multitudes at one and the same time.
They had been what we should shrink to think of;
they became what we should long to be. And one
act had passed between. Holy Scripture says not
only, "Ye *were* ungodly, ye *are* now godly; ye *were*
profane, ye *are* now devout; ye *were* sensual, ye *are*
now spiritual." It says that their past and their
present were severed by a great act, in which *they*
had only been recipients, with their own free-will
accepting the free gifts of God.

" God shone in our hearts," they say, " called us,
wrought and moulded us for this every thing, Who
also is He Who gave us the earnest of the Spirit P;
He loved us and made us acceptable to Himself in
the Beloved; co-quickened us in Christ, anointed us,
sealed us." "The law of the Spirit of Christ freed
me from the law of sin and death." On the other
hand, they say of themselves: ' we *were* compas-
sionated, *were* made free from sins and from the law,
and *were* made servants to righteousness; we *were* re-
conciled, *were* justified, *were* washed, *were* sanctified,
were saved; we received the atonement, an anoint-
ing, the spirit of adoption, access to His grace; their
old man had been crucified with Christ, co-interred;
with Him they had been co-interred, with Him co-

P 2 Cor. v. 5.

raised; in Him they had been re-created unto good works; with Him they had been clothed; in Him made rich; in Him they had been all baptised into one body, all had been made to drink into One Spirit; by His Spirit they had been sealed to the day of redemption[q].' And what was their condition now? You know the deep expression of intimate love and union—they were "*in* Christ." To Him they were united by His Spirit dwelling in them, because they had been made members of Christ, closely united to Him as members to their Head, of His flesh and of His bones, because, as He says, "Whoso eateth My Flesh, and drinketh My Blood, dwelleth in Me, and I in him. . . He that eateth Me, shall live by Me[r]."

Of all this, the poor world could, of course, know nothing, as neither can the natural man now. But it saw the change, and then it scorned, reproached, ridiculed (as it does now), counted Christians as madmen, or—it was converted. While some were moved by miracles or the fulfilment of prophecy[s], and others, "[t]yea, oftentimes were drawn by an over-mastering power of the Spirit against their will, changing their ruling mind suddenly from hatred of the Word to willingness to die for it," others were moved by the superhuman life or superhuman change, which they saw. "[u]Why mention the countless multitude of those who changed from pro-

[q] See the fuller development of the bearing of these statements in Holy Scripture, in Pusey's "Scriptural Doctrine of Holy Baptism," pp. 155—175, § "Passages which speak of Christian gifts, as having been bestowed in the past."

[r] S. John vi. 56, 7.　　　　[s] S. Aug. in Ps. cxlix. 13.
[t] Orig. c. Cels. i. 46.　　　　[u] S. Justin, Apol. i. 15, 16.

fligacy, and who learned continence? For Christ
called not the righteous, nor the sober to repentance; but the ungodly, and profligate, and unrighte-
ous. But that we should be endurant of evil and
subservient to all, He saith on this wise, 'To him
who smiteth thee on the cheek, turn to him the
other also.' Nor doth He will that we should be
imitators of the bad, but He bade through patience
and meekness to lead all from shame and lust of evil
things; which, moreover, we can shew in the case
of many who have come among us, who changed
from violent and oppressive men, having been conquered, either when they traced the endurance of
their neighbour's life, or the strange patience of
fellow-travellers when defrauded, or when they made
trial of those with whom they were engaged in
business."

Celsus mocked at the Gospel for receiving sinners;
"Perfectly to change nature," he said truly, "is all-
difficult[v]." Truly; for man it is impossible. But, then,
on that very ground, the change, when it did exist,
was Divine. "[w]When we see those words which he
saith are uninstructed (as if they were charms,) to
be filled with power, impelling whole multitudes at
once from profligacy to a life wholly well-ordered,
from injustice to goodness, from a recreant unmanli-
ness to a mind striving to despise even death for
the sake of the godliness revealed among them, how
can we fail to admire the power lodged therein? For
the word of those who first ministered and toiled to
found the Churches of God; yea, their preaching
was with persuasiveness, not such as is the persua-

[v] ap. Orig. iii. 69.　　　　[w] Ib. 68.

siveness of those who proclaim the wisdom of Plato or any other philosopher who had nothing but human nature. But the demonstration in the Apostles of Jesus, having been given by God, was persuasive from the Spirit and power. Wherefore their word, or rather the Word of God, ran most swiftly and most forcibly, changing through them many of those to whom sin was nature and custom; whom man could not have changed even by punishing, but the Word transmade, forming and fashioning them after its own will."

Even persecution was the harvest-seed of the Church, not by enlisting sympathies, (which were none, in a people brutalized the more by the exhibition of Christian suffering, except when an executioner here and there came in nearer contact with a sufferer,) but because the superhuman fortitude drew people's thoughts. "[x]Every man who beholdeth so much endurance," is an appeal to a Roman governor, cognizant of facts, "being struck with some misgiving, is kindled with the desire of enquiring, what is the cause of this? and so soon as he discovereth the truth, himself also immediately followeth it."

That change which passed over each converted soul, so that it hated what it before craved; had serene mastery over the passions, to which it was before enslaved; loved to be without what was before the miserable solace of its misery; loved what it before had no taste for;—this was a spiritual fact which could be known only by experience. The experience of the senses tells us the things of sense; the

---

[x] Tertull. ad Scap. end, p. 150, Oxf. Tr.; comp. his Apol. end; and others quoted there, p. 105, note a, Oxf. Tr.

experience of the soul tells us the things which pass in the soul. Beforehand, they seem impossible; experienced, they are known. " I," says S. Cyprian, of his heathen state [y], " when I yet lay in darkness and blind night, and tottering and uncertain with erring steps reeled on the sea of this tossing world, ignorant of my life, alien from truth and light; according to my then ways, I thought what the Divine mercy promised for my salvation, altogether difficult and hard, that one could be new-born, that, quickened to a new life by the laver of healing water, one should lay aside what he had been before, and, while the frame of the body still remained, should be changed himself in heart and mind. How is so great a conversion possible, that suddenly and rapidly *that* should be put off, which, either being part of our natural selves, has hardened in the neglected soil, or, if acquired, has long been engrained, inveterate through age? These things hold secure by deep, far-penetrating roots. While allurements still cling tenaciously, love of wine must needs invite, pride inflate, anger inflame, rapacity disquiet, cruelty stimulate, ambition delight, lust cast headlong. These things said I ofttimes with myself; for, being held entangled with very many errors of my former life, whereof I did not believe that I could be freed, I humoured the vices which clung to me, and in despair of aught better, nurtured my own evils, as being now my own offspring, born in my house."

The method of his conversion S. Cyprian does not relate. For he relates only his own evils, and the

[y] Ad Donat. § 2, 3, pp. 2, 3. Oxf. Tr.

re-creating good ,of God. But see the contrast of powerlessness and power. "But after that, the stain of the former life having been wiped away by the aid of the life-giving water, a light from above, serene and pure, poured itself into my forgiven breast, after that the second birth re-formed me into a new man, drinking in the Spirit from heaven, then forthwith, in a marvellous manner, things doubtful assumed steadfastness, things closed lay open, things dark shone with light; what seemed aforetime diffi-culties offered facilities; what was thought impossi-ble seemed now, achieveable, as it *was* to own, that *that* which, being born after the flesh, lived subject to guilt, was of earth, *that* which the Holy Ghost was now quickening had begun to be of God. Thou knowest and ownest with me, what that death of crimes, that life of virtues, took from me, what it gave me. Now, by the gift of God, not to sin has begun to be the work of faith, as, before, to sin be-longed to human error. Of God, of God, is all my power. From Him I live, from Him I have strength, from Him in that vigour which I have received and ingathered, I have, even while placed here below, some foretokens of what is to be hereafter."

Such are two pictures of powerlessness in his heathen state, of self-power as a Christian, which S. Cyprian gives of himself. Ask yourselves, my sons, "which of the twain belongs to me?" I do not mean to ask as to any of the coarser outbreaks of sin. Deadly sin is compatible with a decent ex-terior, deserving in some things to be thought well of, a general wish to save the soul, a hope that it will be saved, a wish to be on God's side somehow,

a doing some things for God, a vague yearning after
Him. And yet some one unmastered, ever-mastering
sin, makes the heart not whole with God, defiles
perhaps the temple of the Holy Ghost, the body; it
wounds the conscience, cripples the soul, withdraws
it from intercourse with God, its Life, chases away
the Holy Spirit, scares from Communions, the great
preservative against deadly sin, or makes the soul
go to them faithlessly, hopelessly, unprofitably.

But whether it be some one sin, bodily or even
spiritual, which holds you back, whether it be a general torpor, a predominance of sense, a personal ambition, which dulls you as to things spiritual, or a
general self-complacency which stunts your growth,
if your religion is not one of power, it must be that
you have not, generously and without reserve, admitted Christianity as a whole into your souls. For
"the Gospel is the power of God unto salvation."
Christ, of Whom men boast in name, is the Power
of God; and "might" is one of the seven-fold gifts
of the Spirit, and God clothes His own with the
whole panoply of the Divine armoury. Contrariwise,
it is to be part of the self-deceit of the last days, to
own religion as something which *should* form the
soul, "having or holding," S. Paul says, a "formativeness" of godliness, but having" practically denied
or repudiated "its power." Perhaps it may be some
eclecticism out of Christianity, some new-modelling
of the old truths, giving new, unmeaning, alien meanings to the old doctrines. Perhaps it will think that
it renders homage to our Lord, because it owns,
while it criticises as a superior, some of the virtues

z μόρφωσιν 2 Tim. iii. 5.

of His Humanity, and will deem that it shews Him reverence in pronouncing "Ecce Homo [a]," while it has less of awe of Him than Pontius Pilate who crucified Him, and puts Him to more deliberate shame. But whatever that would-be "formativeness of godliness" may be, which the times of Antichrist may invent, be sure that a powerless religiosity is a sign of belonging not to Christ, but of being still under the power of the evil one. " [b] His servants ye are, whom ye obey." There is a strong one who was bound and spoiled, and there is a Stronger than he, Who overcame him by His Death, and bound him. But bound though he be, while he has no power to hurt thee without thy will, he still masters those who place themselves within his grasp. Flee him, and he cannot follow thee. Betake thyself to Jesus, and the blasted one crouches at the presence of his Conqueror and his Judge. Mistrust thyself, but mistrust not God's Almightiness. Look well whether there is any part of the Divine armoury which thou hast neglected. Hast thou mistrusted the omnipotence of prayer, or forgotten meditation on the love of God for thee, or thoughts on the four last things, which close and must close this fleeting life, Death, Judgement, Heaven, Hell; or on God's aweful holiness, trifling irreverently with His sacred attributes, and neglecting His inward calls; or forgetting Him from morning to evening, all the more confidently because

---

[a] My ground for thus warning the young as to the character of one single book, was, that even respectable journalists had been misled, and were misleading them. My words apply to the book only, not to the author, of whom and whose motives I know nothing.   [b] Rom. vi. 16.

thou rememberest Him a little then, and this thou thinkest must needs be enough, and God could not ask for more; or going to a monthly slovenly Sacrament, forgetting almost beforehand, but most certainly afterwards, Whose Presence was to be and was vouchsafed to thee; or holding on a little while by strength from God, and then, through unwatchfulness or tampering with evil imaginations, falling into the same sins as before? Or hast thou secretly thought that the real remedy for thy relapses would be, as others have done, to confess thy sins, and interpose thy Lord's absolving Voice, "Thy sins be forgiven thee," between the living and the dead, thy heap of dead putrefying sins and thy future of life, and hast held back for some shame or awkwardness, or secret pride?

It is a hard thing to say, (God grant that it may not be so!) but I more and more fear that what is wanted in so many, amid this powerless religiousness, is an entire conversion of heart. "[c]Thou shalt love the Lord thy God with all thy heart, and with all thy mind, and with all thy soul, and with all thy strength; and thy neighbour as thyself." Where is this whole-hearted, loyal obedience, when self is stealthily enshrined in so many hearts, and God seems to be made for man, not man for God? A "weak Christian" were a contradiction in terms. For to be a Christian at all is to be a member of Christ, Who is Almighty God; it is to have a claim to *His* might, Who has all power in heaven and earth; it is to have Him for your indweller, Who is all-holiness, all-hallowing. To be a weak Christian

[c] S. Luke x. 27.

is to have but a weak will to be a Christian, to have
been made a Christian, yet half to repent of the love
of God towards thee in making thee a Christian.
Lean on Him, look to Him, watch unto Him, Whose
strength is made perfect in weakness, and past weakness shall not hinder thee. He beholdeth thy conflict Who willeth to crown thee; He Who upheld
the martyrs in their sufferings will uphold thee.
Only be thou strong in the Lord and in the power
of His might; He will overcome in thee Who bid
thee "[d] Be of good cheer; I have overcome the world."
He saith to thee, "[e] To him that overcometh will I
grant to sit down with Me in My throne, even as I
also overcame, and am set down with My Father in
His throne."

Only be earnest now, at once, as if the yawning
gulf of hell were open before thee, and thou couldest
only cross it on that narrow wood, thy Saviour's
Cross. He holds forth His nail-pierced Hands unto
thee; He bids thee " come, and I will uphold thee."
Only remember Him ; and now, for His love's sake,
remember those the wearied victims of their own
weak will and of man's lusts, who long to be freed
from their sickening existence, and who may yet be
His, Who died for them and for us [f].

[d] S. John xvi. 33.   [e] Rev. iii. 21.
[f] There was to be a collection for a Penitentiary.

Y

SERMON XVII[a].

THE PRAYERS OF JESUS.

S. John xi. 41, 42.

"And Jesus lifted up His eyes and said, Father, I thank Thee that Thou hast heard Me; and I knew that Thou hearest Me always."

Marvellous, among the mysteries of this strange mysterious world, is the mystery of prayer. Mysterious in its simplicity, boundless in its might, endless in its efficacy. It needs no gifts of nature, no knowledge, save the knowledge of God, no spoken words, no plainly conceived thoughts, no cultivation of the mind. The simplest soul, to which God has made Himself known, has a power above all created intellect, reaching where the acutest intelligence loses itself, influencing the destinies of its fellowmen, beyond man's mightiest power or his most piercing intelligence. For it is supernatural. Outwardly, it is a few words from the inmost soul, or a deep unspoken longing, darted up, our human soul knows how, gone so swiftly that we cannot follow it. We seem to have done nothing. If we were in earnest, it gave vent to our soul's deep desire; it may

[a] Preached at S. Giles', Oxford. Lent, 1862.

have been for the salvation of souls, for the mitiga-
tion of all this horrible dishonour to God's holiness,
for the staying of the withering unbelief around us,
of the wasting of souls for whom Christ died, for the
arresting of one single sin, for the gaining of the last
grace needed for a soul balancing between sin and
God, Hell and Heaven. The prayer has sped. We
hear no answer, we see no sign: perhaps, until we
are in eternity, we shall never know what became of
it. But it had an inward power, a Divine might
from God to God, a covenanted omnipotency with
the Omnipotent. God has pledged His truth, that
is, Himself, that, if it has been asked according to
His Will, He will give it. God became Man, to
give us this power over Himself. God, become Man,
taught us how to use it. There was a necessary difference in part, in the *subject* of His prayers and of
our's. There was, of course, a difference between
the frame of mind, in which Jesus, as Man, prayed
to His Father and our's; the difference between the
All-Perfect and the imperfect, the All-Holy and sinners. Jesus needed not prayer for Himself. He
neither needed nor could pray on those two great
subjects of our prayers, even apart from the memory
of our past sins. *He*, the All-Perfect, could not pray
against temptation or for spiritual gifts. For "[b]in
Him dwelt all the fulness of the Godhead bodily."
The Godhead was, from the moment of His conception, the source of perfect Holiness to the Man Jesus.
"I sanctify Myself," He says[c]. "[d]He sanctified Himself the Man, in Himself the Word; for Word and

[b] Col. ii. 9.   [c] S. John xvii. 19.
[d] S. Aug. in S. Joh. Tr. 108. fin. p. 977. O. T.

Man are One Christ, sanctifying the Man in the Word." His Human Mind was ever united with God by His Personal union.: His Divine Soul, in His Mother's womb, ever had the beatific Vision of God, and the fruition of eternal bliss in Him. He could not pray against temptation, before Whose All-holiness and the Brightness of Whose Godhead those temptations which His blasted creature was allowed to present to Him; shrank away into their inherent nothingness, as wax melteth before the fire, and is seen no more. Satan was allowed to tempt Him from without; but the darkness of His evil angel disappeared in the Presence of His light. Darkness was dissipated, as it approached Him, the true Light. No motion or emotion was possible to His Mind, which could be apart from that Will of His Father which He came on earth to fulfil. No inward conflict, no balance of will, no faintest velleity, which could be against the Mind of His Father, could arise in His All-Holy Soul. Thus far He was separated from us by the necessities of His Being. He came, not to redeem us only but to re-create our nature, to yield a perfect obedience to His Father, to be a new Beginning of our race, in Whom our human nature should again exist perfectly. That sacrifice which He offered had not been spotless, could one single emotion ever have arisen in the faintest conception of His soul, desiring any thing other than the All-Perfect Will of God. Such emotions, when they arise in our regenerate souls, are not sin, unless, by some consent, we make them our's. But we mourn them as an iniquity of our nature, as a part of "this body of death" wherewith we are encompassed. We confess that, although not truly sin in us, they "have the nature of sin." It were horrible, as well as blasphemy, to conceive of any thing which should have cast even the faintest, passing, shadow, over the God-united soul of Jesus. He " was born without spot of sin, to make us clean from all sin." He ever beheld all things in their reality. He could not pray for things as uncertain, Who saw all things, which are or shall be, perfectly in the mind of God. Have you been, at any time, tempted to think, that it lessens the encouragement from our Blessed Lord's example, or that He could have less perfect sympathy with you, because He could not have any of your imperfections? Would you, if you could, have your Redeemer less "separate from sin," or His Human Nature, the Deifier of our nature, less in-oned with His Godhead? Christ Jesus, God and Man, is, as to His Manhood, the perfection of creation. The Holy Trinity, Father Son and Holy Ghost, created no imperfect work, when the Son united with Himself that All-Holy Manhood. His Manhood has a closeness to God, nearer than any other union save that oneness of the Persons of the Ever-blessed Trinity; yet, in all eternity, Jesus, as Man, will be the First All-Perfect Eternal Adorer of God's Eternal Majesty.

What we lose in our Example, we gain, beyond all price, in the perfection of our Intercessor. These were His chief prayers on earth, our salvation; for to this end He came on earth. He never prayed for Himself Alone, Whose whole Being was for His Father's glory in the salvation of mankind. Even in that mysterious Agony in the Garden, when, to heal our infirmity, He clad Himself with our fear, that He might array our unstayedness with the solidity of His virtue[e], then, when He bowed under the weight of our sins and His Father's displeasure at our sins, and His own knowledge, how we should waste the fruits of His Passion in ourselves, and how some for whom He died, would perish everlastingly; then when, for our sakes, His Human Will seemed to shrink, and He prayed, "[f]O My Father, if it be possible, let this cup pass from Me, yet not as I will, but as Thou," then too, Scripture says[g], "He was heard." What then He really prayed for, then too, with His full Human Will, was His Father's Will. For the Cup passed not away; yet He was heard.

Jesus ever prayed. The Psalmist said in His Person; "[h]I am prayer." His whole Being was prayer. He said aloud to the Father, "I knew that Thou hearest Me always." His life was an ever-present speaking to the Father, an ever-present hearing of His every desire by the Father. As the holy "Angels do always," our Lord says[i], "behold the Face of My Father," while yet they minister to those little ones whom He giveth to them in charge, so and much more did Jesus, whatever besides He wrought for us, behold the Face of His Father and obtained all which He willed. That continual Intercession at the Right Hand of God, which S. Paul speaks of as the object of His life in heaven[j], must have been His Life on earth too. For He says, "Thou hearest Me always." His Me-

[e] S. Leo. Serm. 3. de Pass. [f] S. Matt. xxvi. 39. [g] Heb. v. 7.
[h] Ps. cix. 4. [i] S. Matt. xviii. 10. [j] Heb. vii. 25.

diatorial office began with His Incarnation. When
God the Word took our human flesh, He became at
once Man and our High Priest according to that
nature which He took. Those thirty years, during
which He seemed outwardly to do nothing for man,
were not lost for man. For He was ever God. His
Human Soul was, in His speechless Infancy, illumined by His indwelling Godhead. His Human
Soul ever beheld the Father and ever read His Will.
He says of Himself in the Psalm, "[k] Lo I am come
to do Thy Will, O God." He "came to do it;" then
He ever did it from that time when He came. And
what was that Will? Our Redemption. For that
Redeeming Act, which was the end and close of
His three and thirty Human years, all His life was
a preparation. He opened His eyes upon this world
of our's, yea rather of His, into which He was born,
to love it and each soul in it. From the hour of
His Birth, He knew for what He was born; He beheld the Cross, the Scourge, the Nails, the Crown
of Thorns; He felt beforehand in Spirit that last
Death-pang, which should complete our Redemption; He offered all unceasingly to His Father for
our salvation. Thirty years of intercession were
the preparation for His Ministry in winning souls
to His Father. Thirty three years of unbroken self-
oblation for the sins of men were perfected in His
Atoning Death. Outwardly, He underwent circumcision; He was carried to and fro, to Egypt, to
Nazareth; He received the worship of the Magi,
the shepherds; He went up to the Temple; He was
the Carpenter. Inwardly, He was the perpetual In-

[k] Ps. xl. 7.

tercessor.for all around Him, for the whole human race. In those adult years which the Gospel records, few are the glimpses into His inner life. That unceasing thanksgiving, adoration, prayer to His Father, flash forth to us in single instances for our instruction. We hear here and there of those lone nights spent on the mountains, to teach us, from time to time, whatever our employment, to retire from the world and be with God. From one of those nights before the choice of the Twelve, the Church learned, from the first, those seasons of fasting and prayer, before she sends out those whom they left to be their successors, or ordained to be shepherds of the flock. When, on His Baptism, Jesus looked up to Heaven and prayed, came down His Father's Voice, proclaiming to the whole world unto the end of time, "[1] This is My Beloved Son in Whom I am well-pleased." That gaze and prayer to the Father brought down that Voice from Heaven, that we might know how the windows of heaven will open to us, to pour down righteousness upon us. On prayer followed the marvellous Transfiguring, not so much a miracle as the cessation of a miracle, whereby the inherent light which, from His Indwelling Godhead, belonged even to His mortal flesh, had been, through those long years, repressed. "[m] He went up into a mountain to pray, and as He prayed, the fashion of His Countenance was altered," to teach us the fruit of prayer, how, in and on prayer, our souls are bedewed with heavenly light, and our heavy earthliness is transformed into the heavenly beauty of grace, and of us it is said, by grace not by

[1] S. Luke iii. 22.   [m] Ib. ix. 28, 29.

nature, "This is my beloved son," beloved in the
Beloved. In that one prayer for S. Peter, "[n] I have
prayed for thee, that thy faith fail not," there gleamed
forth, in a single ray, that individual love for the
souls whom He has bought with His Precious Blood.
As S. Paul says, "[o] He loved _me_ and gave Himself
for _me_," so Jesus prays, not for those only whom
God had given Him out of the world, not for all
those only who through Him should believe, but
for each single soul. He died for, He prayed for,
He intercedes for, not the whole of His redeemed,
as a mass, but, with that discriminating love, with
which He prayed for S. Peter or S. John, according
to their need. So, in this confused throng of human
souls, His discriminating Eye, enlightened by the
knowledge of His Godhead, sees the needs of each,
and prays for each according to its needs. Jesus
prays for thee. On the Cross, with expiring Eye
and pierced Hands and gored Feet and dislocated
Frame and yet more wounded Soul, on which the
consolations of His Godhead descended not, He remembered thee, He prayed for thee.

Well might He bid us by the Apostle to "[p] pray
without ceasing," Who, in the days of His Flesh, had
offered for us such unceasing prayers! Well might
He bid us pray for all men, Who, among all the heap
of mankind in all these eighteen hundred years, has,
one by one, singled out us, remembered us.

Such then were the subjects of His prayer. Once
only in all those years is He related to have prayed
for Himself, and then, too, in that Agony, He wept
those tears of Blood from His whole frame, not for

[n] S. Luke xxii. 32. [o] Gal. ii. 20. [p] 1 Thess. v. 17.

Himself, but for us. "He, the Teacher of peace," says a father[q], "and the Master of Unity would not that we should pray singly and severally for ourselves, so that, when any should pray, he should pray for himself alone." And what He taught us, that of course He did. He began His great High Priest's Prayer, "[r] Father, glorify Thy Son, that Thy Son also may glorify Thee." But His glorifying, what was it but our marvellous gain? What was that glory, but our's in Him? That mankind, and we among them, should know Him and the Father in Him; that we should discern His Godhead under the veil of His Flesh, and in Him find our Redemption, Sanctification and eternal Bliss.

Jesus is the Pattern of our prayers, more (so to speak) in the circumstances of prayer than in the substance of His Prayers. For we are sinners, and we have need to ask forgiveness; our penitence for past sin at best is not deep enough or loving enough, and we have to pray for a loving sorrow; we are weak and unstable, and need to pray for steadfastness: we have a fountain of temptation from within, and ever need to pray that we may be cleansed; we are far short of what, by God's grace, we might have been or might be, and have to pray for a flood of light, of grace, of love, to enlighten us as to the depth of our own misery and the boundlessness of His love; to remove from us all hindrances to our prayers; to kindle our coldness; to give us that loving confidence, to which our Father Who giveth it us, will never say us nay.

I should keep you till midnight, if I were to say

q S. Cypr. on the Lord's Prayer n. 4. p. 180.   r S. John xvii. 1.

but a little of all the great things which our blessed Redeemer's prayers tell us, in those, so to speak, attributes of His Prayer. But just look with me for a while on these; the thanksgiving, with which He accompanied it, the simplicity, the earnestness, the continuousness, the perseverance.

Look at the Thanksgiving. Lazarus, he whom He loved, was still in the grave. He had Himself just groaned in Spirit and troubled Himself, when, standing in sight of the opened tomb, He said, "Father, I thank Thee, that Thou hast heard Me." When He stood alone with the seventy, rejected by His own whom He came to redeem, He gave thanks to His Father for those whom He had given Him. "*I thank Thee, O Father, Lord of Heaven and earth, that Thou hast hid these things from the wise and prudent, and hast revealed them unto babes." He went to His Agony and Bloody Sweat and to the Cross, with Psalmody and a jubilee of thanksgiving. "*When they had sung a hymn, they went out into the mount of Olives." It was probably the great Halleluia Psalm, the great "Praise" as the Jews called it, which He sung with His disciples and taught them to sing, as He went forth to bear our sins and the sins of the whole world. Look at that meek Holy Face, radiant with Divine Love and Joy and Thanksgiving! Whither goest Thou, Lord, so full of resplendent irradiating gladness of Thanksgiving? To die the Atoning Death of shame, to drink the Cup of the Passion to its dregs!

My brethren, your prayers would be quite changed, they will be transfigured, as they shall have more

<hr>

* S. Luke x. 21.   † S. Matt. xxvi. 30.

of thanksgiving in them. What so spoils prayer even
in people whose hearts are right with God? I will
take but four things. Coldness, want of childlike
confidence, mistrust of God, hopelessness of being
heard. I do not speak now of the sad hindrances
to the inflow and overflow of Divine graces to us,
but of the way in which it spoils our prayers. Of
course, nothing can be more true, than that we
deserve nothing of God, except Hell ; that there
is nothing in us, why God should look on us ; that
we have been ungrateful to Him for His graces
before, and shall be so again; and that it is a mere
prodigality and squandering of His bountiful love,
to bestow anything upon us. Very true; but what
then ? Why this is the very ground and fountain-
head of our thanksgiving, that, we being what we
are, what we have unmade ourselves, God loves us
with all that Infinite love. God had no reason for
which to create you, except His Infinite love. He
made you, to be a partaker of that His unutterable
love. He loves you, not because you are worthy
of His love, but that you may love Him and have
His love. Thank Him for this; and where is coldness ? It is melted away in that burning, consum-
ing Fire of His Infinite Love. Where is mistrust?
Mistrust of Him Who gave the Son of His love to
die for thee ! Mistrust of Him, Who is daily loading
and overloading thee with His benefits, in Whose
Love thou livest and movest ! Move, if thou canst,
in this world, out of the circle of His love, and so
so mistrust Him. It is only while we think of
our poor, wretched, thankless selves, that we can
mistrust God or pray so coldly. Go out of your-

selves, and go forth into that Ocean of love, wherein
thou art bathed. Thank God, for what He has made
thee, the object of His love, the son of His love
in the Well-Beloved Son, nay, one with Him "in
Whom He is well-pleased." He looks on thee, not
in thyself, but as He has made thee, the bearer of
His image, the temple of His Spirit. Thy voice in
prayer is the voice of the Holy Spirit; for God has
said, "ᵘ the Spirit itself maketh intercessions for us
with groanings which cannot be uttered." It is, to
the Father, the Voice of Jesus; for He Who dwelleth
in us is the Spirit of Christ. Thank God for all the
blessings which you know, as they are showered
daily upon you; thank Him for having saved you
from any sin and misery; for enabling you to check
any temptation; for keeping from you any which
you would not have resisted; thank Him for all His
unmerited love, and that He has concentrated on
you all the wonders of His Redemption, that He
died for you, as much as if in all this wide world
of the redeemed, there had been none besides to die
for. God has made us such, that we are influenced
more by our deeds than by our thoughts. Thank
God, as best thou canst, when thou prayest, for all
His special love of thee, from thy birth till that
hour; thank Him that thou art yet His child, the
child of His infinite Love, and thou wilt not fear
that God will not hear thee.

Again, another hindrance to prayer is want of simplicity. We think so much of ourselves and so little of God, as if, after all, God heard us for something
of our's, not for His own gift of prayer in us, or for

ᵘ Rom. viii. 26.

His Son's sake, with Whose effectual prayers our
poor prayers are united. As though we should be
"heard for our much speaking;" as though there
ought to be some eloquence of words, some appro-
priate language with which to approach God's great
Majesty, something which should move God. Our
true eloquence towards God is our need and our
sense of it. The eloquence which pleads with God
is within, in the heart. The soul which longs, cries
with a loud voice to God. No matter, if thou canst
not form a thought or stammer out two words. God
will put together thy broken thoughts. Plead to
Him as the parched ground pleads, with no voice
but the cracks which rend it, or as the ravens with
their unintelligent cry. Cast down thine empty
soul before Him; shew Him its folds, its collapses,
its wrinkles, its voids. All the gifts and graces
which adorn the Court of Heaven, have been purchased for it by the Blood of Jesus. They are thine.
He has said to thee "Son, all that I have, is thine."
Thy title-deeds are thy needs. Ask with the longing of the heart: and all is thine. Jesus teaches
thee simplicity in asking, by the simplicity of His
prayer. Those seven words on the Cross, which
reach to the end of time, how few and simple are
they! In that dread Agony in the garden, He went
away, saying the same words.

What can one say of the earnestness of prayer,
which S. Paul speaks of, when He beheld all that
hideous mockery and blasphemy of the scourging,
the reed, the thorny crown, the buffeting; when He
felt beforehand the weight of all our sins, from Adam
to the end; knowing, as none besides could know,

how they wounded the love of God and offended
His Majesty; knowing too how we, the price of His
Blood, should waste our ransom; and bore it all, as
if He had been the guilty, we the innocent? Then
He let all our weakness come upon Him, that He
might impart to us His strength; He seemed to
shrink from suffering, that He might teach us how
to conquer in Him Who suffered for us, suffereth
in us, that He may conquer in us. At the beginning of His prayer, He was "ᵛ sorrowful and very
heavy." "His soul exceeding sorrowful even unto
death." Twice His Father seemed as though He
heard not; He desisted not, but prayed more earnestly. As the Agony increased, the intensity of
His prayer increased; and the Angel came, the messenger of His Father's love. How has not that
intenser prayer taught His saints, never to let go
prayer, though it seemed as if there were none to
hear! Never is prayer more heard, than when it
seems not to be heard. Never is the ear of God
closer to our hearts, than when we seem alone in the
world, and God draws us still to hold fast to our
prayer, and, in the end, the light comes. "ʷBlessed
be God Who hath not withdrawn my prayer nor His
mercy from me." He Who has left in thee the power
of that seemingly powerless prayer, has left with
thee His own mercy and salvation, and the earnest
that thou shalt behold His Beatific Face in joy.

For we should know for certain and as matter of
faith, that whatever we ask for, that, if good for
us, we shall have. For us too, in our measure, our
Dear Lord said, "I knew that Thou hearest Me al-

ᵛ S. Matt. xxvi. 37, 38.   ʷ Ps. lxvi. 20.

ways." The Father will hear His Well-Beloved Son in us and for us, if we trust ourselves with Him. You have often, I doubt not, marvelled at that word of our Lord, "[x]What things soever ye desire, when ye pray, believe that ye receive them, and ye shall have them." Perhaps ye shrink back from them; perhaps ye thought that they were for Apostles, that they were for those only whom God inspired with the holy confidence which asks according to His Will because it knows it. Alas! we know not God. On this ground, prayer so often fails, because we have no trust that God will give us what we ask. True, that as to those greater things which do not belong to us and which concern not our salvation, God will not give us any confidence, because He does not will us to ask Him *them.* He would not give us confidence to ask a miracle, unless it be that great miracle which He so loves to work, the salvation of a soul. But try God. God loveth to be put on trial, to have His faithfulness tried and proved. Ask Him perseveringly as to something which lies near your soul, if only you are sure that it is not against His Will or hurtful to you. Ask Him for confidence in Himself and then ask Him in confidence this thing you need. There must be some very great ground in His Goodness, if He gives it you not. You will find unmistakeably that He has given you, instead, something which, you will see, is better for you; just as a tender mother would give her young child something else instead of the knife which it wants and with which it would wound itself. But remember, it is not a lazy, desultory prayer,

[x] S. Matt. xi. 24. add S. Matt. xxi. 22.

now praying; *now* forgetting; *now* asking earnestly,
now remissly; which Jesus sanctified by His continuous Prayer, which God has promised to hear.
Continuous prayer has, like every thing else, to be
learned. Be regular, at least, with all thy appointed
times of prayer. That is continuous prayer, according to thy measure, which goes to God at those fixed
times of morning and evening, when God by nature
itself calls thee, or when, by the Church, He invites
thee. But much more is *that* continuous prayer,
which commends to God, first all the actions of the
day, and then, the beginning of those acts, that they
may be done according to the Will of God. Then
labour, sanctified by self-offering, may be prayer;
then the soul will rest the rather, its labour done, in
God. O what are our thoughts of God that we do
not find prayer our chief rest, that we do not, of
ourselves, fill up our voids with prayer? There
have been, there are, souls, whose home is prayer,
whose labour is prayer, whose rest is prayer; and
bright and sunny are their minds, for the light of
God's love rests sweetly on them.

Once more. Our Dear Lord never prayed for Himself alone, neither do you. It were a poor thing, if it
were possible, to get to heaven by one's self. What?
To think to reach the abode of eternal love and God
Who is love, and bring none with us whom we have,
at least by our prayers, won to God! In one sense,
indeed, we cannot pray, in public or private, without
praying for others. Our Lord has mercifully hedged
us in with the "Our Father," in which He taught us
to pray. Yet even thus our self-love creeps in, and
we rather pray for ourselves *with* others, than for

z

ourselves *and* others.   Common prayer goes up too
often, I fear, practically from a number of souls, each
praying for itself in the common words, than as the
one voice of all, each praying for all.   And so we
all lose.   The more we pray for others, the more we
have the prayers of others.   If in our Litany this
evening we each prayed for all besides, then we had
each of us some 600 intercessors in this one Church;
we do not go back with our own poor prayers only,
but we go back with all the fruit of those 600 prayers,
and the wider we extend our prayer for all who, this
night in this city, shall be about to sin, or shall be
in sin, or under temptation, or weak, or unbelieving,
the more our own prayers will have been heard for
ourselves (for they will have had more love in them)
the more prayers God will have heard for us.   And
so the wider the circle of our love and prayer expands to the whole Catholic Church and the whole
world, for the conversion of all sinners every where
and the glory of God in their salvation, the larger and
brighter is the space of God's love into which we
enter, the more our own souls would be expanded
by Divine love.   I said, "if it were possible, to be
saved alone."   I should almost doubt whether it were
possible.   Quite alone, it would be well-nigh impossible; for it would be to be saved without love.   O
Love of Jesus! Blood of Jesus! where are ye?   Were
ye poured out on this cold earth, only to yield such
fruits as we see now ?   God the Father willeth you
to pray and to give you abundantly what you ask.
"ˣThe Father Himself loveth you," Jesus saith.   God
the Son became Man, suffered, prayed, in part to give

ˣ S. John xvi. 27.

force to your prayers. You never pray alone; you pray, by virtue of His Merits, united with His Almighty intercession at the Right Hand of God. God the Holy Ghost helpeth your prayers. O why do sin and unbelief so gain the upper hand? Why does this world, at the first thoughtful, but superficial look at it, *seem* to be rather the devil's world than God's, but that love is cold, and trust in God is cold, and prayer is cold? You, each of you, have might to change, at least, some portion of the world. Few can argue, fewer can speak persuasively; if they do, it is all, except for prayer, at best, but a passing strain, which dies away at the Church-door. None can do, what is God's prerogative, bend the human will. But you can do more. God has given you a Diviner might. It is with Himself. God made you His children, in part, that you might, by prayer, win others of His children, who forget Him. Jesus left you a portion of His work to do for Him. God waits for you. Pray, as far as God gives you now, simply, humbly, earnestly, regularly, perseveringly, for others with yourself; unite your prayers to your Redeemer's prayers; your prayers for others will return into your own bosom; God will hear for yourself your prayers for others: and it will be part of that Ocean of joy, into which you shall enter, that as the prayers of others have been heard for you, so shall there be some there, who, through your prayers shall have been won to the faith in God, to love of God, to everlasting life in God.

SERMON XVIII[a].

THE MEANS OF GRACE, AS A REMEDY AGAINST SIN.

Col. i. 27.

" Christ in you, the hope of glory."

THE whole of the Christian life is supernatural. Above nature and man's own power are the enemies of his salvation. The Author of his salvation is Almighty God. Sin is the natural offspring of man's corrupt nature. Above nature is every act whereby it resists sin; above nature is every act whereby it pleases God; yea the poorest, lowest motion of the will towards God is more above nature, than the highest conformity of the soul with the Will of God is above that poor act; for every motion of the will towards God is the working of Divine grace. Degrees in holiness are but degrees of the workings of the self-same Spirit of God. The least gift of grace is as infinitely above nature, as the Creator is above the creature. Degrees of Divine grace are but different measures, in which the same Infinite Love putteth itself forth to save us.

Into this ocean of Divine grace we were plunged when we were made children of God. What is it

[a] Preached at S. Mary's, Oxford. Lent, 1859.

to be made a child of God? Is it to be called only
by that great title of love? Is it to have some distant promise only, dependent upon our future faithfulness to the motions of His grace? Does God then
love in name or in deed? Does He call us what He
does not make us? No, He Who bids us love one
another, not in word but in deed and in truth [b], is
Himself the Pattern and the Source of the love which
He enjoins us. He calls us by no empty title, no
mere shadow of truth. "[c] Behold what manner of
love the Father hath bestowed upon us, that we should
be called the sons of God." Not "called" only. "[d]For
they who are called and are not, what profiteth them
the name, where the substance is not?" Not "called"
only; for it follows, "Beloved, now *are* we the sons
God." Not "sons" only, as the creatures of the
Great Father, but "sons" by being members of
Christ, the Eternal Son of God. As he says, "[e] Ye
are all the children of God by faith in Christ Jesus."
"*For*," he adds, "as many of you as have been
baptized into Christ have put on Christ." "Since
Christ," says a Father [f], "is the Son of God, and thou
hast put Him on, then having the Son in thyself and
being transformed into His likeness, thou hast been
brought into one kindred with Him:" an actual son
of God through the union with Him Who Alone is
by Nature the Only-Begotten Son of God.

This is the end of our being, for which God created us, union with Himself through the Only-Begotten Son of God. This was the fruit of the Incarnation, that we, being redeemed by His Blood, should

[b] 1 S. John iii. 18.   [c] Ib. 1, 2.   [d] S. Aug. ad loc.
[e] Gal. iii. 26, 27.   [f] S. Chrys. ad loc. T. x. p. 70. ed. Ben.

be taken into oneness with Him. This He ante-dated in each one of us, before we had the power of reason; before we had, as yet, the aweful capacity of rejecting Him, or choosing something else instead of our God; before that, reversing the end for which He created us, we could choose the evil and refuse the good. He took us out of ourselves and our state by nature, gave us "that good which by nature we could not have;" imparted to us the Trinity; the Father and the Son dwelling in us through the Spirit. For we are "born of the Holy Ghost;" and where the Holy Ghost is, there is the Father and the Son, for they are indivisible. Indivisible also is their Presence. So our Lord said, " g We will love him, and make Our abode with him."

This then is our hope; this, our sanctification; this, our defence; this, our armour at which devils tremble; this, the seal upon our soul, which if we keep, the evil one toucheth us not; "this h, the loosing of death, destruction of sins, abolition of the curse, freedom from the old man," garment of light i, " h entrance into Paradise, ascent into heaven, life with the Angels, participation of future blessing and those good things which eye hath not seen nor ear heard nor have entered into the heart of man," that we were made members of Christ, and being His members, then "we dwell in Christ and Christ in us, then we are one with Christ and Christ with us."

"Christ in you, the hope of glory." S. Paul opens

---

g S. John xiv. 23.　　　h S. Chrys. in S. Matt. Hom. xi. n. 6.
i S. Cyril Jer. Procatech. n. 16. The like accumulation of titles of Baptism occurs in S. Basil exhort. ad S. Bapt. n. 5. p. 117. ed. Ben.

to us, in few words, a whole body of theology, a treasure-house of the Divine Love, the unutterable riches of the Divine condescension. Christ, as our Redeemer, our Reconciler with the Father, our Eternal High-Priest and Intercessor, is the only Hope and Refuge of us sinners. His wide-open Side is our Hiding-place from the accusing foe, our own conscience, and our sins. But here S. Paul says something more. Plainly he does not unsay what he ever said, but he adds to it. Christ is *also* our Hope, in that He is our Indweller, our Sanctifier, our Transformer; the Author of our holiness, the sanctifying principle of our actions which are wrought in Him and to Him, and are by Him inwrought in us. Christ is not only without us, our Redeemer our Lord our God; but "*in* you also," he says, "is the Hope of Glory." "This," he says, "is the riches of the glory of this mystery which was hidden from ages and generations, but now hath been made manifest to His saints." Christ, God and Man, our Redeemer; Christ in you, your Indweller by His Spirit. As Christ says of the confession of Himself; "[k] It is not ye that speak, but the Spirit of your Father which speaketh in you," so of Him the Apostle saith, "[l] I can do all things in Christ in-strengthening me." Wonderful interchange of Heaven and earth, the Creator with His creatures! The Apostle hath all power over himself in Christ; he in Christ, and Christ in him, "instrengthening" him. Whence he could yet more boldly say, "[m] Not I, but Christ liveth in me." He was co-crucified with Christ; his former self was nailed to the Cross of Christ,

[k] S. Matt. x. 20.　　[l] Phil. iv. 13.　　[m] Gal. ii. 20.

and was dead; dead he was to all his former hopes,
wishes, thoughts; dead to everything which once
he had prized, out of Christ; and now, having been
made partaker of Christ, his spiritual life was from
Christ, living in him by His Spirit. When he taught,
Christ taught in him; when he prayed, Christ prayed
in him, for he prayed by the Spirit of Christ within
him; and "[n] the Spirit which helpeth our infirmities,
maketh intercession for us with groanings which cannot be uttered." Christ laboured in him, as he saith,
"[o] yet not I, but the grace of God which was with
me." Christ suffered in him, as, when he was yet
a persecutor, Christ, in His members on earth, suffered through him, as he said "[p] Saul, Saul, why persecutest thou Me?" Hence an early saint and Martyr[q] said of his Lord, "He is not one who only
looks upon His servants, but Himself also wrestleth
in us, Himself engageth, Himself on the issue of
our conflict alike crowneth and is crowned." He
was present in His own conflicts; the champions
and maintainers of His own Name He uplifted,
strengthened, animated. And He Who once over-
came death for us, ever overcomes it in us. "[r] How
did Christ rejoice there, how gladly in such His
servants did He both fight and conquer, the Guardian of their faith, and giving to believers so much
as he who taketh of His hand believeth that he
receiveth."

This then is the groundwork of the Christian life;
this the foundation of the building, its base on earth,

[n] Rom. viii. 26.   [o] 1 Cor. xv. 10.   [p] Acts ix. 4.
[q] S. Cyprian Ep. x. 2. p. 23. Oxf. Tr. See others; Ib. n. a.
[r] Ib. 41. p. 21.

its summit in Heaven; whose "Builder and Maker is God." Herein our great strength lieth, which, if we betray it not to the Delilah of our besetting sin, no craft or power of our spiritual enemies can impair; that, as the soul is the life of the body, so God, unless we part with Him, is our soul's life, our soul's defence, our soul's impregnable fortress. Whoso hath been by Baptism made a member of Christ, in his soul God resides as in His Palace and Temple, so long as the soul receives not wilfully into itself His rival and His enemy, deadly sin. "God never forsakes, unless He is first forsaken." Our Christian birthright, if we barter it not for some vile self-indulgence, God's gift to us, is His own sanctifying Presence in our soul. It is a gift beyond all gifts, but containing all gifts. Grace is higher than all created things; above the glory of the stars, superior to all Angelic natures, infinitely removed above the highest intelligence, which God Himself could create. For every created being is but the receptacle of Divine grace. His grace it is, which is the light of the most exalted intelligence; His grace is the fire of love in that being who cleaves most closely to Him by love. Faith, hope, charity, are its Divine fruits; without them it will not abide in the soul, through them it acts; but itself is more than they. The understanding it enlightens, the affections it kindles, concupiscence it restrains, weakness it makes strong, but Itself is more than its fruits; it is not only "comfort, life or light or fire of love." All these and all gifts are poured out into the soul by the Holy Spirit Which is given us[s].

[s] Rom v. 5.

This is at once the beginning of the spiritual life and the pledge of its completion. "[t] The earnest of the Spirit" is a present gift; the pledge, if we be faithful, of enlarged gifts, until we have reached that fulness, for which God created us and Christ redeemed us. "The power given you to do," saith the same saint and Martyr[u], "will be according to the increase of spiritual grace. For, not as is the wont of earthly gifts, is there any measure or rule in obtaining the gift from Heaven. The Spirit, poured forth liberally, is pent in by no bounds, nor restrained by contracting barriers within a fixed pre-scribed space. It flows on unceasingly; it flows on exuberantly. Only let our hearts be athirst, be open to it. What measure we bring thither of faith to hold, so much of the inundant tide of grace do we receive within."

This grace is, in itself, perfect, because the in-dwelling sanctifying grace of God is one and the same. The grace in the life of glory of those who shall attain hereafter, will be given for other ends, it will bring with it other gifts, such as the light of glory whereby the creature can behold God. It-self will be no other, can be no other. That cre-ated being which God has made to be the nearest to Himself, to receive from Himself the utmost which it pleaseth Him to bestow upon a creature, is united to Himself, beautified, endowed, beatified; nay, those who have spoken most exactly have not been afraid to say, deified, by grace; since S. Peter says "there-by are given us exceeding great and precious pro-

[t] 2 Cor. i. 22. v. 5. Eph. i. 14.
[u] S. Cypr. ad Donat. n. 4. Treatises. p. 4. Oxf. Tr.

mises, that by these ye might become partakers of the Divine nature[v]."

Such is the gift of God. That gift it lay in the purpose of God to enlarge to us without measure and without bound. To the soul, which is in the grace of God, everything within and without may be the channel of enlarged grace. "[w]God is good and doeth good." He communicates Himself, because He is good, and there is nothing good in itself except Himself. He could not impart good without Himself. He made His rational creatures, in order to impart Himself to them. Nor is there any bound to His giving, except His creatures' capacity of receiving. The soul which has received Him, can, because it has received Him, receive Him more fully. God has found entrance into his soul, and, entering it, enlarges it for Himself. He gives "[x]grace upon grace." Each grace makes the soul long for larger grace, and the longing which He gives, He cannot disappoint. He gives the longing, in order that He may fill it.

What should not enlarge the grace of a soul in grace? "[y]All things work together for good to them that love God." But man's only real good, is to be in the favour of God, to be united to God. To one already in the grace of God, they work together to good by guarding, keeping, enlarging, that grace which is his one real good.

i.) Prayer enlarges grace. For what is to call upon God, save to call Him into thyself? The soul in grace asks according to the mind of God. And to

[v] 2 S. Pet. i. 4.　　　[w] Ps. cxix. 68.
[x] S. John i. 16.　　　[y] Rom. viii. 28.

such our Lord saith; "[z]Whatsoever ye shall ask the Father in My Name, He will give it you." "Ask and ye shall receive that your joy may be full."

ii.) Thanksgiving increases grace; for thanksgiving is a special ingredient of acceptable prayer. "[a]In everything by prayer and supplication with thanksgiving let your requests be made known unto God, and the peace of God, which passeth all understanding, shall keep your hearts and minds through Christ Jesus." Thanksgiving is the very end of creation, the object of grace, the tenderest form of the love of God. How should it not draw down more grace from Him, Who gave us grace that we might praise Him? And yet, in this world of the love of God, what does not give to a soul in grace occasion of thanksgiving? What temporal mercies surround us! The daily supplies of our daily needs, our sleep, our food, our health, our powers, the delights of intellect, of knowledge, of feeling, of taste, of perception of beauty, of music, of light, of air, of motion, of affection, love, good actions, loving-kindness, our natural spirits or elasticity of mind, those daily, hourly, momentary mercies of our God, are so many natural calls to thanksgiving, and with each thanksgiving comes a fresh afflux of grace from our Father. We cannot raise one thought to God; by His grace, in adoring love, or momentary thankfulness, or admiration of His Goodness, or contemplation of His Perfections, or longing to be less unlike Him, but instantly comes some fresh gift of grace into our soul.

iii.) Faith increases grace. We intensify our faith

[z] S. John xvi. 23, 24.　　　[a] Phil. iv. 6.

('so God has willed) by acting in faith and grace;
and thereon He gives us larger grace.   Meditation
on the Object of our Faith increases faith.   "[b]With
the mouth confession is made unto salvation."   And
who has not felt faith increased by the confession
of faith?   Who has not known his faith deepened,
while with his heart and his lips he was reciting
to God his faith in God?

, iv.) The Word of God heard or devotionally studied increases grace.   Who has not known words
of Scripture borne in upon his soul with power and
meaning unknown before, or the fire kindle within
him as he was saying psalms to God?

v.) Intercession for others is a·duty enjoined us.
We cannot say 'Our·Father' without it.   Who, if he
knows what the love and the grace of God is, can
help being grieved for those who forget Him, their
only Good, and praying for them?   Intercession for
others is the natural utterance of the soul in grace.
It seems more of nature than of grace; yet of it, it
is said, "[c]My prayer shall return into mine own
bosom."

· vi.) Again, what a joyous easy opening for grace
is Almsgiving for the love of Christ.   We cannot
refrain from it, if we have any love of God.   For
He says, "[d]Whoso hath this world's goods and seeth
his brother have need and shutteth up his bowels
of compassion from him, how dwelleth the love of
God in him?"   And yet for this, which, if we love
God, we cannot help, our Lord promises such overflowing rewards.   "[e]Give, and it shall be given unto

[b] Rom. x. 10.   [c] Ps. xxxv. 13.
[d] 1 S. John iii. 17.   [e] S. Luke vi. 38.

you; good measure, pressed down and shaken together and running over, shall they give into your bosom."[*] Yet all this overflowing reward is surely not reserved for the world to come. It is not the way of God, to reserve anything wholly for the life to come, which is consistent with our state of being here. Our love to others for His own sake He rewards with double interest, with grace here at once, which grace, if used, He will anew reward in Eternity with His own Eternal Love.

vii.) It would seem no such great thing for *us* who have been so much forgiven, to forgive from the heart any who have wronged us. It is a condition of salvation. If we forgive not, we should perish. Yet to this duty, though essential to salvation, God annexes a reward. "'Forgive, and ye shall be forgiven." Men, upon praying for one who had injured them, have felt themselves bathed with Divine grace.

viii.) Great faithfulness in our several callings is only to avoid sin. We should sin if we are not exactly faithful. Yet great faithfulness in our ordinary duties is known to be a special channel of grace. And contrariwise, if we strongly purpose what is pleasing to God, yet through human infirmity forget it, our loss is not complete. We lose through our forgetfulness and distraction what through greater care we might have gained, but we do not lose the grace which it gained for us, strongly by His grace to have willed the Will of God. To long fervently in the morning to do all to the glory of God, wins for us grace in proportion to the love

[f] S. Luke vi. 37.

with which we long, even if in the burden and heat of a busy day we forget it far oftener than we remember it. If, when we came to this house of prayer, we desired earnestly to pray to God, God accepted our will, even if, through distractions against our will, we lost grace which we might have gained, had we never learned to be distracted.

ix.) Temptations, when they come from within, seem to obscure the Presence of God, to confuse and darken the soul, to sully its loyalty to its God, almost to enlist it in a rebellion against its good Father. Be they what they may, Jesus, as He once revealed to a faithful soul, is present within the heart; else it could not hate them. Tempest-tost though it be, while the waves rage and swell, the soul, like the ark, mounts up the higher heavenwards, the more the waters prevail. Never is God nearer, than when He seemeth to be furthest away. Even to S. Paul He must have seemed to be less present in them. Else he would not so earnestly have "g thrice besought the Lord, that the thorn in the flesh, the minister of Satan to buffet him, might depart from him." Yet his Lord knew that it was best for him, that it should remain, that it was a pledge of grace, a token of His own victorious Presence. For He answered His faithful servant; "h My grace is sufficient for thee; for My strength is made perfect in weakness." Therefore the Apostle adds, when he had learned its value, "most gladly will I rather glory in my infirmities, that the power of Christ may rest upon me."

x.) Afflictions are grace-tokens, visible signs of His

g 2 Cor. xii. 8.   h Ib. 9.

healing Presence, for He saith, "[1] When thou passest through the waters, I will be with thee, and through the rivers, they shall not overflow thee."

xi.) What should not minister to grace, when even those infirmities, without which no one can be in this life, may be the means of enlarging the treasure of grace in the soul? They are guardians of grace by keeping the soul humble. " I have learned in truth," said a holy man[k], whose soul was often conscious of the Presence of its holy inhabitant, "I have learned in truth, that nothing is so efficacious to obtain, retain, recover grace, as at all times to be found before God not high-minded but fearing." Wonderful transforming power of the grace of God, which can make our failures a corrective of grave faults; our shortcomings a means of our advancement; our undeliberated close-cleaving weaknesses, not a bond to hold us back, but a band to bind us closer to our Saviour's Side.

Such is the ordinary atmosphere of grace, into which the baptised Christian is brought by being made a member of Christ. He may inspire grace in every breath. There is scarce an act, a word, a thought, through the day, which we do, speak, accept or refuse, but may have its fruit of grace. Grace is spread around him, like the manna, to gather day by day according to his need. Like the manna, sweet is it to the taste; like the manna he gathers he knows not how much, but sufficient for his day.

Such, I might rather say, are some of the ordinary occasions, through which grace, day by day, may

---

[1] Is. xliii. 2.   [k] S. Bernard in Cant. Serm. 55. n. 9.

come to our souls. For who could count up the marvellous ways, in which grace finds our souls? Grace begets grace, and grace grace. It multiplies itself, as men multiply money by compound interest. For God, Who saith, "[1] what he layeth out, it shall be paid him again", makes Himself our Debtor, that He may repay us with usury what He constantly supplies to us, that we may give it anew to Him.

Into this state of habitual grace God brought us without waiting for our wills, if only, when we had our wills, we cast it not away by main force out of our souls. And then there are all those gales of actual grace from Heaven which we all of us have known, which visited us unasked, uninvited, unthought of; which did not cease to visit us, though we neglected them; which came to us especially at critical turning-points of our moral being, bidding us with Angel-voices, "[m] Arise up quickly, gird thyself and follow Me." Great powerful drawings are they or withholdings in greater needs, and yet our everyday companions, about our path and about our bed, at our down-sitting and uprising, watching us like our guardian Angel, and succouring us in our time of need.

One act of God brought us into this rich and abundant superfluence of grace, by which God would make us saints, if we would. This grace He strengthened in us, if we willed, at that turning-point of our life, when the power of thought expands, and the will strengthens, and we feel energies and capacities unknown before, and it may be, passion too awakens, and the opening world invites us, and exuberance

[1] Prov. xix. 17.   [m] Acts xii. 7, 8.

A a

and buoyancy of spirits would live in the present or an earthly future. Then, when the world, and, it may be, the flesh and Satan, the three-fold enemies whom at Baptism we renounced for God, leagued anew with fresh force against us, God too anew marked us for His own by His seal in Confirmation, and strengthened us with the seven-fold gifts of His Spirit. Then, if we willed, Christ, in a nearer way than before, "dwelt in us and we in Him," yea "became one with us and we with Him," when we first sacramentally ate the Flesh of Christ and drank His Blood. O wonderful union of man with God! O marvellous inventiveness of Divine love, devising for us, while yet in the flesh, the closest union with Himself! He doth not wait for our being perfected. It were more than condescension enough, that the Creator should vouchsafe to unite Himself with us, the lowest of His rational creation. Unbelief has started back at the greatness of God's humility, that God the Son took into Himself in the Virgin's womb His Sinless Humanity. But that He should yet further, not redeem us only, but unite us, one by one, with Himself; and this, not as the beatitude of Eternity, but while yet in sinful flesh and sinners, surely His condescension could have found no lower depth, to which to humble itself; and that, for us. Men have been wont to treat strong words as to the goodness of Christ towards us, as though they were excessive and unguarded. The excess is not of man's words, but of our Lord's unspeakable condescension, at which all human thought staggers; in uttering which, all human speech falters; but which human speech could not exaggerate, or, say what we will, man's heart cannot conceive, man's tongue cannot utter, anything beyond the unutterable condescension of his God.

What words are these, my brethren! They are not man's words, but God's, for our sakes made Man, the Eternal Word, speaking the words of Eternal Truth which He Is, "[n] I am the Bread of Life." "I am the Living Bread which came down from Heaven; if any man eat of this Bread, he shall live for ever, and the Bread which I will give is My Flesh which I will give for the life of the world. My Flesh is meat indeed, and My Blood is drink indeed. He that eateth My Flesh and drinketh My Blood, dwelleth in Me and I in him. As the Living Father hath sent Me and I live by the Father, so he that eateth Me, he too shall live by Me." So our Lord saith of Himself; and what do we, but echo His words of grace as to ourselves, if we say with them of old; "[o] we lay Him up in ourselves and place our Saviour in our breasts," "[p] we partake of the Body of Him Who hath Life in Himself, Who for our sakes tabernacles in our body, Christ, the Son of the Living God, One of the Holy Trinity: " "[q] He feeds us with His own Blood and by every means entwines us with Himself: " "[r] Wishing to shew the longing He hath for us, He hath mingled Himself with us, and blended His Body with ours, that we might

[n] S. John vi. 35, 51. &c.

[o] S. Clement Al. Pædag. i. 6. See this and others more fully in the writer's three Sermons on the Holy Eucharist 1843, 1853, 1871, and in his " Doctrine of the Real Presence."

[p] S. Cyril Al. Hom. in myst. cœnam T. v. P. ii. 378.

[q] S. Chrys. in S. Matt. Hom. 82. n. 5. p. 1092. Oxf. Tr.

[r] S. Chrys. in S. Joann. Hom. 46. n. 3. p. 199. Oxf. Tr.

in a manner be one being, as the body joined to
the Head, drawing us on to greater love." " ˢ We
are called Christ's body and members in receiving
through the Eucharist the Son Himself within us."
" ᵗ Since the Flesh of the Saviour became Life-giving,
as being united to That which is by nature Life,
the Word from God, then when we taste It, we
have Life in ourselves, we too being united with It,
as It is to the indwelling Word." *We* have need
of many words, because we need to have the self-
same thing said over and over again to us ; yet what
is any of this or all which man could say, compared
with the majestic simplicity of our Lord's words,
" He that eateth My Flesh and drinketh My Blood
dwelleth in Me and I in him ?"

And this life, this ever-increasing life, this indwelling of our Saviour, we may have, year by year,
and week by week, as often as we will ; we may receive Him, not as a Wayfarer to tarry for a night,
but, as He saith, to dwell in us and we in Him, to
live by Him, to live for ever by His Life, yea by
Himself Who is Life living in us. What accumulated treasure of grace in a few months !   What in
a life !

And are we not then richly endowed against the
assaults of sins ?   " ᵘ If God be for us, who can be
against us ? "   We have, if we will, not grace only,
a perpetual ever-living fountain springing up with
fresh supplies, but we have the Author of grace
within us.   We have grace beyond our wills, without our wills, visiting us, encompassing us, seeking

---

ˢ S. Cyril Al. in S. Joann. vi. 55. fin. L. iv. p. 364.

ᵗ Id. Ib. in vi. 53. p. 361.   ᵘ Rom. viii. 31.

an entrance to us; but we cannot will to have grace and not have it. We have grace without any consent of ours forecoming us, drawing us, all but overpowering us. We cannot have deadly sin, which should overcome grace, without the full consent of our will. Deadly sin cannot master us, cannot surprise us, cannot find entrance into our souls, cannot overpower us, without our will. Christians enter with half-consent into the precincts of sin; they hide from themselves perhaps, that they mean to sin; they take the first step towards it, and do not tell themselves that they mean to complete it; but God so wills to save us, that He will not allow any man to be surprised into it. He does not allow man at last to fall into it, unless man tear himself away from God's withholding Arm, and deafen himself to the tender pleadings of God's restraining Voice within him, "Why will ye die?"

Satan too, well knows this. He knows the limits of his power. He sees that impenetrable armour of light and grace, through which no darts of his can pierce. He knows that in our Christian panoply there is no crevice open for him to inflict a deadly wound. He knows that, while we are invested with the grace with which, without our wills, God clothed us, all his assaults are vain, unless we with our wills unbind it. Prostrate as men lie before him, no soul ever did or ever shall "lie at the proud foot of" this "conqueror, but when it first did help to wound itself."

And therefore his first temptation always is, to lead men to disuse whatever God has given them as channels of His ever-renewing grace. Those who have forfeited their earthly lives to man's law have borne witness again and again, how the life of sin, which so ended, began in neglecting public prayer. But it may be said more broadly, every course of sin, howsoever it ended, whether in its natural end in Hell, or whether God arrested the sinner, began in doing despight to actual grace in neglecting against conscience what to that age were means of grace. Who, well nigh, has ever been steeped in sin, without having, at the outset, through sloth or false shame, laid aside the armour of his childhood's prayers? Hurried, said in bed, forgotten, at last disused! The soul is at last scarce conscious of the change which has come over her: she goes out like Samson, careless as to her foes, and knows not that the Lord has departed from her.

But what, some of you may ask, if we have done this? What if all these treasures of grace are nothing to us now? What if we dare not think, that God the Holy Ghost dwelleth in us any more, that any of our acts are done through the grace of God, that the grace which we have had is of any avail to us now, except to increase our condemnation from having despised and wasted it?

And is it nothing then, nay, is it not everything that God's Eye once rested upon thee in love? Is it not everything that, before time was, in all eternity thou wast in the mind of God? In His eternal purpose of love He created thee; in His eternal love He, in time, redeemed thee; in His unchanging Love He once sanctified thee. Thou mayest wilfully have wrested thyself out of the arms of His love, whereby He would have held thee to Himself. Thou hast not got beyond the wide circle of His grace. Thou mayest have chilled, deadened, buried in sin, thy love for God; thou hast not extinguished the love of God for thee. He brought thee hither to ask anew His grace. Thou hast asked the Holy Trinity, Father, Son and Holy Ghost, to have mercy upon thee. Thou hast asked the Lamb of God, Who taketh away the sins of the world, to have mercy upon thee. Thou hast asked this, by virtue of His Cross and Passion and Precious Death. Whatever of these, if but one prayer, thou hast truly prayed, by the grace of God the Holy Ghost thou prayedst it, and ere thou hadst uttered it, it had ascended to the Throne of thy Loving Father, bedewed with the Blood of thy continual Intercessor, the Incarnate Son.

No too late is there on this earth, while thou hast yet the heart to ask for the grace of God. For without the grace of God thou couldest not ask, couldest not have the faintest longing for it. Too late it never is, till the door is shut. Yet think how it would have been with thee, hadst thou been cut off with that same suddenness, with which one, in prime of youth and strength, was, yesterday, in a few minutes, summoned before his God. Think of thyself; one moment in thine accustomed round of business, thy recreations, thy plans for the future, thy hopes, thy fears, and then (which is to be added) thy use or thy neglect of the grace of God,—the next to give an account of thy stewardship, how thou hadst used or neglected that grace. Dare not to live as, if the choice now were thine, thou wouldest not dare to die.

Yet faint not thou, despond not, however often

thou mayest have relapsed into thy besetting sin. Though thou wert defiled with ten thousand sins, though thou hadst ten thousand times promised to God that thou wouldest forsake thy sins, and hadst broken thy promise as often as thou madest it, still, while God continues to thee the heart and longing to repent, His grace is yet around thee; thy Maker, thy Redeemer has still His Eye of love upon thee. He will not part with thee, if thou wilt but yield thyself to Him. He still opens to thee the full Treasure of His grace, the whole ocean of His Love. He still says to thee, if thou wilt, "Son, all which I have is thine."

Ask Him, by His love for sinners, to give thee true sorrow for love of Himself that thou hast offended Him; and thy Redeemer, Who knows better than thou the value of thy soul for which He paid so dear a Price, Himself counts thy return an addition to the joy of His Humanity. His Heart, in the everlasting repose of His Divine Love, will have one joy the more from thy return to His fold and to His grace; for He Himself hath said, that He, the Good Shepherd, will say to those His friends in the courts of Heaven; "[v]Rejoice with Me, for I have found My sheep which was lost."

But wouldest thou know, that thy past sins are blotted out, wouldest thou have *that* fulfilled in thee, "[w]though thy sins be as scarlet, they shall be as white as snow; though they be red as crimson, they shall be as wool;" wouldest thou be washed anew in His Blood, Who shed that Blood for thee, Whom alas! our sins again crucify; wouldest thou

[v] S. Luke xv. 6.   [w] Is. i. 18.

hear His absolving voice, "Thy sins be forgiven thee," and have fresh grace whereby thou mayest have the mastery, wherein thou hast been mastered; you know how He still pronounces, through man, the forgiveness of our sins, how He confirms in Heaven, what by His authority is done on earth. We too may tell you, "We speak that we do know, and testify that we have seen." Absolution will not make "one step 'twixt thee and heaven." Thou mayest have the same battle to fight: nay, it may be of God's mercy, that He may make you a good soldier of Jesus Christ, conquering through Him, wherein thou wast conquered. Thou wilt still be encompassed with the body of this death, and yet "[x] be more than conqueror through Him that loveth us," and give thanks to God, "[y] Who giveth us the victory through our Lord Jesus Christ."

But whether, my son, thou hast never quitted thy Father's home, or whether thou art returning thither, let not a false fear of others keep thee back from frequent use of the means of grace. Every gift of God is abused by man, and so the means of grace also. But they who abuse them most, are they who least use them. We do nothing well, which we do not do habitually. The worst prayers are those which are most seldom said; the most indevout worshippers in Church are those who, in proportion to their abilities, come here the least frequently; the coldest and most profitless Communions are those of the most occasional communicants.

For all neglect of the means of grace is, in fact, indifference to grace, and those who will not have

[x] Rom. viii. 37. [y] 1 Cor. xv. 57.

grace when it is offered to them, cannot command it at their own will. God gives in proportion to our longings; we cannot remain indifferent for months, and then, because Christmas or Easter are come, obtain at once, of our own will, the hunger which Christ will fill. Joys of earth soon pall with the use; joys of the spirit pall with disuse. Are we in ourselves strong or weak? whole or sick? rich in grace or poor? fervent or cold? When thou findest bodily weakness diminished through want of food, bodily cold relieved by absence of fire, bodily sickness mitigated by neglect of means to restore health, then try it as to thy soul. Else, when thy Saviour crieth aloud unto thee, "[z] Come unto Me, all that travail and are heavy laden, and I will refresh you," turn not thou away. Christ calleth thee; Eternal Wisdom inviteth thee; thy Redeemer willeth to dwell in thee; the Author of thy life willeth that thou shouldest live by Him. He Who died that thou mightest live, willeth that in thee too should be fulfilled, "not I, but Christ liveth in me." He Who, by His Blood, purchased everlasting glory for thee, willeth that in thee too that should be accomplished; "Christ in you, the Hope of glory."

Fail not then thy Redeemer, and He will not fail thee. Forsake not Him, and He Who held thee fast when thou wast ready to fall, or didst fall from Him, will not forsake thee. Seek Him in your daily prayers, your daily needs; seek Him in the daily duties, in which He gives thee grace to find Him; seek Him by self-denial; seek Him by sorrow for

[z] S. Matt. xi. 28.

having forsaken Him; seek Him by thanksgiving
that He has sought thee and found thee; seek Him
by aspirations for His Love; seek Him by longing
to be less unlike Him; seek Him in His House
and at His Holy Altar, and thou shalt find new
life, new power over sin, new faith, new love; and
whether He now reveal it to thee, or whether for
thy good He for the time withhold it from thee,
thou shalt find in the end, that He was thy Com-
panion by the way. He held thee by the hand;
He strengthened thee; He Who is in you the Hope
of Glory was also, indwelling in you, the means of
grace. He thine Eternal Life, the Eternal Truth,
was Himself the Way for thee unto Himself in
Everlasting bliss: to which He of His Infinite Mercy
bring us all, to Whom with the Father and the Holy
Ghost.

SERMON XIX[a].

THE THOUGHT OF THE LOVE OF JESUS FOR US THE REMEDY FOR SINS OF THE BODY.

1 Cor. vi. 15.

"Know ye not that your bodies are members of Christ?"

" The Word made Flesh" changed by that act the whole relation of the creature to the Creator. Before, God sustained His creatures in being by His abiding will. The angels, who had chosen Him and abode in their first estate, evermore beheld His face, and, each according to his order among the heavenly intelligences, drank in, through that beatific sight, fresh effluences of love, knowledge, wisdom, holiness from God, Who alone hath all, dispenseth all. But the Creator and the creature were still distinct. God chose man, the lowest of all, to knit together in his nature the Creator and the creature. Could there be envy in heaven, surely the blessed spirits must have envied our race, that God should have chosen us, not themselves, to unite His whole creation to Himself in our nature, not in theirs. Nay, it has been a received opinion, that Satan fell through envy at the Incarnation revealed beforehand by God to him, while the rest adored His love displayed there-

a Preached at S. Mary's, Oxford. Lent, 1861.

in. I know not what can give us thoughts so intense
of the self-forgetting, unenvying love of those blessed spirits, as that they, the higher, the spiritual, who
had ever done the will of the Father, should be willing, nay, (since such was the will of God) joy to be
passed over, and to see us the fallen, the corrupt,
the debased, the steeped in sin, preferred to themselves. True! the blessed purpose of God is to unite
all things under and in One Head, "in Christ, both
which are in heaven and which are on earth [b]," the
happy spirits and our hapless lost race. Their ranks,
it is a pious opinion, broken by the fall of the apostate angels, will be filled in their several orders by
man, redeemed, restored, sanctified, beatified. Angels
and men will be so one around the throne of God,
that into all their orders, according to the measure in
which men shall have received the grace of God and
have used the grace which they received, man will
be admitted, like and equal to the angels. But even
this equality has not been enough for the boundless
condescension of the love of God. He was not content to bring back His lost sheep on His shoulders,
and to invite His friends, the heavenly hosts who
never fell, to rejoice with Him, as though it was His
own gain. It sufficed not to the lowliness of His love
to do any thing, however exalted, by any act of power
or will, out of Himself (so to speak) for us. He willed
to give us a closeness of union with Himself, which
He gave not to the Seraphim with their burning love,
joining in one for ever our poor human nature with
His own Divine, man with God. And this for all
eternity. This is our prerogative. If, by His mercy,

[b] Eph. i. 10.

we attain and are accepted in Him, then, the very
last and lowest of all those to whom in that day He
shall say, "Come, ye blessed of My Father," shall
have a nearness to Him which no other created intelligence, save man, however filled with God, shall
have. We shall have that same nature which our dear
Redeemer has united with the Godhead, which in
Him is deified. On earth, He was "not ashamed to
call" us "brethren[c]." In heaven, if we attain, however low in that heavenly society our place through
our own ill-deserts may be, we shall still have that
special nearness of love. Jesus,—call Him which
we will, God-Man or Man-God,—He in Whom our
nature is united with the Divine by an union closer
than any other save that of the Holy Trinity in itself [d]; He, in His Human Nature, will be our Brother still. Not the penitent robber alone, although,
before his wondrous gift of penetrating faith, stained
with the countless sins of his career of blood; not
Magdalene alone, "out of whom Jesus cast seven
devils,"—these through their miraculous faith and
penitence became indeed glorious saints,—but that
poor sinner of us all, whom, after countless sins, God
shall save at the last, so as by fire, the lowest and
last of all, shall still have that great prerogative of
love, that his once deeply stained, now purified,
glorified nature will be the same as that of Jesus.
Truly, envy must be impossible in heaven, that the
blessed angels should not envy us such nearness,
which they must have seen on earth so little valued,
so forgotten,—alas! this is not enough for our ingratitude,—so trampled on.

c Heb. ii. 11.   d S. Bernard, de consid. v. 8, n. 19.

This, then, is the first most comprehensive claim of Jesus on our love. God Who in all eternity, before creation was, knew our fall in Adam, fore-ordained, in one, the remedy for our fall and the union of His creation with Himself. He knew that we should be the lowest and most debased of His rational creation; and so, to manifest how deep and low His condescending love could reach, He chose our nature, in which to be for ever glorified. This is our comfort on the way. This was the joy of Martyrs, that visibly, as S. Stephen, or with the mental eye, they saw Jesus, as man could see Him, in His glory, Man in the glory of the Godhead, although the Godhead itself they could not, while in flesh, see. This is the more than compensation for the fall of Adam, that, "encompassed," as we are, "with infirmities," our souls at stake but ready to yield to the cravings of our poor flesh or themselves dazzled with the meteor-blaze of some shadowy greatness, yet it was with a soul like ours, save sin, and with sinless flesh of our mould that God, in Jesus, suffered, God died. This soothes even that aching memory that we have offended God, and, in lesser things, cannot, while encompassed with this body of death, say, "I have made my heart clean; I am pure from my sin [e]," that God became Man, "without spot of sin to make us clean from all sin." Wheresoever we shall be in those "many mansions," whatsoever our reward, yea, though through our own fault we were the last and least in the outermost court of those who see God, this gift of God will abide with us. Jesus, in that special way, is ours; He is our near Kins-

[e] Prov. xx. 9.

man, our Brother, our more than Brother. Jesus must love me with a special love, for He has not the nature of angels, but this of mine. Conceive a mendicant, in the poorest outward lot, who had the blood of the most ancient kings, noble as the noblest which human greatness ever dignified. Men would respect his ennobled blood, even in his outward penury.. "ᶠA potsherd with the potsherds of the earth!" Our kindred is with Him Who is God. He Who took our flesh is in that ineffable, unapproachable glory. Yet even that glory is as nothing. Even heavenly glory, except as it implies nearness to God, would be as nothing. The joy, the bliss, the being of Heaven, is not glory, but love. For "God is loveᵍ." And Jesus is ours, will be ours, to love us and be loved by us in all eternity, not as He deserves but as we can, with that special love of kindred.

And how did He love us? Rather, ask we, how did He not love us? What did He withhold from us, for love of us? His glory? God the Holy Ghost chose no other human word to express it, than that He "emptied Himselfʰ." He, the fulness, the boundless ocean of all being, He, full of majesty, glory, might, wisdom, holiness, became as though He were nothing, had nothing, of all these. His creatures bandied words with Him, the All-wise, as though they could "entangle Him in His talkⁱ." They blindfolded the All-seeing: they challenged Him to prophesy; and He Who saw them through and through, at Whose command were "ᵏtwelve legions of angels,"

ᶠ Is. xlv. 9.   ᵍ 1 S. John iv. 8.   ʰ ἑαυτὸν ἐκένωσε: Phil. ii. 7.
ⁱ S. Matt. xxii. 15.   ᵏ Ib. xxvi. 53.

He Who was and is one with the Father, ended this mortal life, which, being Himself without beginning, for us He vouchsafed to begin, as He began it. He began it an outcast; circumcised as though a child of sin; He ended it as though a blasphemer, perfected in sin, on whom man must execute the judgement of God, "giving Himself to be numbered with the transgressors[1]." What, then, did He withhold from us? What *could* He withhold, when He withheld not that which was nearest to His Divine heart, and was willing that all those horrible things should be believed of Him, as if *He* were the blasphemer against His Father. In those dread hours on the Cross, what part of His sacred Body did He reserve from suffering for us? The Psalms fill out the Gospels, and tell us how "all His bones were out of joint[m]:" limb stretched and strained from limb by the dislocation[n] of the Cross. Or His soul? The three hours of the Passion were but the fulfilment, in act, of the anticipated sufferings of those thirty-three years. By His Divine fore-knowledge He saw all: He had all ever present to His soul. Not one pang of soul or body was ever hid from His soul. He had no distractions. For that end came He into the world, and He knew why He was come. "I have a baptism to be baptized withal," He saith, "and how am I straitened till it be accomplished[o]!" He knew, when twelve years old, His Father's business. His fore-runner knew that He was "the Lamb of God, which taketh away the sins of the world." David and Isaiah and Zechariah, His servants the prophets, had fore-

[1] Is. liii. 12.   [m] Ps. xxii. 14.

[n] התפרון   [o] S. Luke xii. 50.

told circumstances of His Passion. How should not
He Himself know it? Being God, He must have
known all. Outwardly He was the Babe, the Child,
the Carpenter[p], the Prophet Who spake and did the
words and works of God. Inwardly, in a waveless
mirror, He beheld, not as we do, successively, but
in one distinct vision, all the depths of His Passion;
not those outward circumstances only, but all which
made them what they were to Him, all which He
alone could or can know, because in Him alone they
could be fulfilled. Those intimations with which He
stilled His apostles' eager hopes, were but flashes of
light from that serene atmosphere of certain knowledge in which He ever lived. But so, what bursts
on us so awefully as "the hour" of His enemies,
and "the power of darkness[q]," was the one unbroken sight of His life. Day by day during those
thirty-three years it drew nearer. *We* have only some
indistinct conception of suffering before it comes.
When it comes, God mitigates it to us. *He* saw it
all distinctly before it came, and knew that the Father would not mitigate it to Him, when it should
come; that it was not fitting that He should mitigate it to Himself. He "knew from the beginning
who should betray Him ... being one of the twelve.[r]"
He knew the denial, the forsaking even of the beloved disciple for a time; He ever knew of the dread
agony in which all His limbs were swathed with
"a winding-sheet of Blood[s];" He ever knew that
mysterious loneliness, when it should please the Father "to make to meet on Him the iniquities of us

p St. Mark vi. 3.   q S. Luke xxii. 53.   r S. John vi. 64, 71.
s Hymn in Paradise for the Christian Soul, P. vi. p. 66, ed. Oxf.

all '," what it would be to bear in one the iniquities of us all, all the sins of the whole human race. He knew all, and suffered all, day by day, in will, in thought, in steadfast vision, before He suffered in act. He knew even that extremity of agony, when, withholding the consolations of His Divinity from His suffering Humanity, He endured what, but for the support given by His Godhead, His human frame could not endure. His Father's face was hid from His human soul, and instructing us how to hold to God in extremest darkness, He cried, "My God, My God, why hast Thou forsaken Me?" He knew all, and withheld no one moment of such suffering for love of us.

We know He did not, could not withhold anything which He *could* suffer for us. He suffered all which human nature could suffer, and yet be holy. He could not know that one great anguish of our's, the memory of sin or hopelessness as to the consequence of sin ; but so, He substituted for them the actual bearing of our sins and of His Father's wrath, and that utter forsakenness.

Yet all these had their end. "He saw," too, beforehand " of the travail of His soul, and was satisfied ". " He saw " the joy which was set before Him" when He " endured the Cross ". " He knew that His Father was glorified, even when He seemed to be forsaken of Him. If one may reverently speak, deeper than all suffering besides must have been the sight of those souls, whom He knew that His own Passion could not win to God. Gleams of this inner grief too flash out to us, when He " beheld the" de-

---

' Isa. liii: 6, 10.   " Ib. 11.   " Heb. xii. 2.

voted " city " which would crucify Him, and " wept over it [w] ;" when " He was grieved for the hardness of their hearts [x] ;" when " He sighed deeply in His Spirit and said, Why doth this generation seek after a sign [y] ?" We know, some of us, some of that deep oppression, when in our crowded metropolis we see the throng upon throng of souls utterly forgetful of God, on whose faces every passion is by turns expressed, in whom everything is seen, except some trace of the love of God; and yet there is no one to drag them from the pit, to win them to love Jesus. And *He*, the fountain of love, had in His heart love, to which all created love, if it could be gathered and condensed into one, would be as nothing. He knew the love, the joy, which He prepared for those who would have Him. He knew the hell " prepared for the devil and his angels," to which He should have to sentence those who would not have Him, who to the end would say, " On Thy conditions we will have none of Thee." As He saw Judas all those years shutting out every grace, steeling himself against every act or word of love, " a devil [z]," yet so close to Himself; so in all that wild multitude who cried, " Crucify Him, crucify Him," He saw who would repent, but He saw who would go on unrepentant from wickedness to wickedness till they should perish. He saw how those poor thoughtless boys with whom He was surrounded would, rejecting His apostles, ripen into such a death-crop of wickedness that the Jewish historian believed that, had the Romans

---

[w] St. Luke xix. 41.   [x] S. Mark iii. 5 ; and vii. 34, and the comment in the Christian Year, Twelfth Sunday after Trinity.

[y] St. Mark viii. 12.   [z] St. John vi. 70.

tarried, the city must have been destroyed by the immediate judgement of God[a]. He saw further on yet. He saw all who would in each age reject Him. He saw how those called by His name would corrupt each other, drag each other down to the pit; how the price of His blood would be rent from Him by those for whom He was to shed it. Unutterable, inconceivable by man must have been that suffering when He bare the sins of the whole world. Yet this had its abundant fruit and contentment of His love. More piercing yet to His Divine love must have been the thanklessness of those for whom He died. This wounded His love for the glory of His Father; this grieved His holiness; this, in those who repent not, was remediless. Yet all this ingratitude He beheld, ever present to His soul; He beheld it, and yet He loved us, ungrateful.

Loved us? what doth He now? Has it ever occurred to you to think, my sons, what Jesus is doing now? You know that He is in that unspeakable glory, that inconceivable joy, sitting in that place where God is most seen in His majesty, and which thence is called His Right Hand, arrayed with all power in heaven and earth. True! He " upholdeth all things by the word of His power[b]." Thanks be to Him for the mercies of His Providence. He saith Himself, "My Father worketh hitherto, and I work[c];" sustaining in being by the continued operation of His Will the whole order of created things, which exist, not by laws alone, as if laws were their creator, but by Him and for Him, their Author. He governeth also the Church, sanctifying her by His presence,

[a] Jos. de B. J. v. 13, 6.   [b] Heb. i. 3.   [c] St. John. v. 17.

upholding His truth in her, enlarging, chastening, renewing, pouring new life into her, receiving into Himself each new member of her, the infant or the convert, by virtue of His sacred promise, " Lo, I am with you alway, even to the end of the world [d]." But I would ask you something nearer to ourselves individually. Has it been a matter of habitual thought to you, what Jesus doth for us individually; what He so doth, that it is, in a manner, said to be His life? You will any how have remembered now. " Who ever liveth to make intercession for us [e]." " Ever liveth to." What less can this mean, than that this is His unceasing act in heaven; this, His life of love for us; this, reverently to speak, the object of His present Being there? There He liveth, as " He Who *was* dead, and is alive for evermore [f]," in that self-same Body, which for us He took, which for us was crucified, which for us bore the prints of the nails and of the spear. As He died, so He arose; as He arose, so He ascended; as He ascended, so shall He also descend, in like manner as the Apostles saw Him go into heaven [g]. When He cometh again to judge, " every eye shall see Him, and they also which pierced Him [h]." They shall behold Him, as their sins pierced Him, the Redeemer Whom they would not have. The beloved disciple beheld Him, as He is now, in the midst of the throne, bearing the marks of His Passion, " a Lamb, as it had been slain [i]." Calvary lives on in heaven, and pleads for us still. Our dear Redeemer's Passion is not only an event

[d] St. Matt. xxviii. 20.

[e] Heb. vii. 25, ix. 24, Isa. liii. 12, Rom. viii. 34, 1 S. John ii. 1.

[f] Rev. i. 17.   [g] Acts i. 11.   [h] Rev. i. 7.   [i] Ia. v. 6.

which took place 1800 years ago, and on which men dare look coldly back as an event which had been. It lives on still, transfigured in that unspeakable glory. There, on that once veiled Brow of majesty, translucent with the light of Deity, are the marks of the thorns which pierced Him. There, are the glorious scars which He shewed to Thomas, now beaming with the light of love, pleading to the Father for us. There, is that once rifted Side, through which from His pierced Heart gushed forth the water and the blood. There they speak for us, sinners. Day by day (for there is no night there[k]) for these more than 1800 years, hour by hour, has Jesus, in that glorified, once wounded Body, pleaded for us.

To plead for us is part of His Being. As well might you conceive of Him, as absent from heaven, whither He has ascended, whence He is to return, as conceive Him intermitting to plead. He changeth not, wearieth not in His love. The best of us more often forget than remember Him. We are distracted by our business, our interests, our earthly aims, our earthly needs; alas, by our vanities and our sins. He forgetteth not us, whom He redeemed at so dear a price. While men forget Him, turn away from His grace, deafen themselves to His voice, drown His secret inspirations, immerse themselves in brutishness, or frivolity, or toil, that they may not hear Him, He remembers them, He intercedes for them; and for His intercession and merits' sake, every grace which still knocks at their hearts for entrance, when all before it have been rejected, is

[k] Rev. xxii. 5. 6.

given them. Once He merited for us, in those dark dread hours upon the Cross. Ever since, in every successive generation, He has gained for each individual in our whole race, our every grace. Whether we are using, or whether any is shutting out His grace, he owes to that all-prevailing intercession every grace which he has had, or that last grace, that he is not yet reprobate.

And all this, my sons, has been, is, shall continue to be done for us through the body. By taking our flesh, our whole human nature, soul and body, God the Son gave us, in His own Person, that special prerogative of nearness to Himself. That all-holy, meritorious Passion was wrought through the sufferings of His all-holy Body on the Cross. That continued intercession is made through that pierced but all-glorious Body at the Right Hand of God.

But then with what sacredness does this invest our bodies, my sons! Limb by limb, they are the same bodies as that which God the Son took, which for us was crucified, which now is in glory at the Right Hand of God. All sin is misery, because it is rebellion against so loving a Father; all aggravated sin has its deeper misery, that it does, in fact, make a mock and sets at nought the Cross of Christ. Sins of the flesh have yet this special misery, that they degrade that body which Jesus took, degrade it below the beasts which perish. To sin as to the flesh is to insult Christ. It is to insult Him, because they are the like bodies to that which He took and glorified, but also because He has made these, our very own bodies, His. His they are, because He bought them at so dear a price; His they are, because in baptism we put on Christ[1]; His they are, because by His gift, the gift of the Holy Ghost, they are the temples of the Holy Ghost[m], the dwelling-place of the Trinity, as He says, "We will come unto him, and make Our abode in him[n];" His they are, because "now are we the sons of God[o]," being made members of Christ, the only-begotten Son of God; His they are, because He has said, "He that eateth My flesh, and drinketh My blood, dwelleth in Me, and I in him[p]."

You have still warm, generous, hearts. Think of the sacredness of all besides, body and soul, who, with you, have been made members of Christ. Every one around you was, with you, made a member of Him, your Redeemer, a temple of God; every one of them was, with you, created, redeemed, sanctified to be eternally blessed in the infinite fulness of the love of God. Whether they retain or have lost the knowledge of it, or never knew it, this is the one end of their being, to prepare to live for ever with God, and to have their bliss in Him. What intense selfishness, then, (I say not, to corrupt, you are too young for such guilt, but) to aid or participate in sin, which should separate them for ever, from the end of their being, the bliss in God. People sin together, they do not repent together. Sin by sin is drop by drop, filling up the measure of sinfulness, after which, worn out in mind and body they sink degraded and dishonoured into a premature grave. How are they to repent? How are they to know of the love of Christ, who know of nothing but

[1] Gal. iii. 27.   [m] 1 Cor. vi. 19.   [n] S. John xiv. 23.
[o] 1 S. John iii. 2.   [p] S. John vi. 56.

of the sins of those who bear the name of Christ?
People speak of them as a class. Terrifically large
as the class may be, each soul has her own individual
history; each was redeemed by the Blood of Jesus;
each sin brings on another, and makes it more difficult to return: each is one of those steps, which,
one by one, lead to death. They are forgotten here.
What would it be to see on the Left Hand, one who
had ever been a partner in sin?

Trials you have or will have, my sons. But trials
which are only of God's allowing injure neither body
nor soul. He will give the victory Who allows them.
He Who, probably under the self-same trial, said to
His great Apostle S. Paul, "My grace is sufficient
for thee; My strength is made perfect in weakness[q],"
will suffice for thee, He the Omnipotent. But in all
the experience which in these many years I have
had in the trials and difficulties of the young, I have
mostly found that the trials *began* from their own
wills, from curiosity, from example, from imagination, antedating far the time when, in God's providence, those trials, through which He would have led
them safely, would come, forming a new trial to
themselves, not in, but contrary to, the way of nature, and aggravating oftentimes exceedingly those
trials which, in the way of nature, would have come
to them. Imagination, corrupted by corrupt reading, corrupt speaking, corrupt hearing, corrupt sight,
has too often defiled the soul where the Holy Ghost
dwelt, divided the will, or decided it to rebel, long
ere it was any question of any other sin. One who
has so acted upon and bent to evil his own will, dare

q 2 Cor. xii. 9.

not speak of his trials as given to him, as men speak, "by the God Who made Him." They come to him as he has unmade himself. Whatever they are, they are aggravated often to a fierceness which he had never known, had he not, alas! kindled his own fire. From some temptations, and those most desolating to body, mind, and soul, he might have been wholly free.

But now, my son, if thou art liable to temptation, from which thou mightest have been blessedly free, or over which thou mightest have had, by God's grace, an easy victory, the experience which I have learnt from advice to others, may be useful to thee. Observe well, whence mostly thy temptation begins now; from imagination? or from the eye? or from past memories? or from over-fulness of food? For there the entrance on thy battle lies. It is for thy soul. You know those words of God, "when I fed them to the full, they assembled themselves by troops [r]—." You remember the experience expressed by the heathen proverb, "sine Cerere et Baccho—" It is not my experience only; it has an apostle's sanction. If you would use the same self-discipline to gain "an incorruptible crown [s]," which those use who for victory in a race are "temperate in all things," very much trial might still be saved you. I am not setting before you now hard things; I am not even speaking of the fasting which our blessed Lord says His disciples [t] would use—very much temptation as this, as well as every other precept of Christ, saves to those who obey Him,—I am speaking only of that self-discipline which your companions

[r] Jer. v. 7.   [s] 1 Cor. ix. 25.   [t] St. Luke v. 35.

at times use, in order to fit their frames for a race.
That moderate use of God's creatures which He
gives us for food, and that bodily exercise, which
keeps the body in a tempered, unluxuriant state, save
the soul from many trials. I have, I think, never
known a case in which, after victory for a time, there
came one of those sad relapses, but that carelessness
or remissness as to prayer, and some sudden over-
repletion of the body with food and wine ou the one
hand, or indulgence in unlawful imaginations on the
other, were the proximate occasions of it.

At the beginning, any distraction is lawful. In
temptations of this kind, flight is true warfare, is
victory. Elude any trial thou canst, in whatsoever
lawful way thou canst. To put yourself under
circumstances where the sin cannot be committed,
until the fever is over; to occupy yourself so as to
forget it; to use, as I said, bodily exercise; to interest
yourself in any lawful object, are at times helpful.
When imagination is busy, you know how the very
earliest Christians, those close on the Apostles' times,
used the sign of the Cross.[u] I know nothing so power-

[u] "In all our travels and movements, in all our coming in and
going out, in putting on our shoes, at the bath, at the table, lighting
our candles, in lying down, in sitting down, whatever employment occupieth us, we mark our forehead with the sign of the
cross."—*Tertullian de Coronâ*, v. 3, p. 165. O. T. This treatise is
probably A.D. 201.

"Let us not then be ashamed of the cross of Christ; but though
another hide it, do thou openly seal it on thy brow; that the
devils, beholding that princely sign, may flee far away trembling.
But make thou this sign when thou eatest and drinkest, sittest or
liest down, risest up, speakest, walkest; in a word, on every occasion; for He Who was here crucified, is above in the heavens."—
S. Cyril of Jerusalem, Catechetical Lectures, iv. 14, p. 40, O. T.

ful in removing evil imaginations, distractions, bad memories and thoughts, as to retrace on the forehead, the seat of thought, the baptismal cross. Used religiously, I never knew it fail. I have known the thoughts by which a person was beset so entirely scattered, that he was not even conscious what they had been. The soul was like a clean sheet, on which every trace had been utterly effaced; like a serene blue sky, from which every cloud had disappeared.

But in the trial itself, especially in that sort which (those whom it concerns will know what I mean) comes when no one is by, no help˙ or possibility of human help for the time is there, no way of eluding it, but the conflict must come; I know but of one effectual remedy—to clasp the hands together, and pray earnestly to God for help. All the outward resources, which I learned from books and advised, were forgotten when they were most needed. No fear of God's temporal punishments of the sin, nor even the commencement of those punishments, availed. Fear-

"Let us not then be ashamed to confess the Crucified. Be the Cross our seal, made with boldness by our fingers on our brow, and in everything; over the bread we eat and the cups we drink; in our comings in and goings out; before our sleep; when we lie down and when we awake; when we are in the way, and when we are still. Great is that preservative: it is without price, for the poor's sake; without toil, for the sick; since also its grace is from God. It is the sign of the faithful, and the dread of devils: for He has *triumphed over them in it, having made a show of them openly;* for when they see the Cross, they are reminded of the Crucified; they are afraid of Him Who hath *bruised the heads of the dragon.* Despise not the Seal, because of the freeness of the gift; but for this the rather honour thy Benefactor."—*Lect.* xiii, 36 pp. 161, 162, O. T.

ful and common those punishments are, which I have
seen and known and read of. I have known of manifold early death ; I have seen the fineness of intellect
injured; powers of reasoning, memory impaired; nay,
insanity oftentime, idiotcy; every form of decay of
mind and body; consumption too often, torturing
death, even of a strong frame. I have said how,
when God put forth His judgements less visibly,
He visited it with severe chastisement of all kinds,
as He sees good for each, but none escape, even
though some may not know why they are stricken.
Lesser degrees of these punishments were God's
warning voice. At first bodily growth checked,
eye-sight perhaps distressed or impaired; that fine,
beautiful, delicate system which carries sensation
through the whole human frame, in whatever degree, harmed, and for the most part, in that degree
irreparably. When these warnings were neglected,
further decay, with scarce an exception, visibly followed. In vain I repeated, warned, said how my
very brain had reeled with the histories of these
visitations of God on that sin. All failed, faded
away. That prayer with hands clasped to God I
never knew to fail, for God was not called to aid
in vain. If the trial lasted, the victory was more
complete.

And when thou so prayest, my son, think how
Jesus hallowed this poor body: think how He suffered
in this body for love of us. Look up at thy Redeemer, as for thee He hung upon the Cross; or as
for thee He intercedes in heaven. Behold Him there,
"from the sole of the foot even unto the head[v],"

[v] Is. i. 6.

made for our sins, as we had by our sins unmade ourselves, "all wound and bruise and oosing sore," "no soundness" in that tender frame. Look well at that holy frame, racked on that hard bed of the Cross; look at every limb tightened, distended, dislocated; that sacred Back furrowed with harrowing lashes; those Feet, which went about doing good, rent with those nail-pierced gashes; see those Hands, Whose touch healed and saved, Which were even then stretched out wide to bless the whole world, wrung with that riving iron, and torn yet more by the weight of His holy Body suspended by them; but above all, look at that thorn-crowned Head, on Whose radiance the Angels gaze with joy: look at it, scarred with the bruises from that rough felon band, bearing yet the shame of the spitting, drooping with its own weight on that breast of love, stained with the purple streams of His own Blood; and that yet open, mild, forgiving Eye, which looked with pity on Mary Magdalene, and won the blaspheming robber to sue for pardon from his Lord. How does that calm full orb of love speak to thee? Does it not say to thee, "Poor wanderer, this have I endured for love of thee; I loved thee and gave Myself for thee[w]; I thought of thee, and knew how ill thou wouldst requite My love; yet still I love thee. Love Me at least now." Wilt thou not look up to Him and say, "By Thy Grace henceforth I will love Thee. Bind me by Thy love, that I may love Thee, Lord; let me rather die than again profane the body, which Thou didst so redeem, and wound Thy love."

Or, if thou art so drawn, look up, look up above

[w] "Who loved me and gave Himself for me." Gal. ii. 2.

all those suns upon suns which were made by Him;
look to that light unapproachable, where God dwelleth [x], and gaze ou that Glorious Form at the Right
Hand of God. All else is spirit. "God is a Spirity."
All the choirs of angels, cherubim and seraphim,
thrones, dominions, powers,—the ten thousand times
ten thousand, and thousands of thousands, are all
spirits. *One* Body is there, above all, adored by all,
loved by all with adoring love, beauteous above all
created beauty, shining above all created light, paling
all by the glory of His light, for "the Lamb," Scripture saith, "is the Light thereof [z]." A light streams
through that Deitate Body, which absorbs all created
light, (as, amid the full radiance of the sun we see the
moon's pale light no more,) the light of the Godhead
united in one Person with the Manhood of Jesus.
There, with a special lustre of their own, stream forth
the rays of Divine light and love from those two
pierced Hands, those once wounded Feet, that opened
Side and Heart. There, at that moment, the moment
of thy temptation, they intercede for thee; there they
have interceded for thee, when thou wastedst their
intercession. *There*, is that human Eye resting still
in love upon thee. There It sees thy trials, thy fainting heart, thy longings to amend, thy falls, thy repentance, thy renewed falls, and still It has loved,
still loves thee. Those glorious scars in all that
Majesty of heaven, seem to say to us, "So do I love
you, that I would come down from heaven again, to
be crucified again for you, if so I could win one soul
more to love God."

He is not ashamed to wear in heaven the tokens of

[x] 1 Tim. vi. 16.   [y] S. John iv. 24.   [z] Rev. xxi. 23.

His humiliation ;. be not thou ashamed of Him and His service. Look to Him; catch, in mind, that loving, all-glorious Eye, as it beholds thee, and say, "Saviour, save me; let me not again degrade the body which Thou hast vouchsafed to take, which Thou hast so glorified, and in which Thou vouchsafest still to remember me, Thy poor sinner, redeemed with Thy Precious Blood."

Look, in which way thou willest, to Jesus; and He Who, while on earth, touched the poor fevered body, and "rebuked the fever, and forthwith, it departed from [a]" the sufferer, will slake any fever of thine. Only, will with thine whole heart to be freed; will to be *that* for which the Father created thee, the Son redeemed thee and intercedeth for thee, the Holy Ghost sanctifieth thee. Remember that He willeth to "[b] fashion this our" now "vile body, that it may be made like unto His glorious body," and resolve by His grace to degrade no more the body which He so longs to glorify with Himself. Be earnest, and in place of those things which thou thyself hatest afterwards, destroying thyself alone, or others for whom with thee Christ did die, there will enter in "some sweetness of things eternal," the foretaste of everlasting joy in thine own Lord.

[a] S Luke iv. 39.   [b] Phil. iii. 21.

SERMON XX[a].

CONTINUAL COMFORT THE GIFT OF GOD
ON CONTINUAL SORROW FOR SIN.

S. MATTHEW v. 4.

" Blessed are they that mourn: for they shall be comforted."

WE live in an aweful world. Look which way we will, within us or without, on God's revelation of His holiness, or His unutterable condescension, the unspeakableness of His free infinite love, or His just condemnation of sin, the marvellous fertility of His ways in winning us to Himself, and the almost boundless prodigality of the riches of divine mercy, or that dreadful condition of His creature, which has made itself for ever incapable of His love,—our existence is an aweful gift. The infinity of His condescension in our redemption, and the endless sufferings of those who have to the end shut out God, are in sad harmony together. It can have been for no light cause that God abhorred not the Virgin's womb; that God was born; God, in the likeness of man, and having united that Man for ever with Himself, went about among us, partook of all our sinless infirmities; God (not the Godhead) suffered; God the Lord of glory

a Preached at S. Mary's, Oxford. Lent, 1863.

was crucified [b]; God, not the Godhead, but He Who "[c] in the beginning was with God, and was God," died. To persevere in sin against such inventiveness of the love of God, what is it but "an Angel's hope⁻ less fall [d]?" God has done more for us than for them. The mysteries of the redemption were wrought for man, not for the devil and his angels.

The Gospels are full of love, for they are full of the words and works of Jesus. Yet you can scarcely open a page of them, but your eye will fall upon words of awe. False then, as well as deadlily delusive to the soul, is that teaching, which so dwells upon that infinite love of God as to blot out the thought of His aweful holiness, and shuts out from sinners the wholesome terror of hell, until they fall into it irremediably.

Even God's words of comfort shew the unreality of such pictures of this our being, in which God has entrusted us, His creatures, with that aweful choice, upon which our eternity depends, freely to choose or to refuse for ever Himself, the All-Good. One special office, one title of God the Holy Ghost is, to be "the Comforter." Our Comforter is Almighty, is God. His Presence is an especial gift of our departing Lord to His Church, to ourselves. "[e] I will pray the Father for you, and He shall give you another Comforter, that He may abide with you for ever; even the Spirit of Truth; Whom the world cannot receive." Another Comforter! Another to replace Himself! And He, God proceeding from God, to abide with us

[b] 1 Cor. ii. 8.   [c] S. John i. 1.
[d] Keble's Christian Year, Thirteenth Sunday after Trinity.
[e] S. John xiv. 16, 17.

and in us, if we will, for ever. But then what a condition of life does this open to us! An Almighty, ever-present, divine Comforter implies a continual, universal, unceasing need of comfort.

Comfort! The world hates the thought. For comfort implies sorrow, and the world would have none of it; or, at the most, it would have it only, when it cannot escape it, when sorrow does come. Even then, it would have as little as may be to do with supernatural comfort, or, alas! with the Comforter. Then, too, it would rather remove or displace its griefs with fresh cause of grief; fresh pleasures, again to pall; fresh joys, again to fade; fresh hopes, again to fail; fresh honours, ambitions, delights, vain-glories, to perish with this perishing world! As our Blessed Lord prophesied, so it is; "'Whom the world cannot receive, because it seeth Him not, neither knoweth Him." The world shrinketh from the Spirit of Truth, because it clings to its errors; it loathes the thought of the Comforter, because it would be all-sufficient to itself in its joys, and would know no sorrow.

But is then sorrow only for those afflictive visitations of God, by which He awakens men out of sin's death-sleep to themselves and to Him? Is there no abiding sorrow, no abiding consolation, no supernatural sorrow, and supernatural comfort? Our Lord does not speak of any passing feeling or quickly-fading grace when He pronounces the blessedness of the poor in spirit, the merciful, the pure in heart, the ahungred and athirst after righteousness. So neither is it a passing grace, much less is it mere natural sorrow over those causes of sorrow, with which God,

f S. John xiv. 17.

in His love, mercifully besprinkles the absorbing
pleasures of this life. Rather it is an abiding sorrow,
sweeter than all life's sweetnesses; for it. is a sorrow
from God, unto God, according to God; a sorrow,
the fruit of grace, the parent of joy, the condition of
supernatural consolation, "Blessed are they that
mourn: for they shall be comforted."

Is this our home? are we in Paradise? are we in
that state, in which and for which God made us? are
we in possession of our heavenly birth-right? are
we at rest in ourselves? are we satisfied with our
past or present? is our future secure? is our relation
to God what we wish? True! we have consolations
of nature, which, when pure, are earnests of the love
of God. We may have unspeakable consolations of
grace. But consolations (as I said) imply a need
of consolation; they imply a sorrow of heart, which
has to be comforted.

Our Lord's words are so large, that they must com-
prise all mourning which is not sin, or "of the nature of sin." In itself, the word "mourn" almost
always belongs to a tender sorrow. It is originally
the mourning over the dead[g]; it is the inner feeling
expressed by tears; it is sorrow over that, which has
been and is not. In this sense too "blessed are they
that mourn." Nay, since this sorrow is so universal,
since Almighty God has, in His all-wise love, appointed, that almost every death should be single
and alone, each of the deaths of those hundreds of
millions of our race radiating its sorrow in various
degrees to others, who, in their turn and at their
time are to become fresh centres of sorrow, the uni-

[g] The word is πενθεῖν.

versality of this law of individual suffering shews
how great an instrument in the purifying of souls
such individual suffering must be. The "Father and
God of the spirits of all flesh [h]," Who "doth not
afflict willingly nor grieve the children of men[i],"
makes human suffering the corrective of human sin.
Well then may we think that our Lord meant to
include in His blessing this universal wail of His
creatures, to whose fall He annexed that remedial
sorrow! Only the sorrow must have that condition, which is presupposed in any blessing from His
mouth, that it be "a sorrow according to God[k]," in
conformity with, subdued to, following the track of,
His All-Holy Will.

He who had known all earthly joy and glory and
wisdom and fame, the first of his day, with whose
wisdom none competed except to be vanquished,
was chosen as the organ of revealing the blessedness of sorrow. "It is better to go to the house
of mourning" [i.e. where they mourn the life just
fled,] "than to go to the house of feasting: for
that is the end of all men; and the living will lay
it to his heart. Sorrow is better than laughter: for
by the sadness of the countenance the heart is made
better[l]." Blessed is a joy according to God, abounding in thanksgiving, bounding upward to its God,
holding His gifts unvaryingly from Himself, de-
lighting not only in them, but because they are
choice gifts of its Father's Hand. But deeper far
is a "sorrow according to God." For in joy we love
God in, for, with, His gifts; in sorrow the gifts

[h] Num. xvi. 22.   [i] Lam. iii. 33.   [k] 2 Cor. vii. 10.
[l] Eccl. vii. 2, 3.

are gone, and we adore God mutely for His wisdom in withdrawing them, and love Him for Himself. Mourning drives a person into himself. It takes off the false glare of this showy treacherous world. It wakens up old memories, which he would wish buried for ever. It is a lightning flash on a precipice before his feet, and, below, the pit of hell. It speaks of death, and of what is to be after death. It shews him to himself as a whole; how evil acts have become habits; how things in him, seemingly unconnected, are bound together by one unseen thread, and that thread sin, or of sin; how all or most of his good has been cankered by this secret unsuspected worm; how self has been, in all, his secret law, his lawgiver, his idol, his god. Blessed, then, is the outward condition of mourning, blessed far above all outward joy, is that sorrow which becomes, through repentance, the vestibule of heaven.

Yet piercing as is the unveiled sight of that resurrection of man's buried sins; crushing as is their accumulated number, as they exhibit themselves all at once to his gaze, (faint image of the Judgement Day, because our Lord's reproachful look is not there!) or as they throng in long procession, another, and another, and another, until the brain turns dizzy at the sight of self; shocking as it is to see what seemed good deeds look mere counterfeits, with which we deluded conscience and which we passed off upon God—be the sight a baptism of fire, there is a rainbow in the thick cloud, there is, in the sight, an earnest of God's mercy. God would not have shewn us the sight in this life, but that He willed us to repent, and to forgive us.

"No interval separates the tears of the sinner and the mercy of the Saviour." God who "said 'Let there be light,' and there was light," now, by the greater Omnipotence of His love, says of repented sin, Let it be as though it had never been; and forthwith it is not, to condemnation; it exists only in memory, the safeguard of humility, the quickener of forgiven love. Yet not only so. Sorrow is evermore, through God, the parent of Divine joy. Whatever has been our course, whether preserved in Baptismal grace and in the main ever looking heavenwards, or brought back to ourselves and to God by affliction, one is the experience of all, who are now in a state of grace and know themselves. "It is good for me that I have been in trouble, that I might learn Thy statutes;" "Thou in faithfulness hast afflicted me [m]."

Deep were those thoughts of one still young, who having thanked his God for all His marvellous love in childhood, boyhood, and in the bolder range of "reason's aweful power," went on in words which once were here well-known familiar tones [n]:—

> "Yet, Lord, in memory's fondest place
>   I shrine those seasons sad,
> When, looking up, I saw Thy Face
>   In kind austereness clad.
>
> "I would not miss one sigh or tear,
>   Heart-pang or throbbing brow;
> Sweet was the chastisement severe,
>   And sweet its memory now.
>
> "Yes, let the fragrant scars abide,
>   Grace-tokens in Thy stead;
> Faint shadows of the spear-pierced Side
>   And thorn-encompassed Head."

[m] Ps. cxix. 71, 75.

[n] Lyra Apostolica, n. 23; Chastisement, (Dr. Newman's).

And so it is unto the end. Not success, but checks; not praise, but dispraise; not gain, but loss; not this world's joy, but sorrow, are, to hoar hairs, God's choicest gifts, sorrow turning into joy, privation crowned by the riches of His consolation. The touch, from which the flesh shrinks, is the token of the presence of that Spirit of burning, which scorches to save.

" I would not part with one pang that I have had, no not for the whole world," were the almost parting words°of one, who had high rank, wealth, political position, talent, brilliant wit, popularity, and a closing year of intensest bodily suffering.

Yet although these are part of a law of God, they do not work their effects by force of that law. Despair, not repentance, would be the natural fruit of chastisement; passionate, profitless grief would be the natural produce of deep loss; discontent, the result of bodily suffering. Not of itself, but by the brooding of the Spirit of God over the troubled chaos, is it hushed into order and repose, and yieldeth life; only through the healing presence of the Comforter does " the sorrow of this world," which " worketh death," become " the sorrow according unto God;" which "ᵖworketh the repentance unto salvation not to be repented of."

Yet neither the sorrow through which God brings back the dead soul to life, nor those other sorrows through which He quickens it anew to deeper, more inward life in Him, or burns out what might ex-

° The words were said, a day or two before the death of him who spoke them, to Bishop Bagot, of Oxford, who told them to me.
ᵖ 2 Cor. vii. 10.

haust or weaken or choke that life, can come up to the full meaning of our Lord's words. For then He would rather have said, "Blessed are they that have mourned," or, "that shall have mourned;" not, "the mourning," that is, "they who are ever mourning[q]."

This leads us to a deeper thought as to our Lord's words. For now we have two seeming contradictories, an abiding mourning and an abiding joy. We have joy, yea exceeding joy, an exulting, bounding joy[r], as a Christian duty,—a triumph[s] given to us by God in Christ; and Christ Himself pronounces us blessed, if we are ever mourners.

Plainly, then, the mourning must be something quite other than the world means by it. For mourning may have peace; nay, rather, true mourning will always have a deep still peace; but how should it have exuberance of joy?

It has the joy all the more, because it is habitual. Look at any deep loss of this earth, which has severed life in twain, because for the time it has severed

[q] I find this in S. Gregory of Nyssa (De Beatitud., Or. iii. Opp., tom. i. p. 781):—"The Word seemeth to me, in that prolonged action of mourning, to suggest something deeper than I have said, leading us on to conceive of something beside this. For if He had pointed only to repentance for transgression, it had suited better with this, if those had been pronounced blessed, who 'have mourned' (τοὺς πενθήσαντας), than those 'who are habitually mourning' (τοὺς εἰσαεὶ πενθοῦντας); as, to compare *their* condition who are in a diseased state, we pronounce those happy who have been cured, not those who are in a continual course of cure."

[r] ἀγαλλιᾶσθε, S. Matt. v. 12; ἀγαλλίασις, Acts ii. 46; ἀγαλλιᾶσθε χαρᾷ ἀνεκλαλήτῳ, 1 Pet. i. 8: add Acts xvi. 34, 1 Pet. i. 6, iv. 13.　　　　[s] 2 Cor. ii. 14.

those who were as one. Time flows by; the im-
passioned grief is mellowed; there comes a serene
calm, it reigns and is the habitual state of the soul.
But the survivor is not as before. Life is gilded
from above; duty done to God, love to God, kindness
and love to man, natural affections, bring a peaceful
joy; yet, deep below, there is one unchanging feeling, such as that which, after years had passed, burst
from the aged Patriarch's soul, "Joseph is not."

I said mourning (the word which our Lord uses)
especially relates to sources of joy, which we have
had and have not. What is it, which the whole human race had and has lost? What is it, which we
all more or less deeply lose, and which we never in
this life can recover? Innocence was that great gift
of God to man in Paradise, blameless life, unclouded
intercourse with God. "What we now," says a
Father[t], "conceive of only by imagining, all were
shed around that first man, immortality and bliss,
self-rule untyrannised, life without grief or care,
passed in things divine, gazing on the All-good
with unveiled mind. Such were we. How then can
we but mourn, contemplating our present wretchedness by the side of our then blessedness? What
in us was lofty, lowered; what was in the image
of the heavenly, inearthed; what was destined to
reign, enslaved; what was created for immortality,
corrupted by death; what was passionless, exchanged
for this passionate and perishing life; our unenslaved
freewill now lorded over by ills so many and so great,
that we cannot easily count the tyrants over us!
For each of the passions in us, when it gains the

[t] S. Greg. Nyss., l. c., pp. 785, 786.

mastery, becomes the lord over its slave, and, like a
tyrant, seizing the citadel of the soul, afflicts our
subjected nature by the things subdued to him,
using at his will our thoughts as his servants. So
are anger, cowardice, rashness, our passions pleasurable or painful, hatred, strife, mercilessness, harsh-
ness, envy, flattery, memory of injuries and unfeel-
ingness, and all the contrary passions, so many
tyrants and masters, enslaving the soul, as a prisoner
of war, each to his own dominion."

A storm without might be great peace within.
Strife is afflictive, but leaves, by God's grace, no sting
or stain of sin. Few and fleet are our pilgrim-years
here; and God has engoldened our transient dwelling-place with multiplied radiancy of His love. Not
the strife, but the defeat; not even our want of self-
mastery, as such, but our own free evil choice, is life's
deep sorrow. The embitterment of life is sin against
the infinite love of our all-good God.

The bitterness is sweetened by forgiveness; the
gentle, still, deep, sorrow remains; the deeper, because the more still. Think of one deeply loved who,
under whatever temptation, had been guilty of the
blackest ingratitude to father, husband, friend; (it
is the very picture of us in the Prophet, " Go love
a woman, loved of a husband (himself) yet an adul-
teress, according to the love of the Lord to the children of Israel, who look to other gods[u];") could the
forgiven ever cease to mourn? would not the exceeding tenderness of forgiving, unreproaching love,
draw forth the deeper sorrow?

What were all created love, gathered and concen-

[u] Hos. iii. 1 : see Comm.

trated into one, compared with the love of God for each of us? I would not say, it were nothing. Very beautiful is pure, created, love, because it is His highest creation, the image of His Being, Who is Love. But all conceivable love, which God has created, or shall create, or could, if He so willed, ever create, were but finite; and His love to each one of us is infinite. And against this infinite love we have sinned! Each act of wilful sin casts back upon God this His infinite love, compares His creature with Himself, and tells God to His face, "I choose this pleasure, this pride, this vanity, this lie, this misery rather than Thee, and Thine infinite love." What, when such sins have been accumulated? What, when years of life have been spent in such preference of self, self-will, ambition, vilenesses, to God? What, when at best all love which we return for that infinite love is so poor, so mean, so self-seeking, that people would be ashamed to offer it all to any good creature of His, whom they deeply loved!

And all this, on repentance for love of Himself, God has forgiven, blots out, ignores, reproaches not. "God is a God of the present." He accepts the disobedient penitent son, who told Him to His face, "I go not," yet goes at last, as if he had, from the first, done His will. Should we not have hearts of stone, if this untiring, despised, provoked, overcoming, and then unreproaching love of God, did not melt us? And can we then enjoy the manifold, daily, ever-varying goodness of our God, and not mourn that we ever sinned against it?

This mourning is not sad, or dejected, or downcast. It casts no cloud over the brightest cheerfulness which God spreads over life. Rather, it is the supernatural source of comfort above nature. For He who gives the sorrow gives also the joy. In all eternity, redeemed man cannot forget what he has been. His own special blessedness would be less, if he could. For our bliss will be, by God's mercy, in the infinite love of our God; and we should know less of that infinite love, if we did not know how much He had forgiven us, how His victorious love had won us to Himself. S. Peter's bliss would be less, if he could forget that look which won him back to himself and to his Lord. S. Mary Magdalene would be less blessed in her Lord's love, if she could forget His love, when she washed His feet with her tears. The robber would not, if he could, be deprived of the memory of his Lord's love, which pardoned that his last blasphemy on the cross, accepted the confession which that love itself had given, and admitted him alone of His redeemed to His side in Paradise.

But since the memory of forgiven sin will intensify the joy of heaven, so penetrated will it be and trans- figured with Divine love, then neither, by the grace of God, will it cast any shadow over life's pure joys here. Nay rather, there is no true joy without it. True joy can never be in partial ignorance, or in looking away from oneselves. The self which we would flee from, meets us unbidden; any chance word, any old remembrance, awakens it. Some word of God suggests it. We are in doubt and must have misgiving about ourselves; and that misgiving re- lates to eternity and our eternal doom! God will not, in His mercy, let us rest, where rest is disease or death. There is no health, until the last drop of bad blood has been squeezed out or transmuted by His grace. Our only joy can be, not in ourselves, but in God; not in ignorance that we are sinners, or how deep our sins, but in pouring out all our sins at the feet of Jesus and in His forgiveness. And then man's true joy is in thankfulness to God, and to Jesus God-Man, for atoning, pardoning love. So God transmutes our poverty into the riches of His grace; our short-comings into the overflow of His love; our badness into the occasions of His goodness; our hateful memories of what is hateful, sin, into channels of His purifying grace, the joy of redeemed love.

Our humility, repentance, hatred for sin, meekness and tenderness to our fellow-sinners, safety against relapse, thankfulness to God, growth in grace, all are involved in the vivid memory that we are forgiven sinners. Blessed, then, is the mourning, in itself, which is the guardian of our restored grace, which makes us of one mind with God, hating what He hates, and tender with His tenderness, compassionate towards our fellow-servants, even as He had pity on us.

But through the exuberance of His love, the bitter waters are turned into sweetness by the wood of His Cross. *They shall be comforted.* Comfort is not the mere negation or absence of sorrow. It is not (as men's comfort 'is) a powerless sympathy, soothing, in a measure, for the love which there is in it, but not reaching to the depths of the wound below. God's comfort, as " His Word," "is with power[v]." The comfort is from the Almighty Comforter, Who comforts, not in word but in deed. It were little in

[v] Ps. xxix. 4; S. Luke iv. 32.

comparison, had He said, that their mourning should be ended, that their tears should be wiped away. He says much more, "They shall be comforted." Their comfort is not, then, from within, but from without; it is an action upon the soul, and that from God, who vouchsafes to take, as one of His titles, "the Father of mercies" (mercies as manifold as our needs) " and the God of all comfort[w]."

We have then an abiding, supernatural comfort from an Almighty Comforter. Mourning and comfort meet together; "[x] deep crieth unto deep," the depth of men's misery to the depth of God's mercy. Wherever the cry of the soul is, *there* is the ear of God. "Thou preparest the heart; Thine ear hearkeneth thereto[y]."

It bespeaks, as I said, one universal troubled state of men's being, that God the Holy Ghost should have that title and office towards us, the Comforter. Yet this being so, what is in itself evil is, by the touch of God, transformed into a superabundance of good. "Where sin abounded, there the grace superabounded[z]." Where sorrow comes, there is a proportioned superabundance of consolation.

But consolation were as nothing without the Consoler. What man needs is God. Natural joy cannot content the heart, which was made for God. Nothing can content it, except what is from God and to God. *The* joy of consolation is that it is the touch of God. "They shall be comforted" by the Comforter, a continual action of God on the soul, meeting the soul's continual desire.

[w] 2 Cor. i. 3.　　[x] Ps. xlii. 7.　　[y] Ib. x. 16.
[z] ὑπερεπερίσσευσεν, Rom. v. 20.

And so that last treasure of man's innocence, for which he mourns, the intercourse with God, is, by his mourning, restored to him. Not that consolation, or any spiritual sweetness, must be our end. Nothing in ourselves must be our end, but God only. Our end is, by God's grace, to become holier, less unlike God, less ungrateful to Him for His forgiving love. Our sorrow must not take its eyes off from God. We wish, if we could, to make amends to Him; we cannot tell Him often enough to satisfy ourselves, "Would, O God, for love of Thee, I had never, never, displeased Thee!" We know that we cannot change the past, whatever it has been; but we can oppose a strong contrary will to that will, wherewith we offended God; and speaking thus to God strengthens our will and longing, as speaking to man, except in the view of God, weakens it. For God looks on the soul which He has led by His grace to look up to Him; He strengthens the soul, which looks to Him, its Strength. Every such longing of the soul is a portion of the unutterable groanings of the Spirit[a], whereby He suggests desires mightier than words can utter, more than the heart knows how to contain; "Would that I had ever loved Thee!" And what the Spirit suggests within is heard on high. For it is the voice of God, which means more than our thoughts can grasp, pleading with God, by virtue of *His* merits Who, being God, for us sinners became Man.

This is the special value of the deep penitential character of the prayers of our Church. This is why we, instinctively, love the Litany; why, before

[a] Rom. viii. 27.

D d

the Holy Communion, the deeper confession after the Commandments, and that in which we own " the burden of our sins intolerable," suit our heart so well.   It is in the presence of the deepest love, that the sense of forgiven sin is deepest.   The penitence which suits Lent, in another way suits Easter or Pentecost, or the reception of our Lord's Body and Blood.   The sorrow of forgiven love is a festival-joy; for we sorrow, because we have been, are, so unworthy of that infinite love, wherewith God hath loved us, wherewith He loveth us.

God grant, my sons, that ye may have no deeper cause for sorrow than ye now have, that ye may not need that mighty burst of sorrow, wherewith a soul is restored from death.   Yet there must be, I fear, among you some, whom deadly sin crept over, in years yet earlier than yours even now are, less deadly then, because you knew not its whole deadliness.   One cannot but have fears, when the body is so much pampered, and the "[b] keeping under the body," which an Apostle thought needful to himself, is so despised.   Abuse not what I have said, as though ye might have the pleasure of sin now, the joy of forgiven sinners hereafter.   To sin, in hope of God's forgiveness hereafter, is one of the forerunners of the sin, for which there is no forgiveness, because there is no repentance.   Your Saviour, Who hath revealed Himself to you, looketh to " see" in you " of the travail of His soul," and to be " satisfied." God the Father Who loved you in all eternity, and Who made you in and for His infinite love, looketh and waiteth, that ye should answer the end for which

[b] 1 Cor. ix. 27.

He made you. 'God the Holy Ghost, by Whose agency, ere you knew good or evil, ye were severed from the world, and Who made you sons of God and members of Christ, Who has ever put every good thought into you, Who now perhaps is reminding you of your high nobility and suggesting to you to live worthily of your birth of God, waiteth to give you all the treasures of His grace, love, joy, peace, the unutterableness of His consolations. Defraud not God of yourselves. Defraud not yourselves of God. Give to God that which is His, His image, the price of the Blood of God, yourselves. Say to God, "I am Thine. Would, for love of Thee, I had ever lived to Thee; would that I had never disobeyed Thee, never preferred anything to Thee! Would that I may never more so offend Thee!" Say it from thy heart of hearts, and thou wilt know a joy, which if thou hast never so wholly given thyself to God before, thou hast never yet known, the joy of a personal love of God, as thine own God, the individual love of Jesus, Who saveth thee from thy sins. Blessed are they who so mourn, for they shall be comforted.

O God, Who didst teach the hearts of Thy faithful people, by the sending to them the light of Thy Holy Spirit; Grant us by the same Spirit to have a right judgement in all things, and evermore to rejoice in His holy comfort; through the merits of Christ Jesus our Saviour, Who liveth and reigneth with Thee, in the unity of the same Spirit, one God, world without end. Amen.

SERMON XXI[a].

SUFFERING, THE GIFT AND PRESENCE OF GOD.

HEB. xii. 6.

" Whom the Lord loveth, He chasteneth."

IN all heathen antiquity, there are scarcely more
touching words, than that inscription at Athens, "To
the unknown God." It was a feeling after a Divine
Power whom they knew not of, from whom they believed that they had suffered, with whom they wished
to be at peace. It was a confession of ignorance;
but, in its ignorance, the people did the best which
it could. It is the voice of human nature, yearning
after its unknown Creator, dissatisfied with its traditional idolatry, and groping blindly after a Being
on Whom it depended.

That unknown God S. Paul preached to them.
Were S. Paul present among us, would he have to
preach to us an unknown God? Does he still, by
the Holy Ghost, preach One Whom men know not?
Alas! if it be so, it is the God Whom men think
that they know better than He knows Himself, better
than He has revealed Himself, Whom yet they know
not, and are self-satisfied not to know. They leave
no crevice, as these Athenians did, through which

---

[a] Preached at S. Mary's Oxford. Lent, 1864.

some ray of His glorious light might shew them their darkness.

We see this in extreme cases. Our Lord said "[b]My Father worketh hitherto and I work." When then men, to remove from themselves the pressure of an Omnipresent God and of His interference with themselves, relegate back *their* deity to some boundless time, when he is to have created, once for all, this order of things, and tell him flatteringly that it is unbefitting his wisdom to concern himself with his creation, for that it would imply that he knew not how to make it perfectly at first, we know that their Epicurean deity is not our's, the Living God.

Or those, who, by a strange reversal of this theory, will not allow God to have revealed Himself to us once for all, who think that the old Theology of Holy Scripture, as taught by the inspired Apostles, was well enough for days past, but that now we want a re-adjustment in conformity to some discoveries of science (which have, in truth, no bearing on Theology) or of our (God bless our simplicity!) advanced "moral sense," or our more just appreciation of what is becoming to God,—we see, in them, the same disease in another form. These too shrink from having a Lord, Who has not to account to *them* for the wisdom of His revelations, nor to justify to *them* the holiness of His aweful justice. They mislike a God, Who is independent of them, and on Whom they must consequently be dependent. And so they flatter Him, and praise Him for His wisdom, Who has made *them* so wise, and tell Him, that they are sure that He cannot have meant any thing which they

[b] S. John v. 17.

cannot approve of; that their reason is His gift, and that He cannot contradict Himself. But since, after all, those sayings which they would persuade God to unsay, are His, and express truth as to Him, then clearly God is to them too, so far, an unknown God. God is other than they believe. We and they do not worship the same God. Our God is not their god, nor is their's ours.

Again, when people deny or explain away the doctrine of the All-Holy Trinity, it is clear that we do not worship the Same God. The belief or disbelief is not about abstract doctrines, (as men speak); it relates to the very Being of God, to God Himself, in His ever-blessed eternal existence, Father, Son and Holy Ghost. They deny *His* Being Whom we adore.

Again, in that aweful doctrine of the everlasting punishment of those who to the end shut out God and will not have Him, they who say that God would be cruel if He so punished sin, plainly do not believe in God, such as He has revealed Himself through our Divine Lord. They reject our God in His aweful Holiness, and believe in a god whom they have invented to themselves. Never shall we see the solemn seriousness of all those questions, which men so recklessly bandy, until we see that they are not abstract questions or opinions, but that they involve the very Being of God.

But then, as to ourselves, who hold the whole true faith in God, may not God, practically or in a degree, be to some of us an "unknown God?" Is not our idea of God, (or at least has it not in some degree been?) as of one, who has turned us into this

world to have our own way as much as we can without (we tell ourselves) shocking deadly sin; to be
as prosperous, as we can; to get on in life, to go to
Church on Sunday of course, and have to ourselves
the rest of the week, so that we say some prayer
morning and evening, and our grace at meals; else, to
have all the outward prosperity which we can; to be
as comfortable as ever we can; to eat, drink, sleep,
talk, work, rest, dress, gain or spend, accumulate,
be men of the world, flatter and be flattered; to take
our ease and be merry, fare sumptuously every day,
only that we now and then give a sixpence to Lazarus, and, if we are rich, an annual guinea or two to
some charitable or religious object?

But where then is the chastening of the Lord, that
we be "[c]not condemned with the world?" where, the
"[d]much tribulation, through which we are to enter
the kingdom of God?" where, the tribulation which
His own were to have in the world[e]? where the blessedness[f], which our Lord pronounced on those who
weep now, for they should laugh? or His woe on
those who laugh now, for they shall mourn and weep?
Where, "[g]the infirmities," through which "the power
of Christ may rest upon" us? Where, "[h]the suffering with Christ" that we may also reign with Him?
Where "[i]the partaking of the sufferings," that we
may also be partakers of the consolation? Where is
there room for that mark of predestination, conformity to the sufferings of Christ? Where the dread of
being reprobates, "[k]if ye be without chastisement

[c] 1 Cor. xi. 32.   [d] Acts xiv. 22.   [e] S. John xvi. 33.
[f] S. Luke vi. 21. 25.   [g] 2 Cor. xii. 9.   [h] 2 Tim. ii. 12.
[i] 2 Cor. i. 7.   [k] Heb. xii. 8.

whereof all are partakers, then are ye bastards and not sons?" "Hope not," says a father[1], "to be without the scourge, unless thou think to be disinherited; for 'He scourgeth every son whom He receiveth.' Is it every *one?* where wouldest thou hide thyself? Every one, and none excepted, none without the scourge! What? 'every one?' Wouldest thou know how truly 'every one'? Even that Only One, Who had no sin, was yet not without the scourge." "[m]Thou art over-delicate, if thou wouldest have thy gladness with the world, and afterwards reign with Christ."

And is not then God still an "unknown God" to "the world," which thinks that it believes in Him? Is He not unknown to them in His aweful Holiness, unknown to them in His tenderest mercies? These two opposed ignorances are inseparable. "[n]Mercy and truth are met together." It is in the aweful unsearchable depths of God's Holy Justice, that we see the real depths of His Infinite mercies. In the depths of God's judgement we see something of the depth of our sinfulness. In the depth and width of our sin, we see something of the depth and breadth and height of the Atoning love of God, made Man. We see the depth of our disease in the death to which it leads, and the suffering which its cure involves. Our suffering some portion of the penalty of sin brings us in sight of the eternal fires, and, while flesh and soul shrink from the faintest touch of God's aweful Justice, it sets us in reverent sympathy with *His* Sufferings, "upon Whom God made to meet the iniquities of us all."

[1] S. Aug. in Ps. xxxi. [32 Eng.] n. 26. [m] S. Jer. Ep. 14. ad Heliod. n. 10. Opp. i. 36. Vall. [n] Ps. lxxxv. 10.

Happy is the poor world in this alone; that, although God is an "unknown God" to it, this ignorance comes from ignorance of itself, not from wilful denial of the attributes of God.

This, then, is the first, most comprehensive, yet most special way, in which God is the consolation of the afflicted, that He has revealed, that sorrow is a token of His Love. This does not depend upon any self-persuasion; there is no room for self-deceit or mistake. It is more than if God revealed it to ourselves. We have often thought perhaps, "If God did but tell me, that He loves me!" If He has sent you sorrow or pain, He has told you that He loves you. Suffering is in the order of our salvation; it is in order to our salvation. In the mercy of our God, it arrests the sinner; it deepens the loving sorrow of the penitent; it proves and advances the all-but-perfected. It exhibits us to ourselves; it enhances the love of our Redeemer; it is God's instrument to make us of one mind with Himself. It awakens the sleeper: it is the voice of the Redeemer piercing the cold ear of those dead in sin, that they may arise from the dead, and that He may give them life. Every touch of sorrow or pain, from the stunning blow or want which recalls the prodigal son to himself to the last rack which dissolves the martyr's form, is a token of the love of God. "Is one in grace? God tries him. Is one in his sins? God corrects him⁰." God can sanctify the blessings of this life, through abundance of thanksgiving. But the grace of abundance of thanksgiving for our daily, hourly, momentary blessings, the blessings of body

⁰ S. Greg.

and soul, of nature and of grace, within, without; of love or of understanding; is perhaps the rarest on earth. Endless thankfulness is a joy of the perfected in heaven. He has not trusted man upon earth with gifts, which should only be the occasion of present sensible thankfulness. "PLook and see; thou shalt find that all saints suffered adversity. Solomon alone was always encompassed by all which his heart could crave, and therefore perhaps, he," who was once so wise, who once chose God above all things, "fell." Him too God wearied by satiety of prosperity; "qHe gave him his desire, but sent leanness withal into his soul." Rare instance of one, wearied but not soured by the nothingness of the world, and whom the unsatisfactoriness of all created things enjoyed and drained to the dregs, drove back to his first choice, the God Who, in His youth, chose him and from his birth, yea in eternity, loved him and called him, "the beloved of the Lord."

But chiefly it is sorrow, bereavement, heart-pang, disease, misfortune, shame, fear of death and hell, its sin's bitter fruits, which turn the amazed and scared soul to God. Sorrow must follow sin. "Thou," says S. Augustiner of his heathen youth, "Thou wert ever with me, mercifully rigorous and besprinkling with most bitter alloy all my unlawful pleasures, that I might find pleasures without alloy." These sorrows neglected, there follow heavier scourges, until the soul yield itself to God, or die. Sorrow is it also, some sudden check or grief, by which God mostly keeps the soul from false security, from seek-

p S. Jer. Ep. 22 ad Eustoch. n. 39. ii. 122. Vall.

q Ps. cvi. 15.   r Conf. ii. 4.p. 20. Oxf. Tr.

ing itself instead of its God, from relaxing in fervour, from self-dependence, from mistaking nature for grace, from substituting a mere pleasurable activity for the service of God, from lingering on the way, from seeking some other reward out of God, Who is Himself the " exceeding great Reward " of His own. Then also affliction, privation, suffering, are the perfecting of His own. It keeps them in humility, which, in God's hands, is the safe-guard of every grace ; and it prepares the crown, which is reserved for those who have, by His grace, endured to the end. " In My Father's house," our Lord says, " there are many mansions." " ˢStar differeth from star in glory." Everlasting bliss, although perfect to each, may vary from the very highest capacity of containing God, with which He could endow a creature, to the lowest of one who so choked and narrowed himself by love of created things, as scarcely, at the last, to admit God and the grace of God. Whatever the degree of the capacity of each and its eternal bliss, each soul was formed through suffering. " ᵗGod alloweth no one bad to be happy." If any seem to be happy, it is, because men know not, what happiness is, because they see not the sinful soul, nor the spectres which haunt it, nor its secret fears, nor the worm of remorse, which, by God's mercy, gnaws it, when alone. " ᵘThe Cross is ever prepared, every where awaits thee; thou canst not escape it, run whithersoever thou willest; for, go whithersoever thou goest, thou bearest with thee thyself, and ever thou findest thyself: turn thee above, below, without, within;

ˢ 1 Cor. xv. 41.   ᵗ S. Aug.   ᵘ Imit. of Christ ii. 12. 4.

in all thou wilt find the cross." There are those, whom God in His mercy drags, as it were, to heaven; souls, who shrink from every cross, who desire every ease, and from whom God in mercy withholds the temporal good which would ruin them, and gives, for their salvation, the trial from which they shrink. By His marvellous Providence, while through His grace they endure patiently the temporal suffering which they shrink from, God purifies them by the fire of suffering, that they perish not by the fire of Hell. To the highest souls, where there was least to purify, He gave the extremity of suffering. "ᵛ Take away the strife of the martyrs, thou hast taken away their crowns; take away their tortures, thou hast taken away their beatitudes." The sword pierced even through the spotless soul of the Mother of Jesus, and she, upon whom the Holy Ghost came, and the power of the Highest overshadowed her, must have suffered, by a spiritual martyrdom, a sharper agony than that which parts body and soul, when, by the Cross of Jesus, her Son and her Redeemer, Simeon's prophecy was fulfilled, "the sword shall pierce through thine own soul also."

This then is the great comprehensive comfort in every ache of mind or body, that we know infallibly from God's infallible Word, that it is a token of His love. Be it disease or loss of bodily health or strength, or of clearness of intellect, the consequence of sin; be it the shame with which God "ʷ filleth the face that they may seek Thy Face, O God;" be it the first terror of Hell, which, by God's grace,

ᵛ S. Amb. in S. Luc. L. iv. n. 41. Opp. i. 1345.
ʷ Ps. lxxiii. 16.

scares the yet unconverted sinner towards the wide-
open arms of Jesus on the Cross, or the last sharp
pang of death, which lets the imprisoned soul go
free, to meet its God for Whom it yearned and faint-
ed, we know, by God's own word, it is His love.

Yet it is not only love, working through some
fixed or some general rule of His Providence. It is
something far nearer, more tender, more blessed. It
is God's own personal act. It is our Redeemer's own
medicinal Hand. "*I* have afflicted thee." "*As
many as I love, *I* rebuke and chasten." "*Happy
is the man, whom *God* correcteth." "*Blessed is the
man, whom *Thou* chastenest, O Lord, and teachest
him out of Thy law." "*Whom the Lord loveth, *He*
correcteth; even as a father the son, in whom he
delighteth." What a volume of consolation there is
in that word, "I." It is not then, as men atheisti-
cally talk, fate or fortune or luck, just as if there were
no God. Nor is it this or that human agent. In
one sense, it is man's chicanery, or oppression, which
robs of subsistence; or man's malice, which robs of
good name; or man's false tongue, which poisons, or
alienates for the time, the loved heart, or chills the
friendship. Whence all this evil-speaking, but from
man? Whence this wrong-doing, or subtle injury, or
piercing unkindness? They are not from God. Sin
cannot be from the All-Holy. But it is from Him,
Who ordereth all things well, that the evil, done by
man's free-will, reacheth *thee*. He Who "ordereth
the service of angels and men in a wonderful order,"
perfected the patience of Job through the envy of

---

x Nah. i. 11.   y Rev. iii. 19.   z Job v. 17.

a Ps. xciv. 12.   b Pr. iii. 12.

Satan, and the estrangement of his wife, and the un-
kind judgement of his friends.   To think of the human agents, through whom the trouble comes, and
fret against them, is like the poor dumb animal which
runs after the stone which strikes it.   Poor beings,
they do but hurt themselves.   Remember that "I;"
"*I* have afflicted thee."   Then is the rising displeasure turned into submissive cheerfulness, or joy.
"Let him curse," said the royal penitent of the reckless insulter of his miseries, "because God hath said
unto him, 'Curse David[c].'" "[d]Who shall say to Him,
What doest Thou?"   Yes! this is the deep comfort
of each sorrow, as it comes; "*I* have afflicted thee,"
I, Who love thee; thy God."   This is the deep re-
assuring truth, that it is not man's caprice, nor a
fixed iron law, nor a combination of events; but, our
own God.   This is the deep inward peace in every
trial, that He orders each particular blow or weight
of sorrow, or fretting care, or harassing discomfort or
unrest, in His All-wise love, fitting each trial to our
own particular temperament.   He gives to each of us
just our own trial, what, by His grace, will most
amend *us*, what will bring us most to Himself, what
will most draw out the good which He has implanted
in us, or burn out the evil which would most es-
trange or ruin us.   Not till that Day, which shall
most fully reveal us to ourselves, when the secrets of
our hearts, their hidden tendencies, shall be disclosed, shall we know how the things, over whose
loss or absence we have been tempted to repine,
would have corrupted or ruined us; how, what kept
us low, kept us also lowly; how distress or sorrow or

c 2 Sam. xvi. 10.   d Job ix. 12.

aching care or fretting anxiety loosened our grasp from the world, to fix it upon God.

This too is not all. It is not an All-Wise God, unseen, unfelt, at a distance, guiding all things in perfect wisdom for the good of each individual creature which He had made. Great were this, yea, in one sense, all: for it is His individual, infinite, Personal love. He Who loves us infinitely, loves us individually. But this too not afar off, not only in the heaven of heavens. "*e* I am with him in trouble; I will deliver him and bring him to honour." Trouble is the special Presence of God to the soul. "*f* When thou passest through the waters, I will be with thee; and through the rivers, they shall not overflow thee; when thou walkest through the fire, thou shalt not be burned, neither shall the flame kindle on thee." He Who, present with them, soothed to the three youths the flames of fire, so that they fanned softly around them, and were to them an unharming robe of glory; He Who, ever-present with His disciples, then appeared to them, when the storm was at its highest and its waves were boisterous; He, still present to the soul, now soothes to His own the fire of affliction, that, while it burns out the dross, it should not touch the soul, but should yield it pure, transfigured and translucent with the fire of love. He Who baptizes with a baptism of blood, holds His own, that, although immersed and sunk deep down, the waters should not come in to the very soul itself, but should only wash away its stains through His most precious Blood.

Can there be more yet than the Presence of God

e Ps. xci. 15.   f Is. xliii. 2.

with the soul? Yes the end of that Presence is more
to the soul itself, than that Presence itself. For it is
the earnest of His abiding Presence, yea, of union
with God. Suffering, the due reward of our deeds,
becomes, by His Mercy, the means of conforming us
to the Son of His love. While we feel in ourselves
the likeness of the penitent robber, and say with
him " we indeed justly," and feel that the searching nails pierce far less than we deserve, and that
even that cross of shame were nothing to us, seeing
that we deserve "ᵍshame and everlasting contempt,"
we are brought very nigh to the Cross of Jesus.
While we suffer for our own sins, and bear about us
less than their deserved chastisements, God gives us
yet an outward likeness to His Cross, in that it *is*
suffering. For "ʰon Him were laid the iniquities of
us all." But we still hang, as it were, by His Side;
His healing compassionate look falls upon us; from
His All-Holy Sufferings there goeth forth virtue to
sanctify our's. Those nailed-pierced Hands are still
stretched forth to heal and save us; that mingled
flood of water and of Blood still gushes forth to save
us from sin's guilt and power; that sacred Side, "the
Rock of ages rent for me," is wide open to us to hide
us from our sins and from the accuser, that, buried
there, we may drink of the exhaustless Well of life,
that in it we may have the earnest of everlasting life
and glory.

Hence is deserved suffering by God's mercy such
a token of predestination, that it brings us near to,
makes us partakers of, the Sufferings of Christ. If
we are chastened, then God owns us as children;

ᵍ Dan. xii. 2.   ʰ Isa. liii. 6.

"'if children, then heirs; heirs of God and joint-heirs with Christ, if so be that we suffer with Him, that we may be also glorified together." Hence the Apostle triumphs in this communication of the sufferings of Christ; for so he goes on; "ᵍ The sufferings of this present time are not worthy to be compared with the glory which shall be revealed in us," and again, "ʰ If we be dead with Him, we shall also live with Him; if we suffer, we shall also reign with Him."

These are eternal truths, which the Eternal Truth has revealed. We believe them because they are His word; and "ⁱ Thy word is truth." But there is one, my son, whom thou must know also, ere thou canst know what in this life we can know of the Infinite love of God, for us made Man, for us, as Man, dying, to pay the penalty of our sins. Thou must know—it is often a horrible sight, but thou must know thyself. We cannot really know Jesus, until we know what sin is, what is the penalty of sin, what is the blackness of the ingratitude and offensiveness of our own sins. All revelation hangs together. Only in that aweful mystery of the endless doom of him, who, to the end, and *in* the end, perseveres in rejecting God, do we see what the terrible malignity of sin is; only through the knowledge of the malignity of sin can we know the Divine love of Him Who died for us, while we were sinners and because we were sinners; only by the gloom of the undying hate of Hell and the loss of God and the aweful light of its lurid fires, do we know, in contrast, something

ᶠ Rom. viii. 17.   ᵍ Ib. 18.
ʰ 2 Tim. ii. 11, 12.   ⁱ S. John xvii. 17.

E e

of the intensity of the bright love of Jesus, or of the blackness of our own ingratitude in sinning against that deep love.

Suffering, to the poor world, seems but a thing to be got rid of; or, if we cannot be rid of it, to complain of to others, to obtain their sympathy for, to murmur and rebel against. Bereavement seems to it a thing to be simply forgotten; the aching of the secret heart, a thing to be drowned in feverish joy. Without sin and hell, suffering were but a blot in God's creation; a caprice or powerlessness of the ruler or "rulers of the world," as man would then conceive of them, which unreasonably or enviously allotted suffering here, meaning to make it up somehow hereafter. Suffering, in the world of the good God, must have some tremendous meaning, or it is the more utterly unaccountable. Be not wiser than God. Trust God, for a little while, with His own creation, with His own revelation. A few short years, and by His mercy thou shalt know and feel, and in all eternity thank Him for that wonderful condescension of His Love, which created thee with that mysterious power of free-will, that thou shouldest, of thy free God-enabled will, choose Himself. So great a good is it for thee, thyself of thy free-will to love Him Who eternally loved thee, ere yet thou wast, ere the world was, that He created thee free, with a free generous devoted love, to choose Him and to love Him, although the failure in that free-choice involved the creation of Hell, the giving of His Only-Begotten Son to die for us, the infinite Sufferings of Jesus, sustained but not abated by His Godhead, the peril of thine own eternal loss.

" Stand in awe and sin not[k]." No one who feared
Hell ever fell into it. They "[l]fled from God dis-
pleased to God appeased," and He received them in
His everlasting love.

But, as thou wouldest have, or hast had, comfort
in thy suffering, comfort thou others; as thou prizest
thine own soul, so dearly bought, prize thy brother's. God does not comfort us for a selfish comfort.
"Blessed be God," burst forth S. Paul, "Blessed
be God and the Father of our Lord Jesus Christ
the Father of mercies and the God of all comfort;
Who comforteth us in all our tribulation,that we
may be able to comfort them which are in any trouble, by the comfort wherewith we ourselves are comforted of God [m]."

There is a class of shortlived, half-willing, half-
unwilling sufferers by man's sins, worn down to an
early, dishonoured grave by the sins of man and
their own, for whom your help is asked this evening[u]. God has His own among them also. For them
also Christ died. One of them was nearest to the
Cross and earliest at the grave of Jesus, when Apostles had fled. There are among them, who wish
to be delivered from the bondage in which they are
held, who loathe the sin by which they sustain their
living death, in whom the chastening hand of God
is working, by His grace, weariness of sin and a
longing to be free at least from their misery, which
may be transformed into the glorious freedom of
children of God.

We, in this place, have been behindhand in this.

[k] Ps. iv. 4.   [l] S. Aug.   [m] 2 Cor. i. 3, 4.
[n] A collection for a Penitentiary.

E e 2

Those, whom the law has reached, have been gathered together into a prison, like the prisonhouse of Hell [o], rather than what a Christian prison should be, a reformatory ; a prison, worse in one respect than Hell, in that the remaining sparks of natural goodness, which had survived the wreck of innocence and domestic love and purity and good name and the grace of God, are trodden out. Here too there should be homes for the houseless, havens where those who half or weakly long to be freed, might "knock and it should be opened" and they should have no need to sin for their nightly lodging or their daily bread.

As there could not be any more horrible sight than to see on the left hand any one, who had ever been a partner in sin, and to hear the "Depart ye cursed," so it will be one of the joys, now above the thought or imagination of man's heart, to see at the Right Hand, one whom by any self-denying deed of our's we had aided to set free. "Forasmuch as ye have done it to one of the least of these, ye have done it unto Me."

[o] Such was, in 1864 (when this was preached), the want of classification in the prison, that those who had the authority to remove these occasions of temptation from the streets of Oxford, shrank from using that power towards the young, lest they should be hardened by the more corrupt, with whom they would be associated.

SERMON XXII[a].

JESUS, THE REDEEMER, AND HIS REDEEMED.

1 Cor. ii. 2.

" I determined not to know any thing among you save Jesus Christ, and Him crucified."

ABSTRACT yourselves for a moment from yourselves and all around you, and ask yourselves, 'What would be the aspect of a redeemed world?' A world, I mean, which knew that it was redeemed. For we know that Christ is "[b] the propitiation, not for our sins only, but also for the sins of the whole world." Now too the Spirit of God broodeth over the face of the moral chaos, wherein all nations lie which know not Christ; now too He partially lifteth up the veil[c] spread over them. From the fall until now, every grace which has visited every soul of man on this earth; every remorse or sorrow for any crime or sin which has been committed; every struggle for self-mastery, even though it ended in defeat, has been the working of God the Holy Ghost, purchased by the Precious Blood of Jesus. Never, until by God's mercy we attain, shall we know any thing of the

[a] Preached at Christ Church, at a College Service, 4th Sunday in Lent, 1874. [b] S. John ii. 2. [c] Isai. xxv. 7.

reign of Jesus; how He ruled in hearts, which knew Him or knew Him not; how He gave to Joseph or even to Scipio his chastity; or to Regulus his self-sacrifice; or how, at this moment, He is, through the Holy Spirit, "engraving the image of God upon every piece and parcel of the rational creation."

But, while it is well for us, not to forget the vastness of the empire of our Redeemer, our immediate object is with ourselves, who know of our Redemption. And so I ask you to think, away from all things which are around you or in you, what would or should be the aspect of a world, which knew itself to be redeemed. Redeemed *from* what; *to* what; by Whom, and how!

Redeemed (to say but a portion, and yet in one sense the greatest) *from* an endless antipathy and rebellion and loss of God, our only Good! The most thoughtful think that, even in the lost, the suffering of the loss of God is greater far than any suffering of sense. It is, they say, to the soul which God made for Himself, an intenser suffering to be borne towards God by the necessity of its being, and yet to be held back from God by the obstinacy of an obdurated will, than to endure those pains, "prepared for the devil and his angels." And this commends itself to one's reason. For Hell would not be Hell, if we could accept it as "[d] the due reward of our deeds." If we could ever so little love God, it would not be Hell, and we should not be there. Obstinate hatred of God, as He Is, is an essential part of Hell. But, apart from the overpowering love of our redemption, and the unwearying grace which

[d] S. Luke xxiii. 41.

our Redeemer merited and bestows upon us, we could not cease to be alien from God; we could not love Him, we could not (aweful as it is to say it) but hate His Presence in heaven. We know how those who give themselves up to sin would, except for some remaining pleadings of His grace, loathe being amidst any worship of God. They would loathe or scoff at the name of Jesus: its mention would create or awaken antipathy to Him, as, many of His people who rejected Him have a horrible pleasure in blaspheming Him, as "the hanged."

Little as we, in the light of the Gospel, can bear to think it, the centre of our redemption is a redemption from eternal hatred of God. We cannot bear to think it, because His Holy Spirit still pleads with us; still, we hope, dwells in us; because, within and without, God tells us, 'I am thy Father, I have redeemed thee, thou art Mine[e].' But hatred of God, terribly as it sounds, are familiar words in God's word. We have heard (we cannot say how often) of that sanction of the second commandment, how God visits sin "upon them," He says, "that hate Me." And yet what is it, which the second commandment forbids? It says nothing of murder, adultery or any wrong of man to man. It forbids only the setting up an idol in the heart, and "[f]serving the creature more than the Creator." Such, it implies, come to hate God. What, when Love came into the world and went about doing good, what was the result to those who rejected Him? "[g]Now have they both seen and hated both Me and My Father." God, in His condescension speaks of

[e] Is. xliii. 1.   [f] Rom. i. 25.   [g] S. John xv. 24.

the hatred of His creatures to Himself as a common thing. "ʰ The haters of the Lord" is a recognised title. Love says of Himself, "'It is written in their law, 'they hated Me without a cause:'" "ᵏ Marvel not, if the world hate you: ye know that it hated Me, before it hated you."

Could you imagine yourselves living without one look or word or act of love? Yet there can be no love in Hell. All its inmates must live in one unchanged unmitigated hatred of God and of one another. Every hateful passion must exist in all its intensity: for its miserable inmates cherished them with their heart's blood unto the end; and 'change of place,' the heathens knew, 'does not change the soul.' Conceive then one wild hatred, scorn, spite, bitterness, malice, rage, fury, inflicted unceasingly, unceasingly endured; look where one will, all those alas! countless faces of evil men or devils, all scowling and venting their restless misery in an unextinguishable fiery hate, and, if there be one partner of sin or of godless passion here, the fiercer hate. It would make us mad here. *There* there is no relief of madness; no relief of death.

I have spoken only of what is inseparable from the thought of a soul passing out of this world, fixed in sin. I have said nothing of the unquenchable fire, or the worm (of which our Lord warns so tenderly that we may not incur them), save of the fire and the worm which scorch and gnaw within.

But so, I have mentioned but the skirts of that, *from* which Jesus has redeemed us.

And *to* what has He redeemed us? "'¹ Eye hath

ʰ Ps. lxxxi. 15.   ¹ S. John xv. 25.   ᵏ Ib. 18.   ¹ 1 Cor. ii. 9.

not seen, nor ear heard, nor hath it entered into
the heart of man to conceive." But as the mere
counterpart of what I have said of Hell, think of
that boundless capacity, that multiplicity of love.
Every one of those millions of millions of beings,
full of love and of love of us. And there will be
no sameness in their love. Out of each, love will
stream forth with its own individual beauty and
loveliness of love. And we ourselves should be so
full of love, that we should joy in their bliss as our
own; we should have our own joy mirrored and reflected back to us in the joy of all besides; nay,
God has invented for us this capacity of bliss, that,
while we ourselves are capable only of that glory
and love, for which our poor attainments may have
fitted us, we shall joy in the joy of all those exalted
glorious spirits, as if it were our own; nay we shall
joy in the glory of the God-united Humanity of our
Lord. While we have the unutterable Bliss of loving
and thanking Him, that He, at such a price, bought
us, His joy and glory shall be part of our joy, because we shall belong to Him; we shall be His, and
He ours; for so He hath said, we are "[m]members of
His Body, of His flesh and of His bones," and He
will have said, "[n]Enter thou into the joy of thy
Lord."

"[o]O what will be that bliss, where there shall
be no ill, where no good shall be hidden from us;"
"where shall be full, certain, secure, everlasting,
bliss," and every power and faculty of our frame
shall be concentrated in the love and praise of God;

[m] Eph. v. 30.   [n] S. Matt. xxv. 21.
[o] S. Aug. de Civ. Dei xxii. 30. Opp. viii. 609.

"praising Him unceasingly, because we shall unceasingly love; where God Himself shall be the satisfying unsating fulness of bliss; all which heart can desire, life and well-being, and food and abundance and honour and glory and peace and all good." "He Himself shall be the end of all our longings, Who shall be endlessly beheld, loved without cloying, praised without weariness," where we shall have all which we long for, and shall not be able to long for what we shall not have. Free-will we shall have, but inseparably cleaving to its unchangeable Good, which is God, " free from all evil, filled with all good, enjoying unceasingly the sweetness of eternal joys, forgetting its failings, forgetting its pains, yet not forgetting its deliverance, so as not to cease to be thankful to its Deliverer." Yet this too shall be the special bliss of the redeemed; this is a joy, which Angels cannot know. "We shall know," says the same father[p], "that we *have been* miserable; for the Psalm saith, '[q] I shall sing of the mercies of the Lord for ever;' and nothing truly can be sweeter to that Heavenly City, than that canticle to the glory of the grace of Christ, by Whose Blood we have been set free."

This we can in some way imagine, though we cannot imagine that intensity of God-sustained love, or its fulness or variety, which can be ever the same, ever-fresh; unexhausted because passionless, yet with a mighty force, of which passion is but a poor picture, because passion has no rest, unless exhausted. We can imagine in Heaven the satisfaction of seeing in God the hidden causes of all which

[p] S. Aug. l. c. n. 4.   [q] Ps. lxxxix. 1.

puzzled or perplexed us here, and the beautiful harmony of all His works and ways. But the Bliss of bliss, that which is, above all, the Bliss of Heaven, of which all other bliss is, (so to say) but an accident, is the Beatific Vision, the sight of God, face to Face. "[r] All abundance would be poverty, without the sight of God." "[r] The vision of God is the true contentment of the soul." "We shall see Him, as He Is," Him, Who Alone Is, and from Whom all besides have their being and beauty, Whose perfections are not separate from Himself, but are evermore visible in Him. One in Him and with Him are that inconceivable Beauty and exhaustless Wisdom and unchangeable Truth, and Goodness which knows no bounds, and essential Holiness, and all-sustaining Omnipotence, and all-containing Providence, and infinite Mercy, and "splendour of Divine Majesty." Yea, in His simplicity of Being, absolutely One shall we see the Ever-blessed Trinity, Each Person the Object of our special love, yet Each inexisting in the Other. The Father "[s]ever communicating Himself to the Son by that ineffable, co-eternal, consubstantial, Generation, and the Father and the Son, in the Procession of the Holy Spirit, Who is the love of the Father and the Son, communicating Himself to His Spirit, Who, not in Person but in Substance, Essence, goodness, wisdom, charity and majesty, is the same as the Father and the Son." And in that love, which God Is, we shall see and taste and feel that individual love, with which in all eternity God loved our own poor selves, and in time created, redeemed, guided,

[r] S. Greg. [s] S. Laur. Justin. de perfect. grad. c. 13. p. 610; 1.

guarded us all our lives through, and which, having brought us thither, will inundate us with itself and hold us inseparably united with God, in one exstacy of eternal joy.

And *how* were we transferred from *such* misery to *such* bliss? You know well, in faith. Jesus, "'the Just one, died for the unjust, that He might bring us unto God." "ᵘ The Lord laid upon Him the iniquities of us all." It will be part of the joy of eternity to know that wondrous device of the one co-eternal love of the Father and the Son, how, beyond the condescension of the Incarnation, they willed thus to restore our ruined race, thus to combine the tenderest mercy with God's aweful holiness, that "ᵛ while we were yet sinners, Christ died for us." Angels do not yet wholly understand it; for they too rivet their sight ʷ on the Sufferings of Christ. They too are interested in them. For "ˣ He Who raised up man from his fall, gave grace to the angels who stood, not to fall; rescuing the one from captivity, upholding the other from it, and so was redemption unto each, freeing the one, preserving the other." And if angels have yet to learn, and to them "ʸ is made manifest through the Church the manifold wisdom of God," well may we be content not to know *why* God chose this way of restoring us, till we see it in Himself.

Almost as little can we know of the actual Sufferings, whereby it seemed good to the Father and the Son, that God the Son, in our human flesh,

---

ᵗ 1 S. Pet. iii. 18.   ᵘ Is. liii. 6.   ᵛ Rom. v. 8.

ʷ παρακύψαι 1 Pet. i. 12. See Bp. Wordsworth Ib.

ˣ S. Bern. Serm. 22. in Cantic.   ʸ Eph. iii. 10.

should make atonement for our sins. We can repeat His bodily sufferings, as the Gospel tells us of them. But it tells them so simply, and His sacred Body was so tender! Yet we can see how they came without pause, one upon the other, Wound upon Wound, the flesh torn with the scourges, every sense so rudely racked, the sacred Side furrowed by those harrowing lashes, the crown of thorns piercing the nerves of that gentle Head, the limbs dislocated (as the Psalm describes them[z]); and around, all those hateful and hating faces, the gibes, the blasphemies, the imputations of blasphemy to Him Whose Will was ever one with the Father's; His Mother's grief.

Bodily pains we think that we can picture. We have heard in detail of the sufferings of the Martyrs, of the flesh-rending hooks, the hot-iron-plates, the rack, the scourge, till wound came not on the flesh but on the wounds. But the mental pains, the weight of sin upon the Innocent and All-holy, its loathsomeness to the Undefiled, its horror, we sinners can not imagine. We have heard of a conscience haunted by the memory of one sin, till reason was overthrown. But before Jesus and in His sight and heavily upon Him weighed, one by one, the sins of the whole world; the sins of all those millions of millions of human beings, which had been, were, or should be; which in each generation are born, sin, and pass away, penitent or impenitent. Then He, as it were, felt their creeping sickening touch, their horrible defilement. His God-united Soul saw all those countless sins, which no imagination could reach unto, each in its own enormity and aggrava-

---

[z] Ps. xxii. 14.

tion, its foulness or its atrocity. He felt them resting on Himself. Sinners as we are, we cannot but be horrified at some sins. He knew, as no mere creature could know, the hatefulness of sin. He knew, as none else could know, the displeasure of His Father at the sins, which He came to bear. He knew, for whom He bare all those miseries in vain, who would not be redeemed, and He felt the agony of parting with them. "[a] The suffering of His compassion" has been thought to have been "greater than His Passion;" yet Scripture says so calmly, "[b] He bare our sins in His own Body on the tree." He bare their weight in His Agony in the garden for those three long hours; and that Bloody Sweat, those great tears of Blood, which His Agony forced out from His whole Body, that pressure of sin, and hiding of His Father's Face which issued in that mysterious cry, "My God, My God, why hast Thou forsaken Me?" are to us a witness of that Suffering.

Of those indignities which accompanied the Crucifixion, men have thought, the Jews were the instruments, though they were but the executioners of our sins. Of those yet intenser mental sufferings we cannot think that we had not our portion; He bare the sins of each one of us; else they had not been atoned for.

Once more, then, what should we think would be the aspect of a world, which knew itself to be so redeemed? We know what it will be in Heaven. Personal love, adoration, admiration, thanksgiving to the Redeemer. We have heard the song of the "[c] ten thousand times ten thousand and thousands of

[a] S. Bonaventura.   [b] 1 S. Pet. ii. 24.   [c] Rev. v. 11-13.

thousands;" " Worthy is the Lamb which was slain, to receive power and riches and wisdom and strength and honour and glory and blessing." And this was echoed on the earth: "and every creature which is in heaven and on the earth and under the earth, and such as are in the sea and all that are in them, heard I saying, Blessing and honour and glory and power be unto Him that sitteth upon the throne, and unto the Lamb for ever and ever." And this love to the Redeemer must issue in Divine love for those, whom with us He redeemed. "Herein," says the Apostle of love, "[d]herein is love, not that we loved God, but that He loved us, and sent His Son, a propitiation for our sins. Beloved, if God so loved us, we ought also to love one another." Why seems there then to be so little of this personal loyalty and devotion? Why so little of that superhuman love? Personal religion there doubtless, thanks be to God, is among very many. But where is the ardent self-denying love of the early Christians? Where is the fiery faith of S. Paul? Where is there to be seen any burning love of God and our Redeemer? Where any longing for the interests of Jesus, as if they were our own? Where any oppressive thirst for more souls, to be glorified in Him? Where any distress at the unconverted alas! millions in London, who know Him not and dishonour Him? Well and a gain is it, if we have a life-long abstinence from heavier sins!

Were the first Christians different men, or had they a different faith? Whence had they that love to one another, that Heathen exclaimed, "[e]See how

[d] S. John iv. 10, 11.   [e] Tert. Apol. n. 39, p. 82. Oxf. Tr.

these Christians love one another?" Whence had they their patience under injuries by the sight of which, as by something above nature, Heathens were converted[f]? How were they "[g]fenced by a most careful and faithful chastity," while in our metropolis, the desecrated victims of man's sins[h] are counted by tens of thousands? Why were they "[i]known by no other sign than the reformation of their former sins?" They had worse temptations, doubtless, than we, surrounded as they were by the corrupting mass of heathen sin without, and the feverishness of accustomed sin within. They conquered "through Him that loved them." They conquered through love of Jesus crucified for them. They conquered, because "[k]neither death nor life nor principalities nor powers, nor things present nor things to come, nor height nor depth nor any other creature were able to separate them from the love of God, which is in Christ Jesus our Lord."

Jesus, the long-longed-for, came not chiefly to reveal truths, but to love us, to shew us something of that Infinite love, which it shall be a joy of eternity to behold; to love us, with all that boundless, unchanging, inconceivable, Divine, eternal love, with which the Father loved Him. '[l]As the Father hath loved Me, so have I loved you; continue ye in My love.' This love pervaded all His life; it was concentrated in that act, which closed His earthly life,

[f] S. Justin M. Apol. 1. i. n. 16, p. 12. Oxf. Tr. [g] Tert. Apol. n. 9. p. 24. See references to S. Justin M., Tatian, Athenagoras, Minutius Felix. Ib. n. h. [h] "We are," said one to a missionary Priest, "what you men have made us." [i] Tert. ad Scap. n. 2. p. 145. [k] Rom. viii. 37-39. [l] S. John xv. 9.

when, to complete our Redemption, He gave up His Spirit to the Father on the Cross of suffering and shame. He came to be the Centre of our being, the magnet to draw us up, where He is, in Heaven. "I," He says, "^m if I be lifted up from the earth, will draw all men unto Me."

This was the might of the preaching of S. Paulⁿ, that he "^o bare the name of Jesus before the Gentiles and kings and people of Israel;" "^p Christ the power of God and the wisdom of God." In this alone he gloried, "^q the Cross of our Lord Jesus." "^r He might have gloried in the wisdom of Christ, in the majesty, in the power of Christ, and he had spoken truly: but he said, 'in His Cross.' For where was humility, *there* was majesty; where was weakness, *there* was power; where was death, *there* was life." This flashed forth from the mouth of S. Peter, when

^m S. John xii. 32.

ⁿ "Whence, thinkest thou, so great and so sudden light of faith shone in the whole world, save from the preaching of Jesus? Did not God call us in the light of this name to His own marvellous light, that to us, so illumined and seeing light in His light, Paul might with good reason say, Ye were sometime darkness, but now are ye light in the Lord? This name the same Apostle bare before kings and the Gentiles and the children of Israel; and he carried that name as light, and illumined his country. And he shewed to all the light on the candlestick, preaching in every place Jesus, and Him crucified. How did that light gleam on and dazzle all who beheld, when going forth, like lightning, out of the mouth of Peter, it strengthened the bodily feet and ankles of one blind man, and illumined many spiritually blind! Did he not shed light abroad, when he said, In the name of Jesus Christ of Nazareth, arise and walk?" S. Bern. Serm. xx. in Cant. xv. 6. p. 1316.

^o Acts ix. 15. ^p 1 Cor. i. 24. ^q Gal. vi. 14.
^r S. Aug. Serm. 161. n. 4.

F f

he said " ⁸ By the name of Jesus Christ of Nazareth, Whom ye crucified, Whom God raised from the dead, by Him doth this man stand before you whole. Neither is there salvation in any other; for there is none other name under heaven given among men, whereby we must be saved." This made "ᵗ the kingdoms of the world the kingdoms of our Lord and of His Christ." By this ᵘ God gave power to boys, girls, female slaves, a Magdalene ᵛ, power to overcome the inventiveness and the might of incensed power to torture. By this, He kindled that "fire" of love, which He "came to send upon the earth ʷ;" by this He won us to Himself, "ˣ that we should not henceforth live unto ourselves, but unto Him which died for us and rose again:" by this He taught us His "new commandment," that we "should love one another, as He has loved us ʸ," with a self-denying, self-sacrificing love.

By this alone, my sons, ye will conquer in the strife, through which God wills to perfect you, that ye may be fitted to enter into His joy. Look up to the Cross of Jesus, or think of His saving Name, Jesus. "Is any sad," says one ᶻ, who knew well its power, "let Jesus come into the heart, and thence spring into the mouth; and lo, where the light of that name dawneth, every cloud flies away and serene light returns. Does any fall into sin and run desperately to the snares of death? If he call on the name of Jesus, will he not forthwith breathe anew

---

ⁿ Acts iv. 10, 12.   ᵗ Rev. xi. 15.   ᵘ See in Serm. xxiii. p. 456-459.   ᵛ See the touching Acts of S. Afra; Ruinart Acta sincera mart. p. 501.   ʷ S. Luke xii. 49.   ˣ 2 Cor. v. 15.
ʸ S. John xiii. 34.   ᶻ S. Bernard l. c. n. 6. p. 1317.

in life ? In whom did ever hardness of heart, torpor
of sloth, rancour of mind, languor of lukewarmness,
stand before the face of that saving name ? In whom
did not the dried-up fountain of tears burst forth
more plenteously, flow more sweetly, when he called
on Jesus ? To whom, when shivering and trembling
in perils, did not this name of Jesus, invoked, forthwith give confidence, dispel fear ? On whom, when
tossed and eddying in doubts, did not certainty suddenly flash, when he called on that glorious name ?
Who, when mistrusting and ready to fail in adversity, lacked fortitude, when that name of help fell on
his ears ? For these are sicknesses of the soul ; that
is medicine. Nothing so restraineth the vehemence
of anger, allays the swelling of pride, heals the
wound of envy, restrains the dissipation of luxury,
quenches the flame of lust, dispels the pruriency of
all unbecomingness. For when I name the name of
Jesus, I set before me Him meek and lowly of heart,
all-holy, and the self-same, God Almighty, to heal
me by His example and strengthen me by His help.
All these things together fall on my ear, when I
hear the name of Jesus."

And now Jesus from His Cross preaches to us, as
one little token of our love, which is all too little if
it is life-long, "As I have loved you, do ye also
love one another." We hear from those, who went
prepared to disbelieve, that those who must be af-
fected by this Indian famine are 38 millions ; that
one of the six famine-counties, which may perhaps
be saved, contains $4\frac{1}{2}$ millions, but that in each village about $\frac{1}{3}$, i. e. $1\frac{1}{2}$ millions of human beings like
ourselves are undergoing slow starvation ; that the

famine is most terrible, and suffering is rapidly increasing. I use the very words. Picture to yourselves your own little brothers, sisters, mothers emaciated, hunger-gnawed, and so have pity on those scarce able to lift their powerless arms to receive help, living skeletons only, else with skin and nerves which can suffer, famine-stricken, hanging between life and death. For them too Jesus died; them, as every soul of man, Jesus loves; do good as you can to them for Jesus' sake. At the Great Day Jesus will own it to you, "Ye have done it unto Me."

SERMON XXIII[a].

JESUS AT THE RIGHT HAND OF GOD, THE OBJECT OF DIVINE WORSHIP.

REVELATIONS v. 11—13.

" And I beheld, and I heard the voice of many angels round about the throne and the beasts and the elders: and the number of them was ten thousand times ten thousand, and thousands of thousands; saying with a loud voice, Worthy is the Lamb that was slain to receive power, and riches, and wisdom, and strength, and honour, and glory, and blessing. And every creature which is in heaven, and on the earth, and under the earth, and such as are in the sea, and all that are in them, heard I saying, Blessing, and honour, and glory, and power, be unto Him that sitteth upon the throne, and unto the Lamb for ever and ever."

ONE is the Church of the redeemed ; One is their God, their Lord, their Head ; One Spirit knits the whole in One, pervading all, filling each separate member according to the capacity of each to receive Him ; endowing each with his own special gifts, and

---

[a] Preached at St. Mary's Oxford, Lent 1867, as part of the series on "Jesus, as the Conqueror."

in all diffusing the love, the wisdom, the holiness, the righteousness of God. One they are, because He who pervades all the whole mystical body of Christ— militant, expectant, triumphant,—is one and indivisible.

And as they themselves are one through the in-oneing Spirit, so the Object of their being, their bliss, is one; only, that while our praises, and thanksgivings, and intercession ascend together to the eternal throne, those above, being already perfected, need no prayer for graces for themselves. No *Miserere* can mingle with their unceasing, endless Halleluias, save for us in our pilgrimage, whom they long to be brought safe through, to swell the sweet concord of redeemed praise.

One, also, is the object of their worship; one only object can there be of divine worship, Almighty God. This was the fundamental central doctrine of the old law: " [b] The Lord our God is one Lord; And thou shalt love the Lord thy God with all thine heart, and with all thy soul, and with all thy might." "Thou shalt fear the Lord thy God: Him shalt thou serve, and to Him thou shalt cleave, and swear by His name [c]." This doctrine our blessed Lord emphasised at the threshold of the Gospel, when He rebuked His bad rebellious spirit and dismissed him from His sacred presence with the words, "Get thee behind Me, Satan. For it is written, Thou shalt worship the Lord thy God only, and Him only shalt thou serve [d]." "Since then," says St. Augustine [e], "we serve both the Father and the

[h] Deut. vi. 4, 5.   [c] Ibid., x. 20.   [d] St. Matt. iv. 10.
[e] c. serm. Arian. c. 29, Opp. viii. 643.

Son and the Holy Spirit with that servitude which is called *latreia*, and we hear the law of God enjoining that we should shew this to no other but the Lord our God only; doubtless our one and only God is the Trinity Itself, to which, one and alone, we, by right of piety, owe such a servitude." Hence it was rightly objected to the Arians that, owning (as they did, and as Socinus did in later times) that our Lord was an object of divine worship, and yet holding God the Son to be a creature, they were, in fact idolaters. It would have been but the revival of the old Polytheism within Christianity. "Who told them," says St. Athanasius[f], "'Abandon the worship of the creation, and then draw near and worship a creature and a work?'" "They," said another[g] as to the heathen, "whereas they ought to have worshipped the true God, offered the divine honour to the creation. To this censure are they too liable who call the Only-begotten Son of God a creature, and yet worship Him as God. For it were due, either if they call Him God, not to rank Him with the creation, but with God Who begat Him; or if they call Him a creature, not to offer Him divine honour."

Nor, plainly, does the humility of the Incarnation make any difference herein. For He deified our nature in Himself by taking it; He could, and did, empty Himself of the visible glory of His Godhead; He could not, by becoming man, cease to be God. He became man, "not by conversion of the Godhead into flesh, but by taking of the Manhood into God." "We worship not a creature," says St. Athanasius[h];

[f] ag. Arians, i. 8, p. 191, Oxf. Tr.   [g] Theodoret on Rom. i. 25.
[h] Ep. ad Adelph. § 3, p. 912, 913, Ben.

"God forbid! For such an error belongs to heathens and Arians. But we worship the Lord of the creation, the Word of God Incarnate. For although the Flesh, Itself by Itself, is a portion of the things created, yet It became the Body of God. And neither, severing the Body, being such, by Itself apart from the Word, do we worship It; nor, wishing to worship the Word, do we remove Him from the Flesh; but knowing, as I said before, the Scripture, 'The Word was made Flesh,' we own Him, although being in the Flesh, to be God. Who, then, is so senseless as to say to the Lord, 'Remove from the Body, that I may worship Thee?' or who so ungodly as, with the frantic Jews, on account of the Body, to say to Him, 'Why dost Thou, being a Man, make Thyself God?' Not such was the leper; for he worshipped the God, being in the Body, and knew that He was God, saying, 'Lord, if Thou wilt, Thou canst make me clean;' and neither, on account of the Flesh, did he account the Word of God a creature; nor, because the Word was the Artificer of all creation, did he make light of the Flesh, wherewith He was arrayed; but he worshipped as in a created temple the Creator of all, and was cleansed. So also the woman with an issue of blood, believing and only touching the hem of His garment, was healed; and the sea, tossing its foam, heard the voice of the Incarnate Word, and ceased its tempest; and the blind from his birth, through the spittle of the Flesh, was healed by the Word; and greater and more marvellous still (for this, perchance, shocked even the most ungodly), when, the Lord being upon the Cross itself, (for the Body was the Lord's, and in It was the Word,) 'the sun was darkened, and the earth shook, the rocks were rent, and the veil of the temple was rent in twain, and many bodies of the saints which slept, arose.' "

The confusion, created by heretics, arose in the ignorance or misbelief of the doctrine of the Incarnation, the fruitful source of manifold heresy. For men, in one or the other way, parted with the belief that our Lord's Divine Nature, being Divine, was unchangeable; that It could not be confused; that It could receive no accession to Itself, so as to be a complement of Itself. For It was all-perfect. When, then, God the Word vouchsafed to take our nature upon Him in the Virgin's womb, He did not unite to Himself a pre-existing nature, so that It should have a distinct personality, but " created that manhood which He took, by taking It, and took It by creating It[i]." His Manhood, real and perfect as It was, was but an adjunct of His Deity. He took our nature, that for us He might suffer, that for us He might die; that He might bear our sins, that He might offer a full price and ransom for us; that He might be our High Priest for ever at the Right Hand of God; yea, that, having redeemed us, He might, by taking a manhood joined to His own Nature, make His Flesh lifegiving, and " through His flesh akin to us might draw up to Him all humanity[k]." " He used it as His instrument for the operation and the shining forth of His Godhead[l]." Yet His Personality is not human but Divine. When, then, we adore Christ, our God, we adore not His Deity and

[i] Hugo de S. Vict., Summa Sent. i. 15. t. iii. p. 431.
[k] Ps. Basil in note k on S. Ath. ag. Arians, p. 444, Oxf. Tr.
[l] S. Ath. ag. Arians, iii. § 53, p. 475, Oxf. Tr.

His Humanity separately, but His Deity clothed
with His Humanity. This the Church of God proclaimed that she had received from the first, that
" God the Word Incarnate, with His own Flesh was
worshipped[m]," rejecting with anathema, the opposite
heresies, that Christ is worshipped in two natures,
thus introducing two acts of worship, one appropriated to God the Word, the other appropriated to
the Man; or again, with either destruction of His
Humanity, or confusion of the Godhead and Manhood, or the assumption of " one nature from both
concurring."

This Divine Nature, then, of our Lord in His
Humanity, St. John exhibits as a distinct Object of
the praises and thanksgivings of the Church Triumphant. For he saw the beatified beings, whom he
was admitted to behold, at times prostrate in adoration before the Lamb, at times as adoring at once
Him Who sitteth on the Throne, and the Lamb.
At one while, he shews us the four living creatures
and the four and twenty elders falling down before
the Lamb, having, every one of them, harps and
golden vials full of incense, which are the prayers
of the saints. We hear the new song of redeemed
love: "[n] Worthy art Thou . . . for Thou wast slain,
and hast redeemed us to God by Thy Blood out of
every kindred, and tongue, and people, and nation;
and hast made us unto our God kings and priests."
"[o] Worthy is the Lamb that was slain to receive
power, and riches, and wisdom, and strength, and
honour, and glory, and blessing." And again, the

[m] Conc. Const. ii. can. 9; Conc. T. vi. p. 212 Col.
[n] Rev. v. 8—10.   [o] Ib. 12.

song is echoed from the whole Church, triumphant, militant, and expectant: "[p] every creature which is in heaven, and on the earth, and under the earth, saying, Blessing, and honour, and glory, and power, be unto Him that sitteth upon the throne, and unto the Lamb for ever and ever." And again, all that great white-robed, palm-bearing "[q] multitude, which no man could number, of all nations, and kindreds, and people, and tongues, stood before the throne, and before the Lamb, saying, with a loud voice, Salvation to our God which sitteth upon the throne, and unto the Lamb."

This same, which St. John exhibits in being, as God shewed it him, St. Paul sets forth as the end of the humiliation of the Son of God. God humbled Himself, emptied Himself, to exalt that Manhood which He humbled Himself to take, and then, in Him, all our humanity. In Himself the Son could not be exalted. For He was Co-eternal, Co-equal with God. But He willed to be One Person with the Humanity which He humbled Himself to take. He humbled Himself, so closely to unite Himself with man, that all which could belong to His Manhood might be spoken of Him as God; what belonged to Him, as God, might be spoken of the Man Christ Jesus. Was it not so? They of old said boldly, "the Passion of Christ my God [r]," "the sufferings of God [s]," "God was dead and buried [t],"

[p] Rev. v. 13. [q] Ib. vii. 9, 10.

[r] S. Ignat. ad Rom. n. 6. "God suffered;" S. Melito ap. Anast. Hodeg. 12. See St. Ath. ag. Ar., p. 444, n. i. O. T.

[s] Tert. de Carn. Christi, c. 5. [t] Vigil. c. Eutych. ii. 502, ib.; see also Petav. de Inc., ii. 2. 12, 13; iv. 15. 5 sqq.

because, although God could not suffer or die, He Who for our sakes died and was buried and rose again was Almighty God. "[u] Because of the perfect union of the Flesh which was assumed, and the Godhead which assumed It, the names are interchanged, so that the human is called from the Divine, and the Divine from the Human. Wherefore He Who was crucified was called by Paul 'the Lord of glory;' and He Who is worshipped by all creation, of things in heaven, in earth, and under the earth, is named Jesus." God the Son plainly could not be exalted; for He was, in all eternity, "in the form of God." It was the equality with God which He *had*, of which He "held it no desirable thing" to retain the manifestation; but He humbled Himself by "taking upon Him the form of a servant" of God, by "coming to be (by His Birth) in the likeness of man;" (not mere man, being still what He was, Almighty God) "and, being found in guise as a man," [i. e. being, again, not mere man, but personally God, clothed with our humanity,] "He humbled Himself by becoming obedient even unto death, and that the death of the Cross," the shameful, the accursed, the transgressors' doom.

The counterpart of the exaltation relates to the self-same. The humiliation was the veiling of His essential glory, which He had, co-equal with the Father, before the world was, by taking our manhood. The exaltation was of Himself, not in Himself, but in regard to that Manhood which He had taken. *He* was exalted, because the Manhood was exalted, which He had made an adjunct of Himself. His

[u] S. Greg. Nyss. in Apoll., t. iii. 265. 6.

Manhood had no separate existence, but was assumed to His own Personality. "His Godhead was in It; the Body was God's [v]." " Being God and Man, He was One Christ [w]." St. Paul then speaks of Him as being super-eminently exalted by God, because the Manhood was exalted, which was His own. "Wherefore," since He so humbled Himself and was so obedient, " God super-exalted Him, and gave Him that Name," which is excellent and glorious "above every name,"—that saving Name, which was predicted by the angel, which was given beforehand at His Circumcision, which received its full meaning and fulfilment when on the Cross He poured out His Blood, and paid the price of the redemption of the whole world, " [x] that at the name of Jesus every knee should bow, of things in heaven, and things on earth, and things under the earth; and every tongue should confess that Jesus Christ is Lord, to the glory of God the Father." It is, as if he described our worship 1800 years before. All things human have manifoldly changed, are changing. The worship of Jesus, our Lord and God, changes not, being, like Himself, eternal.

And so is fulfilled that solemn prayer of our Lord, " [y] Father, glorify Thou Me with Thyself with that glory which I had with Thee before the world was." The Son never ceased to be in that glory, in that oneness with the Father, in which He eternally Is. But as, when on earth, He spoke of Himself, as " the Son of Man Who *is* in heaven [z];" because, as God,

[v] St. Ath. ag. Ar., iii. § 31, p. 444, O. T.
[w] Ath. Creed.　　[x] Phil. ii. 9—11.　　[y] St. John xvii. 5.
[z] Ib. iii. 13.

He is there and every where eternally; as He said to the Jews [a], " What and if ye see the Son of Man ascend up where He was before?" although His Divine Person alone, not His Manhood, which was now in one with It, had been there before; as He said, that "[b] the Son of Man hath power "on earth to forgive sins," although " none" has that power " but God alone [c]," and the Son of Man had it, only because He was God the Son; as " the Son of Man was Lord of the Sabbath [d]," which " the Lord " God had "blessed and hallowed [e]," because He was One Substance with God Who had so hallowed it; as He saith that the Son of Man shall, in that great day which shall decide eternity, " come in His own glory [f]," although the glory in which He shall come is the glory of the Godhead, since He also calls it " the glory of the Father [g];" as it is said, that in that day " the Son of Man shall send forth *His* angels [h]," although those blessed spirits are " the ministers of God" only, " to do His pleasure [i]:" so He, being One Person with God the Son, is glorified with that glory which He had with God before the world was, although then the Manhood existed not.

This worship of " the Word made flesh " began from the moment that He took that Flesh. Elisabeth owned Him as her Lord, ere yet He was born: " Whence is this to me, that the Mother of my Lord should come unto me [k]?" This worship the angels paid Him unseen, when He lay in a manger-bed.

[a] S. John vi. 62.   [b] St. Matt. ix. 6.   [c] St. Mark ii. 7.
[d] Ibid. ii. 28.   [e] Exod. xx. 11.   [f] St. Matt. xxv. 31.
[g] St. Mark viii. 38.   [h] St. Matt. xiii. 41.   [i] Ps. ciii. 21.
[k] St. Luke i. 43.

The shepherds heard their songs of joy, "Glory to God in the Highest, and on earth peace, good will toward men[1];" but, unseen, they worshipped Him, where they told the shepherds that they would find Him; for they obeyed that command, "When He bringeth the First-Begotten into the world, He saith, 'And let all the angels of God worship Him[m].'" This worship they must have paid Him, as He ascended from choir to choir above the highest heavens, as they owned Him the King of Glory. "Lift up your heads, O ye gates; and be ye lift up, ye everlasting doors; and the King of Glory shall come in. Who is the King of Glory? The Lord of Hosts,"— their own Lord, Who took this title of "Lord of Hosts" from them,—"He is the King of Glory[n]."

But what on earth, which Prophets had foretold would be His, where kings were to worship Him, where all nations were to serve Him, which He had claimed as His own, but which, as Man, He had left for that "far country[o]," whence He was to return? What on earth? His own Person could not but be, It was, It is, It will be to the end, the centre of the faith, the object of attack, the rock on which His Church should be founded, on which the waves of unbelief would dash themselves; the magnet attracting love and hate, adoration and blasphemy. Had His religion been a philosophy, no need to destroy it: it would have taken its place among the things of earth, and have died. Had it been a mere worship of what men call the Deity (meaning something about as vague as what the old heathen believed), it would

[1] S. Luke ii. 14.   [m] Heb. i. 6.   [n] Ps. xxiv. 9, 10.
[o] St. Matt. xxv. 14.

have been admired, have caused no uproar, have been
forgotten. But the Jews, and His own "little flock"
and the heathen presently, alike understood the issue. Was Jesus what He claimed to be, God? or was
He what the Chief Priests and Pharisees called Him
to Pilate "a deceiver?" There was no middle term;
Either Almighty God, One Substance with the Father indwelling in the Father and indwelt by the
Father, through the absolute numerical Oneness of
the Divine Nature, or,—less than man; not such 'as
Socrates or Græcia's wise men, but—it is well to face
the alternative, to look it straight, full in the face,
—not even an upright man, such as many whom we
reverence now on earth, but a deceiver. The Jews
sought to extinguish His Name. Either they were
Deicides, or He was such as they between whom
they had crucified Him; yea, worse than they, by how
much spiritual seduction from loyalty to our God
and Father, spiritual falsehood, taught in the Name
of and against the God of Truth, is worse, more desolating, more destructive than sedition of a conquered nation against their temporal masters. And
so they forbade to teach in His Name; they gave
authority, (it is doubtless, according to the wont
of Holy Scripture, but one instance out of many,)
they gave authority to Saul, while "yet breathing
out threatenings and slaughter against the disciples
of the Lord," to "bind all who should call on the
Name of Jesus [p]." To that same Jesus, the converted Saul, when struck to the earth by the majesty of
His appearing, submitted his whole soul, all which
he was, all his life, as to his Lord: "What shall I do,

[p] Acts ix. 1, 14, 21.

Lord q ?" To Him he prayed, as washing away his sins,. when baptized ; "calling on the Name of the Lord r." To Him he prayed thrice s in that distressing temptation which he calls "the thorn in the flesh," that it might depart from him, and received answer, "My grace" (imparted manifestly upon that prayer) "sufficeth for thee," yea, and (it lies in the words) "shall suffice." And should this be an insulated act? What religious act of any religious man is an insulated act? Where we have found help, *there* we again seek it; where it has been opened to us, *there* we again knock; of Him Who has given to us, we again ask. Much more in S. Paul. One word, one act, opens to us a large vision into his inner life. Man's fickleness waves to and fro; stayed and steadfast is the soul whose centre, whose attraction, whose lodestone is Christ! His strength was perfected in this one weakness; His might, upon S. Paul's prayer, resided upon him as its home. What, then, of those other weaknesses in which his soul rested content, in which to be weak was to be mighty? He whose life was the life of Christ in him t; he, in whom what he wrought, Christ wrought u; he, in whose body Christ was evermore magnified v; he, who could do all things in Christ instrengthening him w; he, in whose heart Christ dwelt, and by whose mouth Christ spake; in whom Christ was! Whence could he have this closest union and communion with Christ, but that that intense prayer in his weakness, which he mentions the rather becuase it was an-

q Acts xxii. 10.   r Ib. 16.   s 2 Cor. xii. 8.
t Gal. ii. 20.   u Rom. xv. 18.   v Phil. i. 20.   w Ib. iv. 13.
See further in Dr. Heurtley's "Prayer to Christ," p. 15.

swered otherwise than he asked it, was but one flash which shines forth from his God-illumined soul.

St. Paul prayed not only to Jesus but in that corresponding act, wherein we are so mean and niggard towards Almighty God, he thanks alike God and Jesus. He thanks Jesus as his Lord for that Divine act of grace which was the turning-point of his whole life : " I thank Christ Jesus our Lord Who instrengthened me, that He accounted me faithful, putting me into the ministry,, being a blasphemer and persecutor and insulter[x]."

And what of others? What were his manifold benedictions but prayers to his Lord and God, Christ Jesus, either by Himself or with God the Father[y] with Whom the Son is One, that He, Jesus, would be present with the spirit of those whom He blessed ; that Jesus would, equally with the Father, pour peace, love, faith, grace, mercy into their souls ; that He would comfort their hearts and stablish them in every good word and work? S. Paul gathers into one thought the whole body of Christians, as, "all who call upon the Name of" our common " Lord, Jesus Christ[z];" he speaks of all who were Christ's disciples in sincerity and truth, as those who "call on the Lord with a pure heart[a]." Devotion and prayer to Jesus was the characteristic of Christians. He, One and the same Lord of all, was ever-abounding in wealth towards all who call upon Him, gushing forth in one ever-flowing munificence of grace and love to all everywhere who looked to Him for aid ; not of any temporary, fleeting graces, but of " grace upon grace," grace heaped upon grace, grace issu-

[x] 1 Tim. i. 12.   [y] 1 Cor. i. 3.   [z] Ib. ver. 2.   [a] 2 Tim. ii. 22.

ing in salvation. For so had the prophet foretold, "Whosoever shall call upon the Name of the Lord [b]" (i. e. as is plain from the context [c], the Lord Jesus,) "shall be saved." Momentary prayer obtains the grace it asks for; abiding prayer obtains abiding grace; prayer for perseverance obtains the grace of perseverance; prayer, persevering to the end, obtains grace in the end; grace in the end yields the soul to salvation.

What one of the glorious company of the Apostles did, in so central a point of Christian faith, self-evidently all must have done. To Jesus, probably, S. Peter addressed that prayer about the choice to Judas' vacated place: " Lord, discerner of the heart of all [d]." To Jesus, in that most perfect imitation of His close of His earthly life, in entire resignation and Divine love, S. Stephen yielded his soul in His own prayers as Man, "Lord Jesus, receive my spirit;" "Lord, lay not this sin to their charge [e]." How did he, whom Jesus loved, fall unreproved at *His* Feet [f], on Whose breast he once lay, ascribing to Him the incommunicable " glory and might [g]," which belong to God only ! How does he thank Him for His ever-abiding, ever-present love [h], and for that more than atoning, more than forgiving act; that act, in one, atoning, forgiving, re-creating, sanctifying; " Who loveth us, and washed us from our sins in His own Blood [i] !" How does he pray for grace and

[b] Rom. x. 13; Joel ii. 32.

[c] For it continues, " How shall they call upon Him, in Whom they have not believed?" See Alford, *ad loc.*

[d] Acts i. 24.   [e] Ib. vii. 50. 51.   [f] Rev. i. 17.

[g] Ib. 6; comp. 1 Tim. vi. 16; Heb. xiii. 21: 1 Pet. iv. 11, v. 11.   [h] ἀγαπῶντι.   [i] Rev. i. 4, 5.

peace, to issue to the Churches, at once from the Eternal God, and from Him in Whom the Godhead was enshrined, with Whom It was united by that hypostatic union, which was closer, more inter-penetrating, than any union, save of the Persons of the self-inexisting Trinity in Unity !

And since the Father and the Son are One, and our Lord had said, as meaning one and the same thing, that "whatsoever ye shall ask of the Father in My Name, He may give it you[k]," and "Whatsoever ye shall ask in My Name, that will I do[l];" so S. John, summing up the end and object of his own teaching, "that ye may know that ye have eternal life, and that ye may believe in the name of the Son of God[m]," adds, as to Him of Whom he had so spoken, "and this is the confidence which we have towards Him, that if we ask anything according to His Will, He heareth us. And if we know that He heareth us whatsoever we ask, we know that we have the petitions which we have asked from Him." What a volume of accumulated prayer, asked of and granted by the Son of God ! "We know that whatsoever we have asked for, that"—not we *had* simply, but, "we *have*," an ever-present possession of all we ever asked Him.

Ere yet S. John had left the earth, the heathen Pliny knew of the Christian worship that, "in meetings before day-break, they sang responsively a hymn to Christ as God[n]." "Very many Psalms and songs of the brethren,"we are early told[o], "written from the beginning by the faithful, hymn Christ the Word of God, entitling Him God." The heretic, Paul of

[k] S. John xv. 16.   [l] Ib. xiv. 13.   [m] 1 Ep. v. 13—15.
[n] Plin. Ep. x. 97.   [o] Caius, A.D 210, in Eus. H. E. v. 28.

Samosata, in order to make way for his heresy of the simple humanity of Christ, had to do away with those Psalms to our Lord Jesus Christ, feigning that they were recent[p]. Morning by morning they echoed those lauds in Heaven: "Glory to God in the highest [q]." They prayed, as we still carry on their prayer: "O Lord God, Lamb of God, Son of the Father, Who takest away the sins of the world, have mercy upon us;" and the rest of that prayer, which, in deepest thankfulness, you have said so often to Him, blessing Him, that He Alone is Holy, He Alone is the Lord, He, Jesus Christ, "with the Holy Ghost in the glory of God the Father." Evening by evening, as they came to the setting sun, they hymned Father, Son, and Holy Ghost, and Him, through Whom we approach to God, God and Man; "Worthy art Thou to be hymned at all times with holy voices, Son of God, Who givest life; wherefore the world glorifieth Thee[r]."

"The world glorifieth Thee!" Ere the second century had expired, Tertullian, enumerating the narrow bounds of those world-empires which had passed away, appeals to the Jews: "Why speak I of the Romans, who guard their empire by the outposts of their legions, nor can stretch the might of their

---

[p] Ep. Conc. Antioch. in Eus. H. E. vii. 30.

[q] The beginning of the hymn is given in the ancient *de virginitate*, in S. Athan. Works, and by S. Chrysostom, Hom. 68 in S. Matt, as a morning hymn; the whole, with variations, in the Apost. Const. vii. 47. See further Abp. Ussher, who thinks that it is one of the early hymns mentioned by the writer in Eusebius (see p. 87) De Symbolis, n. 3, Works, vii. 335, 6.

[r] See in Routh, Rel. S. iii. 515. S. Basil (de Sp. S. c. 29,) speaks of it as " ancient,' of its " evidence, from its antiquity."

reign beyond those nations? But the reign and
Name of Christ is stretched forth everywhere; everywhere He is believed; by all those nations He is
worshipped; everywhere He reigns; everywhere He
is adored; He is given equally to all everywhere;
kings stand in no greater favour with Him; no bar-
barian hath an inferior joy; no dignities or birth con-
fer distinct merits; to all, He is the same; to all, the
King; to all, the Judge; to all, Lord and God[s]."

This seemed to the Heathen "madness[t], that, after
the immutable, everlasting God, Parent of all, they
alleged, that Christians gave the second place to
a Man, Who had been crucified;" "they worshipped
exceedingly One Who had lately appeared[u];" "the
Son of Man, under the plea that He was the Great
God[v];" "the leader of their sedition, Whom they
called the Son of God[w]." "That great Man, Who
was crucified in Palestine because He brought into
the world this new religion[x]." "You put your trust

[s]Adv. Jud. i. 7, p. 213, Rig. [t]S. Justin, Apol. i. 13, p. 9. Oxf. Tr.
[u] Celsus in Origen, c. Cels. viii. 12. [v] Ib. 15. [w] Ib. 14.
[x] Lucian de morte Peregrini, t. i. 565, Gr. "I come now to the
Passion itself, which is wont to be objected to us as a reproach,
that we both worship a Man and One who was by men afflicted by
a notable punishment and excruciated." Lact. iv. 16. "'But,'
one saith, 'the gods are not therefore your enemies, because you
worship God Almighty, but because you both believe that one,
born man, and (what is infamous to vile persons) put to death by
the punishment of the Cross, still survives, and you adore Him
with daily supplications.'" Arnob. i. 36. "A man, punished
capitally for guilt, and the cross's sad wood, they relate, are their
worships, fitting altars for lost and guilty men, that they should
worship what they deserve." Cæcil. in Minut. Fel. p. 86, Ouz.
"We worship the gods with joy, feastings, songs, plays, revellings, and wantonness; but you a crucified man, Whom they can-

in a mere crucified man and still, though neglecting God's commandments, hope to obtain good from Him[y]." "Who has persuaded you," a Proconsul asks[z], "that leaving the venerable and true gods from whom you obtained weal, and had love among the people, you transferred yourselves to one dead and crucified, who could not even save Himself?"

And the Apologists answered the Jews that so had their own Prophets foretold in express terms (as they did), that Christ should both suffer, and be worshipped, and be God; nay, they say that the Jews admitted this[a], only that they dared to deny that Jesus was the Christ. They worshipped One, (they said,) not Man only but God. "We worship," they said[b], "One God, the Father and the Son, and do not give an excess of worship to Him Who appeared of late, as though, before, He were not. For we believe Himself Who said, 'Before Abraham was, I am[c].'" They told the Heathen that what these counted madness, they with reason did, "having learned that He, Who was born Jesus Christ, Who was crucified under Pontius Pilate, was the Son of the true God[d]." "We are no worshippers of insensate stones, but of the Only God, before all and above all, and of His Christ, being indeed God the Word before all ages[e]."

not please who enjoy all these things." Heathen judge to St. Epipodius; Ruinart, Act. Mart., p. 64.

    [y] Trypho in S. Justin Dial. n. 14, p. 83. Oxf. Tr.
    [z] Acta Lucian. et Marcian. Martyrs in the Decian persecution, Ruin. p. 153. They had been Magicians Ib. 152.
    [a] S. Justin, Dial. c. Tryph. n. 68, p. 160, Oxf. Tr.
    [b] Orig. c. Cels. viii. 17.   [c] S. John viii. 58.
            [d] S. Justin, Apol. i. 13, p. 5.
    [e] S. Melito, Apol. in Chron. Pasch., p. 259; Gall. i. 678.

To this they exhort them: "Believe, O man, in Him, Who is Man and God. Believe, O man, in the Living God, Who suffered and is worshipped[f]."

. This was the confession of the Martyrs.

"The common people knoweth Christ as one among men, whence one might the rather suppose us worshippers of a man. We say openly and, while ye torture us, mangled and gory we cry out, We worship God through Christ: believe Him a Man; it is in Him and through Him that God willeth to be known and worshipped[g]."

To Him they cried, when their tortures were past human endurance. We still have their broken words faithfully preserved. To Him they looked for aid, for Whom they suffered; yea, Who in them was persecuted, and suffered. To Him they prayed: "Christ, I pray, have mercy; Son of God, help[h]." "Christ, my Lord, let me not be confounded." "I pray, O Christ, give endurance. Thou art the hope of Life[i]."

---

[f] S. Clem. Coh. c. 10, p. 30. Sylb.

[g] Tert. Apol. n. 21, p. 50. Oxf. Tr. Maximian afterwards " commands that the *worshippers of Christ* [Christicolas], unless they would sacrifice to idols, should perish by exquisite deaths." Pass. S. Victor, &c., Ruinart, p. 301. " We have so persecuted *the worshippers of Christ*, that I think that thou almost alone remainest," Judge to S. Alexander, about A. D. 178. Ruin. p. 66.

[h] Saturninus, Acta Mart. in Baron. A. 303, n. 48.

[i] Thus Dativus, Ib. n. 44, " So, while he is wholly in Christ and, now worn out, invokes Him with his last words, he breathes out his blessed spirit." Alexander, in Act. Epipod. et Alex, n. 11 ; Ruin., p. 66. Saturninus Jun., Ib. n. 54, " O Lord Jesus Christ, Hope of the hopeless, grant me to finish my course, and to offer the shedding of my blood for a sacrifice and libation, for all their sakes who are afflicted for Thee." S. Theodotus in Ruinart., p. 354.

Him they confessed before their judges, as the object of their adoration: "I am the servant of Christ; Him I confess with my mouth, hold in my heart, adore unceasingly[k]." "There is no king beside Him Whom I have seen[l]; and I adore and worship Him; and if for His worship I die a thousand deaths, His will I be, as I have begun. Christ from my mouth, Christ from my heart, tortures cannot take[m]." "The sacrifice of prayer and deprecation, of compunction and praise, I must offer to the Living and True God, to the King of all ages, Christ[n]." To Him they offered themselves as a living sacrifice: "Father, Son, and Holy Ghost I adore; the Holy Trinity I adore; beside Whom there is no God. I am a Christian. I sacrifice myself to Christ God[o]." "Lord God of heaven and earth,—Jesu Christ, to Thee I bend my neck as a victim, Who abidest for ever, to Whom is

[k] Alexander in Acta S. Felic. n. 3. in Ruinart, Acta Mart., p. 22. "Christ, with the Father and the Holy Spirit, I confess to be God; and it is meet that I give back my soul to Him Who is both my Creator and Redeemer." Acta S. Epipod. Ruin., p. 65.

[l] In a vision. Ib.

[m] Acta S. Genesii ex mimo Martyris; Ruinart, p. 284. *Q.* "What God do you worship?" *Polemon.* "Christ." *Q.* "What, then, is He another?" *Pol.* "No but the same, Whom those, too, confessed a little before." Acta S. Pionii, n. 9, about A.D. 250, Ruin., p. 129. "What God do ye worship?" *Pionius.* "Him Who made heaven," &c. *Q.* "Sayest thou Him Who was crucified? *Pion.* "I say, Him Whom the Father sent for the salvation of the world." Ib., n. 16, p. 134. "We render honour to Cæsar; fear and worship we yield to Christ, the true God." S. Donata in Act. Mart. Scillit. A.D. 200; Ruin. p. 80.

[n] Act. SS. Martr. Petri, Andreæ, &c.; Ruinart, p. 147.

[o] *Consular.* "Cease, Euplius, from this madness. Adore the gods, and thou shalt be free." *Euplius,* "I adore Christ, I detest dæmons. Do what thou wilt, I am a Christian,"—*C.* "Unhappy

glory and majesty for all ages P." In thanksgiving
to Him, their God, they closed their lives : " Us
Christ governeth, Who hath brought us to this glory.
Glory to Thee, O Christ, Who hast vouchsafed to
gather us with the holy Martyrs q." "Thanks be
to Thee, O Christ; keep me, who suffer these things
for Thee.—I adore Christ r." "The eternal kingdom,
the undefiled kingdom dawneth, O Lord Jesu Christ.
We are Christians. We serve Thee. Thou art our

one, adore the gods, Mars, Apollo, Æsculapius." *E.* "Father, and
Son, and Holy Spirit I adore; the Holy Trinity I adore; besides
Which there is no God."—*C.* "Sacrifice, if thou wouldest be
freed." *E.* "Now I sacrifice myself to Christ, God. I can do no
more. In vain thou essayest; I am a Christian." Acta Euplii,
n. 2; Ruinart, p. 440. "I never sacrificed, nor sacrifice, save to
the One God, and our Lord Jesus Christ His Son, Who was born
and suffered." Acta S. Crispini, Ruin., p. 494. "We sacrifice to
our Lord Jesus Christ," &c. Acta S. Mammarii in Mabillon,
Analect. t. iv. ap. Ruinart, p. 367, n. 2; add Acta Mart. Lugd.,
n. 14.; Ruin., p. 56. S Symphorosa about A.D. 120, says, "Thy
gods cannot receive me as a sacrifice, but if I be burnt for the name
of Christ, my God &c. Ruinart p. 19.

p Acta S. Felic. in Baron. A. 303, n. 123; add Acta S. Afræ
in Ruinart, p. 502.

q Acta Olympii in Baron., A.D. 259, n. 30. "Bl. Crispina said,
'I give thanks to [my God, and my] Christ. I bless the Lord,
Who has vouchsafed thus to deliver me from thy hands.'" Acta
S. Crispinæ, Ruin., p. 496.

r Acta Euplii, Ruinart, p. 439; add Acta Mart. Scillit. fin.
Ruin., p. 78. Act. Lucian. et Marcian., n. 7; Ib., p. 154. Acta
S. Afræ, n. 3; Ib. 502. Acta S. Irenæi, n. 5, p. 454; Acta S.
Philippi, n. 10; Ib., p. 450. Acta Probi, Ib. 481. S. Ampelii,
Baron. A. 303, n. 52; S. Felic. Baron, l. c. Acta S. Ignatii;
Ruinart, pp. 12, 698 : "I give thanks, O Lord, because Thou hast
vouchsafed to honour me with perfect love, to be with Thy
Apostle Paul placed in iron chains." Ep. Eccl. Smyn. de Mart.
S. Polycarp. n. 14. Cotel. Patr. Ap. ii. 199.

Hope; Thou art the hope of Christians. O God most Holy, O God most High, O God Almighty, we give Thee praise for Thy Name [s]."

Such, then, was the Will of the Eternal Trinity towards us, Father, Son, and Holy Ghost, not only that we should be admitted to the blissful adoration and intuition of the Triune God, through the Incarnation and Atoning Death of God the Son, but that He Himself, our Redeeming Lord and God, should, in His Humanity, be a distinct Object of our contemplation and adoration and thanksgiving and joy. One indeed is God, and the God-enabled eye of the blessed shall see the truth which our Lord enounced: "I am in the Father, and the Father in Me [t]." They, being empowered to see the Essence of God, must see, how "the Holy Ghost reposes and habitates in God [u]," how "All the Father embosometh the Son [v]," and how "the Father is the natural Place of the Son [w]." The Father has in Him the Son; and, again, He is in the Son, because of the identity of the Substance. "Each is contemplated, and is truly in the Other [x]." "The Union is not as that of our Lord's Godhead and Humanity (intimate as was the blending of Both in the One Person of our Lord), but as

[s] Acta Thelicæ in Baron l. c. A.D. 303, n. 41. Ruinart p. 212.

[t] S. John. xiv. 10.

[u] S. Dionys. Rom. in S. Ath. ag. Arian., p. 46, Oxf. Tr.

[v] An orthodox expression in the Macrostich, Ib. p. 116, the correlative of S. John i. 18: "The only-begotten Son, Who is in the bosom of the Father."

[w] S. Cyril, Thes. vii. t. v. p. 5, quoted in S. Ath. ag. Ar., p. 399, n. a. "The Son is the place of the Father, as the Father, too, is the place of the Son." S. Jerome in Ezek. iii. 12. Ib.

[x] S. Cyril de Trin. vi. p. 621; Ib. p. 403, n. i.

the whole Power, Life, Substance, Wisdom, Essence
of the Father is the very Essence, Substance, Wisdom, Life, and Power of the Son." So that he who
sees the Essence of the Son, or the Son as He Is,
must needs see the Essence of the Father and of the
Holy Ghost. For they are One. And he who adores
God the Father must needs, by one act, adore the
Son and the Holy Ghost, since the Holy Ghost is
"co-glorified and co-worshipped with the Father and
Son;" and the Trinity is worshipped in the Unity,
which It is, and the Unity in the Trinity, which co-
exist and in-exist as One.

Yet *there*, too, we must retain a separate love and
thankfulness for that which in their Oneness of Being Each separate Person has done for us. For although inseparable are the works of the Trinity, and
the Father so loved the world that He sent His Only-
Begotten Son to die for us; yea, and according to
His Sacred Humanity that is true, that "the Lord
God and His Spirit sent^z" Him, yet it was One of
the All-Holy Trinity Who vouchsafed to take our
nature upon Him, and, in it, unsuffering to suffer
for us through that Flesh which He took. Why
does the heart so throb at the Name of Jesus? Why
is it so jubilant? Why so instrengthening? Why
does it so melt us, if we are dry? Why does it
so kindle us, if we are cold? Why does it diffuse
in us such serenity, if we are sad? Why, if we are
half-dead, does it give us life? Why, if we sit in
darkness, does it flash light into our souls? Why,
if we are quivering in temptation, does it give us
strength? Why, if we are terrified at our past sins,

y Thomassin de Trin. 28, 1. Ib.   z Isa. xlviii. 16.

does a ray burst forth from it, which transmutes the dark cloud into the crimson tinge of His Blood? Why, but because it is the " Name Which is above every name; " because the Name of Redeemer is in one way mightier than that of Creator, (for it cost more to redeem our souls than to create them,) be- cause it is the Name of God, for us and for our sal- vation, become Man.

Every thing good and Divine on earth is a coun- terpart of something more wondrously beautiful or visibly Divine in Heaven. We cannot think of Jesus here but with adoring love, or loving adoration. We must cease to believe in Him, ere we could cease to adore Him. But Jesus cannot cease to be. Nay, rather, we are told that when God shall be all in all[a], and all shall be subdued unto Him, and the whole multitude of His elect shall be perfected, and Christ, i. e., Whole Christ, Himself in His Human Nature our Head, and we His, as yet, imperfect members, shall be subject to God through the entire subjection of His whole redeemed Body in their whole compass and their entire selves to the mind of God[b],—then, too, His kingdom shall have no end[c]; then, too, more than before, " shall every knee bow in the Name of the Lord Jesus, and every tongue confess that Jesus Christ is Lord, to the glory of God the Father[d]; " then, too, the Humanity of Christ, and God manifest in that Human Form, will be a distinct joy and ado- ration in Heaven. For then, too, that " river of liv- ing water[e]," that torrent of pleasure, that unceasing

[a] 1 Cor. xv. 28.
[b] See Fathers in Petav. de Trin., iii. 5 ; de Incarn., xii. 18, 13.
[c] St. Luke i. 33.   [d] Phil. ii. 10, 11.   [e] Rev. xxii. 1.

effluence of beatitude, that overstreaming fulness of joy which shall, with its multitudinous bliss, inundate the souls, and minds, and senses of the beatified, shall issue forth from the one throne of God and of the Lamb. There, amid all the varied fruition in that blissful Paradise of God, where all curse is done away for ever, the central joy is, that the one Throne of God and of the Lamb shall be in it; and St. John speaks as though we should see Them with one vision, and adore Them with one adoration, and bear the Name of God and of Jesus, as One Name, upon our foreheads. For, having spoken of the Throne of God and of the Lamb therein, he adds, "And His servants shall worship *Him*, and shall see *His* Face; and *His* Name shall be on their foreheads [f]." And again, "The Lord God Almighty is the temple thereof, and the Lamb [g]." There shall be no visible temple, for God shall, if we attain, be our place. In Him we shall see Himself; in Him we shall contemplate, adore, praise, thank, bless Himself. Yet then, too, we shall be in Christ; for not God only, but the Lamb also, shall be our temple. "And the glory of God shall enlighten" that city of the blessed; His uncreated glory filling it with the beatific, illumining, transporting light of His Godhead; and yet then, too, undimmed by that essential Light, shall shine out the glory of the Humanity of Jesus; undimmed by It, because, although seen distinctly, It is the selfsame, "The glory," Jesus says, "Which I had with Thee, before the world was [h]." It shall shine with a separate, transporting lustre, an illumining, beatifying beauty. For so God says, "The glory of God

f Rev. xxii. 3, 4.   g Ibid. xxi. 22, 23.   h St. John xvii. 5.

did lighten it, ánd the Lamb is the Light thereof."
We could not even imagine it otherwise. Heaven
would not be a Christian's heaven without Jesus.
No, even in this land of shadows, amid the necessary
distractions of this life's duties, amidst our infirmities, whether self-contracted or incidental to our way-
faring condition, it would be misery to think that our
poor praises and thanksgivings here for His redeeming love would be all; that we should not endlessly
love and praise Him for that mercy which itself "en-
dureth for ever." Our thanklessness is well-nigh intolerable to our better selves now. But to think that
we should never see Him, to praise and adore Him, —
not worthily of Himself, for *that* were impossible to
created love (His Blessed Mother, by reason of her
creatureship, could not adequately praise Him), but—
to the utmost of our created capacity, it would leave
(which is impossible) an unfilled blank, an unsatisfied
longing, in Heaven. It is our joy and consolation
now to think of that great white Throne, and, in faith,
to behold Him there; to see those Eyes, which once
wept over Jerusalem, now beaming not only with the
human love of God-man, but with the Infinite Love of
His Godhead; to behold those Hands, once stretched
forth to heal, once nailed on the Cross; or those Sacred
Feet, which went up and down to save the lost, and
which we, with Magdalene, would so long to dare to
touch, and (if it could but be) to kiss with penitent
love; or, even chiefly, that wounded Side, riven, that
we might hide ourselves therein, pouring forth from
those Wounds which for us He received, not His
Redeeming Blood as once, but the radiant Majesty of
His Divine love, lighting and love-enkindling the

utmost bounds of God's creation, wherever there is a being which can love. Our consolation and joy is to know that, wherever our place be, although the last and lowest, *there* too we shall " ever be with the Lord[i];" there we shall speak to Him, adore Him, love Him, as our own Jesus; "My Lord and my God[k]." " O, it is good for us to be here[l]." Would that we could, in thought at least, be thus with Him in the holy mount! Would that we could ever bear about with us the dying of the Lord Jesus, that He could be our life, as He is invisibly our life's Source!

But there is an aweful gulf, an aweful Day, an aweful aspect of our Divine (would we may say our Dear) Lord, between; the gulf of death, the Day of Judgement, the truth that " we believe that Thou shalt come to be our Judge." Yet He Who shall be our Judge is Omnipotent to save. He has " the keys of death and hell;" He, not Satan, its prince and our accuser; He shall be our Judge, Who died that we might not die the second death; Who liveth that we might also live through Him, in Him, to Him, with Him; through Him, by His redemption; in Him, by His Sacraments and His Spirit; to Him, in our lives, by His grace; with Him, in eternity, to adore and to love Him.

Only now, in the day of salvation; now, in this season of penitence; now, while the door is not shut to; now, when He anew calleth thee, turn to Him, if thou hast not yet turned; resolve, by His grace, to break off any deadly sin if thou yet be in one; if not, pray for true, abiding, loving sorrow, that thou didst ever displease Him; pray, day by day, for that His

i 1 Thess. iv. 17.   k St. John xx. 28.   l St. Mark ix. 5.

great gift, perseverance against that sin, perseverance unto the end; remember, whenever thou canst, His poor (and now, those penitent sinners who, with thee, have been snatched from the jaws of hell[m]). Pray Him, with the penitent Robber, " Lord, remember me when Thou comest in Thy kingdom; though last, least, lowest, Lord, remember me;" and He Who came, not to destroy men's lives but to save them, will in that dread Day remember thee, deliver thee, that thou too mayest for ever behold His Face, for ever have the beatitude of adoring Him, of loving Him, of being loved by Him.

[m] There was a collection for a Penitentiary.

SERMON XXIV[a].

ISAIAH: HIS HEAVINESS AND HIS CONSOLATION.

Isa. vi. 8—10.

" I heard the voice of the Lord, saying, Whom shall I send, and who will go for us? Then said I, Here am I; send me. And He said, Go, and tell this people, Hear ye indeed, but understand not; and see ye indeed, but perceive not. Make the heart of this people fat, and make their ears heavy, and shut their eyes; lest they see with their eyes, and hear with their ears, and understand with their heart, and convert, and be healed."

Such was the heavy burden laid upon Isaiah in his fresh youth, probably at much your age. Like S. Paul, he had seen the glory of God; he had seen, as man could in the flesh see and live, God Himself; he had witnessed the burning love of those fiery spirits of love, the Seraphim; he had felt, in that aweful Presence of the All-Holy, the sinfulness of man and his own. Holy and pure he must have been; for even in that dread Presence, while shrinking abashed into himself as " undone," from his unfitness to behold It, nothing flashes into his mind,

[a] Preached at S. Mary's, Oxford. Lent, 1869.

even in that •all-revealing light, no spot of sin is
visible to him in his God-enlightened memory, except some *words*. "Woe is me, for I am a man of unclean lips." Sins of words, as well as sins of deeds,
were one wide offence of his people. He had, in
his prophetic office, often to warn against them. A
national sin is infectious. Individuals partake of
it more or less, at least in its lighter shades, because it *is* the national character. It is, perhaps,
the last to be extirpated. For an impatient, God-
unhonouring not God-dishonouring, word, Moses had
lost the hope of those fourscore years, that he should
bring his people into the land which God had promised them. "ᵇBy thy words shalt thou be justified,"
says our Lord, "and by thy words shalt thou be
condemned." Isaiah did not excuse himself, that
they were *only* words. His words (not such as men
now think nothing of), whether they were of impatience, or untempered zeal, or harsh reproof, or
whatever they were, rose in his soul, and called
out the penitential cry, "Woe is me ! for I am undone ; because I am a man of unclean lips, and I
dwell in the midst of a people of unclean lips : for
mine eyes have seen the King, the Lord of Hosts."
Perhaps God, as He often does in those whom He
early calls, had awakened in him the longing to
speak to his God-forgetting people in the Name of
God. Perhaps, as God had awakened in Moses,
while yet in Pharaoh's court, the consciousness that
he was to be God's instrument in delivering his
people, and had so filled his soul with the thought,
that he wondered that they understood not the mean-

ᵇ S. Matt. xii. 17.

H h 2

ing of his slaying the Egyptian, so He had kindled in Isaiah the burning longing to be employed by God to His degenerate people. God discloses Himself to the hearts which He has prepared. And now at the sight of God, he felt how all-unfit he was to speak in the Name of the All-Holy God. "Woe is me! for I am undone." His longing must have lived, if he could but be fitted for the mission which he longed for. But the sight of God had pierced his soul with the conviction, how holy His words must be, because they are the words of the All-Holy; how holy ought to be the lips which would take those words upon them; how pure *he* should be, who would be the messenger of God the All-Holy to sinful man. Job defended himself long against the unjust inferences of his friends from his miseries. When God revealed Himself to him, he said, "[c]I heard of Thee by the hearing of the ear, but now mine eye seeth Thee; wherefore I abhor myself, and repent in dust and ashes." And now, like him, Isaiah is as one dead. The sentence, which guilty man of himself deserves from the Holy God, was, already in his feeling, fulfilled on him, "I am cut off." Then followed that wondrous type of the Incarnation first, and then of the Holy Eucharist, the living heavenly Fire in a visible form, the Coal from the Altar; and that, which the incorporeal Seraph out of reverence touched not, was approached to his lips, the type of Him "by Whom the guilt of the world is purged[d]." "This has touched thy lips, and thine iniquity is gone, thy sin is atoned for." And then God, the

[c] Job xlii. 5, 6. [d] See passages of Fathers in "Doctrine of the Real Presence," pp. 119 sqq.

Holy Trinity; Whose praises he had heard sung by
the Seraphim in their Trisagion, which the Church
has caught .up from them,—willing that he should
have the reward of a spontaneous self-oblation, elicit
in words the devotion which They had inspired, and
ask, "Whom shall I send, and who will go for Us?"
And Isaiah summed up his whole future life in those
two words [e], "Behold me; send me." Then on his
ardent soul was poured the heavy message, "Go,
and thou shalt tell *this* people," (God speaks of them
no more as His own,) "Hear ye on, and understand
not; and see ye on, and know not. Make thou dull
the heart of this people, and its ears make thou
heavy, and its eyes close thou; lest it see with its
eyes, and with its ears hearken, and its heart understand, and it return and one heal it." Startling
office for one so sanguine and so young! Heavy burden to bear for probably sixty-one years of life, to
be closed by a martyr's excruciating death! Outside of that commission there was hope: hope, because the promises of God could not fail of fulfilment: hope, because in the worst times of Israel
there had been those seven thousand which the Prophet knew not of, but whose number God revealed
to him, who had stood faithful to God amid the national apostacy: hope, because when God pronounces
not a doom, we may take refuge in the loving mercy
of Him Who swears by Himself, "As I live, saith
the Lord God, I have no pleasure in the death of the
wicked, but" (the "but" says, "in *this* I have pleasure," on *this* Almighty God dwells with pleasure,)
"in the turning of the wicked from his way, and

[e] הנני שלחני.

that he live; turn ye, turn ye from your evil ways; for why will ye die, O house of Israel f?"

The message was to the people, not to individuals: "Go ye to this people, and say." It related to individuals, only as they were such as the mass of the nation was, as they themselves made up that mass. But a burning zeal enters into the mind of God, Who "willeth that all men should be saved, and should come to the knowledge of the truth g." A burning love enters into the mind of Him, in thought of Whom Isaiah found his solace, "Who died for all h." Yet we know how S. Paul i attests, "my conscience bearing me witness in the Holy Ghost, that I have great grief and unintermitting sorrow in my heart," so that he could wish even to be severed from the Presence of Christ, never to behold Him Who had died for him, in Whom was his life, Who was his life within him, if so be Israel might be saved. And now this, in all seeming, was the thankless office to which Isaiah was called, to be heard, to be listened to, by some with contempt, by others with seeming respect, and to leave things in the main worse than he found them. Even with our little love, we know what heaviness it is, to pass along any of our crowded places of concourse, in the streets of any of those centres of human activity, and to see undying souls, with their master-passions impressed upon their countenances, living for the world, and not for God. But they have their own one talent, whatever it may be: their souls may, we trust, be saved.

f Ezek. xxxiii. 11.   g 1 Tim. ii. 2.   h 2 Cor. v. 14.
i Rom. ix. 1.

Isaiah's commission was far harder, to act towards a loveless faith. His office was towards those, in part at least, who were ever-hearing, never-doing, and so never understanding. And so (so to speak,) he was only to make things worse. So S. Paul says[k], "The earth which drinketh in the rain which cometh oft upon it—if it bring forth thorns and briars, is accounted worthless and nigh unto cursing," not yet accursed, (thanks be to God), yet nigh unto it, "whose end," if it remains such unto the end, "is to be burned." There were better among the people; there were worse; but such was the general character; it was an ever-hearing,—hearing,—hearing (such is the force of the words, "hear ye hearing on[l]," evermore) never wearied of hearing, yet never doing; ever seeing, as they thought, yet never gaining insight; and so becoming ever duller, their sight ever more and more bleared, until to hear and to see would become well-nigh, and to man, impossible. The more they heard and saw, the further they were from understanding, from being converted, from the reach of healing.

Such they were, God says, a little later, in Ezekiel's time. You know how they came to the prophet of God, but had set up every man his idol in his heart, (who was indeed his god,) and how God says, "Are ye come to enquire of Me? As I live, saith the Lord God, I will not be enquired of by you[m]." Nay, so coming, they should only be the more deceived. And of this, Isaiah was to be the occasion and the instrument.

So it was when *He* came, of Whom Isaiah pro-

[k] Heb. vi. 7, 8.   [l] שִׁמְעוּ שָׁמוֹעַ   [m] Ezek. xx. 3.

phesied. They thought that they knew the law, but only to allege their interpretation of it against Him. The more they heard, the more they were blinded. And their imagined seeing and their real blindness, was their condemnation. "If ye were blind," our Lord says, "ye should not have sin; but now ye say, We see; therefore your sin remaineth [n]." This is inseparable from every revelation of God, from every preaching of the Gospel, from every speaking of God inwardly to the soul, from every motion of God the Holy Ghost, from every drawing or forbidding of that judge which He has placed within, our conscience, from every hearing of God's Word. All and each leave the soul in a better condition or a worse. Not by any direct hardening from God, not through any agency of the Prophet, but by man's free-will, hearing but not obeying, seeing but not doing, feeling but resisting, the preaching of the Prophet would leave them only more hopelessly far from that conversion, whereby God might heal them.

And what said the Prophet? Contrary as the sentence must have been to all the yearnings of his soul, crushing to his hopes, he knew that it must be just, because "the Judge of the whole world" must "do right [o]." He intercedes, but only by those three words, "Lord, how long?" He appeals to God. Such could not be God's ultimate purpose with His people; not for this could He have taken them out of all nations, to be a peculiar people to Himself. The night was to come; sin deserved it; but was it to have no dawn? Hope there is yet, but meanwhile a still-deepening night, a climax of woe; and that

[n] S. John ix. 41.   [o] Gen. xviii. 25.

in two stages.' In the first, "cities left without inhabitants;" and not cities only, as a whole, but "houses" too "tenantless;" nor these alone, but "the whole land desolate, and God removes the inhabitants far away, and there shall be a great forsaking in the midst of the land." Nor this only, but when, in this sifting-time, nine parts should be gone, and one-tenth only remain, this should be again consumed: only, like those trees which survived the winters and storms of a thousand years, while the glory, wherewith God once clad it, was gone, its hewn stem was still to live; "a holy seed" was to be the stock thereof.

The vision, opened before him, stretches on until now and to the end. His question, "How long? Until when?" implied a hope that there would be an end; the answer "until," declared that there would be an end. We have, in one, that first carrying away, the small remnant which should return; its new desolation; the holy seed which should survive; the restoration at the end, of which S. Paul says, then "all Israel shall be saved [p]."

And this message fell on one of the tenderest of hearts in its early freshness. As he is eminently the Gospel-prophet, the Evangelist in the old covenant, so he had already been taught by the Holy Ghost the Gospel-lesson, "Love your enemies." He denounces God's judgements; but he himself is the type of Him Who wept over Jerusalem. "My heart," he says, "shall cry out for Moab [q]," who was ever banded against his people. "I will water thee with my tears, O Heshbon; my bowels shall sound like a

[p] Rom. xi. 26. [q] Isa, xv. 5. xvi. 9, 11.

harp for Moab, and my inward parts for Kirhar-esh." Even Babylon, whom he foreknew as God's appointed waster of His people, the world-power who should uproot them and carry them far away, even Babylon moved him in its fall. Present in spirit at a doom which was. to come nearly two centuries later, he was himself in spirit as one of the sufferers. "My loins," he says, "are filled with reeling cramp; writhing pangs have laid hold of me, as the pangs of a woman in travail. I am bowed down, that I can-not hear; I am terror-stricken, that I cannot see. My heart reeleth; horror hath terrified me: the even-tide of my desire hath He made into terror to me[r]." If Isaiah so felt for the destroyer of his people, if he was so horror-stricken for the woes of those yet un-born, what for *their* sufferings who were flesh of his flesh and bone of his bone, whose woes he had to tell them, face to face, woes which would come upon them because they would not hear! O what a woe it is, to see certainly before one those judgement-fires, into which people are rushing madly, because they will not believe them or look at them!

And in this his general grief for his people, there were so many particular griefs, as many as there were forms of evil. All confronted him. For his office lay in the heart of the material prosperity, the intellect, the corruptions, the rebellions, the op-pressions of his people, the city of David[s], once " the faithful, now the harlot-city, where righteous-ness once dwelt, and now murderers[t]." There, in Jotham's sixteen years, was all the insolence of hu-man pride, "high and lifted up[u];" in the next

[r] Isa. xxi. 3, 4.   [s] Ibid. xxix. 1.   [t] Ibid. i. 21.   [u] Ibid. ii. 6, 7.

sixteen years of Ahaz, the whole weight of the king's authority was thrown in against the faith, from his first scarce-veiled insolence in rejecting the prophet's offer in the name of God to give him what sign he would of the verity of His promise in his trouble, to his naked apostacy, when he closed the Temple, suspended its worship, burned his sons in the dreadful worship of Moloch, made every corner of Jerusalem a shrine of idolatry, and desecrated every city by its own idol-chapel [v]. Then came Hezekiah's reformation, in himself personally devout, but powerless over his people; the thickening troubles of his country, unconverted by each successive scourge. "The people turneth not to Him that smiteth them, neither do they seek the Lord of Hosts [w]." And so his burden still had to be, "For all this His anger is not turned away, but His Hand is stretched out still [x]." Under Manasseh, the tide of evil, which Hezekiah's personal influence had stayed, burst out uncontrolled; it swept along with it the boy-king of twelve years also, thereafter himself to give fresh impulse to the current, to flood Jerusalem with monstrosities of cruelty and lust, as worship of their gods [y], and (too late for his land though not for his soul) to turn to God. Martyrdom crowns those only who resist. In witnessing then for God, though in this reign he uttered no recorded prophecy, God, after his threescore years of service, ordered that he should close his life's long martyrdom with a martyr's death. Strange likeness to our Lord, of Whom he spake so much, if, in that reign of terror and of

[v] 2 Chron. xxviii. 2, 3, 23—25.   [w] Isa. ix. 13.
[x] Ibid. xii. 17, 21.   [y] 2 Kings xxi.; 2 Chron. xxxiii. 2—6.

blood, occasion was found for slaying him through distortion of his words[z]!

This great outline of suffering was filled up variedly. Ahaz' scornful rejection echoed on in the unbelieving taunts of the great or the learned. They ridiculed the simplicity of his teaching. It was but fit for babes; they were men, and had outgrown it! "Line on line, rule on rule; a little here, a little there! Whom should he teach knowledge[a]?" They challenged the Almighty to fulfil His prophet's threats: "Let Him make speed, hasten His work, that we may see; and let the counsel of the Holy One of Israel draw nigh and come, that we may know it!"

> "Bricks fell, hewn stone will we build;
> Sycomores are hewn down, cedars will we replace[b]."

Present judgements, they said, they would more than recover; against threatened judgements they had made their covenant with death, and their agreement with hell[c]; if imminent, they looked to strengthen themselves with human help, not to their Maker[d]; if inevitable, they would enjoy themselves to the end; it was, "Eat, drink, and to-morrow die[e]." The leaders misled[f], the judges judged unjustly[g], the rich left no space for the poor[h], their women had lost modesty[i], their men were oppressors[k]; evil they called good, good evil[l]; chastise-

---

[z] See Yebamoth, iv. fin., quoted by Martini, Pug. fid., f. 700, (p. 899, 900, Carpz.)　　[a] Isa. xxviii. 9, 10.　　[b] Ibid. ix. 10.　　[c] Ibid. xxviii. 15.　　[d] Ibid. xxii. 9—11.　　[e] Ibid. 13.　　[f] Ibid. ix. 16.　　[g] Ibid. i. 17, 23; v. 33.　　[h] Ibid. v. 8.　　[i] Ibid. iii. 16. *sqq.*　　[k] Ibid. iii. 5, 12.　　[l] Ibid. v. 20.

ment but engendered increased rebellion ; the whole head was sick and the whole heart faint[m].

Isaiah could but weep for those who wept not for themselves. "I will be bitter in my weeping," he says; "press not on me to comfort me for the desolation of the daughter of my people[n]."

Yet where there is desolation for the sake of God, there is also consolation. Wherein was Isaiah's? Not in the solace of his married life. His daily dress was like John Baptist's, the hair-cloth pressing upon his loins, wearing to the naked flesh, although mentioned only when he was to put it off and himself to become a portent to his people, walking naked and barefoot[o]. His two sons were, by their names, the continual pictures of that woe on his people; the one spoke only of "the speed of the prey, the haste of the spoil[p]," the other was that sad dirge which so echoes through the Prophets, "a remnant shall return[q]," a remnant only of that people who were to be as the sand of the sea, the stars of heaven[r]. What, then, was his solace?

S. John tells us, in connection with that heavy message. "These things said Isaiah, when he saw His glory and spake of Him[s]." Of whom? Of Christ, of Whom S. John was speaking. Isaiah had seen, as man can see, His Deity. He had seen Him, the Brightness of the Father's Glory and the express Image of His Person; yet he had not seen the Son Alone. He himself says, "Mine eyes have seen the king, Him Who Is, the Lord of Hosts." And the

[m] Isa. i. 5.   [n] Ibid. xxii. 4.   [o] Ibid. xx. 2.
[p] Ibid. viii. 3.   [q] Ibid. vii. 3. x. 21.   [r] Gen. xv. 5; xxii. 7.
[s] S. John xii. 41.

Holy Ghost says by S. Paul, that He spake by
Isaiah in these words: "Well said the Holy Ghost
by Esaias the Prophet unto our fathers, saying, Go
unto this people and say, Hearing, ye shall hear,
and shall not understand[t]." Isaiah had not seen
the Beatific Vision: "No man hath seen God at
any time[u]." Yet he says, "Mine eyes have seen
the Lord of Hosts." Not with his bodily eyes did
he behold God, nor with his bodily ears did he hear
His words, but to his inward sight did God disclose
some likeness, whereby he should understand the
nature of the Divine Essence, how God, Father,
Son, and Holy Ghost, in-exists in Himself, although
the Beatific Vision, as He Is, was reserved for the
life to come. He had, in his inmost being, in some
way, unimaginable to us who have not beheld it,
seen the Holy Trinity in Their Unity of Essence,
and *that*, in the Person of the Son Who said of Himself, "He that hath seen Me hath seen the Father[v]."
For it was a Human Form which he beheld, sitting
enthroned as the Judge, and receiving the worship
of the glowing love of the Seraphim. He had seen
Him in His own glory and the glory of the Father,
transfiguring the likeness of that Human Form,
Which is now, with the Father, the light of Heaven; Which, amid the Uncreated Light which God
Is, illumines Heaven also with an Uncreated Light,
(as S. John says, "The Lamb is the Light thereof[w],") because "in Him dwelleth all the fulness of
the Godhead bodily[x]."

How should not this Vision live in him for

[t] Acts xxvi. 25, 26.   [u] S. John i. 18.   [v] Ib. xiv. 9.
[w] Rev. xxi. 23.   [x] Col. ii. 9.

those threescore years, who knew that thereafter, not through some created image, not by similitude, but face to Face he should behold the End of our being, God? So God prepared him to be,—above all others even of those God-inspired men, those men of zeal and longing and love, "the goodly company of the Prophets"—the Evangelic Prophet, in that he had seen the glory of the Lord.

God's Word is consistent with itself. We need not marvel (as some have done) that he should speak so plainly as he does, that that Child to be born to us was to be "the Mighty God, the Everlasting Lord [y]," or that the Virgin's Son should be called "Immanuel [z]," when he had himself seen a Human Form in the ineffable Glory of God. No wonder that he should speak of Him Whom he had seen enthroned as Judge, smiting the earth with the rod of His mouth, and with the breath of His lips slaying the wicked.

This, then, is ever his consolation; this, his joy in trouble; this, his life in death. The surges of this world, higher and higher as they rose, only bore his soul upward toward his God. He, too, was a man of longing. In the darkness of the world God ever brings this light before him; his darkest visions are the dawn-streaks of the brightest light. Does he describe darkness, the image of that outer darkness [a]? Then follows, "The people that walked in darkness have seen a great light." Has he to denounce the utter desolation of all the pride and glory and luxury of the mighty and the beautiful? "Zion, clean-emp-

---

[y] Isa. ix. 6.   [z] Ibid. vii. 4; viii. 8.

[a] Comp. Isa. viii. 22 with ix. 1.

tied, shall sit on the ground." God teaches him straightway to add, "In that day shall the Branch of the Lord be beauty and glory [b]." And then follow the holiness and peace which He would bestow. Has he to say that the refuge of lies, under which the scornful hoped to hide themselves, shall be swept away? He first says, in the Name of God, "Behold, I lay in Zion for a foundation a Corner-stone, a tried stone, a precious corner-stone: he that believeth shall not haste [c]." Has he to denounce woe "on all the houses of joy, in the joyous city [d]?" It is but "until the Spirit be poured out from on high," "and the wilderness shall be a fruitful field, and the work of righteousness shall be peace, and the fruit of righteousness quietness and assurance for ever [e]." Has he to speak of the house of David as the stump of a tree hewed down to the ground? "From that hewn stump of Jesse," he says, "there shall come forth a rod, and a Branch shall grow out of his roots, and the Spirit of God shall rest upon Him [f];" and then follow the peaceful and peace-giving glories of His reign, and the restoration of the remnant of His people. Has he to tell, how in the captivity of Babylon "they that rule over them make them to howl, and Thy Name every day is blasphemed?" Forthwith he bursts into a jubilee of joy: "How beautiful upon the mountains are the feet of him that bringeth good tidings, that publisheth peace, that bringeth good tidings of good, that publisheth salvation, that saith unto Zion, Thy God reigneth [g]."

[b] Isa. iii. 16—26; iv. 2.   [c] Ibid xxviii. 16—18.
[d] Ibid. xxxii. 13.   [e] Ibid. 15—17.   [f] Ib. xi. 1.
[g] Ibid. lii. 5, 7.

Never does that sad message part from his sight. He is like our own loved poet,—

> " Ready to give thanks and live
> On the least that Heaven may give."

He does not live in a bright, ideal future, in " Messianic hopes," as men tell you of. His future is as his present, until " death shall be swallowed up in, victory." It is still " the remnant shall return ; the remnant," he repeats, " shall return to .the Mighty God [h];" they are " the gleaning-grapes left in it; as the shaking of an olive-tree, two or three berries in the top of the uppermost bough, four or five in the outmost fruitful branches thereof, saith the Lord God of Israel [i] ; " " the shaking of an olive-tree, as the gleaning-grapes when the vintage is done [k]." It is what we see before our eyes now, " Ye shall be gathered one by one, O ye children of Israel [l]." And when the Messiah came, it was to be so still. He was to be at once " a sanctuary, but for a stone of stumbling and a rock of offence to both the houses of Israel. And many among them shall stumble, and fall, and be broken, and be snared, and be taken [m]." The words of the aged Simeon but summed up the prophecies of Isaiah: " This Child is set for the fall and rising again of many in Israel, and for a sign which shall be spoken against, that the thoughts of many hearts may be revealed [n]." For such as they were, such did Christ become to them; for the fall of the proud and self-satisfied, for the rising again of those who owned themselves fallen. So Jesus Himself said, "For judgement I am come into this world,

[h] Isai. x. 21.   [i] Ibid. xvii. 6.   [k] Ibid. xxiv. 13.
[l] Ibid. xxvii. 12.   [m] Ibid. viii. 14.   [n] S. Luke ii. 34, 35.

that they which see not might see, and that they which see might be made blind [o]."

And so his soul was prepared for that great paradox of prophecy which God revealed through him, the way of whose accomplishment, St. Peter says, was a mystery to the prophets, the meaning whereof they searched into and sought out diligently; the "sufferings of Christ, and the glory which should follow [p]." He, as no other, spake of the buffeting, the spitting upon, the malefactor's death, the counting with the transgressors, the contempt, the constant companionship with grief [q]. He, as few did, spake of the glorious reign, the everlasting rule; how He should reign in righteousness, and be a hiding-place from the storm to those who seek Him, the shadow of a great Rock in this weary and dry land of our banishment from Him. For these should the message for his people be repealed: "The eyes of them that see shall not be dim, and the ears of them that hear shall hearken [r]."

In this hope and longing he lived, in a future for himself, a future which God had promised to the remnant of his people. He was a man of longing: "In the way of Thy judgements have I awaited Thee, O Lord; to Thy Name and Thy memorial is the longing of my soul; with my soul have I longed for Thee in the night; yea, with my spirit within me I will seek Thee early [s];" "This is our God, we have waited for Him, and He will save us; this is the Lord, we have waited for Him, we will rejoice

[o] S. John ix. 39. [p] *ἐξεζήτησαν και ἐξηρεύνησαν* 1 S. Peter i. 10, 11. [q] Isa. l. 6; liii. [r] Ibid. xxxii. 3.
[s] Ibid. xxvi. 8, 9.

and be glad in His salvation[t];" "Thou wilt keep him in perfect peace, whose mind is stayed in Thee, for on Thee is it rested[u]." For he looked on beyond this world of disappointment and of shadows. He longed to see Him Who had at the beginning revealed Himself to him, the King on His Throne. "Thine eyes," he says, "shall see the King in His beauty[v]." The grave was to him but a chamber where he should hide himself for a little while[w]; then, to behold what "ear hath not perceived nor eye seen, O God, beside Thee, what He hath prepared for him who waiteth for Him[x]." For for Him had his whole life been one long waiting, and He Himself is the everlasting bliss of those who wait for Him.

Every time has its own pressure in this world of trial. And since we feel most what presses on ourselves, each time seems to those who live in it a time of special trial. Sixteen centuries ago it seemed as if the world was reaching its old age[y]. It attests, they said, its own ruin in the tottering state of things. "[z]The time of Anti-Christ seemed to be approaching;" "[a]faith seemed to be in a declining or almost slumbering state; priests were wanting in religious devotedness, ministers in entireness of faith; there was no mercy in works, no discipline in manners;" modesty was violated in both sexes; "[b]the world was renounced in words, not in deeds; men were eager about property and their gains, sought to exalt themselves;

[t] Isai. xxv. 9.　　[u] Ibid. xxvi. 3.　　[v] Ibid. xxxiii. 17.
[w] Ibid. xxvi. 19, 20.　　[x] Ibid. lxiv. 4, (3. Heb.)　　[y] S. Cypr. ad Demetr., Oxf. Tr., n. 2, p. 200.　　[z] Id. ad Fortun. de Martyr. Pref., p. 278.　　[a] S. Cypr. de lapsis. Treatises, p. 156, O. T.　　[b] Id., Ep. xi. p. 24.

gave themselves up to emulation and dissension, were careless about single-mindedness and the faith;" they were sundered by unabating quarrels; "ᶜ bishops were engaged in secular vocations, relinquished their chairs, deserted their people, hunted the markets for mercantile profits."

But for this last trait, one might think that the Martyr-Bishop of the third century was describing our own times in the nineteenth. Sore as moral and religious evil are, because of that horrible risk of human souls, the Gospel (which is impossible) would be false if they existed not. The presence of unbelief and of moral evil is a confirmation of faith. "Now I have told you, before it comes to pass," our Lord says of men's rejection of Him, "that when it is come to pass, ye may believe [d]."

This chequered aspect of good and ill is but what the Prophets, what our Lord, forewarned us of: it does but verify to us His knowledge of the human heart. Only all good is evidence of His power; the evil is evidence, not of His weakness but of ours. All evil is natural, all good is supernatural. Vice, selfishness, crime, impurity, ambition, covetousness, unbelief, are but the natural growth of the human heart. Faith, self-denial, chastity, content, lowliness, meekness, charity, are supernatural, the working of the Spirit of God. Start not back, then, as if some strange thing had happened, if iniquity abound, if faith seems rare, if zeal looks chilled or well-nigh extinct, if high aims or devotedness lie hid, if a low standard seem to have supplanted the measure of Christ. All this is but of nature. What should we

[c] S. Cypr. de lapsis. l. c.   [d] S. John xiv. 29.

look for in what is mere nature but the works of a corrupt nature? What should we expect from the flesh, but the works of the flesh, of which the Apostle tells us? The Gospel, and the grace of God in it, has to lift us above nature. And it does. But God respects the free-will of the creature which He made in His own Image; He will not destroy what is essential to our likeness to Himself. He will lift us above nature, but only if we, by our God-enfreed will, will it. In our mixed selves, we are evidences at once of the fall and of the restoration. We have too much noble in us, not to have been once consistent in the good, in which God created us and endowed us with supernatural grace. We have too much capacity of good, not to be destined for something much nobler than we at the best are. But "[e] He who made thee without thee, will not save thee without thee." The mass of evil is but the refuse which will not be restored. The simplest self-conquest is the presence of a supernatural power, a fruit of the Passion of Jesus, a triumph of His love and of His hallowing Spirit.

Be not dismayed, then, though men who think that they see, see not, or though they see not, because they think that they see. It is but the condition of the victories of faith over the soul, free, if it will, to disbelieve. Be not discouraged, if iniquity abound, or mankind seem to deafen itself in its pleasures or gains, or at the stupidity of an intellect which will not acknowledge a God Whom it does not see, or own its own free-will, which it has used against God continually, and, by repeated choices of its own evil against God's good, has well-nigh

[e] S. Aug.

enslaved to its master-passion, which God would have subjected to it. Jesus foretold at once His victories and His sorrows; His victories in those who willed to look to Him as their Master, their Saviour, their Regenerator, their Life, their Resurrection, their Immortality of Joy ; His sorrows, in those who would not be redeemed.

O that we looked, or that we may look, more to Jesus, "the Author and Finisher of our faith !"   O that we had His interests more at our hearts; that we longed with a burning love, with a fiery zeal, to win more souls to love Him, and to find rest and peace in believing and loving Him! Disappointment there will be, but—

> " E'en disappointment Thou canst bless,
> So love at heart prevail."

Disappointments there will be; but look to Jesus. Ask of Him a heart of fire ; pray Him to touch thy lips with that fiery coal.   Thou knowest not, what He will do in thee, through thee.   Look to Him, simply for Him, that the travail of His soul may be accomplished, and He will work in thee and through thee more than thou darest ask or think. What will it be in that Day to have won one soul to His end-less glory and His love !

And now in these poor wanderers [f] who have, we trust, after all their weary, miserable straying, re-turned to the Good Shepherd, and have been by Him brought back into His fold, remember Him, remem-ber the price of thy own soul, remember thyself.

[f] For a Penitentiary.

𝕿𝖍𝖆𝖓𝖐𝖘 𝖇𝖊 𝖙𝖔 𝕲𝖔𝖉.

SERMONS by the REV. E. B. PUSEY, D.D.

PAROCHIAL SERMONS, Vol. I., for Season from Advent to Whitsuntide.

1. The End of All Things.
2. The Merciful shall obtain Mercy.
3. Prepare for Seasons of Grace.
4. God with Us.
5. The Incarnation a Lesson of Humility.
6. Character of Christian Rebuke.
7. Joy out of Suffering.
8. God calleth thee.
9. The Fewness of the saved.
10. Fasting.
11. Review of Life.
12. Irreversible Chastisements.
13. God's Presence in Loneliness.
14. Barabbas or Jesus.
15. Christ Risen our Justification.
16. The Christian's Life in Christ.
17. Our Risen Lord's Love for Penitents.
18. How to detain Jesus in the Soul.
19. The Christian's Life hid in Christ.
20. Increased Communions.
21. Heaven the Christian's Home.
22. The Christian the Temple of God.
23. Will of God the Cure of Self-Will.

TWENTY-THREE SERMONS. 8vo., cloth price 6s.

PAROCHIAL SERMONS Vol. II.

1. Faith.
2. Hope.
3. Love.
4. Humility.
5. Patience.
6. Self-knowledge.
7. Life a Warfare.
8. The Besetting Sin.
9. Victory over the Besetting Sin.
10. Prayer heard the more through delay.
11. Re-creation of the Penitent.
12. The Sin of Judas.
13. The Ascension our Glory and Joy.
14. The Teaching of God Within and Without.
15. The Rest of Love and Praise.
16. Faith in our Lord God and Man.
17. Groans of Unrenewed and Renewed Nature.
18. Victory amid Strife.
19. Victory through Loving Faith.
20. The Power and Greatness of Love.
21. Our Being in God.
22. The Sacredness of Marriage.

TWENTY-TWO SERMONS 8vo., cloth, price 6s.

PAROCHIAL SERMONS Vol. III.

Reprinted from the Plain Sermons by Contributors to the "Tracts for the Times."
Revised edition.

1. Sudden Death.
2. Conversion.
3. The Cross borne for us and in us.
4. Real Obedience in all things.
5. Christian Life a Struggle, but Victory.
6. The Value and Sacredness of Suffering.
7. The Christian's a Risen Life.
8. Victory over the World.
9. Obedience the Condition of Knowing the Truth.
10. Pray without ceasing.
11. Conditions of Acceptable Prayer.
12. Distractions in Prayer.
13. Baptism the Ground and Encouragement to Christian Education.
14. Holy Communion, —Danger in Careless Receiving.
15. Holy Communion. — Privileges.
16. Christian Kindliness and Charity.
17. Obeying Calls.
18. The Transfiguration of our Lord the Earnest of the Christian's Glory.
19. Christian Joy.
20. God's Glories in Infants set forth in the Holy Innocents.

TWENTY SERMONS 8vo., cloth, price 6s.

PAROCHIAL SERMONS Preached and printed on Various Occasions.

1. The Day of Judgement. 6d
2. Christ the Source and Rule of Christian Love. 1s. 6d.
3. The Preaching or the Gospel a Preparation for our Lord's Coming. 1s.
4. God is Love. 5. Whoso Receiveth One such Little Child in My Name Receiveth Me. 1s. 6d.
6. Chastisements Neglected, Forerunners of Greater. 1s.
7. The Blasphemy against the Holy Ghost. 1s.
8. Do All to the Lord Jesus. 6d.
9. The Danger of Riches.
10. Seek God First and ye shall have All.
11, 12. The Church the Converter of the Heathen. Two Sermons.
13. The Glory of God's House.

THIRTEEN SERMONS. 8vo., cloth, price 6s.
The above Sermons may also be had separately.

SERMONS PREACHED AT ST. SAVIOUR'S LEEDS, On Repentance and Amendment of Life, with a Preface by Dr. PUSEY.

1. Loving Penitence.
*2. The Nature of Sin.
*3. The Sinner's Death.
*4. God's Merciful Visitations.
*5. The Last Judgement.
*6. Hell.
*7. Love of Christ for Penitents.
*8. The Returning Prodigal.
*9. Death to Sin in the Death of Christ.
*10. Virtue of the Cross.
11. Looking unto Jesus the Groundwork of Patience.
12. Looking unto Jesus the Means of Endurance.
13. Union with Christ, &c.
14. Hopes of the Penitent.
15. Bliss of Heaven, "We shall be like Him."
16. —— "We shall see Him as He is."
17. —— Glory of the Body
18. Progress our Perfection.
19. Daily Growth.

NINETEEN SERMONS. 8vo., cloth, 7s. 6d.
The Sermons with asterisk prefixed are not by Dr. PUSEY.

Lightning Source UK Ltd.
Milton Keynes UK
UKHW021627261118
332986UK00012B/843/P